Paola Ravasio

Black Costa Rica

Paola Ravasio

Black Costa Rica

Pluricentrical Belonging in Afra-Costa Rican Poetry

Würzburg
University Press

Dissertation, Julius-Maximilians-Universität Würzburg
Graduierten Schule für die Geisteswissenschaften, 2018
Gutachter: Prof. Dr. Brigitte Burrichter, Prof. Dr. Heike Raphael-Hernandez

Impressum

Julius-Maximilians-Universität Würzburg
Würzburg University Press
Universitätsbibliothek Würzburg
Am Hubland
D-97074 Würzburg
www.wup.uni-wuerzburg.de

© 2020 Würzburg University Press
Print on Demand

Coverentwurf: Leonardo Ureña

ISBN 978-3-95826-140-2 (print)
ISBN 978-3-95826-141-9 (online)
DOI 10.25972/WUP-978-3-95826-141-9
URN urn:nbn:de:bvb:20-opus-202981

We all need histories that no history book can tell, but they are not in the classroom – not the history classrooms, anyway. They are in the lessons we learn at home, in poetry and childhood games, in what is left of history when we close the history books with their verifiable facts.

Michel-Rolph Trouillout, *Silencing the Past*

Meinem Papa Battista Ravasio zugeeignet.
(Monza 10.08.1938 – San José 21.05.2015)

Custu libru esti po Maria Bonaria,
sa mamma mia.

Content

PREFACE

UNTIL WE CAN BE BOTH VISIBLE AND BELONG, THE WORD "HOME" WILL REMAIN FOR US AMBIGUOUS, IRONIC, AND EVEN SARCASTIC.

WE WILL STILL BE "STRANGERS AT HOME".[*]

---

[*] *Charting the Journey* Editorial Group.

The Journey Begins

The following is a story about Costa Rica. A story of the past read in poetry written by Costa Rican women. Black women. The substance of this story articulates a Caribbean arrival that disturbed Costa Rica's imagined *white* 'exemplary and exceptional difference' in the Central American region and transformed itself into a hyphenated way of being, that is, into Afro-Costa Ricans. In the voices of these Black Costa Rican women a historical imagination will be traced, one that refuses to be forgotten; that refuses to be assimilated; that refuses to remain circumscribed within the nation's boundaries.[1]

The poets here discussed are *Afra*-Costa Ricans Eulalia Bernard (*1935 Limón, Costa Rica), Shirley Campbell (*1965 San José, Costa Rica), and Dlia McDonald (*1965 Colón, Panamá). The gendered term *afra-* is used purposively across this study in order to emphasize that its object of study is constituted *specifically* by Black women poets who are contributing to an emerging literary tradition.[2] During the first readings of their work, a recurrent question haunted my investigator-gaze, for the women upon which this interpretative journey is charted across do not represent a homogeneous nor monolithic group of writers. They do not speak all the same themes with similar tones nor aesthetic forms. Their poetry does not portray similar concerns in an exact manner. Contrarily, it is rather difficult to find a single guiding content or poetic form that is common to Bernard, Campbell, and McDonald. Even ethnic criteria, erotism, linguistic and national issues are deployed through multifold aspects, granting singularity to each of these women's poetic vain. What, then, makes it possible for their prolific poetry to be approached by an overarching critical discourse? How can their diversified lyric be encompassed as independent entities whose particularities are nonetheless relatable? How can their poetry be engaged in specific detail, while exposing their singular aspects as sharing a common lyrical thread?

In *La isla que se repite* (1989), Antonio Benítez-Rojo explains every "text is a pre-text" that is "born when it is read by the Other: the reader."[3] He in fact commences his book with the plea to "start *rereading the Caribbean*, that is, to do the kind of reading in which every text begins to reveal its own textuality" (emphasis added).[4] His words should help grasp the approach that has given origin to *Black Costa Rica,* given that the following pages voice my own critical reading of these women's *pre-texts*, weaving them into a finite corpus of texts in the form of a *story of the past*. Likewise, for Doris Sommer "[s]ubalterns write creative literature as well as active *history*" (emphasis added), which is why she pleads in *Proceed with Caution, When Engaged by Minority Texts in the Americas* (1999) for a "selective, differentiated understanding of reading" that can appropriate "resistant texts".[5] Central to

---

[1]   Cf. "Introduction" in Grewal et al, *Charting the Journey*: 1f., which inspired this opening paragraph.
[2]   The gendered term is taken from De Costa-Willis, who defines "Afra-Hispanic literature" as "the writing of Black Spanish-speaking women of the Caribbean and Central and South America" ("Afra-Hispanic Writers": 204).
[3]   Benítez-Rojo, *The Repeating Island*: 23.
[4]   Ibid.: 2.
[5]   Sommer, *Proceed with caution*: 21 and 7.

my reading of Afra-Costa Rican poets is in fact the author's plea to *learn* and *teach to read* literature by focusing on the "tangents [that] lead to places that some readers have not visited".[6] As a result, the present study engages Afra-Costa Rican poetry with the purpose of grasping, and here I appropriate Gloria Anzaldúa's words (*Borderlands* 1987), the deep structure of meaning below their literacy so as to "see in surface phenomena the meaning of deeper realities".[7] In order to capture this, a hermeneutical *close reading* is necessary.

My hermeneutics of Afra-Costa Rican lyric turns to the rhetorical with the purpose of engaging the pre-texts through a reader-response criticism in which, as proposed by both Benítez-Rojo and Sommer, the texts *teach the reader how to read*. Therein, in their pre-textual character, lie internal meanings that the literary scholar-reader deciphers through a critical process since, as enlightened by Raymond Williams (1977), "meaning is always *produced*; it is never simply expressed".[8] The poems are not invoked here so as to *let them speak for themselves*, an affirmation which is coherent with Gayatri Spivak's (1988) critique of the "epistemic violence" of postcolonial studies. Mainly, "the first-world intellectual masquerading as the absent non-representer who lets the oppressed speak for themselves."[9] Rather, the pre-texts are thoroughly and philologically dismembered so that the deep structure of meaning can be extracted by a hermeneutical gaze that intertwines the enquiring investigator's purpose with textual *silence*. By focusing on these silent spaces – i.e. *what is not said explicitly*[10] – I carry out connections between the texts' poetic nuances and the sociohistorical process concerning the *coming of age* of the Afro-Costa Rican minority. In this sense, *Black Costa Rica* aims to tell a *story of the past* by addressing the ways in which three Afra-Costa Rican poets deploy a *pluricentrical sense of belonging* through specific lyrical figures of speech.

This study has as a point of departure the historical, philosophical, and literary debates that have emerged since the 1990s regarding the Costa Rican imagined community. It goes however beyond them by establishing a critical dialogue with postcolonial Caribbean scholars in the attempt to address an *other* Costa Rica. A *Black Costa Rica*. I do so by carrying out a *"historically backwards-looking"*[11] hermeneutic that explores a *pluricentrical*

---

6   Sommer, *Proceed with caution*: 21.

7   The quote is taken from the discussion Anzaldúa is carrying out when defining *la facultad* as "the capacity to see in surface phenomena the meaning of deeper realities" (Anzaldúa, *Borderlands*: 60). She is referring to the capacity that oppressed people inhabiting a borderland (be it racial, religious, or a gender one) (have) de-velop(ed) as a strategy for survival. "It's a kind of survival tactic that people, caught between the worlds, un-knowingly cultivate." (p. 61) For Anzaldúa, "the females, the homosexuals of all races, the darkskinned, the outcast, the persecuted, the marginalized, the foreign" (p. 60) are the people caught between worlds.

8   Williams, *Marxism and Literature*: 166.

9   Spivak, "Can the Subaltern Speak?": 292.

10   Cf. Spivak, who quotes Pierre Macherey when discussing ideology and the consciousness of the subaltern: "What is important in a work is what it *does not say* [emphasis added]. This is not the same as the careless notation 'what it refuses to say,' although that would be in itself interesting: a method might be built on it, with the task of *measuring silences*, whether acknowledged or unacknowledged. But rather this, what the work *cannot* say is important, because there the elaboration of the utterance is carried out, in a sort of journey to silence" ("Can the Subaltern Speak?": 286). For Spivak, the question of what the work *cannot* say is what be-comes important concerning the subaltern consciousness (cf. p. 287).

11   Cf. Ette, *Literature on the Move*: 19, where the author mentions "historically backwards-looking" as one of the possible methods for analyzing a *travelogue*: "Can the reasons for the fascination and radiance of the (literary, scientific and perception-scientific) genre of the travelogue be found only in its concern with determined

sense of belonging. This concept is approached here as a *(g)local* continuum stretched across a historical dimension and expressed through specific lyrical figures of speech. By taking note of oxymoron in McDonald, metonymy in Campbell, and language mixture in Bernard, I trace a story of the past across the first half of the twentieth century in Limón, Costa Rica in an outer/supra/infra-national form. The following study contends that *pluricentrical belonging* in Afra-Costa Rican poetry sheds light upon how the Afro-Costa Rican community participates of the similarity/difference continuum Stuart Hall (1990) takes the Caribbean to represent, withholding in its essence *la isla que se repite* that Antonio Benítez-Rojo describes. The coming of age of the Afro-Costa Rican community mirrors as well Paul Gilroy's *Black Atlantic* thesis regarding the multinational position Blacks occupied in Costa Rica's unrealized democracy, which came to be thanks to the building of the railroad to the Atlantic and the subsequent United Fruit Company's Plantation system.

The term "West Indian" is consciously discarded here when referring to Afro-Costa Ricans so as to avoid reproducing an error traceable to Christopher Columbus's arrival at the Caribbean instead of India. In order to clarify an ambiguous terminology, it must be underscored now that the term "Afro-Costa Rican" does not represent the people born out of mestizaje during the colonial epoch (1570–1870), for their participation in the racial cartography of the population was ideologically whitened in the process of imagining the nation. Instead, as the anthropologist Michael D. Olien defined it, the term "Afro-Costa Rican" corresponds specifically to the descendants of the Afro-Caribbean population (mainly Jamaicans) that migrated to the region as volunteer workers to build the railroad, work at the Panamá Canal and the United Fruit Company's banana enclaves (1870–1948), and who have been politically recognized as Costa Rican citizens since 1949.[12] This transnational re-accommodation determined the present-day constitution of the country's largest ethnic minority, which is of migrant origin. It is worth pointing out that while the 2001 national census portrays a substantial smaller percentage of Afro-Costa Ricans (1,9%), the 2011 census shows that Afro-Costa Ricans represent 7,8% of the nation's population – against 2,4% of people polled who identified themselves as of Indigenous origin and 83,6% as white- or mestizo-descendant.[13] Against this historical backdrop, Afra-Costa Rican writers are approached here as embodying one of the multiple histories of the country, specifically regarding diverse nation~diaspora dynamic/s that changed the racial cartography not only of Costa Rica, but of the Central American countries and their Caribbean regions as well.

Consequently, this book is installed within a widening focus of Afro-Latin American studies. On the one hand, Central American writers of Caribbean descent illuminate in a particular manner the region's relationship to Blackness as constituting a history of its own, where the migration of insular Afro-Caribbeans to the Central American isthmus bridges

---

objects, the examination of cultural otherness, or […] in the apparently easy appropriation of the text by a (contemporary or historically backwards-looking) audience?" Ette refers to a reading that focuses on the contemporary aspects the text may be able to elucidate, as well as a lecture that throws light upon the historical aspects contained by the travelogue. My approach to Afra-Costa Rican poetry is exclusively a historically backwards-looking reading practice.

[12] See Herzfeld, "Language and Identity": 119–121; and "Vida o muerte del criollo limonense": 17, where Olien's dateless manuscript is quoted.

[13] PNUD, *Situación socioeconómica*: 18f. See also INEC, *Costa Rica a la luz del censo 2011* (2014).

Black Studies with Latin American Blackness *beyond* the colonial experience of mestizaje and the African Diaspora, past the traditional contexts of Africa, the U.S., Brazil and South America,[14] incorporating, on the other hand, *women* voices to the cultural spectrum. My work focuses on literature written by women connected to a double diaspora, but who are nonetheless *more* than *Daughters of the Diaspora* (DeCosta-Willis 2003).[15] Otherwise said, being born and schooled in the country, these women have *become* Costa Rican, redefining what was imagined as "Costa Rican" in the first place.[16] In fact, it was through education that Caribbean-descendants were slowly integrated into the host country. Even if this eventually led to being caught between exclusive cultural identities, developing what W.E.B. Du Bois termed "double consciousness" (*The Souls of Black Folks* 1903) and what constitutes the theoretical premise from which this study departs.

In the opening pages of "Of Our Spiritual Strivings", Du Bois tells of an encounter he experienced, which allowed him to conceive the reality of his racialized existential difference. One day at school, the boys and girls were exchanging visiting-cards, until one girl refused "peremptorily" his card. "Then it dawned upon me with a certain suddenness that I was different from the others;" he continues, "shut out from their world by a vast veil."[17] For the author, this veil is the reason that African Americans have "no true self-consciousness" and instead recognize themselves only "through the revelation of the other world". Defined by the author as "this sense of always looking at one's self through the eyes of others", *double consciousness* emerged from an incompatibility drawn out between being Black and being North American. Du Bois attests a *veil of race* as that responsible for the yielding of this "twoness", that is, of "two unreconciled strivings" that are caught between two simultaneous identities.[18]

The experience of double consciousness as defined by Du Bois is also evident in Afro-Costa Rican literature, given that the myths and imagery drafted during the nation-building process at the second half of the nineteenth century determined that 'Black' and 'Costa Rican' were contrary to one another. In fact, Dorothy Mosby considers Afro-Costa Rican literature expresses double consciousness because of a "difficult negotiation of difference and national identity."[19] Specifically, a whitewashed identity confronted by Blackness. It first took literary form with Eulalia Bernard and Quince Duncan (*1940, San José, Costa Rica), who represent the first Afro-Costa Rican writers to enter the national canon and to publish with national state-funded publishing houses from the 1970s onwards. Their literature claims belonging to Costa Rica from an ex-centric perspective, i.e. located outside the country's political and ideological center and instead rooted in the Caribbean province of Limón, which is connected furthermore with the Central American Caribbean region and beyond it with the Caribbean islands. As a result, their texts reproduce social, political, ethnic, and cultural issues from a spatial and ethno/racial identification that contests the

---

[14]   Cf. Wade, "Afro-Latin Studies: Reflections on the field" (2006).

[15]   See Cohen, "The Diaspora of a Diaspora: The Case of the Caribbean" (1992).

[16]   "Blacks born, nurtured and schooled in this country are, in significant measure, British, even as their presence redefines the meaning of the term" (Gilroy, *There Ain't No Black in the Union Jack*: 203).

[17]   Du Bois, *The Souls of Black Folks*: 6.

[18]   Ibid.: 7.

[19]   Mosby, *Place, Language and Identity in Afro-Costa Rican Literature*: 234. As Mosby has pointed out, "the national dominant discourse [signaled] that the two positions [were] mutually exclusive" (p. 236f.).

original imagined community, which they critically represent by intertwining aspects of the marginalization of Afro-Costa Ricans in the country.[20]

Scholars such as Ian Smart (1984), Dorothy Mosby (2003, 2012), Consuelo Meza and Magda Zavala (2015) have argued that Afro-Costa Rica literary double consciousness represents the desire to belong to the national imagination and the impossibility or difficultness in achieving this. These arguments have however superficially acknowledged the issue of the Costa Rican imagined community, focusing rather on the literary naming and claiming of ethnic, cultural, and linguistic differences, which for Mosby dictate an *"incompatibility* between being Black and Costa Rican" (emphasis added). The author follows Smart, who first claimed Eulalia Bernard's poetry mirrors how the desire of belonging to Costa Rica "is more a desired goal than an achieved one". Meza, instead, affirms Afro-descendant Central American women writers deploy a *fragmented conscious-ness* ("framentación de la conciencia") due to the hegemonic discourses of the Central American mestizo countries.[21] The purpose of the ensuing discussion is to overcome the use of 'double consciousness' when approaching Afra-Costa Rican poetry and instead turn to 'pluricentrical belonging' in order to comprehend the glocal aspects intrinsic to their writing, thus avoiding explaining its multicultural features by way of exclusive, binary identities.

If on the one hand Antonio Benítez-Rojo considers that the Caribbean basin "is still [...] one of the least known regions of the modern world",[22] then the literature of the Central American Caribbean holds an even more unfamiliar position in literary scholarship. As proclaimed by Werner Mackenbach (2008), its literary production has suffered a double exclusion. It has remained at the margins of literary canons vis à vis nation-building projects in their own Central American countries, while also being displaced towards the sidelines because it has been overshadowed by studies on insular Caribbean literature.[23] Coherently, Quince Duncan (2009) affirms Afro-Central American writers have in fact been *systemati-cally silenced* by literary critics.[24] Which is why this book approaches the Costa Rican Carib-bean as representing an exemplary silenced area, or echoing Spivak, "the silent, silenced center".[25]

The attempt to overturn this, most recently approached from a transareal perspective, focuses mainly on the cultural continuum in the region. Such studies explore literature in the present epoch of accelerated globalization along the processes of transference and circulation between centers and peripheries, as well as through migratory movements. Literary production is thus approached from the multiple cultural and dynamic intertwinements that exist between areas, rather from static notions of traditional spaces

---

[20] Ovares/Rojas, *Cien años de literatura costarricense*: 232.
[21] Mosby, "Roots and Routes": 10. See also, Mosby, *Place, Language, and Identity in Afro-Costa Rican Literature*: 234. Smart, *Central American Writers*: 91. Meza, "Memoria, identidad y utopia": 123.
[22] Benítez-Rojo, *The Repeating Island*: 1.
[23] Mackenbach, "El Caribe y la literatura Centroamericana": 107f. See also from Mackenbach, "Representaciones del Caribe en la narrativa centroamericana" (2008).
[24] Duncan, "Corrientes literarias afrocentroamericanas": 513.
[25] Spivak, "Can the Subaltern Speak?": 283.

like the nation.[26] Accordingly, Mackenbach affirms it is necessary to avoid thinking the Caribbean only in relation to nation-state projects and instead it is pertinent to study the processes of cultural production between these areas intra-, inter-, and trans-regionally. Mainly because the Central American Caribbean comprises a transnational Afro-Central American imaginary that shares cultural, ethnic, and linguistic features across the region's territories as outer-national communities. That is why the author explicitly discourages the use of the term *Nationalliteratur* for Central American Caribbean literature.[27]

Focusing *solely* on the transareal continuum without taking into consideration the nation-building projects from a transformative perspective can lead however to a certain homogenization of the diversity of experiences that renders invisible the multiplicities and particularities of each community in their specific and particular historical contexts. The internal diffractions remain thus partially covered up and hence evasive to the whole of the sociohistorical processes determining such differences. Because of this, *Black Costa Rica* is innovative since it aims to make visible how *pluricentrical belonging* illuminates a literary expression referring both to a *transareal* dimension on the one hand, as to *national* particularities on the other by simultaneously placing emphasis on the similarities (the global features) and the differences (the local specificities). Otherwise put, a keener awareness of Costa Rica's ideological and historical specificities regarding the irruption of the Caribbean diaspora in Costa Rica's nation-building process may offer a deeper understanding of the complexities concerning the global dimension of diverse nation~diaspora dynamic/s. Therefore, with the purpose of extracting how these women's poetry reflects a national dimension of transnational, global processes concerning Black diasporic minorities, I analyze Afra-Costa Rican poetry at particular historical junctures and in the light of specific state projects that motivated the Afro-Caribbeans to arrive in Costa Rica. As well as against the later socio-historic conditions in which nationalist movements against Black immigrant laborers emerged, together with posterior assimilation projects such as education policies.

"I'm Just a Girl"*

Costa Rican women writers of Caribbean descent represent a fairly new literary voice that is becoming a novel object of study along with other Afra-writers from the Central American region. Voices that have been constricted to the margins, being "virtually invisible and unheard until quite recently."[28] The recent scholarly interest in these voices is in

---

[26]   See for example Ette (ed.), *Caribbean(s) on the Move* (2008); Ette et al (eds.), *Trans(it)Areas.* (2011) and *El Caribe como Paradigma* (2012); Ette/Müller, *Worldwide* (2012); Cortez/Ortiz/Ríos (eds.), *Hacia una historia de las literaturas centroamericanas III. (Per)Versiones de la Modernidad* (2012); Ortiz Wallner, *El arte de ficcionar* (2012), and Meza/Zavala (eds.), *Mujeres en las literaturas indígenas y afrodescendientes en América Central* (2015). And beyond the Caribbean area, see Ette, *TransArea. A Literary History of Globalization* (2016) and *Writing-Between-Worlds* (2016).

[27]   Mackenbach, "El Caribe y la literatura Centroamericana": 115.

*   Song title by Hortense Ellis (1979) compiled in *Studio One Women. The Original.* UK: Soul Jazz Records (2005).

[28]   Gallego, "On Both Sides of the Atlantic": 73.

itself part of a broader academic concern regarding Black Caribbean female writers' *visibility*.[29] Nonetheless, the (until recently) relatively scarce literature on Afra-Costa Rican poets reflects how the Central American Caribbean has been overshadowed by both Latin American and insular Caribbean literary studies. Since the Central American region has been approached as a cultural, economic, and political appendix of Latin America, its literature has been traditionally constricted to a marginal position, representing, as named by Amelia Chaverri (2005), 'the periphery of the periphery.'[30] Therefore, an all-Black female-based corpus is not gratuitous.

On the one hand, the current Black poets of Costa Rica *happen* to be women nowadays. "No debo ninguna disculpa" from poet, teacher, and communal leader Prudence Bellamy, a.k.a. *la niña Prudence* (*1935), represents one of the first pioneer works in the country. Her father was from Barbados, her mother from Jamaica. In 1966 she went to Oregon to study "supervisión escolar" and later became the first Black woman to act as the principal in the "escuela n. 2" in Limón.[31] Both Bellamy, who was incorporated to Limón's Hall of Fame in 2010,[32] and Eulalia Bernard stand as forerunners of Black female poetry in Costa Rica, together with less visible Afra-Costa Rican oral poets Joyce Anglin, Carol Britton, and Marcia Reid, while Kyria Perry and Queen Nzinga are two poets breaking ground in the country.[33]

That women writers are becoming more visible in the literary scene is most likely due to similar socio-historic conditions like those outlined by Ajua Maria Mance (2007) regarding African American women writers in the U.S. She states their literary productivity flourished in determined epochs because they had "access to education and resources that enabled them to produce and publish their work", this as a consequence of Black people in North America having a wider access to education, as well as sociopolitical and economic conditions yielding more jobs and hence financial well-being for Blacks in general.[34] The same explanation applies for Afro-Costa Ricans. Once President José Figueres Ferrer paved the way for naturalization (1949), opportunities were slowly extended to the Black population who was integrated in the sociopolitical and economic structures of the country through lawful citizenship. Because of integration through a national, monolingual education system, Costa Rican-born Caribbean-descendants could access new work oppor-

---

[29]   See for example, Cudjoe (ed.), *Caribbean Women Writers* (1990); Boyce/Savory (eds.), *Out of the Kumbla* (1990); Condé, *La parole des femmes. Essai sur des romancières des Antilles de langue française* (1993); O'Callaghan, *Woman Version: Theoretical Approaches to West Indian Fiction by Women* (1993); Anim-Addo, *Framing the Word: Gender and Genre in Caribbean Women's Writing* (1996); Chancy, *Framing Silence. Revolutionary Novels by Haitian Women* (1997); Condé/Lonsdale (eds.), *Caribbean Women Writers: Fiction in English* (1999); O'Haigh, *Mapping a Tradition. Francophone Women's Writing from Guadaloupe* (2000); Sharpley-Whiting, *Negritude Women* (2002); and De Costa-Willis, *Daughters of the Diaspora* (2003).

[30]   Amelia Chaverri, "América central debe ser nombrada": 201. From here on, all phrases quoted with single quotation marks (') refer to my own translation of the non-English texts.

[31]   Rosario, *Identidades de la población de origen jamaiquino*: 169.

[32]   *Afrodescendientes de valía*: 13f. See McDonald, *Pregoneros de la memoria*: 27, where Bellamy's "No debo ninguna disculpa" is reproduced in its entirety. See also Álvarez, *Cuentos y leyendas* (2008) for Bellamy's contribution to Costa Rican traditions in Limón with "El Garden Party" (p. 135), "Harvest Sunday" (p. 136), "La Escuela Dominical" (p. 138), and "Marianela y yo" (p. 185).

[33]   Personal interview with Dlia McDonald on December 12th, 2015 (San José, Costa Rica). Cf. Zavala, "Para conocer a las poetas afrodescendientes centroamericanas": 111 and 112.

[34]   Mance, *Inventing Black Women*: 21.

tunities and thus acquire a better livelihood as 'Costa Ricans'. Black Costa Rican women have benefited particularly from this process, specifically regarding education. The 2011 socioeconomic situation of the Afro-descendant population in Costa Rica (PNUD 2013) shows Black Costa Rican women present higher levels of schooling than their counterparts, both in the urban as in the rural areas.[35]

The choice to focus on poetry written solely by Black Costa Rican *women* responds on the other hand to the need of acknowledging that their lyric expands and strengthens the consolidation of a female literary production particular to a *Black Costa Rica* that however also plays an important part in the establishment of Afra-discourse/s in Central America. If in fact Black women writers represent – in the words of Evelyn O'Callaghan in her study of fiction by Caribbean women (1993) – "the 'alterity' of white femaleness", their "outsiders' voices" are hence the most peripheral regarding that of white, male discourse.[36] Black Costa Rican women poets are therefore caught within a movement of *doubled "double displacement"*.[37] That is, *Black* and *women*, and recalling Mackenbach's 'double exclusion', *Central American* <u>and</u> *Caribbean-descendant*. Proof of this displacement is the fact that even though these women have produced and published in the last decades, they have published either in other countries or with independent publishing houses by their own means. Bernard's *My Black King* (1991) was published by the World Peace University of Oregon, while *Ciénaga/Marsh* (2001) was presented by the independent Costa Rican publishing house Asesores Editores Gráficos. Campbell's *Rotundamente negra* (1994) appeared in Arado and then was reprinted (2006) by the Costa Rican independent publishing house Perro Azul, while *Naciendo* (1988) was published by herself thanks to money granted by the Board of Port Administration and Economic Development of the Atlantic Coast of Limón (JAPDEVA), moreover currently out of print. She has furthermore published in Spain a compilation of poems entitled *Rotundamente Negra y otros poemas* (2013) with the publishing house Torremozas. Mc-Donald found institutional support and published *...la lluvia es una piel...* (1999) with the Costa Rican Ministerio de Juventud, Cultura y Deportes (later reprinted in 2010 with Asesores Editoriales Gráficos), as did Bernard for *Ritmohéroe* (1982), published by the Editorial de Costa Rica. McDonald's other compilations – *El séptimo círculo del obelisco* (1994) and *Sangre de madera* (1995) – were however self-published with assistance of her colleagues from a poetry workshop.[38] Whereas *Todas las voces que canta el mar* (2012) was published in Mexico by Sediento Ediciones. Though her first prose work (*La cofradía cimarrona* 2018) represents the first novel published by a Black female writer in the country, this was published by the independent house Guayaba.

While Afra-Costa Rican writers have struggled to obtain recognition in their own country, the fact that their literature circulates with greater presence in the international scene makes evident that they represent an emerging *local* literary current contributing to the establishment of a *global* diasporic community through literary acts, as defended by

---

[35] Black women living in urban regions present the highest average of approved school years (10.2 years) opposite Black women living in rural areas (6.6 approved years). Men, on the other hand, are lower both in the urban as in the rural areas (9.4 years; 5.9 years, respectively). PNUD, *Situación socioeconómica*: 30.

[36] O'Callaghan, *Woman Version*: 25.

[37] Cf. Spivak, "Can the Subaltern Speak?": 295.

[38] Mosby, *Place, Language and Identity in Afro-Costa Rican Literature*: 209.

Wendy Walters (2005).[39] Compilations like *Central American Writers of West Indian Origin* (Smart 1984), *Daughters of the Diaspora* (DeCosta-Willis 2003), and *Mujeres en las literaturas indígenas y afrodescendientes en América Central* (Meza and Zavala 2015) have referred to their writing by reuniting their literature with that of other Black women writers in Central and South America. These studies shed light on why Afra-Costa Rican poets are important spokespeople regarding emerging literary Afra-voices, discourses, and female-centered cultural production. As affirmed by DeCosta-Williams, "literary texts of Afra-Hispanic women reveal an emerging feminist consciousness, as these women treat female subjectivity, explore sexuality and the female body, and examine silence, voice, and language."[40] In fact, specific issues of womanhood constitute an important part of McDonald's, Bernard's, and Campbell's poetry, which (specially in Campbell and Bernard) lay side by side the social and political issues of their communities, both local as global. Bernard's code-switching, Campbell's poetization of *historia*, and – although not approached here – McDonald's poems on the pain of absent love confirm the author's claim.

Dorothy Mosby's groundbreaking *Place, Language and Identity in Afro-Costa Rican Literature* (2003) has rescued not only these Afra-voices, but also those Afro-Costa Rican writers who have written both in English and in Spanish in the country since the beginning of the twentieth century. Nonetheless, any person who holds in their hand recent anthologies and critical compilations (published in the country) regarding Costa Rican poets, can notice by glancing at the table of contents how Afra-writers oscillate to a large degree between international recognition and national *voicelessness*.[41] As outlined by Carole Boyce Davies and Elaine Savory Fido in their Introduction to *Out of the Kumbla* (1990), the concept of *voicelessness* addresses "the historical absence of the women writer's text" in literary canons regarding specific issues like slavery, colonialism, or social and cultural issues. Mainly because "the Caribbean male text [has assumed] primacy" in literary criticism.[42] For the authors, "voicelessness" refers to a question of invisibility and "exclusion from the critical dialogue" that leads to women's articulations on such subjects to remain "unheard". As a consequence, the "Caribbean women (writer)", they argue, "has been historically silenced in the various 'master discourses'."[43] Something that Gloria Anzaldúa had referred to with a similar tone in her book *Borderlands/La Frontera*:

---

[39] Walters, *At Home in Diaspora*: x.
[40] De Costa-Willis, "Afra-Hispanic Writers and Feminist Discourse": 205.
[41] For example, Bernard and Campbell appear in the selection of thirty-eight women poets compiled by Mora/Ovares in *Indómitas Voces. Las poetas de Costa Rica* (1994), each with only two poems despite their abundant lyrical production. Black poets do not figure either among the twenty-five poets reunited in *Martes de poesía en el Cuartel de la Boca del Monte* (1998). In Corrales Arias's anthology *Sostener la palabra. Antología de poesía costarricense contemporánea* (2007), Dlia McDonald represents the single Black Costa Rican writer among sixty-seven other poets. Refreshing is however *Noches de poesía en el farolito. Una Mirada a la poesía costarricense en el 2007*, edited by Paula Piedra and published by the Centro Cultural Español in Costa Rica, which dedicated the month of April to Afra-Costa Rican poets, with Kyria Perry, Prudence Bellamy, and Dlia McDonald as spokeswomen thereof.
[42] Boyce/Savory, "Introduction": 2.
[43] Ibid.: 1.

the dark skinned woman has been silenced, gagged, caged, bound into servitude…
For 300 years she was *invisible, she was not heard.* Many times she wished to speak,
to act, to protest… She remained *faceless* and *voiceless*…[44] (Emphasis added)

Spivak's consideration regarding subaltern voicelessness in the context of colonial production also becomes relevant to the position Afra-Costa Rican writers have withheld in the country's literary historiography as "the muted subject of the subaltern woman".[45] The author claims that if "the subaltern has no history and cannot speak, the subaltern as female is even more deeply in shadow."[46] Shirley Campbell refers to this *shadowing* in an interview with Javier Bragado (2017), where she indicates Afro-Latin American wo/men writers have been muted because their voices have been structurally marginalized in their own countries and because it is hard for them to access the means that belong to the elite. She goes on to clarify that because they are poor, they cannot take advantage of those means of production in the same manner. As a consequence, Afro-writers, specifically women, have been made invisible (*invisibilizados*).[47] This, however, does not signify that they *cannot speak.* Accordingly, Myriam Chancy (1997) states the subaltern is always speaking and reproaches Spivak for condemning the subaltern to voicelessness and hence to a non-liberation from silence.[48] Black female voicelessness in Costa Rica is thus perceived to be a structural problem regarding literary markets and institutionalized knowledge rather than these women lacking the capacity of speech *per se.* Silvia Solano Rivera and Jorge Ramírez Caro (2016) point out, in fact, that Quince Duncan is the most visible of the Afro-Costa Rican writers discussed in recent important compilations of national literary historiography, such as *Cien años de literatura costarricense* (Rojas/Ovares 1995) and *Breve historia de la literatura costarricense* (Quesada 2008). Mainly, they affirm, because he was a university professor and winner of various (inter)national prices.[49] Even if the authors asses that the aforementioned studies dedicate only a few lines to Duncan's work, thus lacking deeper attention, the *Afro*-Costa Rican text has nonetheless assumed primacy, shadowing to a certain extent its female counterparts.[50] Which is why the present book strives to make audible *Afra*-Costa Rican voices by putting them in the spotlight. In so doing, *Black Costa Rica* brings to the surface the rhetorical figures of speech across which these women poets do in fact speak.

---

[44] Anzaldúa, *Borderlands*: 44f.

[45] Spivak, "Can the Subaltern Speak?": 295.

[46] Ibid.: 287.

[47] Bragado, "No éramos negros" (11.02.2017). "[N]osotros estamos arrinconados en los pueblos más pobres, en la periferia y es difícil acceder a esos medios que son propiedad de la élite." She goes on to state: "tenemos el obstáculo de que somos pobres y no tenemos el mismo acceso a esa misma producción."

[48] For Chancy, "Spivak's understanding of subalternity preempts dialogue since its initial question presupposes an absence of the ability to communicate" (*Framing Silence*: 32, see 29–33). Spivak questions "[w]ith what voice-consciousness can the subaltern speak?" and which are the mechanisms "rendering vocal the individual […]?" ("Can the Subaltern Speak?": 285.)

[49] Solano/Ramírez, "Poética de la liberación en Shirley Campbell Barr": 156.

[50] In her article "I will be a Scandal in your Boat", Myriam Díaz-Diocaretz (1990) refers to this shadowing by affirming the "patriarchal paradigms of women's 'inferiority' and their subsequent exclusion have been applied […] to the cultural expressions produced by women, namely literature, and particularly *poetry*" (emphasis added, p. 88).

Consequently, the main interest behind an all-Black woman-based corpus is to fend off the voicelessness that hovers over contemporary Afra-Costa Rican poets in their own country by engaging their literature with the history of Black Caribbeans in Costa Rica. The present study explores how Afra-Costa Rican poets express resistance to the double exclusion/double displacement phenomenon through a historical imagination that "is often not recognized by nation-states or by traditional models of literary study".[51] A historical imagination that can be specifically Costa Rican and yet inherently *global*. Therefore, the purpose here is to decipher what these women's writing *say* on subjects like the origins of the Black Caribbean diaspora in Limón, about linguistic relations of power between the region's Creole and the official state language, and on a complex subject like invisibility and silence regarding Afro-history in their own countries as across the globe. Their lyric is approached here as emerging from deeper within the shadow itself and contesting it with literary practices that resist their historical marginalization and *invisibilización* as subjects and articulators of Costa Rican history.[52] Their work is hence understood as actively overturning Black female voicelessness in Costa Rican cultural memory.[53]

One of the main contentions this study departs from is the fact that these Black women writers are counter-hegemonic cultural agents since they produce resistance literature that is "involved in a struggle against ascendant or dominant forms of ideological and cultural production."[54] For Barbara Harlow (1987), resistance literature allows a reconstruction of history for those who have "been denied an active role in the arena of world politics", so that through it, relations of power can be compensated on the cultural, political, and economical levels by making them visible through/by/in literature.[55] Coherently, Mosby (2012) asserts Afra-Costa Rican poetry performs a type of resistance literature because it transcends the limits of the nation-state and forms a collective bond outside national frontiers, confirming Mackenbach's dismissal of *Nationalliteratur* as an appropriate genre for Caribbean-descendant writers of Central America. Meza refers to Central American Black (and Indigenous) women's literary production along the same line, affirming it represents a movement of cultural resistance with its own aesthetic forms and contents.[56]

---

[51] Walters, *At Home in Diaspora*: x.

[52] See Barbas-Rhoden, *Writing Women in Central America*: 13.

[53] Jan Assmann (1988) defines *cultural memory* ("kulturelles Gedächtnis") by "its distance from the everyday" and as the objectification of culture through a stock of texts, images, rites, and practices whose maintenance stabilizes and conveys a knowledge of a shared past that rests upon the self-consciousness of a group ("Collective Memory and Cultural Identity": 129). It has two modes of expressing itself; one in the form of the "potentiality of the archive" and the other, in that of "actuality" (p. 130). It is therefore subdivided in a 'functional memory' (*Funktionsgedächtnis*) – embodied or inhabited by individuals/collectivities – and distinguishes itself from a 'storage memory' (*Speichergedächtnis*). The former refers to "the life story that one 'inhabits'" through "vital recollections that emerge from a process of selection, connection, and meaningful configuration" (Assmann, *Cultural Memory and Western Civilization*: 127). While the latter preserves historical knowledge in the form of a passive storing of material archives and – like Pierre Nora's *lieux de mémoire* (1989) – relies on the support of institutions and professional specialists so that it can be preserved, conserved, organized, and circulated as cultural knowledge (Assmann, "Collective Memory and Cultural Identity": 130). For Jan and Aleida Assmann's relevance in the study of literature, see Erll, "Literatur und kulturelles Gedächtnis" (2002) and *Kollektives Gedächtnis und Erinnerungskulturen* (2005).

[54] Harlow, *Resistance Literature*: 28f.

[55] Ibid.: 22.

[56] Meza, "Memoria, identidad y utopía": 122.

Likewise, Mosby considers these women "participate in the literary construction of transnational Blackness" in the region, a project she defines as simultaneously creating and addressing an imagined community from Belize southwards to Panamá.[57] She refers thus to Nicaraguans June Beer and David McField, Quince Duncan and the three Afra-Costa Rican poets here mentioned, as well as Panamanian Gerardo Maloney as examples of this transregional construction of literary Blackness.

By relating the transnational features to national specificities, the following pages attempt to show Afra-Costa Rican voices produce a *re-narrativisation* of the power and knowledge field regarding Limón and the history of postcolonial Costa Rica.[58] This, furthermore, from a perspective that privileges an internal vision.[59] That is, as in-group members of the Afro-minority themselves. They complement with their voice/s Quince Duncan's prose fiction[60] and the novels of historical reference by Tatiana Lobo (*1939 Puerto Montt, Chile) and Anacristina Rossi (*1952 San José, Costa Rica), which acknowledge and tell a silenced history concerning the fundamental role that the Black communities in Limón had in the modernization and industrialization of independent Costa Rica. However, given that the present study focuses exclusively on Black Costa Rican women's voices that have not been made quite as audible, Lobo's and Rossi's novels of historical reference are not approached here.[61]

To critically study Afra-Costa Rican poetry from a historically backwards-looking gaze signifies mainly making visible what Abena Busia (1990) identifies as the "voice re-found", i.e. the recollection of past fictions that reclaim stories and re-write histories from the perspectives of Black women.[62] The present pages thus set out to demonstrate how these writers add new voices, perspectives, and stories regarding Costa Rica's historical imagination, *revis(it)ing it*. Much like Etsuko Taketani (2014) draws on African American countermemories of Pearl Harbor as "radical black narratives of the Pacific" that diverge profoundly from official U.S. historical memory,[63] the ensuing discussion approaches Afra-

---

57   Mosby, "Roots and Routes": 26.

58   Cf. Hall, "When was 'the Post-Colonial'?": 250 and 251, where the author refers to post-colonial discourse as a "re-narrativisation" that displaces critically the "grand historiographical narrative" by "new forms [that have emerged] to disrupt the settled relations of domination and resistance inscribed in other ways of living and telling these stories."

59   See Martínez-San Miguel, *Coloniality of Diasporas*: 141, where she echoes the authors of *Éloge de la Créolité* (1989), who state Édouard Glissant's *Malemort* (1975) and Frankétienne's *Dézafi* (1975) represent a new literary paradigm that articulated Caribbean identity from an *internal* perspective/vision.

60   Duncan has published both novels as short story compilations: *El pozo y una carta* (1965), *Bronce* (1970), *Una canción en la madrugada* (1970), *Manconía* (ca. 1971), *La rebelión pocomía y otros relatos* (1979), and *Cuentos Escogidos* (2004) (Mosby, *Quince Duncan*: 19). His prose work corresponds to *Hombres curtidos* (1971), *Los cuatro espejos* (1973), *La paz del pueblo* (1978), *Kimbo* (1989), the bilingual text *A Message from Rosa/Un mensaje de Rosa* (2007), *Final de la calle* (1979), and his only theatrical text, *El trespasolo* (1993) (Cf. Mosby, *Quince Duncan* [2014]).

61   Lobo published *Calypso* in 1996, while Rossi first released *Limón Blues* in 2002 and later *Limón Reggae* in 2007. Regarding the term "novels of historical reference" and its differentiation from "historical novels", see Mackenbach/Sierra/Zavala 2008: 8.

62   Busia, "This Gift of Metaphor": 289.

63   Taketani, *The Black Pacific Narrative*: 3 and 4, respectively. The author engages in his book "the black Pacific", which he defines as "alternative memories of the war [...] namely, the literary and cultural production of African American narratives of the Pacific" in the geopolitical context of the twentieth century and specifically as "a major theatre of World War II." (p. 6)

Costa Rican poetry as alternate Black narratives of Costa Rican historical imagination. Their voices are *multilingual* – as Bernard code-switches. Their perspectives are *gender and race* oriented – as Campbell deploys the subject of *historia*. And their stories are *transhistorical* – as McDonald's poetics of landscape reveals it. The present study contends their literature disrupts the settled relations of domination and exclusion opposite a national canon, breaking away from it and redefining it as *glocal* poets. That is, as *Black, Central American, Caribbean-descendant, Costa Rican* writers. Much like the compilation of the Essays from the First International Conference on Caribbean Women Writers (1988), the present study "seeks to rescue and give expression to voices that have not always been heard as loudly and as clearly as they should have been."[64] In so doing, it reads an *outernational, infranational,* and *supranational* story of a *glocal* past.

Ask Away...

How is the coupling of the 'local and the global' present in these women's writing? The main contention of *Black Costa Rica* argues certain lyrical figures of speech deploy multifold historical aspects regarding diverse nation~diaspora dynamic/s in the form of *pluricentrical belonging*. With the Afro-Caribbean diaspora in Costa Rica as an exemplary case, this study expands on the interconnectedness between Central America and the insular Caribbean by focusing on the dynamic between national and diasporan imaginings within a single nation. This with the purpose of imagining an*other* Costa Rica. Consequently, the analysis of glocal references in Bernard's, Campbell's, and McDonald's poetry traces how diverse historical dimensions are expressed in the singular (national specificity) and in the plural (global identifications) through *oxymoron, metonymy,* and *code-switching*. Central to this perspective is Édouard Glissant's claim that

> Caribbeanness [...] tears us free from the intolerable alternative of the need for nationalism and introduces us to the cross-cultural process that modifies but does not undermine the latter.[65]

The study on pluricentrical belonging in Costa Rican Black female poets asks, fundamentally, what are the poetic *themes* and which are the lyrical *forms* expressing the glocal in Afra-Costa Rican poetry? What kind of *stories of the past* can be extracted by a close reading of their *pluricentrical* elements? In what (lyrical) ways does the poetry of these Black Costa Rican women reveal a historical imagination that refers simultaneously to both a national specificity and yet simultaneously expresses identification with the socio-historical processes of the circum-Caribbean region? The ensuing pages approach the above-mentioned figures of speech and explains them against a historical imagination with the purpose of reading the story of twentieth century Costa Rica with the Caribbean proletarian diaspora as one of its focal points and as a mirrored reflection of global realities concerning nation~diaspora dynamic/s. Rhetorical figures, sociohistorical processes, and

---

64   Cudjoe, "Introduction": 7.
65   Glissant, "Cross-Cultural Poetics": 139.

hermeneutics thereof are the inherent elements of the following critical expedition into times past.

Structure of the Book

This literary journey is charted across three Parts, divided themselves into three sections each. Whereas Part I exposes the theoretical *Prolegomena* concerning the two concepts which guide the ensuing discussion, Part II *Becoming Afro-Costa Rican* deploys the historical backdrop of the Afro-Caribbean diaspora in Limón and its marginalization born out of neocolonial transnational capitalism and racist nationalism.

The clash of ethnically, linguistically, and religiously defined cultural identities at the turn of the twentieth century – that is, 'white', Catholic, and Spanish-speaking Costa Rica *vs.* the Black Atlantic rooted in anglophone, Protestant, Jamaican culture – represented an important obstacle in the recognition of Caribbean descendants as Costa Rican citizens. *Becoming Afro-Costa Rican* deploys this backdrop. In it, Costa Rica's imagined community is key to understanding what was imagined to be Costa Rican, by whom, and when ("Imagining Costa Rica"). Its fissure is signaled by the incursion of Black Caribbean workers who represented cheap labor for the multinational enterprises of Minor Keith's railroad construction and the United Fruit Company, and who settled at the Limón province by reenacting their own cultural realities as a cultural, deterritorialized diaspora ("Dwelling in Displacement"). Curiously enough, the proletarian diaspora entered Costa Rica at the precise moment that the country was imagining its people and its place in the world as a sovereign community. At this time, labor organization in the United Fruit Company inevitably led to class and racial antagonism on behalf of Costa Ricans with respect to Black workers in Limón, yielding an ethnonational borderland in the country ("The Dialectics of Race and Nation").

Three sections conform Part III, the bulk of the book comprising the critical analysis. *The Following is a Story of the Past* structures the literary analysis of pluricentrical belonging across a chronological understanding of time. It departs with diaspora with *Dlia McDonald – This Train is Bound to Glory*. It continues with the race/nation conflict with *Shirley Campbell – The Memory of Skin: Traces of People Without History*. And it ends at assimilation and marginalization with the discussion of *Eulalia Bernard – The Telling of an InfraNational Linguistic History*.[66] Each section within this third Part is not only dedicated to an individual poet, but each one poetizes a specific figure of speech mirroring an explicit historical imagination. In so doing, *The Following is a Story of the Past* corresponds to a three-layered stor(y)ing of spatially-, meta-historically-, and multilingually-defined Afra-Costa Rican outer/supra/infra-national historical imaginings, respectively.

The first section carries out a close reading of Dlia McDonald's poetics of landscape in *...la lluvia es una piel...* (1999). The selected poems are approached here as deploying an *outernational* historical imagination through a *modernized-nature oxymoron* constructed

---

66   The word *InfraNational* is written here in this manner in order to comprise the idea of the *national* and the *non-national* in a single graphic form.

upon tripartite sites of historical meaning. While the first segment "A Literary Introduction to Limón" explains Limón as an ex-centric province in the territorial imagination of Costa Rica, "En vacaciones íbamos a Limón" approaches the representation of the *train* in McDonald's poetry as a means of transportation withholding historical significance. That is, as a cultural, political, and historical unity that refers symbolically to the origins of Afro-Costa Ricans and to the modernization of the Costa Rican economy due to the building of the railroad to the Atlantic. Together with the representation of nature as the non-human world, which for Raymond Williams (1980) "contains, though often unnoticed, an extraordinary amount of human history",[67] the train will be moreover approached here as analogous to the *ship* in the Black Atlantic in so far both are fundamental historical elements lodged between the local and the global. Following Gilroy, the train's symbolism as the origin of the Caribbean diaspora in Costa Rica stands as well as a poetic representation of "both rootedness and of multiplicity"[68] and hence of *pluricentrical belonging* in Afra-Costa Rican poetry. The last segment, "Spatializing Time Past", deals with the remains of the urbanization of Limón portrayed by McDonald's sites of modernization and of dwelling. These diverse sites of historical meaning in McDonald's poetry are explored as expressing Glissant's *poetics of landscape* and their historical dimension is furthermore engaged following Benítez-Rojo's thesis that the Caribbean is in its essence a *repeating island*. It will be discussed along these pages how the modernized-nature oxymoron welds together dislocated pasts into a shared and single re-presentation of multiple spatialized imaginings of times past as an expression of *pluricentrical belonging*.

Next, Shirley Campbell's *Memory of the Skin*, focuses on the author's equivocal reference to *historia* in *Naciendo* (1988), *Rotundamente negra* (*RN* 2006), and the last section of *Rotundamente Negra y otros poemas* (*RNOP* 2013) entitled "Historia develada". Coupled to their analysis is also the poem "El encuentro" (*Palabras indelebles* 2011). By way of an intertextual analysis, this chapter focuses on Campbell's contribution to *Black Costa Rica* through meta-historical lyric. Analyzed against Gilroy's definition of Black Atlantic subjects as "people in but not necessarily of the modern, western world",[69] an in-depth discussion of glocal references in her poetry will make evident how diaspora, racism, and invisibility are the focal points determining a *supranational* historical imagination made evident by way of a *skin-history metonymy*. The first segment pinpoints the metonymy in the Costa Rican case by a close reading of Campbell's poem dedicated to Carlos (*RN*, III.XII). The global aspects of racism deployed by Campbell's lyrical voice are made evident with historical specificities concerning Caribbean migrant workers in Costa Rica. Specifically, with elite and working-class racism which yielded institutionalized racism (anti-Black legislation) in the first decades of the twentieth century. "The Advocation of an InfraHistory" instead engages the semantic constellations surrounding *historia* in "Historia develada" (*RNOP*). In so doing, it argues Campbell launches a literary combat which advocates a supranational Black *postmemory* that condemns the erasure, invisibility, and silence surrounding what Glissant referred to as a *non-histoire*. This nonhistory withholds

---

[67]   Williams, "Ideas of Nature": 67.
[68]   Cf. Glissant, "Cross-Cultural Poetics": 117, where the author also discusses Wilfredo Lam's and Roberto Matta's paintings as exposing rootedness and multiplicity in their artistic creations.
[69]   Gilroy, *The Black Atlantic*: 29.

forced diaspora and 'the torment of the absolute unknown' at its center, as well as alienation as subaltern cultural effects. This is why Campbell stages lyrical *decolonial violence* following Frantz Fanon's precepts and with the purpose of *un-veiling (develar) historia*. The last segment, then, explores the representation of Blacks in Costa Rican cultural memory only to focus thereafter on how the skin-history metonymy is transmitted across matrilineal structures. In "The Black-Woman-Mother Triad", Campbell's skin-history metonymy becomes a powerful element and an alternative narrative of Costa Rican cultural memory, one whose perspective is not only racialized, but gendered as well. Her poetry stands thus as an exemplary case of what Maryse Condé (2004) termed a "literary combat",[70] given that Campbell's poetic words regain possession of a proper story, memory, history, *herstory*. The analysis of the rhetorical elements of her lyrical combat demonstrates in fact that *she can speak* and *consciously chooses* to use her poetic vain in the service of her political purposes. Through it, Blackness is granted a refreshing and empowering self-esteem that claims its place in Costa Rica by way of a supranational historical imagination.

Code-switching between Spanish, English, and Limon Creole in Eulalia Bernard represents the final discussion on pluricentrical belonging. Bernard's multilingualism is approached in the last section of Part III as performing Gloria Anzaldúa's *mestiza-consciousness* in the form of a *forked tongue* caught between national (Spanish) and outernational languages (English and Limon Creole). By analyzing multilingualism against the sociolinguistic context of Limón, Bernard's poetry is approached as concerned with ethnolinguistic Afro-Costa Rican visibility. Three are the poems here chosen to tell an infranational story of the past. They tell of linguistic assimilation and economic marginalization of anglophone Blacks in Costa Rica. With the help of the poem "What fi do?" (*My Black King* 1991), the first segment, "Limón on the Raw", introduces the socio-historic context of Bernard's threefold linguistic repertoire. Parallel to the linguistic analysis, the unequal relations of power between Spanish, English, and Limon Creole towards the second half of the twentieth century are brought to the surface. This leads the way to the succeeding discussion entitled "On the Path Towards Language", whose content matter is deployed along the linguistic and historical analysis of the poem "Bilingual Campesinos Speak Out", published in *My Black King* in 1991 yet originally recorded in Bernard's 1976 vinyl *Negritud*. The segment argues Bernard's code-switching is deployed strategically as a literary combat with the purpose of fending off what Anzaldúa so keenly referred to as *linguistic terrorism*. It deals specifically with the poet's bilingual claims against linguistic assimilation of Afro-Costa Ricans through monolingual education. The section concludes with "The Cacao People" and the analysis of "Bilingual Economy" (originally written in 1978 and first published in *Griot* 1997). Here, Bernard's code-switching is exposed as a literary combat aimed at demystifying Costa Rica's social democracy by the poet's critical stand on the socioeconomic circumstances regarding the Black *campesinos* at the Caribbean coast. Against the imagined community's territorial and agricultural idea of a democratic Costa Rica, "Bilingual Economy" performs the glocal both formally as thematically, connecting multilingualism with a plurality of histories and locations. The discussion on Bernard's

---

[70] Condé, "The Stealers of Fire": 154.

Telling of An InfraNational Linguistic History is charted upon multilingualism as a performance of *pluricentrical belonging*.

The Scope of it All

The main provocation that has put this study in motion has been Ronald Harpelle's (2001) claim, for whom the Afro-Costa Rican community "has remained a footnote in Costa Rican history and a forgotten part of the national heritage".[71] *Black Costa Rica* overturns this by shedding light on the rarely acknowledged connections between the sociohistorical process regarding the coming of age of the Afro-Costa Rican community, the global dimensions of such processes, and the literature by Black female writers which in turn gives testimony of these. Both overtly as covertly. By focusing on poetry rather than on the already extensively researched genre of the Latin American historical novel,[72] the present study is innovative because it explores the potential of *lyric* in telling alternative version/s of an official history. Afra-Costa Rican poetry is thus approached across the ensuing pages as *poetica sub specie historia*, echoing Aristotle's premise stated in *Poetics*:

> [...] a poet's object is not to tell what actually happened but what could and would happen either probably or inevitably. The difference between a historian and a poet is not that one writes in prose and the other in verse [but] that one tells what happened and the other what might happen. For this reason poetry is something more scientific ('more *philosophical*' – φιλοσοφώτερον) and serious than history, because poetry tends to give general truths ('the whole' – τὰ καθόλου) while history gives particular facts.[73]

In so doing, *Black Costa Rica* scrutinizes the scope of Afra-Costa Rican poetry in Costa Rican cultural memory, while simultaneously acknowledging its belongingness to the broader Black Atlantic.

---

[71] Harpelle, *The West Indians of Costa Rica*: 183.
[72] On the subject see for example Orr, "The Revenge of Literature: A History of History" (1986/87); Foley, *Telling the Truth* (1986); Hutcheon, *A Poetics of Postmodernism* (1988); Harlan, "Intellectual History and the Return of Literature" (1989); Menton, *Latin America's New Historical Novel* (1993); Pulgarín, *Metaficción historiográfica* (1995); Pons, *Memorias del olvido* (1996); Kohut (ed.), *La invención del pasado* (1997); Bravo, "La verdad y el juego en la novela histórica" (2001); Kohut, "Mirando al huerto del vecino: los historiadores frente a lo literario" (2001); Domenella (ed.), *(Re)escribir la historia desde la novela de fin de siglo* (2002); Mackenback et al, *Historia y ficción en la novela centroamericana contemporánea* (2008); Perkowska, *Historias híbridas* (2008); Aínsa, "Los guardianes de la memoria" (2010); Compagnon, "Histoire et littérature, symptôme de la crise des disciplines" (2011); and Mackenbach, "Narrativas de la memoria en Centroamérica: Entre Política, historia y ficción" (2012).
[73] Aristotle, *The Poetics*:: 1451a–b.

PART I – PROLEGOMENA

PLURICENTRICAL BELONGING

A CONCEPTUAL METAPHOR REGARDING HISTORICAL IMAGINATION

Towards a Definition of Historical Imagination

To define history is complex. Its meaning is neither evident nor univocal. Jacques Le Goff (1992) discusses how a "play of mirrors and ambiguities has continued throughout the ages" with regards to the senses the word expresses since Herodotus' *Histories* up to present times, and points to the fact that the different meanings the word has in Romance languages exhibit to a large extent its ambiguity content-wise. Hence, "histoire, historia, storia, etc. express two if not three different concepts", affirms the author.[1] Which is why here I shall start by drawing a line between the meanings of history, deemed fundamental to the conceptualization of *pluricentrical belonging*.

A first meaning refers to (a) a series of events occurred in time passed. A second meaning has to do with (b) the systematic production of knowledge regarding these events, comprising the interpretation of them into a discourse, which is constructed as "that which is said to have happened".[2] Both of these meanings complement each other in the definition of history and cannot be separated from each other. In his study of power and the production of history, Michel-Rolph Trouillot (1995) provides a helpful distinction between these two semantics by stating the former refers to the sociohistorical process (the series of events themselves as *res gestae*), while the latter has to do with the knowledge of that process expressed in writing/textual formulae, i.e. *res gestarum*.[3] As these distinctions make evident, meanings (a) and (b) lie very close to one another since 'history' as (a) represents the object of study of 'history' as (b). Together they conform what Le Goff terms the "duality of history as history-reality and as history-study of that reality".[4] The crucial difference between these two is the fact that meaning (b) has the particularity of having established itself as a western discipline of knowledge, as a discipline that Marc Bloch has conceptualized as "the science of *men* in time" (ironic emphasis added).[5]

In fact, the boundary between these two senses is for Trouillot "often quite fluid" and may result in them overlapping each other, so that the narratives of the sociohistorical process (*Geschichtsschreibung*) dangerously overlap its object of study (*Geschichte*), producing thus "one-sided Historicity"[6] – a central theme in Campbell's poetry. Meaning (b) understands history as a discipline that recollects documents and systematizes past events into ruptured periods by means of explaining objectively their relationships with one another, so that each period consolidates diverse sociocultural scenarios and organizes social practices into a discourse, what Michel de Certeau (*L'écriture de l'histoire* 1975) defined as "the making of History".[7] At the center lies the criteria of certainty since, as stated by Spivak, "the production of history" functions "as a narrative (of truth)."[8] And so here we

---

[1] Le Goff, *History and Memory*: 102.
[2] Trouillot, *Silencing the Past*: 2.
[3] Ibid.
[4] Le Goff, *History and Memory*: 104.
[5] Bloch (1941/42), quoted in Le Goff, *History and Memory*: 106.
[6] Trouillout, *Silencing the Past*: 3 and 4, respectively.
[7] Cf. de Certeau, *The Writing of History*: 6, 10, and 20f.
[8] Spivak, "Can the Subaltern Speak?": 283.

arrive at a third meaning of history which has to do with (c) a *narrative* form as for example particular to tales or fables where storytelling is its purposefulness.

The narrative form has been traditionally opposed to the argumentative procedure intrinsic for instance to the discipline of History, whose objective is to deliver truthful knowledge about the world. On the one hand, the elementary distinction between a narrative and an argumentative form corresponds to one of the classical dualisms of western metaphysics, concretely that of μῦθος vs. λόγος as a distinction between fictive and factual utterances. In this point-of-view, the traditional opposition between a narrative and an argumentative form was drawn around the content of truth the former was denied and the latter granted.[9] This set the epistemological binary of fiction/non-fiction, a "hierarchical axiology" as Derrida defines it,[10] where "'imaginative' or 'literary' truth always turns out to be something less than truth itself".[11] The first tells an imaginary and false story, while the other speaks of a real and true account of things. The twentieth century has witnessed heated debate among poststructuralist scholars of diverse disciplines who wish to supplant and overturn this dualism of western metaphysics by subverting it. Hence, Le Goff claims that the narrative form does not exclude the possibility of its content being true, for example as in a historical novel based upon "historical reality" instead of "pure imagination".[12] Likewise Barbara Foley (1986), who in her study of the documentary novel introduces the reader to "the shifting borderline" between fiction and its counterparts, arguing that "factual and fictive discourses are not immutable essences but are historically varying types of writing".[13] Both belong to the order of discourse, but the value attributed to their individual production of meaning shifts in time depending on the social, historical, and political conditions in which they are created, more than on an essential fictional or factual nature.

---

[9] This first distinction was introduced by Pre-Socratic philosophers and developed to its finest by Plato, for whom truth takes a stronger stand over poetic creation. Take for example Plato's introduction to the myth of judgment in *Gorgias* (523a), where he tells Gorgias to listen to what he is going to tell him next, what Gorgias most likely 'believes' to by a *mythos*, i.e. a fable, but Socrates regards as *logos* – 'an account' (ἄκουε δή, φασί, μάλα καλοῦ λόγου, ὃν σὺ μὲν ἡγήσῃ μῦθον, ὡς ἐγὼ οἶμαι, ἐγὼ δὲ λόγον). He goes on to state where the difference lies between the two: "for what I am about to tell you I mean to offer as the truth (ἀληθῆ)" (ὡς ἀληθῆ γὰρ ὄντα σοι λέξω ἃ μέλλω λέγειν.) He then goes on to narrate the myth. This rhetorical maneuver on behalf of Plato-the writer makes evident how the narrative form (*mythos*) becomes *logos* insofar its content is *truthful*. See Brisson (*Plato, The Myth Maker* 1994), who argues that Plato's attitude towards *mythos* corresponds to a political project with the purpose of imposing his teachings in order to overcome *mythos*'s hegemony in the ancient Greek *Weltanschauung*.

[10] Derrida, "Limited Inc. abc", quoted in Foley, *Telling the Truth*: 13.

[11] Lamarque/Olsen, *Truth, Fiction, and Literature*: 21. The authors carry out a study of the relationship between truth, fiction, and literature and propose a "'no-truth' theory of literature" (p. 1). The authors do not place *truth* and *literature* on a same level and argue that by doing so, literature is being equaled to science or philosophy, which are structurally different from literature or fiction. "There is no significant place for truth as a critical term applied to works of literature" (p. 1). By rejecting an essential link between these two (p. 4), they hence plea 'truth', 'facts', or 'the world' should not become analytical concepts when carrying out a critical study of literature. However, they do attest that the application of truth to the content of literature is possible by contextualizing literary works. The authors consider 'pro-truth' theories help understand the literary value of literature in a mimetic and epistemological approach, since their verisimilitude aims to tell a story untold. Under these considerations, *verisimilitude* holds a central value opposite truth.

[12] Le Goff, *History and Memory*: 102.

[13] Foley, *Telling the Truth*: 15 and 27, respectively.

Nineteenth-century South American historical novels and twentieth-century Central American novels of historical reference exemplify Foley's claim. Doris Sommer (1993) argues historical novels in Latin American countries had a central role in the process of imagining their recently independent nations in the nineteenth century. Her overarching study of such foundational fictions shows how national ideas were grounded in heterosexual love and in socially convenient marriages. Sommer reads in this "rhetoric of love" and of "conquest" political projects to 'woo and domesticate' the newly emerged civil societies, motivating them furthermore to "be fruitful and multiply". Her study makes visible the "inextricability of politics from fiction in the history of nation-building" through an "erotic rhetoric that organize[d] patriotic novels".[14] Contrarily, Mackenbach (2008) sustains the novels of historical reference produced in the Central American region in the last three decades of the twentieth century respond largely to the need of telling stories that have been made invisible and have been silenced by an official historical imagination. Which is why Valeria Grinberg Pla (2008) affirms these novels function as an alternative discursive space opposite the official historiographic discourse. Along these lines, Magda Zavala (2008) also argues Costa Rican novels of historical reference produced in the 1990s express a subterraneous fatherland, which debilitates myths of national identity desired by official discourses.[15] These two literary genres sustain Foley's claim exemplarily because they make evident how the content of truth regarding the textual production of *history* and *fiction* depends largely on political and historical contexts. Literature may be used in favor of ideological processes concerning nation-building processes, where exclusion and marginalization can occur as byproducts of "a tradition written in erasures of the past".[16] While literature can also be used with the purpose of overturning this unequal power structure in the construction of knowledge.

Language and the production of discourses thus have an ideological context, so that their production of meaning is always connected to a power structure.[17] Either in a supportive manner, as for example with Latin American foundational fictions, or in a confronting manner, as in the case of Central American novels of historical reference. In other words, literary genres are inevitably situated within the fields of power which determine their own production and thus their own 'content of truth'.[18] Consequently, the traditional criteria opposing narrative to argumentative discourse "is institutional [and] exists in the contexts of politico-discursive conditions".[19] These critical approaches to the discursive nature of all forms of knowledge have led to the comprehension that "not all narrative is fictional" and that the narrative form is common to other non-fictive discourses, like for example History.[20] Hayden White's contributions in this respect are grandiose, whose approach to the writing of History has demonstrated how "narrative has always been and continues to be the predominant mode of historical writing".[21]

---

[14] Sommer, *Foundational Fictions*: 6, 5f., and 2, respectively.
[15] Mackenbach, "Introducción": 8. Zavala, "Novela de la nación en crisis": 50.
[16] Sommer, *Foundational Fictions*: 4.
[17] Cf. Hutcheon, *A Poetics of Postmodernism*: xxif.
[18] Ibid.: 178, quoting Terry Eagleton, *Literary Theory. An Introduction* (1983).
[19] Hutcheon, *A Poetics of Postmodernism*: 178.
[20] Lamarque/Olsen, *Truth, Fiction, and Literature*: 39.
[21] White, *Figural Realism*: 3.

Consequently, meaning (c) overlaps meaning (b) in that "the making of History" is inseparable of narrativization and is constituted in the long run as a discipline that frames (a) the sociohistorical process as *the story of the past*. The following pages dialogue across the interrelations between meanings (a) and (b) and their representation through a *poetic space of writing* (c). Which is why, attempting to differentiate the subtleties between these meanings, which are necessarily intertwined with each other, I will refer from hereafter to meaning (b) as History with a capital H to indicate the discipline that was consolidated in Europe in the nineteenth century and whose objective is the knowledge of the past. Contrarily, whenever I shall speak of *the story of the past*, I am reuniting meaning (a), (b), and (c) so that together they represent *historical imagination*.

The Supranational, Outernational, and Infranational Historical Imagination

Paul Gilroy's definition of the Black Atlantic as a highly multifaceted network of transnational and intercultural multiplicities and as a "multi-faceted desire to overcome the sclerotic of the nation-state"[1] becomes rather appropriate when approaching Black Costa Rican literature from the perspective of its plural historical imaginations. For, as Joseph Roach (1996) defines the totality of Gilroy's scholarly work, "Gilroy expands the cultural horizons of modern history in a way that does not begin and end at national borders."[2] Instead, it yields historical imaginations in plural forms: diasporic, global, and national, which constitute the foundation of the ensuing discussion.

The Supranational

Although the experience of 'Blackness' is lived in conditions specific to each individual country, with "*supranational* historical imagination" this experience is referred to here as not being circumscribed to an individual nation-state. I do not mean here that Blackness constitutes an essence of a people, nor a medium for a national or proto-national homogeneous community, as criticized by Gilroy.[3] Rather, it refers to the fact that existential, socio-politic, and economic phenomena regarding the conditions surrounding diaspora and Blackness are experienced in similar if not identical patterns across the globe. It indicates thus a diasporized collective identity that overrides territorial frontiers and transcends individual nation-states. Hence its *supra*–national character (i.e. *above, beyond* national borders). Despite the internal diffractions that constitute multiple Afro-descendant collectivities across the globe, Black people share the historical memory of forced uprooting, consequent enslavement, and contemporary oppression as "*Afro-descendants*", thus *belonging* in a way to an overarching imagined community. Even though Benedict Anderson's original coinage of this concept was thought of in relation to nations and the spread of nationalism, the concept is highly useful for understanding how supranational historical imagination and pluricentrical belonging correlate in Afra-Costa Rican literature by way of *diaspora/s*.

Diaspora/s manifest three fundamental aspects. Firstly, *dispersal* to one or more host lands. Secondly, a lasting *reterritorialization* abroad, which may not become necessarily permanent. And thirdly, they maintain social, political, economic, or cultural *ties* with the homeland and among the people living in displacement.[4] Though these elements are considered to be core features of *diaspora/s*, Kim Butler (2001) also notes that "diaspora is

---

[1]   Gilroy, *There Ain't No Black in the Union Jack*: 206.
[2]   Roach, *Cities of the Dead*: 5.
[3]   Gilroy, *The Black Atlantic*: 33.
[4]   Van Hear, "Refugees, Diasporas, and Transnationalism": 176.

[not] a monolith" – which explains the shifts in theoretical approaches on the subject.[5] In *Global Diasporas* (2008), Cohen outlines "four phases of diaspora studies" and explains "Diaspora" in singular and in capital letters as referring to a first phase, which originally was circumscribed to the Jewish experience. Safran's (1991) article reconfigured this exclusivity and expanded the concept to comprise a more wide-ranging group of people in displacement, such as expatriates and political refugees (second phase). According to Cohen, the 1990s witnessed a third reconstitution of the concept influenced by postmodern theory, where deterritorialized identities reordered the conceptual baggage of diaspora/s towards a more "flexible and situational" construction. Currently, diaspora studies incorporate deterritorialized postmodern conceptions to define new diasporas, while still underscoring the homeland as a powerful discourse determining the nature of such.[6]

The term *diaspora/s* is thus used consciously in the plural form throughout these pages so as to avoid "(mis)using diaspora as an overfull metaphor", which according to Walters overrides historic detail and geographic specificity.[7] Diaspora due to enforced uprooting caused by European colonialism, to give an example, differentiates itself in time, place, duration, and circumstances to, for instance, the new African diaspora. While migration movements from Africa to Europe or to the U.S. occur voluntarily since the 1980s,[8] compulsion and trauma were at the center of the former, since dispersal was constituted as a consequence of "a traumatic event in the homeland", i.e. forced uprooting and slavery, constituting it as a "victim diaspora" (Cohen 1997/2008). For Cohen, it is necessary to draw furthermore a distinction between the African victim diaspora and others of the same kind, such as the Armenian, due to the "prolonged time scale of the African slave trade".[9] These diasporas differentiate themselves in turn from Chinese, Indian, and Afro-Caribbean labor diasporas of the nineteenth and twentieth centuries, whose motive force for departure from the homeland where jobs in other countries. Also, "new diasporas" (Van Hear 1998) have developed since the last quarter of the twentieth century due to geopolitical issues, globalization, and human rights conflicts that have extended new patterns of transnational formations which span several societies. These new diasporas are also different from former ones given "the intensity and reciprocity of the ties between emigrant or exiled populations and their countries of origins".[10]

Despite such internal differentiations that refer to a variety of diasporas across place and time, it becomes of upmost relevance to the present study to underscore here what Khachig Tölölyan (1996) affirms as a common aspect regarding the conformation of diaspora/s as a whole. This determines in fact the correlation between pluricentrical belonging and a supranational historical imagination because "like the nation, the *diaspora* is [...] also an *imagined community* whose ligatures are discourse and representation, ideology and the

---

[5]   Butler, "Defining Diaspora": 203.
[6]   See Cohen, *Global Diasporas*: 5.
[7]   Walters, *At Home in Diaspora*: xvi, see xxv.
[8]   Regarding the new African diaspora, see Feldner, *Narrating the New African Diaspora. 21st Century Nigerian Literature in Context* (2019).
[9]   Cohen, *Global Diasporas* (2008): 2 and 42, respectively.
[10] Flores, *The Diaspora Strikes Back*: 22. See also Van Hear, *New Diasporas*: 1–12.

reproduction of a *subjectivity of belonging*" (emphasis added).[11] Tölölyan draws on Anderson's innovative approach to *nations*, who defined these as cultural artifacts and termed them *imagined communities* because, as explained by the author, they are constructed primarily upon a feeling of communion between members of a group who have never met, but still *imagine* themselves as *belonging* to a closed social unit. Moreover, the feeling of belonging to a delimited and independent territory, according to Anderson, does not represent itself through a hierarchal structure, but as a "deep, horizontal comradeship" among anonymous and faceless equals despite socio-economical inequalities between them.[12] In fact, Anderson states that "in the minds of each lives the image of their communion", even though they "will never know most of their fellow-members, meet them, or even hear of them".[13]

Like Anderson, Ernst Gellner (1983) points as well to the communal aspect of *belonging* by affirming "nations are the artefacts of men's convictions and *loyalties* and *solidarities*" (emphasis added).[14] Ernest Renan had asserted a century earlier (1882) that a "nation is a soul, a spiritual principle" corresponding to "a large-scale solidarity" constituted upon the legacy of a shared heritage (the past) and the will to perpetuate such legacy into the future.[15] These 'loyalties and solidarities' find expression among those who recognize themselves as in-group members of a particular nation, who, according to Eric Hobsbawm (1996), become an imagined community by the reification of *a people* thanks to the "invention of emotionally and symbolically charged signs of club membership".[16] In this nation-building process, "the citizens of a country became a sort of community, though an imagined one", affirms Hobsbawm (1994). Its members share certain affective marks, such as places, practices, and cultural and historical memories that reinforce "patriotism with sentiments

---

[11] Tölölyan, "Rethinking Diaspora(s)": 23. Along the same line of thought, Roza Tsagarousianou's book *Diasporic Cultures and Globalization* (2007) rejects considering diasporas as mere annexes to nations by looking into diasporas as transnational actors. She affirms "there is no reason why diasporas could not qualify as imagined communities too. They, too, can be seen as such as they are constructed through the lengthy process of forging links among their members in both local and transnational contexts, of suppressing or neutralizing internal differences, of establishing the context in which common experiences can be developed and past experiences can be interpreted in similar ways" (Tsagarousianou, "Rethinking the concept of diaspora": 60). See also David W. Cavers, "Nationalism, Ethnicity, and the Cultural Politics of Identity" (1994), who refers to three ethnic groups from Nigeria as field cases serving to prove his point. He argues that "[b]oth nations [...] and ethnic groups are 'imagined communities'", since both correspond to social organizations that carry out an "essentialisation of characteristics of a community" to create a common identity for its members. He concludes "there are no intrinsic defining features that make a nation different from an ethnic group" and argues that they should be considered as similar orders of phenomena, i.e. imagined communities (p. 22 and p. 23).

[12] Anderson, *Imagined Communities*: 7. See Lomnitz, "Nationalism as a Practical System" (2001), who carries out an in-depth critique of Anderson's claim on "horizontal comradeship" regarding specifically the Spanish-American case. Lomnitz argues against "the compelling aspect of nationalism [as a] promise of fraternity" (p. 337) stating "comradery" was 'invented' within hierarchical structures and relations of power during the nation-building process. For the author, a 'national community' is hence fallaciously built on imagined fraternity, for an "interconnection between fraternity and dependency" on the state actualize the development of nationalism (p. 339).

[13] Anderson, *Imagined Communities*: 6.

[14] Gellner, *Nations and Nationalisms*: 7.

[15] Renan, "What is a nation?": 19. ("Qu'est-ce qu'une nation?", lecture delivered on March 11, 1882 at the Sorbonne.)

[16] Hobsbawm, "Introduction: Inventing Traditions": 11.

and symbols" of the imagined community.[17] Richard Fox (1990) describes this as conceptions of peoplehood that reflect "ideologies of common ('national') culture", determining the "cultural productions of public identity."[18] Each of these theories emphasize how the sentiment of community cohesion parallels the feeling of *belonging*.

Concerning Afro-descendants across the globe, Stuart Hall affirms Africa represents the idealized homeland of Black slave descendants outside the continent. For Hall, Africa

> 'has acquired an imaginative or figurative value we can name and *feel*.' Our *belongingness* to it constitutes what Benedict Anderson calls 'an imagined community'.[19] (Emphasis added)

What Hall underscores is not an imagined community in the sense of a territorially determined, linguistically, and ethnically essentialized homogeneity of an imagined people comprised under the modern nation-state, for given the plundering of the African continent and its people this is obviously not possible. Instead, he emphasizes there exists an *affective* dimension created by the historical experience of forced displacement that has yielded a sense of *belonging* to an encompassing collectivity with one single traceable "origin": the African victim diaspora.

Going beyond this traumatic origin, Gilroy calls attention to the fact that the memory of slavery and the remains of the plantation societies are not the sole elements unifying Afro-descendants born out of diaspora/s. Instead, this internally diffracted supranational collectivity is unified most strongly because of "the experience of migration" after emancipation, becoming the "racially subordinated migrant labourers" and the Black working-class in the host countries.[20] In fact, Cohen (1992) affirms Afro-Caribbean people are part of a double diaspora not (only) because of the historical memory of the slave trade as descendants thereof, but mainly because of a collective history and an ethnic group consciousness that has faced racism and discrimination in the capitalist system ever since. Cohen thus argues Caribbean deterritorialized communities constitute themselves a double diaspora because (1) the "original collective trauma of slavery" is an important part of Afro-Caribbean collective consciousness and historical memory, which is reinforced (2) "by racism and colour discrimination" in the host lands.

Likewise, Hall affirms that Blacks

> are very much 'the same'. We belong to the marginal, the underdeveloped, the periphery, the 'Other'. We are at the outer edge, the 'rim', of the metropolitan world – always 'South' to someone else's *El Norte*.[21]

Accordingly, Benítez-Rojo considers that the Caribbean poem and/or novel constitute "projects that communicate their own turbulence [...] their otherness, their peripheral

---

17 Hobsbawm, *Nations and Nationalism since 1780*: 90f.
18 Fox, "Introduction": 3 and 4, respectively. The author uses the term "nationalist ideologies" to refer to "the production of conceptions of peoplehood" (p. 2) that have been termed by others as "nationalisms", "subnational identities", and "ethnic nationalisms" (p. 3). "Nationalist ideologies" also circumscribe "racial identities" and "ethnicities". Together, these terms refer to the "cultural productions of public identity".
19 Hall, "Cultural Identity and Diaspora": 232.
20 Gilroy, *The Black Atlantic*: 81.
21 Hall, "Cultural Identity and Diaspora": 228.

asymmetry with regard to the West".[22] Keen to Malcom X's "You can't have capitalism without racism", the authors agree with Kehinde Andrews (2016) upon the fact that "[r]acism is a central feature of Western capitalism".[23] In fact, Gilroy affirms Afro-descendants' story of the past goes beyond the moment that their forefathers were taken from Africa and turned into slaves, since their past/present duality manifests itself as a shared journey "into an incompletely realized democracy that racialises and thus frequently withholds the loudly proclaimed benefits of modern citizenship."[24]

The idea of *supranational* historical imagination refers then to the global dimension of experiences such as diasporic displacement, racialization, marginalization, and exclusion due to Blackness as elements composing a feeling of belongingness to an overarching collectivity. Therefore, it underscores the fact that Black communities in present time – in Costa Rica, Brazil, Colombia, the UK, France, or in North America – share the racialized conditions of their historical ever-present marginalization, economic exploitation, and political racism in a supranational manner. They are mirror images of each other based on similar – if not nearly identical – marginalizing processes, expressing a constant "*changing same*".[25] Hence, Afro-descendant diaspora/s share certain loyalties and solidarities with members of Black communities in other countries[26] because of similar processes of (racialized) marginalization worldwide, for the Black circum-Atlantic populations live "a common experience of powerlessness somehow transcending history and experienced in *racial* categories".[27] Cohen lists being poor and underprivileged, not holding key positions of authority within their (former) host lands, and suffering ghettoization and segregation as examples of this.[28] The case of Costa Rican-born Caribbean descendants confirms the author's claims.

Even though Blacks acquired obstacle-free Costa Rican citizenship in 1949, which in turn made it possible for them to transform their former disadvantaged status by way of social, political, and economic integration to the structures of the country, Purcell (1993) affirms a "lack of congruence between ideology and realization" took place, since Afro-Costa Ricans "experienced increasing economic disfranchisement and displacement."[29] Back in the 1970s, Olien (1977) had already taken note of this unequal reality:

---

[22] Benítez-Rojo, *The Repeating Island*: 27.

[23] Andrews, "Black is a Country": 19.

[24] Gilroy, *The Black Atlantic*: 192.

[25] See Gilroy, *The Black Atlantic*: xi, where he defines "the relationship between ethnic sameness and differentiation" as "a changing same", later referred to again when he engages the discussion of the reproduction of cultural traditions not transmitted as a fixed entity, but instead through interruptions that bring together the different and the same in a complex manner (p. 101); and lastly in his discussion regarding Black cultural tradition, which he defines as a 'non-traditional' tradition redefined as the "living memory of the changing same" (p. 198).

[26] Cf. Cohen, *Global Diasporas* (1997): 58f.: "diasporic communities not only form a collective identity in their place of settlement of with their homeland, but also share a common identity with members of the same ethnic communities in other countries."

[27] Gilroy, *There Ain't No Black in the Union Jack*: 208.

[28] See Cohen, *Global Diasporas* (1997): 139–144 for a thorough explanation of these conditions concerning Black Caribbean migrants in France, the Netherlands, the UK, and North America (also discussed in "Diaspora of a Diaspora" [1992]).

[29] Purcell, *Banana Fallout*: 89, 93, and 45, respectively.

Their position in Costa Rican society had been transformed from that of "foreign laborer" on foreign-owned banana plantations to that of "Costa Rican" filling positions at the middle and bottom of the wealth, authority, and prestige substructures.[30]

Although the situation has changed across the years, the disadvantaged position the Caribbean-descendant population holds in the country has not been truly overturned. The latest PNUD (*Programa de las Naciones Unidas para el Desarrollo*) report regarding the 2011 socioeconomic situation of the Afro-descendant population in Costa Rica (2013) demonstrates how the Black minority in Costa Rica still withholds a disadvantageous position in comparison to other populations in the country, since they portray the highest percentiles of low levels of schooling, of poverty, and of a disadvantaged labor market. It shows that no-education or incomplete primary/secondary schooling is higher among Afro-Costa Ricans (23%) than in the mestizo population (19,3%). Likewise, whereas 16% of the mestizo population over twenty-five years of age has concluded their university studies, only 9% of Afro-Costa Ricans have accomplished this. The report also reveals that Black Costa Ricans hold the higher rates of unemployment in the country (2,3% vs. the country's 1,8%). Moreover, Afro-Costa Ricans have suffered longer from worse working conditions than the rest of the other population groups in the country, such as lower salary wages, reduction in social security benefits, and a limited labor market that obstructs them from developing their individual capacities so as to access better socioeconomic conditions. Lastly, the data displays Afro-descendant homes have higher extreme and non-extreme poverty percentiles as those portrayed by the mestizo group.[31] The PNUD report thus makes evident how the "incompletely realized democracy" Gilroy speaks of is also found in Costa Rica in the form of hindered upward mobility for Afro-Costa Ricans, as well as the impossibility of overcoming inequality in general.

Consequently, regarding supranational Afro-historical imaginations in literature, *diasporan* origins and marginalization due to *Blackness* define the emotionally charged element of in-group membership (Hobsbawm) articulating a large-scale solidarity (Gellner, Renan) with other Black communities in, for example, North America, Europe, Latin American, and the Caribbean. Rather than implying an essentialism regarding Black cultural production, this understanding of supranational cohesion operates across a "unifying notion of an *open* blackness" (emphasis added) and as a politically-constructed racial *solidarity*.[32] Which is why it makes sense that Kehinde Andrews states "Black is a country",[33] for Blackness is a highly charged symbolic, yet *embodied* indicator of in-group membership that transcends the outmoded consideration of territorially defined nations. It points rather to a global community whose fragments are sutured together by way of a common historical memory concerning forced uprooting and slavery, together with contemporary new displacements and experiences of racism and marginalization as consequences thereof.

---

[30] Olien, "The Adaptation of West Indian Blacks": 153.
[31] See PNUD, *Situación socioeconómica*: 30f., 41, 43, and 54.
[32] Gilroy, *The Black Atlantic*: 86.
[33] Andrews, "Black is a Country: Building Solidarity Across Borders" (2016).

In light of such realities, a supranational historical imagination in Afra-Costa Rican writers poetizes, hence, what Juan Flores (2005) refers to as a "transnational reach of black experience".[34] Something that also Taketani sustains, arguing African American literature gives form to the *Black Pacific* by "projecting *a sense of belonging* in a world that extends *beyond* US borders and the world's black belts" (emphasis added).[35] Because of this, Taketani too, like Hall does with Africa, defines the *Black Pacific* as "a sort of 'imagined community'", one that is imagined through "performance of black narratives that invent a shared *history*" (emphasis added) between African American and colored people of the Pacific Rim that "move[s] beyond the frame of the nation-state".[36] *Black Costa Rica* follows a similar line of thought.

The piece entitled "International Negro" by spoken word African American poet Damu mirrors such *supranational* premises. In the poem, Damu reflects primarily, as expressed by the title itself, on the "idea of global interconnectedness among people of color", states his interviewer Sablo Sutton (2004). Otherwise put, "International Negro" plays upon the "idea of global black identity"; or in Damu's own words: "they black like I'm black but you know we're kinda like pieces of the puzzle."[37]

The Outernational

The *outernational* is understood here as a double-faced synonym of the "ex-centric" (Hutcheon 1996), insofar the Afro-Caribbean diaspora/s that settled with time in Limón gave way to a community that existed "both *inside* and *outside* a culturally different and dominant context" (emphasis added).[38] That of the Costa Rican imagined community. On the one hand, they were the backbone workforce that motored the modernization of the country with the building of the railroad, the development of the Limón seaport, and the banana enclaves. Yet Blacks were constricted to the margins in a country that imagined itself as *white*. Moreover, since the Central Valley highlands were originally imagined as the territory representing Costa Rica while the provinces at the Pacific seaside (Puntarenas, Guanacaste) and at the Caribbean coast (Limón) existed at the margins (out-side) of this ideological *center*, the 'ex-centric' refers to the *peripheral/concealed* presence of Limón and its Black inhabitants in the official imagination of Costa Rica.

On the other hand, an *outernational* imagination adds to this position a "diaspora-consciousness" at its metaphoric core, where, as defined by Gilroy (1994), the "historical rift between the location of residence [Limón] and the location of belonging [Costa Rica]" is manifested.[39] Despite reterritorialization in Central America, Afro-Caribbean communities retained a strong sense of belonging to their homeland to the point of not being interested in obtaining Costa Rican citizenship once they resettled here. A return home was,

---

[34] Flores, "Triple Consciousness?": 80.
[35] Taketani, *The Black Pacific Narrative*: 6.
[36] Ibid.: 6f.
[37] Sablo Sutton, "Spoken Word": 224f.
[38] Hutcheon, *A Poetics of Postmodernism*: 35.
[39] Gilroy, "Diaspora": 207.

instead, always at the horizon, which defined these first generations of migrant laborers as a diasporan community. As an ethnonational diaspora in Limón, a "cultural-social-political formation of people" resided as a minority group in the host land, sharing a common ethnic and national origin.[40] That is, *Afro*-Caribbean and, in the case of Costa Rica, Jamaican. Given that their displacement occurred because they possessed "no economic resources other than their labour", Afro-Caribbean wage workers in Costa Rica represented also a proletarian diaspora.[41] Their reterritorialization in Limón was propelled because low-cost migrant labor was recruited from the Caribbean islands towards the end of the nineteenth century in order to carry out the building of the railroad due to labor shortage in Costa Rica. Lastly, Afro-Caribbeans left their homeland because, as Kim Butler defines the labor diasporas of the nineteenth and twentieth century, "shifting world economic conditions allowed imperial powers to redirect workers to sites where labor demands were greatest".[42] Therefore, an outernational historical imagination in Afra-Costa Rican poetry refers mainly to the diasporic origins of Afro-Costa Ricans as a proletarian workforce.

These origins encompass moreover two specific, successive diasporas that constitute the outernational historical imagination present in Afra-Costa Rican poetry. One referring to the African victim diaspora comprising the experience of colonial slavery, the other regarding modern day migratory movements from the Caribbean islands outbound. Cohen makes a difference between the Middle Passage as the first African diaspora and a second, successive diaspora (i.e. double diaspora) regarding Caribbean people of African descent displaced to specific countries like the United Kingdom, Netherlands, or France – to which it is highly pertinent to add here Central America as well. The author considers "migrants of African descent from the Caribbean as a paradigmatic case" of what he first called a "cultural diaspora" (1997), which he later replaced in the second edition of his book (2008) with "deterritorialized diaspora". I find both terms to be complementary and will refer to them across the ensuing pages by coupling them as a single term ("cultural/deterritorialized diaspora"), since Cohen defines Afro-Caribbeans across the globe as diasporic communities that have lost "conventional territorial reference points, to have become in effect mobile and multi-located cultures."[43] In fact, Afro-Caribbeans that settled in Limón and across Central America gradually developed into deterritorialized, multi-located cultures due to their constant transregional movement, consolidating thus plurilocal communities.[44] Which is why Caribbean communities of the Central American Atlantic coast have more in common with each other, than with the ideological imaginings of the mestizo countries they have come to belong to.

For Gilroy, "diaspora is an outer-national term"[45] that overcomes a single, homogenous, territorialized national or cultural identity. Because of this, they are located necessarily *outside* the national imagination and thus outside the imagined community. An

---

40   I follow here Scheffer's conceptualization of "ethnonational diasporas" in "Transnationalism and Ethnona-
     tional Diasporism": 130.
41   I follow here Alan Anderson's conceptualization of "proletarian or labour diasporas" in "Diaspora and Exile":
     24 (echoing Esman, "Diasporas and International Relations" [1986]).
42   Butler, "Defining Diaspora": 201.
43   Cohen, *Global Diasporas* (2008): 124.
44   Cf. Walters, *At Home in Diaspora*: xvi, see xxv.
45   Gilroy, "Diaspora": 207.

"*outernational* historical imagination" tells a story of the past by referring to key aspects of the nation-building process from the ex-centric point of view, i.e. diasporic and peripheral. In the present study, it refers specifically to Afro-Caribbean agency in the urbanization of the Limón province and in the modernization of the Costa Rican economy as 'non'-Costa Ricans located *inside* (as a migrant labor force) and yet simultaneously *outside* the dominant ideological context (the official imagination). As a result, the diaspora of anglophone Caribbean people in Limón consolidated a cultural hinterland in Costa Rica at the turn of the twentieth century in the form of what Gloria Anzaldúa has termed "a border culture, a third country, a closed country".[46]

The Infranational

As elucidated by Frantz Fanon in *Peau noire, masques blancs* (1952), Blacks are citizens of the European nations while paradoxically representing the undesired Others.[47] Yolanda Martínez-San Miguel (2014) explains Fanon's recognition of his Otherness in Paris as "the key paradox" by which "Martinicans are themselves French citizens, yet their race makes them as other vis-à-vis the metropolitan motherland".[48] Something that Nikhil Pal Singh addresses in his book *Black is a Nation* (2004) as a problem of citizenship and civil rights in a land where slavery, racism, and segregation have marked (and continue to mark) particular experiences of nationhood for Blacks (specifically in the U.S.). In studying Martin Luther King's writings, Pal Singh explains that for King "'Negroes' had a separate existence within, and a tortured relationship to, the United States as a nation".[49] As elucidated by these authors, the position Black communities hold within individual nations is deemed as being of second-class citizens due to the color of their skin.

Similar to the case of Afro-Caribbean French citizens and to the experience of African Americans in their own country, Costa Rican-born Caribbean descendants were marked as 'non'-Costa Rican by the Central Valley cultural, economic, political, and cultural center because of their Blackness and of their languages (English and Creole). As a diasporan community, it "endure[d] within a particular state and resist[ed] the cohesion imposed by it" for decades.[50] The aforementioned perspectives are appropriated and applied analogously here, where I attempt to demonstrate an *infranational* story of the past regarding linguistic assimilation and economic marginalization of anglophone Afro-Costa Ricans, deemed as second-class citizens. This semantic is implied by the term "*infranational* historical imagination", whose prefix alone sheds light on this position. Specifically, when racist nationalism in the Costa Rica subjugated Blacks to a peripheral and borderline position due to an ideological and political center that intertwined the ideas of race and nation when defining itself.

---

46   Anzaldúa, *Borderlands*: 33.
47   Martínez-San Miguel, *Coloniality of Diasporas*: 1.
48   Ibid.
49   Pal Singh, *Black is a Country*: 2.
50   Tölölyan, "The Nation-State and its Others": 4.

Lastly, before turning to the definition of *pluricentrical belonging*, it must be underscored that a diaspora consciousness is constituted according to James Clifford both negatively and positively. While the negative aspect refers to "experiences of discrimination and exclusion" that determine its *infranational* position within the imagined community, this yields the *supranational* identification that permits such communities to identify with wider "world-historical cultural/political forces". As a refreshing result, diasporic subjects "feel [positively] global".[51] The charting of pluricentrical belonging across these historical imaginations shall therefore make evident how Afra-Costa Rican poets are, in fact, glocal writers.

---

[51]   Clifford, *Routes*: 256 and 257, respectively (quoting Aihwa Ong).

Pluricentrical Belonging

Pluricentrical belonging is a conceptual metaphor comprising various definitions regarding Black Costa Rican cultural identity. On the one hand, it refers to the in-between space created by the confrontation of the Costa Rican imagined community and the Afro-Caribbean ethnonational proletarian diaspora that gradually transitioned in the twentieth century from migrant to settler status in the country. On the other, it aims to overcome the naming and claiming of double consciousness in Afra-Costa Rican poetry by expanding on the discussion concerning the cultures of the Central American Caribbean from the perspective of a cultural continuum that is best explained across nation~diaspora dynamic/s. The concept thus attempts to establish a "contact zone" that bridges a theoretical gap between imagined communities and diasporic identities circumscribed and simultaneously marginalized by the former.[1] In order to accomplish this, *pluricentrical belonging* stretches fundamentally across a multileveled historical dimension as it has been outlined in the preceding pages.

Joseph Roach's (1996) definition of the "circum-Atlantic world" is, as stated by the author himself, indebted to Paul Gilroy's landmark work on the *Black Atlantic* from where Europe, Africa and the Americas, North and South are understood as bounded together in an economic and cultural system with movements of people at its center.[2] Roach explores the *circum*-Atlantic as opposed to a *trans*-Atlantic world with the purpose of making visible other territories concerning the system of cultural exchanges Gilroy centers between Africa, Europe, and the Americas. For as noted by Clifford, "black South America and the hybrid Hispanic/black cultures of the Caribbean and Latin America are not [...] included in Gilroy's projection. He writes from a North Atlantic/European location."[3] Hence, the concept adds to Gilroy's *Black Atlantic* new territories such as the Southeastern United States (particularly the Gulf of Mexico which borders the Caribbean Sea), the Caribbean archipelago, the Atlantic coast of northern South America (particularly Venezuela and Colombia), and particularly important to *Black Costa Rica*, the Caribbean coasts of Central America.[4] Like Gilroy's Black *trans*-Atlantic, the more inclusive concept of the 'circum-Caribbean' or 'circum-Atlantic' "locates the peoples of the Caribbean rim at the heart of an oceanic interculture".[5]

---

[1] Cf. Neumann/Nünning, "Travelling Concepts": 7.
[2] Roach, *Cities of the Dead*: 5.
[3] Clifford, *Routes*: 267.
[4] Cf. Braziel/Urbina, "Circum-Caribbean Poetics: Tracing Black Atlantic Routes in the Américas" (2016).
[5] Roach, *Cities of the Dead*: 4. For Roach, this interculture is "embodied through performance" – the main object of study in his book. In it, he argues "that the scope of the circum-Atlantic interculture may be discerned most vividly by means of performances, performance traditions, and the representations of performance that it engendered" (*Cities of the Dead*: 5). According to the author, performances reveal a complex dimension where memory and history are closely intertwined, thus focusing on them as forms of cultural production that retain memory of time past beyond the traditional archive. Lastly, the author approaches the "circum-Atlantic performance [as] a monumental study in the pleasures and torments of incomplete forgetting" (p. 7) and excavates circum-Atlantic memory through sites like London and Latin New Orleans.

Black Costa Rica draws first and foremost from Du Bois's double consciousness as the departing theoretical premise, only to expand on it as *pluricentrical belonging*. Central to this is the relationship that historical imagination holds with both *roots* and *routes*. Consequently, it appropriates Gilroy's understanding of the Black Atlantic as an interwoven network extending itself "between the local and the global" and across a system of cultural interchanges.[6] Hence, *pluricentrical belonging* is a conceptual metaphor that refers specifically to Black circum-Atlantic *routes* traced into Central American *roots* – explicitly in the first half of twentieth-century Costa Rica.

Édouard Glissant's understanding of the Caribbean archipelago elucidates this oceanic interculture quite clearly. In *Le discours antillais* (1981), the author poses the question, "[w]hat is the Caribbean in fact?" To which he answers: "A multiple series of relationships."[7] *Pluricentrical belonging* follows Glissant's claim in that it approaches these women's poetry from the interrelationships they hold with a palimpsest of lands, of languages, and of histories – yet deploying local particularities. As already stated, these multiple series of relationships are consequences born out of the original African victim diaspora due to European colonialism; later extended with the Afro-Caribbean cultural/deterritorialized diaspora in Central America due to U.S. neocolonial enterprises in the region, by which nation~diaspora dynamics developed as an integral part of Black Costa Rica.

Since the present study attempts to bring together the intellectual history of Costa Rica's liberal imagined community with the coming of age of the Afro-Costa Rican community in the country, I am obliged then to refer to both the 'here' and the 'elsewhere' as inherent to the idea of *pluricentrical belonging*. Fundamental is the fact that within and across the interrelationships perceived by Glissant, the concept functions as a metaphor for the coming together of *roots* and of *routes* as a "a visible continuity between inside and outside, the dazzling convergence of here and elsewhere."[8] In so being and following Gilroy's premises, *pluricentrical belonging* functions as a concept reevaluating the "problems of nationality, location, identity, and historical memory"[9] by focusing upon the dynamic alliance between the *national* and the *diasporic*. The investigation of *pluricentrical belonging* in Afra-Costa Rican poetry takes into consideration the direct impact the Caribbean diaspora had in the imagination of Costa Rica precisely because the presence of the ethnonational proletarian diaspora in the country made visible the limits of the national perspective.[10]

I qualify the story of the past found 'below the surface' of Afra-Costa Rican poetry as 'pluricentrical' because, on the one hand, it disrupts the *homogeneity* of the liberal imagined community that determined the invention of Costa Rica as a monolithic, unchanging entity of well-proportioned sameness across *empty, homogeneous time* (Benjamin 1989). Considering that mass migrations articulate transnational routes that lastly find fluid anchorage in multiple roots regarding both (the memory of) the homeland as the host countries where they settle with time, diaspora/s acquire a central importance in debates

---

6   Gilroy, *The Black Atlantic*: 29.
7   Glissant, "Cross-Cultural Poetics": 139.
8   Ibid.: 117.
9   Gilroy, *The Black Atlantic*: 16.
10   Ibid.: 87.

concerning imagined communities. The latter are represented (i.e. imagined) as a site of ethnic and linguistic homogeneity, bound to a definite territorial identification, and where differences are abolished and assimilated into an essentialized and harmonized expression of 'one people', "gathering", as Hall (1993) refers to Gellner's affirmations, "*one* people, *one* ethnicity, [...] under *one* political roof". Hall contests the fact that "the history of the nation-states of the West has *never* been of this ethnically pure kind. [...] It has been the main function of national cultures, [...] to *represent* what is in fact the ethnic hotch-potch of modern nationality as the primordial unity of 'one people'."[11] Diaspora/s contest this *unity of homogenic oneness.*

Recalling Gilroy, "diaspora is an outer-national term".[12] Because of this, diaspora/s do not integrate quickly to the host country. On the one hand, sentiments of racism on behalf of the national community hinder integration. On the other, for generations for whom collective histories of displacement are central to their sense of peoplehood, as are those pertaining to the Black circum-Atlantic, these "cannot be 'cured' by merging into a new national community", as stated by Clifford.[13] 'Cured' I understand here as metaphorically referring to 'belonging'. Minority ethnic groups with diasporic origins who with time have transitioned from 'there' into settler status 'here' acquiring a new home, i.e. a new place to belong, retain certain cultural differences that "remain profound and sometimes insuperable" regarding their host/home lands.[14] This ultimately means that an equilibrated hybridity is impossible because of the dynamic existing *between* and *within* these spaces. This is why Walters considers that "Black writers' texts often look beyond the nation-state, demanding reading strategies that see connections in other framework".[15] *Pluricentrical belonging* is the concept that permits this reading strategy.

Nation-states represent the borderland of diaspora/s. These "are caught up with" and simultaneously "defined against [...] the norms of the nation-state".[16] Diaspora/s maintain as well their cultural identity and in-group feelings of solidarity over extended periods of time, as well as the sense of belongingness to their homeland.[17] Both because of exclusion by the host country, on the one hand, and because of class, racial, and cultural hierarchies installed by their presence, on the other. Nonetheless, diaspora/s represent too the borderlands of nation-states. As asserted by James Clifford, these are "traversed and, to varying degrees, subverted by diasporic attachments".[18] They transcend and thus challenge the authority of the national imaginations they integrate to with time since they contest "the construction of a homogeneous national space that travels through empty time from a pristine past (the 'old') to a future (the 'new') not overwhelmed by external influences".[19] In order words, diaspora/s have the capacity of distilling the borders and barriers of the imagined community, be them territorial, ethnic, linguistic, or narrative ones. As stated by

---

[11] Hall, "Culture, Community, Nation": 356.
[12] Gilroy, "Diaspora": 207.
[13] Clifford, *Routes*: 250.
[14] Cohen, *Global Diasporas* (1997): 134.
[15] Walters, *At Home in Diaspora*: vii.
[16] Clifford, *Routes*: 250.
[17] Cf. Esman, "Diasporas and International Relations": 334.
[18] Clifford, *Routes*: 250.
[19] Varadarajan, *The Domestic Abroad*: 35 (echoing Benjamin).

Tölöyan, diaspora/s "are the exemplary communities of the transnational moment"[20] whose deterritorialized cultural and collective identities cannot be easily contained within a single territorially-defined nation-state.[21] This nation~diaspora dynamic is central to the coming of age of the Black community in Costa Rica, which in turn defines literary *pluricentrical belonging*.

While the term is used on the one hand to refer to the cultural continuum installed between imagined communities and their diaspora/s at the Central American Caribbean, *pluricentrical belonging* aims to overcome as well binary oppositions of center/periphery and national/non-national when discussing Black Costa Rican writing. The ensuing analysis will make evident that Afra-Costa Rican poetry has plural centers of cultural identification, some of them determined by deterritorialization/s, others instead firmly grounded upon Costa Rican soil. This means that poetry written by Caribbean-descendant Costa Ricans withholds plural sites of cultural identity that can be traced through the routes of diasporic displacement that with time founded new roots in other territories, thus creating new homelands.

On the subject, diaspora studies point to the necessary relevance and fundamental significance that the homeland has in the conformation of diaspora/s.[22] It may be real, as for Ecuadorians living in Madrid. An idealized construct, as Africa was for the back-to-Africa movements of the twentieth century. Or even a 'myth', which in the case of the Jewish diaspora became a reality. Regarding the subject, Safran expands on how diasporic subjects share the characteristic of retaining "a collective memory, vision, or myth about their original homeland – its physical location, history, and achievements", considering them to be "their true, ideal home and as the place to which they or their descendants would (or should) eventually return".[23] Otherwise put, people in displacement articulate a strong desirability of *return* to the place once called 'home', which in turn defines their diasporic subjectivity. Taking into consideration Kim Butler's (2001) assessment that the diasporan community is quite different by the fourth generation, for it enters another phase in which its members do not forge a common identity with a distant homeland and instead actively reinforce their diasporan identity to counteract assimilation,[24] neither a traditional approach to the issue of the homeland as extensively investigated by diaspora studies, nor a

---

[20] Tölölyan, "The Nation-State and its Others": 5.

[21] Varadarajan's study of the "domestic abroad" brings this aspect to the forefront. Key to the production of a "domestic abroad" is both a lasting connection between diasporic communities and their original homelands, as well as the "claim that these connections need to be and deserve to be acknowledged and empowered through the state institutions of the homeland" (p. 9). The domestic abroad maintains economic and political ties to the original homeland, "produced through state policies and initiatives aimed at institutionalizing the relationship between nation-states and their diasporas" (p. 6) in the form of a "delocalized transnation" (quoting Appadurai), since "state policies take on a *transnational* form" (p. 39). Therefore, the author affirms that "diasporas are playing a critical role in reinscribing both nationalisms and the nation-state structure itself" through *deterritorialization* (p. 36).

[22] Edmondson, "Black America": 167.

[23] Safran, "Diasporas in Modern Societies": 83.

[24] The author suggests "another phase is entered", where "relationships develop between diverse communities of the diaspora to forge a diasporan common identity distinct from an identification exclusively as members of a homeland." Butler affirms "there is a subtle but critical difference between notions of community centered on the homeland and those centered on the diaspora itself" (Butler, "Defining Diaspora": 210).

nostalgia-premised definition of it are undertaken here. These definitions are not pertinent to the study of *pluricentrical belonging* in Afra-Costa Rican poetry given that what once represented the *host land* to migrant Caribbean workers in the past has now become the *homeland* to the new generations of Afro-Costa Ricans, as for example Campbell and McDonald, defined by Mosby as fourth generation Afro-Costa Ricans.[25] She distinguishes them from Bernard since they "are shaped by life in the dominant Hispanic culture of San José" unlike Bernard, for whom Limón is *home*.[26] Moreover, an overrated emphasis and fixation on the issue of the once geographically distant homeland may overshadow the potentiality of writers of diasporic origin in "'making' one's home", affirms Tsagarousianou (2004).[27] Especially given the fact that for diasporic people belonging to deterritorialized diasporas as Afro-Central Americans of Caribbean origin, "homelands are for all practical purposes lost to them" due to multiple displacements from diverse domiciles to one or more host lands.[28] These may be transareal, like Bernard's parents who moved from Jamaica to Limón. Or translocal, like Bernard herself who moved from Limón to San José as a child, or Campbell, from San José to Limón as an older woman. Or even transnational, as McDonald who moved from the Panamanian capital of Colón to San José when just a child.

Black Costa Rica approaches instead *historical imagination* as a highly abstract metaphor for the homeland, from where *pluricentrical belonging* stems out. In *At Home in Diaspora*, Walters approaches 'diaspora' and 'home' as no longer binary opposites. Instead, she argues that Black prose literature "performs a home in diaspora" and thus analyzes the ways in which Richard Wright, Michelle Cliff, Chester Himes, Simon Njami, and Caryl Phillips "use their writings to define and desire spaces of home" while writing outside the place of origin. Her book argues diaspora-consciousness in literature creates the concept of diaspora into a *home* itself, which writers return to via writing. According to the author, "alternative narratives of identity" are thus constructed through the literary act.[29] Expanding on the author's reflections, *pluricentrical belonging* implies diaspora literacies carry in their own paths of displacement a process of creating *home in historical imagination*. The extraction of *pluricentrical belonging* in Afra-Costa Rican lyric aims therefore to delineate above all the creative ability these daughters of the diaspora/s manifest in their poetry when negotiating their Afro-Costa Rican identity through a network of local and global linkages, which are deployed through multileveled historical imaginations. These in turn construe alternative narratives of Costa Rican identity and in so doing draw out feelings of belongingness to plural imagined communities. That is, Costa Rican, Caribbean, and Afro-descendant, which are arranged from diverse perspectives (i.e. infra/outer/supra-national). Because of this, their poetry does not tell *one* single history in no singular manner.

---

[25] Mosby, *Place, Language, and Identity in Afro-Costa Rican Literature*: 168.

[26] Mosby, "Roots and Routes": 21.

[27] Tsagarousianou, "Rethinking the concept of diaspora": 58. The author distances herself from placing too much attention to the homeland and instead argues for, on the one hand, focusing on the potentialities of the diaspora in negotiating their cultural identities and, on the other, on shifting the understanding of diasporas from mobility and displacement to connectivity.

[28] Cohen, *Global Diasporas* (2008): 8.

[29] Walters, *At Home in Diaspora*: x and xiii, see also p. xi.

The ensuing pages instead unearth how Afra-Costa Rican poetry deploys – both tacitly as explicitly – *plural* stories of the past. These stories are also manifold in their aesthetic form, given that they are expressed in linguistic, meta-historical, and spatial rhetoric. These stories are moreover plural because they repeat themselves across time and space. Hence, by tracing connectivity between Black Costa Rica and the broader Black circum-Atlantic across outer/supra/infra-national historical imaginations, *pluricentrical belonging* will be highlighted as a cultural continuum that stretches transareally and transhistorically. When read critically through a historically backwards-looking and analyzed against the discourses drafted by elite intellectuals and politicians located in the Central Valley at the turn of the nineteenth and twentieth centuries, these stories of the past contrast the hegemonic center by incorporating alternative narratives to its foundational discourses.

Pluricentrical belonging, therefore, follows Gilroy's assertion that there is a need of going beyond the national to avoid ethnonational exclusivity when approaching the cultural and political history of communities in contact. Ten years earlier, Édouard Glissant had written in the same tone about the need of national literature to be inclusive of what the author termed the *Diverse*. According to Glissant, national literature "must signal the self-assertion of new peoples, which one calls their rooted-ness, and which is today their struggle. […] It must express […] the relationship of one culture to another in the spirit of Diversity, and its contribution to the totalizing process."[30] Coherent with Glissant's appeal and Gilroy's critique of ethnic absolutism, cultural insiderism, and their relation to exclusionary national or ethnic belonging,[31] *pluricentrical belonging* charts a more pluralistic sense of the country's historic and cultural memory. For in their poetry there are no loyalties or solidarities exclusive to one single imagined community, but a mixture of them that articulates a local and transnational communal imagination. Mirroring Anzaldúa's description of *borderlands* and *borderland consciousness*, *pluricentrical belonging* expresses no "divided loyalties" but rather "a broader communal ground" upon which these poets exist as "crossers of cultures".[32] In so doing, the local and the global become mutually inclusive aspects of their poetry. Through *pluricentrical belonging*, then, a historical imagination can be studied as deploying a discourse that, as described by James Clifford,

> articulates, or bends together, both root *and* routes to construct […] forms of community consciousness and solidarity that maintain identification *outside* the national time/space in order to live *inside*, with a difference.[33] (Emphasis added)

Against 'Hybridity'

'Hybridity' is not the key feature of *pluricentrical belonging*. Nor is 'synthesis of duality'. Not even 'syncretism', defined by Cohen as "the evolution of commingled cultures that are

---

30 Glissant, "Cross-Cultural Poetics": 101.
31 See Gilroy, "Nationalism, History and Ethnic Absolutism" (1990) and "Cultural Studies and Ethnic Absolutism" (1992).
32 Anzaldúa, *Borderlands*: 109 and 106.
33 Clifford, *Routes*: 251.

different from two or more parent cultures."[34] Instead, *pluricentrical belonging* is installed within a *continuum* whose dynamic state of change permeates the idea of an open fluidity.

Even though the concept of hybridity tends to create an image of openness because of the coming together of multiple parts into a complex cultural identity that rejects homogeneity, the concept however declares to a large extent a paradoxically *closed* entity, even if determined by heterogeneity.[35] As stated by Néstor García Canclini (1995), the concept of *hybridity/hybridization* "can suggest easy integration and fusion of cultures, without giving sufficient weight to contradictions and to that which resists being hybridized."[36] Instead, the *fluidity* intrinsic to a *continuum* makes it possible to approach nation~diaspora dynamic/s and its effects in the generations following naturalization as something more than a "disaggregated identity".[37] The concept of *pluricentrical belonging* expands on the concept of a diasporized/diasporic identity by underscoring how it is composed of multiple and separate parts that exist in dialectical tension with one another, thus disrupting traditional understandings of national, cultural, linguistic, territorial, or historical identities. Without discarding neither of these and rather comprising them all in a dialectical tension, *pluricentrical belonging* refers to plural centers of identification that flow and break off into one another along a *mapped rhizome* without sacrificing neither of its elements.

Alongside Gilroy's Black Atlantic as a system of cultural interchanges and Glissant's understanding of the Caribbean as a series of multiple relationships, Deleuze and Guattari's considerations on the *rhizome* (*Mille Plateaux* 1980) as a system of multiplicity, opposed to a fixed dichotomy expressed through the image of roots and radicles, is also highly useful for explaining *pluricentrical belonging* in Afra-Costa Rican poets. Contrary to a binary logic of a fixed cultural identity (either Jamaican or Central American, either Black or Costa Rican), the rhizome *maps* out an intersection of multiple lines that connect in a state of perpetual "construction or collapsing" since these are "breaking off and starting once again" by connecting "any point to any other point".[38] Now, if this rhizome (in this case, the 'sense of belonging' to a specific collectivity) breaks or shatters – as for example through "deterritorialization" caused by diaspora/s –, it does not disappear, but instead finds the way to reunite itself upon its old lines (with its former/distant origins, i.e. Jamaica or Africa). Or by finding new ones on which to expand by "reterritorialization" (i.e. finding new sources in Costa Rica). That is why a rhizome – in this case *pluricentrical belonging* – cannot

---

34   Cohen, *Global Diasporas* (1997): 131.
35   I am indebted to Claudia Fioretti Bongianino (Afro-Latin American Mark Claster Mamolen Dissertation Workshop, Harvard University 12–13 May 2017) for the conceptualization of *pluricentrical belonging* as installed across an open *continuum*. Her keen observation and commentaries led the way for discarding "hybridity" as a central defining feature.
36   García Canclini, *Hybrid Cultures*: xxix. The author insists "that the object of study [must not be] hybridity, but the processes of hybridization" (p. xxxi).
37   See Boyarin/Boyarin, "Generation and the Ground of Jewish Identity": 721: "[Jewish] diasporic identity is a disaggregated identity. Jewishness disrupts the very categories of identity because it is not national, not genealogical, not religious, but all of these in dialectical tension with one another".
38   Deleuze/Guattari, "Introduction: Rhizome": 20 and 21.

be dual nor a syncretism,[39] for these "lines always tie back to one another".[40] Hence, I use the authors' concept and considerations interchangeably with *pluricentrical belonging* so as to contemplate the local and global elements found in Afra-Costa Rican poetry, which are lengthened and prolonged into a network of connectedness between lands and cultures, languages, and histories. As the authors state it, the rhizome is none other than "made of plateaus", proliferating and connecting with other multiplicities (i.e. *centers*).[41] Following this line of thought, the displacement of the Afro-Caribbean diaspora/s ("derritorialization") and its consequent settlement in Costa Rica ("reterritorialization") is understood as the installment of a connectedness that led to the creation of multiple and fluid identifications. In fact, to think of *pluricentrical belonging* as a cultural, linguistic, geographical, and historical continuum allows us to grasp multiple sites of cultural identification as what Anzaldúa described as a subject of *degree-variation* between cultural and historical *shifts*, given that the rhizome reflects "dimensions, or rather directions in motion".[42] As defined by Deleuze and Guattari, "the rhizome pertains to a map [...] that is always detachable, connectable, reversible, modifiable" with "multiple entryways and exits".[43]

Likewise, *pluricentrical belonging* mirrors Anzaldúa's definition of borderlands as being in a constant state of transition and whose members' identities behave, as defined by Zygmunt Bauman (1996), more like *verb(s)* than as *noun(s)*. (To Bauman's keen elucidation, the plural version needed adding.)[44] Therefore, the concept carries in its core the weight of double consciousness as a "borderland conflict", but its main – positive – aspect is the capacity of "straddling the borderlands" as a 'juggling of cultures', as Anzaldúa puts it.[45] In this dynamic movement, Afro-Costa Ricans are neither rigidly Costa Rican nor exclusively Caribbean. The hyphenated way of being determined by diasporic displacement points to the reality of being *more* than the reunion of a disaggregated identity. As affirmed by Anzaldúa, the dual identity of Chicanos as Mexican Americans does not identify with one of these identities specifically. Instead, Chicano-identity is "a synergy of two cultures with various degrees of Mexicanness or Angloness."[46] Expanding on Anzaldúa's assertion, *pluricentrical belonging* in Afra-Costa Rican poetry underscores the shifts within various and diverse degrees of Costa Rican-, Central American-, Caribbean-, and Afro-ness.

Regarding the pluralized cultural subjectivity drawn out by "straddling between two or more cultures",[47] the last chapter of Anzaldúa's extended book-essay *Borderlands* ("La conciencia de la *mestiza*/Towards a New Consciousness") deals precisely with setting ground towards a new consciousness regarding the "struggle of borders",[48] which she terms

---

[39] Deleuze/Guattari, "Introduction: Rhizome": 20: "No, this is not a new or different dualism".

[40] Ibid.: 9: "A rhizome may be broken, shattered at a given spot, but it will start up again on one of its old lines, or on new lines. [...] These lines always tie back to one another".

[41] Cf. Deleuze/Guattari, "Introduction: Rhizome": 11 and 21, respectively.

[42] Deleuze/Guattari, "Introduction: Rhizome": 21.

[43] Ibid.

[44] Bauman, "From Pilgrim to Tourist": 19: "Hence 'identity', though ostensibly a noun, behaves like a verb, albeit a strange one to be sure: it appears only in the future tense."

[45] Anzaldúa, *Borderlands*: 84 and 101, respectively.

[46] Ibid.: 85.

[47] Ibid.: 102.

[48] Ibid.: 99.

"*mestiza*-consciousness". For Anzaldúa, this new consciousness does not bring together severed/separate pieces into one single entity, nor is it interested in balancing opposing powers. Instead, the inherent nature of the *mestiza*-consciousness reveals that she

> has a plural personality, she operates in a pluralistic mode – *nothing is thrust out* [...] *nothing negated, nothing abandoned* (emphasis added). Not only does she sustain contradictions, she turns the ambivalence into something else.[49]

Since *nothing is thrust out* nor sacrificed, *pluricentrical belonging* is not mutually exclusive, but rather inclusive of pluralities where the relationships between center and margin are eradicated. *Pluricentrical belonging* "cannot hold fixity in rigid boundaries", as Anzaldúa describes the continuum between borderlands. Rather, it "shifts through divergence and similarity".[50]

On the other hand, while the traditional binary concepts of center/periphery can be utilized in order to explain exclusion from the national scene due to ethnonational premises, when speaking of fond imaginings of belonging in Afra-Costa Rican poetry they represent however outdated notions. It is rather their "complex interpenetration" that which becomes here paramount. In this sense, *pluricentrical belonging* mirrors Gilroy's claim, for whom the historical relationship between blacks and whites "lies not in the overhasty separation of the cultural forms particular to both groups into some ethnic typology but in a detailed and comprehensive grasp of their complex interpenetration."[51] This interpenetration is actualized with "the flows, exchanges, and in-between elements"[52] caused by the dynamics caught between (and yet born out of) the national/diasporic duo. It is *this* the new focus, where the new 'center' lies. Hence the need for arguing for plural centers as "intercultural cross-fertilisations"[53] that in their plurality and diversity avoid the logic of binary coding and are instead better understood from Benítez-Rojo's perspective, who claims the Caribbean is *a-centric*. For the author, the Caribbean "People of the Sea" stand as a poetic manifestation of de-centeredness, who "tend to roam the entire world in search of the centers of their Caribbean-ness".[54]

Is it 'Pluricentrical' or 'Acentrical' Belonging?

Regarding the Caribbean, Benítez-Rojo claims there is an intrinsic "impossibility of [it] being able to assume a stable identity".[55] The author refers to the similarities (the centrifugal force) and to the differences (the centripetal force) manifested across countries and between Caribbean cultures in order to state that Caribbean identity is in a constant state of flux (i.e. in a movement of *chaos*). He likens this movement to that of the Milky Way, extending itself outward infinitely. In it, it is possible to "detect dynamic regularities – not results – within

---

49   Anzaldúa, *Borderlands*: 101.
50   Ibid.
51   Gilroy, *The Black Atlantic*: 48.
52   Ibid.: 190.
53   Ibid.: 188.
54   Benítez-Rojo, *The Repeating Island*: 25.
55   Ibid.

the (dis)order that exists beyond the world of predictable pathways."[56] Hence, the circum-Caribbean rim comprises a continuity of Caribbean culture/s along a series of cultural discrepancies due to a multilayered process of exchange across time and place. As defined by Benítez-Rojo, the Caribbean functions as a point of transition between the North and South American continents, bridging them together through cultural encounter and exchange ever since Modernity until present times. In the author's words,

> the Caribbean is an important historico-economic sea and, further, a cultural meta-archipelago *without center* (emphasis added) and without limits, a chaos within which there is an island that proliferates endlessly, each copy a different one, founding and refounding ethnological materials like a cloud will do with its vapor[.][57]

The author underscores there is no *one center* that dictates one series of homogeneous cultural codes in each single territory. As a result, the Caribbean archipelago "has the virtue of having neither a boundary nor a center".[58] In this openness, the Caribbean is *centerless*, for it succumbs and tends to unfold within its own center, annihilating it and posing more importance on the historical ripples repeated across time. Hence, the archipelago cannot be reduced to a space such as the Antilles or the Central and South American Atlantic coast. For the author, it represents instead a *meta-archipelago* that extends itself beyond its own geographical (maritime, insular, and continental) limits.

A fundamental problematic now emerges. Is being *a-centered* the same as being *pluricentrical*? I argue across these pages *for* the *pluricentrical* instead of (not against) the *acentrical*, since my approach focuses on the reference to *detailed and designated* historical imaginations. Extracting primordially the writers' capacity of poeticizing realities and histories beyond one single territory, these intertwined multiplicities are named here in exact and detailed specificities. The single elements are furthermore linked to the conjunction of the totality in a cylindrical manner. Afra-Costa Rican poetry can be read as a project that makes visible their otherness and their peripheral asymmetry against the hegemonic cultural center from a renewed perspective, one that transforms their ex-centric position into the conjunction of *plural* manifestations: outer/infra/supra/national, cultural, spatiotemporal, linguistic, historical, rhetorical, and aesthetic. A dynamic concentration of rhizomatic histories can be drawn out in Afra-Costa Rican poetry by paying attention to specific rhetorical figures that in turn make evident precise and concrete aspects of the coming of age of the Afro-Costa Rican minority, thus naming and explaining the *acentrical* with punctual specificities along a traceable continuum. In this sense, the *pluricentrical* is understood as an inverse metaphor of the acentric, insofar to deploy plural centers of identification mirrors Benítez-Rojo's claim that there is no *one* center dictating a homogeneous cultural code, but rather *countless*.

Lastly, *pluricentrical belonging* is not only a conceptual metaphor comprising Guattari and Deleuze's rhizomatic identity, Gilroy's webbed network of cultural interchanges, Glissant's poetic of relation, and Anzaldúa's straddling between borderlands. It mirrors best Stuart Hall's Janus-faced definition of Caribbean identity/ies as exposed by himself in

---

56   Benítez-Rojo, *The Repeating Island*: 36.
57   Ibid.: 9.
58   Ibid.: 4.

"Cultural Identity and Diaspora" (1990). Despite the similarities linking Black communities across the globe upon a 'one-ness' that is the global Black experience to which I referred to with supranational historical imagination, Halls also defines Afro-Caribbean cultural identity/ies as a set of critical, highly significant, deep *differences* constituted by the particularity of each community's history and culture. One must only think about the French Caribbean islands and their particularity regarding anglophone, Dutch-, or Spanish-speaking Caribbean neighbors to fully comprehend Hall's premise. Likewise, Benítez-Rojo explains how the presence of England, Spain, France, and Holland in the region "helped to lend a heterogeneous aspect to the colonial Caribbean", in which despite the shared features throughout the insular region, "other obvious factors [...] keep the area from being coherent."[59] As underscored by Maryse Condé (1999), "[e]ven within the English-speaking Caribbean, people from different areas are intensely, and proudly, conscious of their difference from each other."[60]

Hall critically underlines that it is therefore not possible to speak of 'one experience, one identity' (sameness/continuity) without recognizing its counterpart, the differences (ruptures/discontinuities) which constitute, precisely, the Caribbean's "uniqueness".[61] Benítez-Rojo speaks of *centrifugal* and *centripetal* forces working at the Caribbean that yield differences and similarities among its people, territories, histories, and cultural productions within a dynamic he categorizes as *chaotic*.[62] Like these authors, Gilroy also places central importance to this continuum of sameness within differentiation and to difference across sameness as the theoretical frame of thought that allows him to overcome the binary between diasporic and nationalistic perspectives.[63] A binary focus that according to Benítez-Rojo represents a "constricting violence".[64] Specially because, as defined by the Cuban scholar, the Caribbean has "the furtive image of collective Being".[65] This makes it highly difficult – if not impossible – "to speak and write of the circum-Caribbean literature in unitary terms".[66]

Black Costa Ricans too are 'framed' by two simultaneous vectors installed across a continuum of similarity/continuity and difference/rupture in the Central American Caribbean region. There too persists difference *in* and *alongside* continuity.[67] *Central American English* (1983), compiled by John Holm, is exemplary of such a transareal continuum composed of differences across similarities. The volume gathers a series of linguistic studies regarding the particularities of the anglophone communities of Caribbean origin located at the Central American isthmus.[68] It thus expands on the cultural continuum that exists between the insular anglophone Caribbean and the Central American Hispanic

---

59   Benítez-Rojo, *The Repeating Island*: 34.
60   Condé, "Introduction": 1.
61   Hall, "Cultural Identity and Diaspora": 225.
62   Benítez-Rojo, *The Repeating Island*: 35f.
63   Gilroy, "Diaspora": 209.
64   Benítez-Rojo, *The Repeating Island*: 36.
65   Ibid.: 1.
66   Braziel/Urbina, "Circum-Caribbean Poetics": 7.
67   Hall, "Cultural Identity and Diaspora": 227.
68   See also Zimmer's (2011) study on the spoken Spanish of Afro-Costa Ricans, where she offers a short subsection that refers transareally to Central American English (*El español hablado por los afrocostarricenses*: 25–30).

countries by way of *language*. In this sense, the Afro-Costa Rican community is actually exemplary of the Caribbean cultures located in Central America and that, echoing Hall, inhabit various identities and speak at least two cultural languages.[69]

Pluricentrical belonging in Afra-Costa Rican poetry thus reveals the continuity/discontinuity and repetitiveness/rupture reality these authors take the Caribbean to represent, specified across a trifold historical imagination. The concept mirrors the rhizomatic experience that holds, in fact, *no one-truer-identity as expression of truer origins*. For the rhizome is not reducible to a single one. Because of this, *pluricentrical belonging* in Afra-Costa Rican poetry reflects the glocal along a cultural, linguistic, geographical, and historical continuum, which is expressed by *oxymoron, metonymy,* and *code-switching*.

> *... I have no country,*
> *my homeland cast me out;*
> *yet all countries are mine...*

Gloria Anzaldúa, *Borderlands*

---

[69]   Hall, "Cultural Identity and Diaspora": 225.

PART II – BECOMING AFRO-COSTA RICAN

THE CARIBBEAN AS THE BORDERLAND OF THE COSTA RICAN IMAGINED COMMUNITY

Imagining Costa Rica: "We are Different, We are White"

> The people of Costa Rica have a larger proportion of pure Spanish blood, less intermixed with that of the negro and Indian, than those of any other Central American state; and if they have attained a greater prosperity, and evinced a greater degree of activity and enterprise, materially and otherwise, it may fairly be attributed to this circumstance.
>
> E.G. Squier, *The States of Central America* (1858)

In 1940, an editorial written by Saúl Zapata appeared in *La Prensa Libre* stating that "Negros costarricenses no hay [...] los negros nacidos en Limón, hijos de padres antillanos no son costarricenses."[1] Nowadays, such a claim no longer withholds veracity, for those children of Antillean parents were granted Costa Rican citizenship in 1949 and have since then become part of the sociopolitical structure of the nation-state. Nonetheless, the quoted opinion is exemplary of the attitude manifested by Costa Ricans regarding the settlement of the Black diaspora in Limón at the first half of the twentieth century, expressed mainly as an animosity against Black immigrant workers. At the center of this conflict was an essentialized ethnic consideration of Costa Rican-ness, what Alexánder Jiménez has termed a metaphysical ethnonationalism (*nacionalismo étnico metafísico*).

In *El imposible país de los filósofos: el discurso filosófico y la invención de Costa Rica*, Jiménez (2013) disarticulates the Costa Rican imagery of the *Suiza centroamericana* by relating literature, history, and the imagined community portrayed by the country's intellectuals as founded upon racist, colonialist, classist, and sexist discursive practices. Following Ricœur's studies on the relevance of metaphor and narrative in the disciplines of History, Literature, and Philosophy (*La métaphore vive* 1975 and *Temps et récit* 1983–1985), Jiménez carries out an in-depth analysis of the most significant metaphors, images, and histories delivered by national philosophical discourse and which constituted the invention of the modern Costa Rica nation. According to Jiménez, the liberal project expressed itself through ethnonational categorizations that at the second half of the twentieth century (1948–1980) resulted in a discourse he has termed *nacionalismo étnico metafísico*. He defines the latter as a narrative form whose content operates metaphors, fictions, and imageries mixed with metaphysical argumentations and categories.[2] By studying the writings of twentieth century Costa Rican intellectuals, the author brings to light conservative metaphysical notions like *alma nacional, ser costarricense, ser de la nacionalidad, patria esencial*, and *esencia nacional*, and explains how for most of these philosophers, as well as for their predecessors, the national population's 'rationality' was an irrefutable element of its national essence, which in turn was based on racial considerations. The origins of such discourses are traced next.

---

[1] Quoted in Duncan/Powell, *Teoría y práctica del racismo*: 71.
[2] Jiménez, *El imposible país*: 41f., n. 28 and n. 34.

Amnesias and Selections

"The essence of a nation is that all individuals have many things in common, and also that they have forgotten many things."[3] Ernest Renan, intellectual proprietor of the former quote, explains how modern nations correspond to a historical result brought upon by a series of convergent conditions. As theorists of nations and nationalism have assessed it, the nation is not a natural, self-bred entity born out of historical progress. Instead, a nation is a product of carefully crafted amnesias and selected memories. As discussed by Eric Hobsbawm in *Nations and Nationalism since 1780* (1994), a nation is an entity that came to be in modern sociohistorical conditions in which multifold elements were manipulated – consciously and unconsciously – by ruling and middle classes in the process of crafting group self-representation. One of them is precisely the interplay between what Ernst Gellner (1983) claims are distorting amnesias and deceptive selections regarding the ideological manufacturing of a common past.[4]

When Renan posits the question, "What things are adequate for the creation of a nation?" he responds: "to have a common past and a common will in the present".[5] This explains the nation as voluntaristic, that is, as possible only thanks to voluntary participation and recognition of belonging by its members, as well as the will to continue performing things as such.[6] A common past, instead, corresponds to a discourse delicately crafted by intellectuals working close to the nation-state and whose aim is to create social cohesion between members of the imagined community. This lays the foundation of a single heritage and a common frame of reference concerning, as stated by Hobsbawm, the "invention of traditions" regarding specific glories, men, heroes, places, memories, and things performed under the mantle of the nation's flag, which the in-group members of a nation identify as elements of their 'own history'.[7] In the author's words, "all invented traditions, so far as possible, use *history* as a legitimator of action and cement of group cohesion" (emphasis added).[8] Carefully crafted as a narrative of the nation, a national past generates cohesion among people who have never met, but who share nevertheless a historical reference imagined as common to all.

Hence, an official historical imagination connects diverse generations of an imagined community across what Walter Benjamin called "homogenous, empty time". That is, out of a sort of eternal present that remains fundamentally the same along a supposed linear sequence of historical progress and from which the nation combusts automatically and spontaneously. Benjamin critiques it as 'empty' because temporal progression has been conceptualized as pursuing its course inevitably, which has led historicism to create an "'eternal' image of the past".[9] This *empty time* fabricates a series of time-spatial scenarios

---

[3] Renan, "What is a nation": 11f.
[4] Gellner *Nations and Nationalisms*: 56 and 57.
[5] Renan, "What is a nation": 19.
[6] Gellner lists two definitions concerning imagined communities: (1) a cultural one, where it is stated that people within a nation share a common culture. And (2), voluntaristic, according to which people belong to a same nation if they *recognize* each other as belonging to the same nation (*Nations and Nationalisms*: 7).
[7] See Hobsbawm, "Introduction: Inventing Traditions": 6f.
[8] Ibid.: 12.
[9] Benjamin, "Theses on the Philosophy of History": 260.

that organize a collectivity's self-representation arranged across selected historical memories which have been fixed, developed, justified, and delivered to its members as part of an *official nationalism*.[10] This corresponds broadly speaking to a policy carried out in emergent nation-states where the ruling classes define national symbols and representations with the purpose of securing and preserving their interests. As explained by Anderson, official nationalism functions as a discursive strategy that justifies the ruling class's power in order to retain it and, what is more important, it reifies 'a people' within a delimited territory together with an official state language and a common past.

Hobsbawm explains that at issue is mainly the problem of establishing and maintaining feelings of obedience, loyalty, and correspondence on behalf of the newly emerged citizens of the state, which have come to be thanks to the democratization of nation-states. For the author, the diverse processes of modernization dictate the need of elaborating and updating social bonds to the upper-level governmental organization. In this sense, the main purpose of deploying an official nationalism is the consolidation of social cohesion within a political formation characterized by social disorganization brought upon by socio-economic transformations such as independence and the posterior consolidation of political communities with states and citizens thereof.[11] The discourses crafted by elite intellectuals hence draw a complex re-presentation of the nation structured upon the culture, values, and symbols they embody and through which they desire to create a monolithic and homogenous imagined community, inviting the working class into their nation-building project.

In *Nations and Nationalisms since 1790*, Hobsbawm also refers to the fact that nations are "constructed essentially from above" by those in political and influential positions in society as key actors dictating a national imagery. The author emphasizes nations are "dual phenomena, constructed essentially from above, but which cannot be understood unless also analyzed from below".[12] That is, comprehended from the perspective of the ordinary people, which represent the object of nationalistic propaganda that influences and forms their needs, interests, and fears. As an element of official nationalism, the creation of a common past is one of the principal aspects that allows individuals of all classes to recognize themselves as members of a *shared fellowship*. Furthermore, a common past is articulated and fixed by *the act of writing the nation*. That is, across a narrative dictated *from above* and composed of facts, symbols, and foundational myths through "textual strategies, meta-

---

[10] Anderson draws the concept of official nationalism from Seton-Watson (1977), who specifies it as the doctrine that replaced the principle of dynastic loyalty as basis of government legitimacy. It consists in imposing the nationality of the powerful nations upon all subjects of the empire, drawing smaller states into their own "superior" culture and thus attempting to create a single, homogenous nation (Seton-Watson, *Nations and States*: 148). Anderson echoes Seton-Watson when analyzing how empires and dynasties accomplished naturalization of their power as a means of retaining their privileged place to counteract the threatening popular national movements that were gaining ground at the turn of the eighteenth and nineteenth centuries (see Anderson, *Imagined Communities*: Ch. 6, 83–111). Seton-Watson explains how the leaders of multilingual and multi-religious states within these empires started thinking of their communities as nations and when these ideas reached the larger part of the population, national movements arose demanding their status be recognized (see Seton-Watson, *Nations and States*: Ch. 6: 86–98; p. 143).

[11] Hobsbawm, "Mass-Producing Traditions: Europe, 1870–1914": 265.

[12] Hobsbawm, *Nations and Nationalisms since 1790*: 10.

phoric displacements [...] and figurative stratagems", as signaled by Homi Bhabha (1990).[13] Much like Anderson's approach to newspapers and novels as the specific means by which the imagination of modern nations was carried out through *language* – "not in blood!"[14] –, Michel de Certeau underlines the fact that it is *the act of writing history* at the hands of a political party that which creates a particular space, such as an imagined community and its metaphors.[15] By way of its narrative procedure, an official historical imagination becomes a marker of group-identity that creates the illusion of historic continuity between the past and the present. However, as Benjamin draws attention to it, the image of the past becomes a threat insofar it transforms itself into "a tool of the ruling classes".[16] For as both Anderson and de Certeau have underlined it, the writing of history at the hands of the powerful serves and legitimizes *their* power, as well as prioritizing their views and imagery regarding the imagined community.[17] In fact, Anderson signals the "official rewriting of history" as one of "the policy levers of official nationalism".[18] That is, individual and collective memories of thousands of people must be sacrificed for the sake of a communal past in order to legitimize and create national cohesion. In the case of Costa Rica, Afro-descendant and Indigenous autochthonous collectivities, for example, were sacrificed in this process of nation-building. And it must not go without saying that across time "[c]ulture is made by those in power – *men*" (emphasis added).[19]

Costa Rica was imagined into being like any other nation.[20] That is, by delimiting its territory, centralizing and organizing its political power around the state, and by imagining its citizens as sharing common places, memories, and identity markers that were turned into symbols of nationality, thus homogenizing its population. Central to the mechanism of national cohesion dictated from above was the idea of Costa Rica's 'exemplary and exceptional' character in the region. This discourse was drafted as a proto-nationalism at the independence juncture (1820s–1870s) by the upper-level governmental figures of the

---

[13]   Bhabha, "Introduction": 2.

[14]   Anderson, *Imagined Communities*: 145. For Anderson, novels and newspapers were the innovative means of the print market that carried out this project. In fact, Anderson's innovative contribution to the study of nation building is the role print-capitalism had in the development of communal feelings of belonging. It was through writing that "the independent movements in the Americas became, as a soon as they were printed about, 'concepts', 'models', and indeed 'blueprints'" taking the European independent states as their paradigm (Anderson, *Imagined Communities*: 82; cf. p. 61). Hobsbawm adds education and sport also have an important role in this procedure (cf. *Nations and Nationalisms since 1790*: 142f. and "Mass-Producing Traditions: Europe, 1870–1914": 300f.).

[15]   De Certeau, *The Writing of History*: 6. For the author, "the making of history has referred to writing" for the last four centuries (p. 5f.), to which he adds that this practice "is buttressed by a political power which creates a space proper (a walled city, a nation, etc.) where a will can and must write (construct) a system (a reason articulating practices)" (p. 6), which in the long run "'legitimizes' the force that power exerts" (p. 7).

[16]   Benjamin, "Theses on the Philosophy of History": 257.

[17]   De Certeau, *The Writing of History*: 7.

[18]   Anderson, *Imagined Communities*: 101. See Ch. 6: 83–111.

[19]   Anzaldúa, *Borderlands*: 38.

[20]   Jiménez affirms this at the beginning of his book (*El imposible país*: 82): "Costa Rica ha sido inventada de la misma manera en la cual han sido inventadas otras naciones latinoamericanas y mundiales."

nation-state.[21] During this pre-stage, or first stage, of the nation-building process, the *invention of the Costa Rican difference* came into being.

Inventing an Exceptional and Exemplary Costa Rica

Historian Víctor Hugo Acuña (2002) traces the "invention of the Costa Rican difference" between 1810 and 1870 as a positive image that contrasted admirable traits of Costa Rica to negative features of neighboring countries, specially Nicaragua. The author traces three fundamental periods in the consolidation of this imagined difference: (1) at the independence juncture (1821–1823), when the fundamental components are conceptualized; (2) the period between the 1820s and the 1830s, when the idea of Costa Rica as a 'special and particular' community is developed; and (3) towards the end of the 1830s and into the 1840s, when the foundational elements of the first period are fixed into a national imagery. He states that the liberal period only added the idea of "more teachers than soldiers" to the consolidated imagery, as well as underlining a racial ideology that referred to a white, European-descendant community and to democracy as definite features of Costa Ricanness.[22] Acuña's research rescues the central myths regarding the construction of Costa Rica's national character, which found its strength in the category of 'exemplary difference' – with *racial homogeneity, peace, equality,* and *democracy* as its defining elements.

On the one hand, the austere character of young Costa Rica was celebrated and poverty was exalted as a positive reality. This idea was inherited from colonial times, when Costa Rica was seen as a relegated territory of the Spanish Empire: "siempre fue pobre Costa Rica […] ninguna Provincia está más indigente en toda la Monarquía".[23] The austere and poor character of the recently independent territory functioned as a platform upon which the idea of democracy and social equality was later built upon. Its 'abandonment' gave way to colonial poverty because of the territory's isolated reality, which with time came to positively define a Costa Rican society lacking of socioeconomic inequality when compared to neighboring territories.[24] Due to its peripheral position, which had been the cause for the land's neglect, a "rural democracy" was able to (discursively) emerge[25] in which poverty acted as the main aspect which permitted an egalitarian society to develop.[26] Steven Palmer (1996) states that being isolated and largely ignored as a poor territory during colonial times had left the region with a considerable amount of land to be divided and expanded for a small-numbered society, which was eager to work and was not interested in revolutions nor

---

[21] According to Palmer (2004), after Independence and before liberalism (1830s–1870s), the formation of the Costa Rican state was accomplished along what Hobsbawm conceptualized as "proto-nationalisms", a pre-stage regarding the manipulation of sentimental imaginings of the nation (i.e. nationalism). Jiménez delimits the first stage between 1821 and 1870 (*El imposible país*: 85).

[22] Acuña, "La invención de la diferencia costarricense": 191 and 218.

[23] "Actas del Cabildo de Cartago, 1800–1810", quoted in Acuña, "La invención de la diferencia costarricense": 193.

[24] Giglioli, "¿Mito o idiosincracia?": 193–99.

[25] Pakkasvirta, *¿Un continente, una nación?*: 106.

[26] Cortés, *La invención de un país imaginario*: 28.

in intervening in its neighbors' conflicts.[27] To own land, however, did not mean wealth, but instead functioned alongside the idea of poverty as a positive feature of Costa Ricans as a humble people, states Giovanna Giglioli (1996), since the owning of private property was interpreted as fairly-distributed.[28]

On the other hand, Costa Rica had no long-lasting civil wars, nor long periods of political instability during the nineteenth century. Nonetheless, the few wars and dictator-ships that the country experimented were drawn away by the exaltation of a *peaceful* character when compared to other troubled Central American countries.[29] As the Costa Rican writer Fernando Contreras expressed in 1996 at the *Tertulias del Farolito*, organized by the Philosophy Department of the University of Costa Rica together with the *Centro Cultural Español* on the subject of the imagined conceptions of Costa Rica, the Costa Rican 'us' was invented by means of comparison with its neighbors, fabricating the fiction of its difference into myths of 'a peaceful fatherland'. Thus, Costa Rica was imagined as a privi-leged country in the middle of barbaric neighbors who were always at war.[30]

Together with 'austere' and 'peaceful', features such as 'order', 'harmonious', 'laborious', 'neutral', and 'prudent' were drafted as a consequence of this 'peaceful poverty' and became fundamental political virtues in the discourses pertaining to the Costa Rican imagery. Jiménez too speaks of the invention of Costa Rican traits such as 'order', 'absence of social conflict', and 'democracy' as assumed essential and exclusive characteristics of this 'special' country when opposed to the adjacent nations' tendency to disorder and disaster.[31] These key symbols were conceptualized and refined throughout the nineteenth century, thus *inventing the Costa Rican difference.*[32] They became the basic ideological components of the exceptional and exemplary character that liberal intellectuals later developed in the mature elaboration of the Costa Rican imagined community.

Following both Anderson and Hobsbawm, Steven Palmer (2004) claims an official nationalism was drafted from 1880 onwards by liberal intellectuals working close to the state who disseminated the imaginings of Costa Rica from above and through diverse institutions and activities.[33] In his study of "intellectual racism" (1996), he defines these intellectuals as a group of people composed mainly by public, political and diplomatic figures, journalists, authors and editors regarding the subject of education, as well as philosophers and teachers, among other academic professions. These conformed a privileged group of learned people mostly all based at the San José capital and who were in charge of the articulation of a national culture.[34] Jiménez also accounts for the invention of Costa Rica between 1890 and 1914 at the hands of the coffee oligarchy, which handed down

---

27 Palmer, "Racismo intelectual": 114f.: "[…] su pobreza, insignificancia e ignorancia durante la época colonial [había sido] lo que había dejado a Costa Rica con una división de la propiedad razonable, con tierra para expansión y una sociedad pequeña, asidua al trabajo y racialmente homogénea, en contra de las revoluciones y de la intervención en los asuntos de sus vecinos."

28 Giglioli, "¿Mito o idiosincracia?": 193.

29 For a discussion on the eradication of nineteenth-century wars from Costa Rica's imagery, see Acuña, "La invención de la diferencia costarricense": 198–211.

30 Contreras, "Territorios y fronteras": 67.

31 Jiménez, *El imposible país*: 34.

32 Acuña, "La invención de la diferencia costarricense": 197.

33 Palmer, "Sociedad anónima, cultural oficial": 261f.

34 Palmer, "Racismo intelectual": 100f.

diverse marks of identity to the working class and small coffee producers through the education system and its diverse activities (such as hymns and civic ceremonies).[35] Parallel to the elaboration of elite discourses regarding the imagination of Costa Rica, both authors point to the creation of what French historian Pierre Nora termed in the 1980s as *lieux de mémoire*.[36] During this period, for example, the National Archive (1881), along with the National Museum (1887) and the National Library (1888), the National Monument (1895), and the National Theatre (1897) were built. Also, oligarchical elite intellectuals developed the foundational narrative of the national hero Juan Santamaría (*Campaña Nacional de 1856*)[37] and the building of his commemorative statue (1891). Additionally, the conceptualization of a *national* literature became too a foundational element of Costa Rican cultural memory. Lastly, towards the end of the nineteenth century, *racial homogeneity* was discursively added to these aspects as a central discourse pertaining to the imagery of Costa Rica.

Crafting Social Cohesion: Erasing Mestizaje

Eric Hobsbawm states that ethnicity functioned in Europe as a marker of nationhood only after 1880, reinforced by Darwinism and scientific considerations on 'races', where 'race' and 'nation' were used as virtual synonyms.[38] Accordingly, Steven Palmer affirms that the concept of 'race' was used during the liberal period in Costa Rica to identify ethno-biological differences of its population. He asserts the concept was often utilized as a synonym of nationality under the presumption of elaborating politics of social protection that would avoid Costa Rica's racial conformation from being degenerated.[39] He calls this frame of thought "intellectual racism" and pinpoints its birth in Costa Rica (and also in Guatemala) between 1870 and 1920 as a consequence of social Darwinism and eugenic opinions developed in Europe under the curtain of scientific racism. Intellectual racism rested much like scientific racism upon the idea that humans could be classified according to their phenotypical characteristics, which in turn determined moral, intellectual, and cultural qualities of the group. During this period, the country's leaders and intellectuals tended to adopt the assumptions of social Darwinism in the effort to give birth to a nation in which its racial homogeneity had to be safeguarded from racial contamination. It was in the liberal period that the idea of an exceptional and exemplary country in the region was ripened to a mature state by intellectuals that imagined a political community differentiated upon an ethnic principle of nationality. The idea of whiteness was essential to the

---

[35] Jiménez, *El imposible país*: 86.
[36] Three volumes on the subject were published under the direction of Nora (*La République* [1984], *La Nation* [1986] and *Les France* [1992]) with the purpose of "rethinking France", as the English title underlines it. For a definition of *lieux de mémoire* by Nora, see "Between Memory and History: Les Lieux de Mémoires" (1989).
[37] Cf. Quesada, *Unos y los otros*: 32.
[38] Hobsbawm, *Nations and Nationalisms since 1790*: 108.
[39] Palmer, "Racismo intelectual": 100, 105, and 120f.

imagination of Costa Rica, which contemporary historians, philosophers, and literary critics have critically referred to in recent years.[40]

According to Acuña, racial homogeneity became a central idea of the country's difference in the region towards the middle of the nineteenth century and strongly developed from then onwards as part of an official nationalism.[41] For, as assessed by Palmer, Costa Rica was not belligerent, was not revolutionary, and, furthermore, it was not mestiza nor indigenous.[42] As a consequence, one of the strongest consolidated myths of traditional Costa Rican historiography and popular mentality came to be the 'purity' or 'Spanish-ness' of its inhabitants and where whiteness was considered to be its main constituent, as assessed by Mauricio Meléndez in *Negros y blancos, todo mezclado* (1997).[43] On the subject, Giovanna Giglioli (1998) attests this principle can be found in each and every one of the foundational writers of the Costa Rican imagined community of the late nineteenth century up to the first half of the twentieth century.[44] Likewise, Palmer (1995) affirms that from 1880 onwards, liberals denied heterogeneity and insisted contrarily on racial homogeneity.[45] On the subject, Lara Putnam (1999) defines racial homogeneity as one of the central motives of the liberal nation-building project.[46]

The idea of a white Costa Rican society was moreover supported by foreigners who journeyed to the country (1840–1860s). After three months travelling in Costa Rica, the Scottish traveler Robert Glascow summarized his impressions of the country's racial cartography by stating that its inhabitants were almost all white since they did not mix with the Indigenous populations, concluding that the few people of color had come without a doubt from neighboring countries.[47] The German travelers Wagner and Scherzer also attested a predominantly white population after spending some time in Costa Rica (1853–54),[48] while the North-American E.G. Squier (1858) – quoted in the epigraph – went so far as to state that the country's prosperity and peaceful nature, contrary to the other Central

---

40   See for example Palmer, "Hacia la 'auto-immigración'" (1995), "Racismo intelectual" (1996), "Sociedad anónima" (2004); Giglioli, "¿Mito o idiosincrasia?" (1996); Lobo/Meléndez, *Negros y blancos: todo mezclado* (1997); Jiménez/Oyamboru, *Costa Rica imaginaria* (1998); Murillo, "La piel de la patria" (1998); Zavala, "Novela de la nación en crisis" (2008); Putnam, "Ideología racial" (1999); Cáceres, *Negros, mulatos, esclavos y libertos en la Costa Rica del siglo XVII* (2000); Jiménez, *El imposible país* (2013); Acuña, "La invención de la diferencia costarricense" (2002); Cortés, *La invención de Costa Rica* (2003); and Sandoval/Alvarenga Venútolo, *El mito roto* (2007).

41   The first official document that Acuña has found where racial homogeneity is stated as a constituent of the Costa Rican people dates back to 1856 and it pertains to the annual report delivered by Congress to President Juan Rafael Mora. In it, the foundational attribute of a *laborious* people is placed alongside its racial homogeneity. In it, Costa Ricans are described as 'a laborious and honest people, docile to the laws and respectful to its authorities, *racially homogenous* and because of this united' (Acuña, "La invención de la diferencia costarricense": 212; emphasis added).

42   Palmer, "Racismo intelectual": 114: "[...] el carácter nacional se vio definido cada vez más en términos que lo distinguían del resto de Centroamérica".

43   Meléndez, "Segunda Parte. Las familias": 89.

44   Giglioli, "Los colores de la idiosincrasia": 24.

45   Palmer, "Hacia la 'auto-inmigración'": 77.

46   Putnam, "Ideología racial": 142.

47   Quoted in Fernández, "Robert Glasgow Dunlop": 113: "Los habitantes del Estado de Costa Rica son casi todos blancos, no habiéndose mezclado con los indios como en otras partes de la América española, y los pocos de color han venido sin duda de los Estados vecinos."

48   Acuña, "La invención de la diferencia costarricense": 212.

American countries, was due to its racial homogeneity. "Her revolutions however", he writes, "were less bloody than those of Guatemala and Nicaragua, owing, probably, rather to the circumstance and homogeneousness of its population than to a higher morality or a more tolerant spirit."[49] A few years earlier, in 1851, the Guatemalan Felipe Molina had stated for the international community that Costa Rica had 90,000 whites and 10,000 indigenous people.[50] And last but not least, the Irish man Thomas Meagher referred to Costa Rica as the "Switzerland of the Tropics" in 1860.[51] This has become one of the fundamental metaphors and strongest identity symbols of the Costa Rican nation passed on ever since as the *Suiza centroamericana*. Proof of this is Erick Verg's perception of Costa Ricans in the second half of the twentieth century, which he published in his book *Mañana ist es zu spät…* (1962):

> Costa Rica ist anders. Costa Rica ist so sehr anders, daß ich versucht bin, alles, was ich bisher geschrieben habe, noch einmal durchzugehen und an jeder Stelle, an der ich verallgemeinernd von 'Lateinamerika' oder fern 'karibischen Ländern' gesprochen habe, hinzuzufügen: '… außer Costa Rica'. […] In Costa Rica ist nicht nur die Oberschicht 'weiß', sondern alle. Die Gepäckträger, die Zollbeamten, die Taxichauffeure. Es ist eines der wenigen tropischen Länder, wo der Weise ganz zu Hause ist.

> ["Costa Rica is different. Costa Rica is so different, that I am tempted to go through everything I've written so far and add at every point where I have spoken generally of 'Latin America' or distant 'Caribbean countries': '… except Costa Rica'. […] In Costa Rica not only the upper class is 'white', but everyone. The porters, the customs officers, the taxi drivers. It is one of the few tropical countries, where the white man feels at home."][52]

Costa Rican liberal intellectuals, drawing proudly on the international perception, echoed and reiterated persistently the imaginary origins of a white, Costa Rican people. The 'pure Costa Rican race' ("la raza costarricense tan pura y tan bien formada") was conceived as a matter of praise, to which positive attributes like hard-working and ambitious ("laboriosa y emprendedora") were laid side by side, as proclaimed by the Governor of Limón in 1886.[53] As a result, liberal official nationalism essentialized particular characteristics of the community's heterogeneous population in order to legitimize and create national

---

49   Squier, *The States of Central America*: 466.
50   Felipe Molina, *Bosquejo histórico de la República de Costa Rica* (1851). The text is referred to and quoted by Palmer, "Hacia la 'auto-inmigración'": 77. Also by Acuña, who defines it as a "folleto propagandístico" ("La invención de la diferencia costarricense": 211). In "Sociedad anónima, cultura oficial" (2006), Palmer refers to the book's main purpose as "selling" the country to the foreign world (p. 259).
51   Quoted in Acuña, "La invención de la diferencia costarricense": 213. Cf. also Fernández, "Thomas Frances Meagher, Vacaciones en Costa Rica": 333–448.
52   Verg, *Mañana ist es zu spät*: 143f. English translation is mine. I have chosen to paraphrase "der Weise" [Eng. the *wise* man] into "the white man" to underscore the racial binary that Verg reproduces in his affirmation, where he aligns whiteness with wisdom.
53   Quoted in Putnam, "Ideología racial": 144: "Costa Rica tiene bastante atractivos; – el ilustrado europeo, el progresista norteamericano al contemplar nuestra pequeñez relativa, no dejan de admirar las bellezas naturales del país, mirando en él un vasto campo para su genio activo y iniciador. La exuberancia de nuestro suelo, la benignidad de nuestros climas, y sobre todo las condiciones de *la raza costarricense tan pura y tan bien formada, como laboriosa y emprendedora*, llama con justicia su atención" (emphasis added).

unity *under the tight white, European skin* of imagined Costa Ricans.[54] This feature was increasingly emphasized by the country's elite and intellectuals beyond the liberal epoch into the third (1914–1948) and fourth (1948–1980) consolidation periods of modern Costa Rica,[55] when the idea of racial homogeneity strengthened the perception of the exceptional and exemplary character of the country's uniqueness in the region. By underscoring its alleged European descendance, mestizaje was thus denied.

On the subject, Helio Gallardo (*Fenomenología del mestizo* 1993) explains the ideology of the Latin American *ladino* as the fictional rejection of the mestizo's intercultural being through racial prepositions that denounce an ethnical purity. The ladino considers himself to be white, although he is of mixed race, and identifies himself with occidental and European values. In fact, much like Squier's justification of Costa Rican well-being and prosperity with racial suppositions, the myth of racial homogeneity not only erased ethnic distinctions, pluriculturalism, and colonial miscegenation in the country, but it was simultaneously assimilated to a series of attitudes and attributes that where presumed by Costa Rican intellectuals as inseparable elements of the nation's 'difference'. Jiménez has referred to this discursive process extensively in his book, where he discusses how the nation-building project made an effort to deliver an imagery of a population whose whiteness was equaled to virtue and to moral force, and where the purity of alleged white Spanish blood protected it against social and political problems.[56]

In other words, a white, ethnically homogenous society explained the positive and distinguishing attributes that made it exemplary and exceptional in Central America. Costa Rican people were healthy, hard-working, prosperous, cultured, well-organized, and democratic[57] precisely *because*, as Jiménez underlines it, Costa Rica was imagined as the product of a rational organization derived from the ethnic homogeneity of its population.[58] Racial homogeneity became the attribute that explained its social and political harmony, its economic well-being in the region, and therefore its moral virtue as an exemplary and exceptional community in Central America. Otherwise put, the imagination of Costa Rica went through a process of ideological whitening and finally expressed itself in deceptive metaphysical and racial terms: "we are different, we are white".[59] Racial homogeneity functioned hence as the foundational myth of the nation, crafting cohesion across white-

---

[54] I echo here Anderson, who states official nationalism corresponds to "stretching the short, tight skin of the nation over the gigantic body of the empire" so as to construct the inherently contradictory "merger of nation and dynastic empire" and thus legitimize imperial government (Anderson, *Imagined Communities*: 86). Anderson is quick to clarify that official nationalism is not a model exclusive of empires and dynasties. It is a discourse which is invented, imposed, and transmitted 'from above' even by small nation-states with no great power pretensions, as for example, Costa Rica.

[55] Jiménez refers to the third period (1914–1948) as the crisis of the liberal nation, while the fourth period refers to the consolidation of modern and democratic Costa Rica between 1948–1980 (Jiménez, *El imposible país*: 86–88).

[56] Ibid.: 192 and 206: "la pureza de la sangre blanca española protege contra los problemas sociales y políticos."

[57] Ibid.: 197: "La invocación de la blancura pretendió seducir a un público para el cual ese color se asociaba a los buenos negocios, las buenas costumbres, el buen pensar. [...] Por eso procuraron difundir internacionalmente la imagen de una población blanca y, gracias a ello, sana, robusta, laboriosa, culta, próspera, ordenada, trabajadora y patriótica."

[58] Ibid.: 34: "En cambio, la nación costarricense es imaginada como el producto de una organización racional derivada de la homogeneidad étnica de su población."

[59] Cortés, *La invención de Costa Rica*: 20: "Nosotros somos diferentes, nosotros somos blancos."

ness.[60] Following Gellner, its ideological manipulation permitted the "collective self-worship" practiced by Costa Rican nationalism that lead to a "profoundly distorting and deceptive" idea of the nation.[61]

Historical imagination and an ethnic principle of nationality articulated thus Costa Rican official nationalism in such a manner that the ethnonational element racialized national belonging.[62] No wonder, then, that the Caribbean diaspora became a national issue for the country's leaders at the first half of the twentieth century. For the arrival and subsequent settlement of Black Caribbean wage workers at the Costa Rican Caribbean province would put such imaginations to test.

---

[60] The myths of the nation are defined by Murillo as narratives that condense interpretations of the col-lective past of a population ("La piel de la patria": 47: "Los mitos son narraciones que condensan interpretaciones sobre el pasado colectivo de los pueblos.")

[61] Gellner, *Nations and Nationalisms*: 56 and 57.

[62] Cf. Ovares et al, *La casa paterna*: 44, following Anderson's precepts exposed in *Imagined Communities*.

Dwelling in Displacement in Limón, Costa Rica

Limón – Costa Rica's Caribbean province that spreads over the eastern coastline from Nicaragua to Panamá – is, as described by Harpelle, a place "where cultures came together and where a separate Costa Rican 'identity' was forged."[1] At the turn of the twentieth century, Limón was one of the numerous fragmented territories of the Central American region where the disarticulation of traditions into transcultural re-accommodations took place. Like Bryce-Laporte and Purcell (1982) noted, the Caribbean province of Limón "is in fact very similar to the Caribbean provinces of other Central American countries"[2] in that it takes part in the shared experience of Afro-Caribbean diaspora inaugurated by nineteenth- and twentieth-century transnational capitalism in Central America. Nonetheless, even though the province stands as a typical example of "sociocultural life in the Western Caribbean coastal and insular societies of Central America",[3] Limón represented *otherness* regarding the Costa Rican imagined community at the turn of the century and throughout the first half of the twentieth century. During this time, the province became witness to a transareal movement of people between the insular and continental Caribbean regions, as well as becoming the host land to an ethnonational and proletarian diasporic community. The motor force behind this immigration of Afro-Caribbean people to Costa Rica was, in fact, determined by the attempts of the nation's government to exploit the region's potential richness through the construction of the railroad to the Atlantic.

From 1870 onwards, liberal ideology in Costa Rica became strong and influential in the development of the young nation-state with dictator Tomás Guardia (1870–1882) at its front. The main intention during this period was the modernization of the recently independent territory and of its society through agricultural capitalism, mainly the exportation of coffee. This mentality had become stronger from 1860 onwards, when coffee production in Costa Rica met a significant peak and "coffee growers pressured the government to construct a port on the east coast and a railway connecting the port with the highlands".[4] The railroad was thought of and conceptualized as the ultimate and definite means for participating in the international market through an export economy, which signified for the country's leaders the awakening of enrichment and of progress.[5] As asserted

---

[1] Harpelle, *The West Indians of Costa Rica*: xvi.
[2] Bryce-Laporte/Purcell, "A Lesser Known Chapter": 224.
[3] Bryce-Laporte, *Social Relations and Cultural Persistence*: 2.
[4] Olien, "The Adaptation of West Indian Blacks": 138.
[5] Zapata Duarte/Blanco Obando, "La región Atlántico/Caribe de Costa Rica": 445: "La visión liberal del desarrollo, basada en el impulso de la modernidad a través de la construcción de vías de comunicación y obras civiles que faciliten la creación de riqueza, la movilización de mano de obra, el surgimiento de nuevas actividades productivas y la mejora del nivel de vida de las personas; tuvo una influencia importante sobre el proceso de desarrollo de la región Atlántico/Caribe, en los siglos XIX y XX." See Tomás Guardia's discourse (1882) held for the Council of Foreign Bond Holders and Dr. José María Castro's railroad inauguration speech of the same year, who advocate precisely along the liberal arguments of 'progress' and of 'enrichment of national wealth' (reproduced in their entirety in González/Zeledón, *Crónicas y relatos*: 134f. and 145, respectively).

by Aviva Chomsky (1996), "the goal behind the Atlantic Coast railroad was to promote the national economy."[6]

Before the existence of a modernized transportation system that connected the Central Valley highlands to the Atlantic, Costa Rica exported coffee to the European market through the Southern Pacific port of Puntarenas. This meant that it was necessary for the product to embark on a long journey departing from Puntarenas outwards, either by navigating Cape Horn, southernmost headland of Chile, or by crossing Panama before heading overseas.[7] Because of a slow and expensive transportation system, the country's leaders and coffee producers became highly interested, as Costa Rican historian Ronny Viales (2013) has underlined it, in establishing a less costly coffee-transit-road from the highlands to the Atlantic port and further towards Europe and North America.[8] In fact, Dr. José María Castro, Secretary of Foreign Relations in 1882, emphasized then how the traditional and complicated transit roads of national products had earlier meant the deprivation of its consumption and of its competition in the international market. His speech summarizes the interest Central Valley politicians had regarding the colonization of the Atlantic/Caribbean region in favor of national economic growth and modernization.[9] Consequently, a seaport based at the Atlantic/Caribbean province became of utmost importance, as well as a road that could connect it to the Pacific port of Puntarenas and to the highlands where coffee was produced. The belief in the 'fundamental laws of progress' that would bring a young Costa Rica closer to the 'civilized nations' led Mr. L. Walfran – the first of several engineers to carry out expeditions of the territory and of the difficult road to the Atlantic – to present an article in 1861 advocating the urgency for a road that would allow the young nation-state to enter into the grand narrative of Progress.[10] After Walfran, Captain José Antonio Angulo inspected the region in 1862 and delivered a report to the country's leaders where he "indicated that the Atlantic coast had potential for further commercial exploitation by highland Costa Ricans",[11] thus encouraging further investiga-

---

6   Chomsky, *West Indian Workers*: 21.

7   The German engineer, later nationalized as Costa Rican, Francisco Kurtze details this journey to justify the importance that an Atlantic port would have as a direct entrance into the international world commerce. As he wrote in 1886, "Ese modo de enviar los productos, significaba, primero, el embarque para Panamá; luego, la transferencia al ferrocarril para Aspinwall [alternative name for Colón, Panama], a menudo acompañada de un segundo embarque; y, por último, un tercer cambio, el necesario para poner la mercadería a bordo del barco que había de conducirlo a su final destino. [...] Dispuso [el Gobierno] asimismo, establecer un puerto comercial en el viejo puerto de Limón, en aquella costa; y así poner el comercio de su pueblo en más directa y económica comunicación con el gran tráfico del mundo" (Kurtze, "La Ruta Ferroviaria Interoceánica a través de la república de Costa Rica": 117).

8   Viales, "La segunda colonización": 97.

9   Castro, "Discurso pronunciado": 145.

10   The Gaceta Oficial de Costa Rica published Walfran's conclusions on the subject on June 13, 1861, where he stated: "A partir de esta época, la apertura de un camino al 'Limón' o a Moín ocupa todos los espíritus; hoy más que nunca, se siente esta necesidad, tanto para levantar el crédito público, como para dar valor a los inmensos ternos que la República posee, y para dotar al comercio de la actividad que necesita para enriquecer, o hacer surgir las diferentes industrias que reclama la fertilidad del suelo, y con ellas el bienestar de los habitantes. Para realizar en fin, esta aspiración de todas las naciones civilizadas que se resume en esta sola palabra, 'Progreso', hay una voz inmensa, la voz de todo un pueblo que pide un camino al Atlántico" (Walfran, "Informe": 88).

11   Harpelle, *The West Indians of Costa Rica*: 8. Captain Angulo gathered information on what he identified as the port of Moín, the Matina valley, the territory of Talamanca, and the lands along the Atlantic coast.

tion of the area. His pioneering work led to Juan Mechán's exploration of the territory in 1864, whose report gathered topographic information that instructed how the Government should proceed with the colonization of the land.[12]

After several attempts to establish the construction of an Atlantic railroad, the iron road project was taken on in August 1871 by the North American magnate of Andean railroad construction, Henry Meiggs.[13] The project had been approved by President Jesús de Jimenéz (1869), whose *coup d'État*-successor General Tomás Guardia (1870–1882) later financed through British investment with the coeval liberal ideology in mind: over one hundred kilometers of railway were to be built in favor of the national economy. A few years later, the enterprise was handed over to Meigg's nephews, Henry Meiggs Keith and Minor Cooper Keith, who carried out the completion of the railway. Consequently, the Soto-Keith Act of 1884 was signed between Keith and the government, which has been seen as the "prototype of subsequent concessions to powerful foreign concerns" in Central America. The act granted him a 99-year lease to 800,000 acres of undeveloped land, full and undisputed ownership of the railway that he was to complete, and furthermore was exempted from taxation and custom obligations to the Costa Rican economy.[14]

A mixed route was inaugurated firstly in 1882 under Keith's supervision, which meant the first "direct" connection between the Atlantic and the Central Valley capital, and the railroad to the Atlantic was finally concluded on December 7, 1890 with an extension of roughly 160 km.[15] This would have positive repercussions on the national economy and from then on, Keith would have a fundamental role in the modernization of Costa Rica. He became a central figure not just in the country, but in Central American nineteenth- and

---

[12]   His report summarized his investigation of the area, specifically of Puerto Limón, the Matina river, and of Moín. In it, he describes in detail the geography of the coast; the nature of the coastal land and soil; the extension of its coral reef; the depth of the sea water at diverse strategic points for the building of docks, as well as the nature of the rivers above which the necessary bridges had to be constructed, and the steep hills of the roads leading to the coast (Mechán, "Informe": 100).

[13]   Kurtze's "La Ruta Ferroviaria Interoceánica a través de la república de Costa Rica" (1866) was a first attempt to seek North American investors to participate in the construction of the railroad, but lack of interest on behalf of North American entrepreneurs never led to a definite taking on of the construction. In 1867, the Costa Rican President José María Castro Madriz wanted to construct an interoceanic railroad between Limón and Caldera and hired therefore general John C. Fremont for the enterprise, but this project was never commenced. Two years later, President Jesús Jiménez contracted once again another North American company for the building of the railroad, a project that also failed to be carried out (Viales, "La segunda colonización": 111).

[14]   These conditions were expressed in Article XXII of the famous Soto-Keith Act: "The Government grants to the company 800,000 acres of undeveloped national lands along the railroad line or in any other part of the country, to be selected by the company, with all the natural wealth which said areas contain and the strip of land for the right-of-way for the building of the railroad and necessary structures; and all kinds of material necessary for the construction of the railroad which may be found in undeveloped lands anywhere along the railroad; and two of the lots of national property now measured in the port of Limón, for the construction of wharves, warehouses and stations – all without reimbursement of any sort … The Government cannot lay taxes on said lands within twenty years, counting from the effective date of this concession […]" (quoted in Kepner/Soothill, *The Banana Empire*: 45).

[15]   Viales, "La segunda colonización": 111–114.

twentieth-century economy as well. He became a "captain[] of industry in the modern capitalistic world" and was even referred to as "the uncrowned King of Central America."[16]

Minor Keith's enterprises led to "the import and settlement of West Indian migrant labor" in Costa Rica because of which the country's racial cartography underwent a substantial and definite change at the turn of the twentieth century.[17] The recently independent country had only around 150,000 inhabitants in 1870,[18] thus making the project's first order of business the recruitment of low-cost laborers for the arduous task of tearing down a dense rainforest and tolerating difficult work conditions in a hostile environment. Chomsky's investigation of Minor Keith's gathering of railroad workers refers New Orleans had been his first city of choice for the recruitment of laborers, which, with help of a police commissioner, set off to call upon "cutthroats, robbers, thieves, and other riff-raff". Harpelle comments as well on this, claiming that around seven hundred inmates from this city's prison were sent to Limón, of which "fewer than 25 survived". Furthermore, Chomsky refers that men who had served William Walker in his attempt to colonize the Central American region for North America were also drafted for the job. Parallel to these attempts, hundreds of migrant laborers departed from Jamaica, New Orleans, and Italy to work at the province of Limón. Italians were the first to revolt when their contract conditions regarding payment and living arrangements were not fulfilled. They consequently went back to their home country.[19] Contrarily, the similar environmental characteristics of the insular and continental Caribbean territories made it easier for Black people from the islands to lay the tracks. This small, yet not irrelevant factor is what allowed Afro-Caribbean people to adapt better than Italians and Chinese to Limón's tropical weather conditions. Because of this, as Olien states, "the major workforce for the construction of the railroad was recruited from the West Indies, especially from Jamaica", from where migration began in December 1872.[20]

A substantial number of English-speaking Blacks from Jamaica first entered Costa Rica at the beginning of the 1870s and continued to do so in intermittent waves up to the first half of the twentieth century as migrant wage laborers. Between 1873 and 1874, the *Gaceta Oficial* registered that

> during 1872 ships brought workers from throughout the Caribbean; in December 1872 the first ship from Jamaica arrived, carrying 123 workers for the railroad. In 1873, 894 Jamaicans arrived, as did at least 653 Chinese and 130 workers from New Orleans. In 1874 a railroad official informed the government that there were 2,500 men working on laying the tracks, among them 1,000 Jamaicans and 500 Chinese.[21]

---

[16] The affirmation pertains to Wilhelm Bitter, *Die wirtschaftliche Eroberung Mittelamerikas durch den Bananen-Trust: Organisation und imperialistische Bedeutung der United Fruit Company* (1921), quoted in Kepner/Soothill, *The Banana Empire*: 44. Tomás Guardia also praised Keith, considering him an intelligent, hardworking entrepreneur that served loyally the Republic's interests, for he had been able to satisfy the nation's demands with facts, instead of impressing with promises. See the Presidential speech reported in La Gaceta de Costa Rica (1886), N.A. "Inauguración oficial de los trabajos del ferrocarril al Reventazón": 150 and 153.

[17] Purcell, *Banana Fallout*: 25.

[18] Senior, *Ciudadanía afrocostarricense*: 11.

[19] Chomsky, *West Indian Workers*: 22. Harpelle, *The West Indians of Costa Rica*: 12.

[20] Olien, "The Adaptation of West Indian Blacks": 139.

[21] Chomsky, *West Indian Workers*: 24.

The nationality of the other 1,000 is not mentioned. It has been suggested these were Costa Ricans from the Central Valley.[22] This euphoric migration brought multiple communities from the insular basin, the continental isthmus, and further north from the U.S. in contact in Costa Rica. Puerto Limón grew from an 800-people community in 1875 to having around 1,200 inhabitants in 1876, mostly Afro-Caribbean. By 1883, the national census reported that almost half of the people living in Limón were Jamaican (48%).[23]

Contrary to these figures, at the time of Independence (1821) and when slavery in Central America was abolished (1824), only *eighty-nine* people of African ascendance were accounted for in Costa Rica.[24] A few years before the railroad enterprise took off, the population census of 1864 showed merely *twenty-eight* Black inhabitants in Costa Rica.[25] Historian Rina Cáceres (2000) claims this low number corresponds to institutionalized invisibility. According to the author, there must have been a larger amount of people of African origin in the Costa Rican colonial province than that which was registered in the archives, their presence however made invisible in the country's racial cartography through censuses.[26] Lowell Gudmunson (1984) instead explained such invisibility (i.e. "disappearance") as a two-way *assimilation* process that reduced Afro-American population in Spanish America as a whole. The author explains on the one hand how African people had joined in interracial marriage as a way of bettering their socio-economic position. While on the other, mortality rates and further inter/national migratory movements throughout the nineteenth century played too their part in diminishing (i.e. assimilating = disappearing) the Afro-American population in general.[27] Such an invisibility of Black people in Costa Rica was completely overturned with the arrival of Caribbean workers. The first attempt to construct the Panama Canal under the French man Ferdinand de Lesseps in the 1880s also attracted migrant labor to the isthmus and thus Blacks in Costa Rica "came from other Central American countries or from Panama, [even though] the majority left Jamaica directly for Costa Rica."[28]

By 1910, approximately 20,000 Afro-Caribbeans were estimated to be living in Limón. Harpelle claims that the Panamá Canal Zone and Cuba were the only regions that could claim to be home to more Afro-Caribbeans than the Costa Rican province.[29] It has also been estimated that around 43,000 Jamaicans came to Costa Rica between 1891 and 1911 to work at the banana plantations, constantly moving from one Central American country to another. As proof of the euphoric Afro-Caribbean proletarian diaspora at the turn of the twentieth century, the 1927 Costa Rican census showed at this time the presence of little over 19,000 Blacks in the country, of which 18,003 were living in Limón. In contrast, little

---

[22] Koch, *Ethnicity and Livelihoods*: 64.
[23] Senior, *Ciudadanía afrocostarricense*: 14.
[24] Meléndez, "El negro en Costa Rica durante la colonia": 48. Alvarenga Venútolo (2007) states the participation of Blacks and Mulatto populations in the processes of independence in Latin America, together with Britain's ban on the supply of African slaves, were the causes for the abolishment of slavery in the region ("La inmigración extranjera en la historia costarricense": 4).
[25] Dirección General de Estadística y Censos (1964), quoted in Olien, "The Adaptation of West Indian Blacks": 139.
[26] Cáceres, *Negros, mulatos, esclavos y libertos en la Costa Rica del siglo XVII*: 85.
[27] Gudmunson, "'Black' into 'White'": 42–45.
[28] Bryce-Laporte/Purcell, "A Lesser-Known Chapter": 222.
[29] Harpelle, *The West Indians of Costa Rica*: 31.

less than 10,000 Costa Ricans inhabited the province.[30] The numbers show a drastic change in the conformation of the Costa Rican population and confirm that "by the second decade of the twentieth century the population of the [Limón] province was more or less equally divided between men and women from all over the Caribbean."[31] The province had taken on the form of cosmopolitism. In fact, it was the only territory in Costa Rica in which there were more foreigners than Costa Rican citizens, signaling 2.2 foreigners per national.[32] In 1911, governor Gerardo Lara had already affirmed that the population of Limón was composed of cosmopolitan elements;[33] while a report of 1913 stated (with a racist overtone) that Limón possessed a heterogeneous population composed by nationals, Europeans, North and South Americans, West Indians, Africans, and Asians (therefore the difficult task of maintaining order, according to the Governor).[34] In 1927 almost eighty percent of the population was Caribbean, since of 23,000 foreigners living there, 18,000 were Afro-Caribbean. Evidently, Limón had become "an outpost of the West Indies, particularly Jamaica."[35] That is, Limón was not only multicultural, but mainly *Black*. Which is why Diana Senior's (2011) claim is highly representative: it was principally the Black hands of volunteer workers which built the first miles of the railway to the Atlantic.[36]

Upon arrival, Afro-Caribbeans in Limón dealt with their displacement through the establishment of their own educational, artistic, religious, and specific cultural manifestations in new territory. This made it possible not only for their homeland's socio-cultural patterns to persist in new nations, but for these to be reinforced through new expressions. As a consequence, Jamaicans and their Costa Rican-born descendants occupied an in-between place in Limón, for they maintained economic and political ties with the homeland, while resettling in the host land. By relocating and settling here, they reproduced their cultural traits in Limón as a "continuous adaptation of a minority group to a new cultural environment".[37]

This resulted in the first decades not in the hybridization of two cultures in a single territory, but in their autonomous and independent existence as two separate imagined

---

[30]   With regards to Caribbean immigration to the Costa Rican Caribbean, cf. Olien, "The Adaptation of West Indian Blacks": 139; Senior, *Ciudadanía afrocostarricense*: 34f.; Viales, *Después del enclave*: 46f.; Purcell, *Banana Fallout*: 23–27; Meléndez, "Aspectos sobre la inmigración jamaicana": 61–87; Bryce-Laporte/Purcell, "A Lesser-Known Chapter": 222–224, Chomsky, *West Indian Workers*: 34f. and 44, and Bourgois, *Ethnicity at Work*: 45–65.

[31]   Harpelle, *The West Indians of Costa Rica*: 19.

[32]   Cf. Viales, *Después del enclave*: 46; Meléndez, "Aspectos sobre la inmigración jamaicana": 84. See also Olien, "The Adaptation of West Indian Blacks": 139f. Olien presents a table of the proportion of Costa Ricans to foreigners in the country's provinces in 1927, where Limón is the only province which presented a mainly foreign population.

[33]   Quoted in Putnam, "Ideología racial": 167: "[...] su población, compuesta de elementos cosmopolitas [...]".

[34]   Quoted in ibid.: 156: "[...] ha sido la persecución o castigo de la vagancia, los juegos prohibidos, y demás vicios que vayan en perjuicio de la moralización del pueblo y que, aquí, más que en las otras ciudades de la República, cunden, debido a la heterogeneidad de la población limonense, donde están representadas casi la mayor parte de las naciones del globo, nacionales, europeos, norte y suramericanos, antillanos, africanos y asiáticos [...]".

[35]   Olien, "The Adaptation of West Indian Blacks": 143.

[36]   Senior, *Ciudadanía afrocostarricense*: 12: "Son principalmente las manos negras de hombres del Caribe, quienes construyen las primeras millas de la línea férrea en las inhóspitas tierras del Atlántico."

[37]   Harpelle, *The West Indians of Costa Rica*: 184.

communities. The complexity of these communities was shaped by the transareal reality of being laborers in a foreign land and in constant movement between their homelands and the hosting countries, becoming therefore travelling, mobile, and multi-located cultures in Central America with the Caribbean, Britain, and Africa as multiple centers of 'fond attachments'. Afro-Costa Rican Paul Rodman shares his testimony with Paula Palmer regarding how Caribbean immigrants dealt with displacement and with building a new home while in diaspora as "a tendency to organize themselves in groups for cultural reasons" since "there were many that were interested in seeing to it that the culture was sustained and maintained as far as they could."[38] Even though Afro-Caribbean workers first arrived in Limón as temporary laborers, this reality was overturned with time as they slowly established in the country. An English-speaking, Protestant-majority, Afro-Caribbean community in Limón slowly developed within a Spanish-speaking, Catholic, ideologically whitened mestizo nation. The transcultural identity of Costa Rican-born Caribbean-descendants bear the characteristics in which their forefathers and -mothers coped with their immigration, rejecting to integrate to a country they did not identify with, while at the same time asserting roots in new ground by actualizing a series of cultural constellations that reinforced their outernational identity. With time, a group of people "dwelling-in-displacement"[39] from the Caribbean archipelago gave way to a cultural/deterritorialized diaspora at the Central American Caribbean.

In his first edition of *Global Diasporas* (1997), Cohen outlines four aspects he characterizes intrinsic to "Caribbean peoples as a cultural diaspora", which he slightly reconfigures in his second edition.[40] A return movement to the African homeland is mentioned as one of its fundamental aspects, together with the "cultural retention or affirmations of an African identity". In the second edition, he adds retentions *to the Caribbean* as another important cultural reference, relating his own theory to Gilroy's Black Atlantic thesis.[41] Cohen explains cultural and social activities affirm, reproduce, and create "a diasporic identity" in the places to which cultural diasporas subsequently move.[42] This is accomplished by way of cultural artefacts and expressions that mirror "cross-influences between Africa, the Caribbean and the destination countries".[43] In fact, Jamaicans who had settled in Limón portrayed a strong sense of cultural and national identity as anglophone

---

[38] Palmer, *What Happen*: 178f. For a detailed description of the Afro-Caribbean community life and organization in Limón from 1914 to 1948, see Ch. 7: 83–95, and Ch. 12: 168–213. Palmer offers not only historical accounts of the communities, but also personal testimonies and accounts from the members of the communities.

[39] See Clifford, *Routes*: 254.

[40] Cohen, *Global Diasporas* (1997): 144–151. These are "Retention and affirmations of African identity" (pp. 144–146); "Return movements, literal and symbolic" (pp. 146–148), "Shared cultural expressions" (p. 148–150), and "Social conduct and popular attitudes" (p. 150f.). In the second edition (2008), the author refers instead to the Caribbean diaspora as his "principal case study of a deterritorialized diaspora" (p. 124; cf. pp. 130–135). He slightly modifies the aforementioned aspects so as to be more inclusive of Caribbean identity, modifying the first two into: "Retention and affirmation of an origin in Africa" (p. 131) and "Symbolic and vicarious links" (p. 132f.). See also "Shared cultural expressions" (p. 133f.) and "Social conduct and popular attitudes" (p. 134f.).

[41] Cohen, *Global Diasporas* (2008): 130–135.

[42] Ibid. (1997): 138.

[43] Ibid.: 144.

Caribbean people, reproducing cultural artefacts and social patterns from the colonial motherland in Costa Rica. These gave Caribbean migrant laborers and their families a feeling of easy rooting in Costa Rica, not having to abandon nor reject their customs or cultural expressions which manifested their adhesion to the British crown as Caribbean subalterns.

As documented by Paula Palmer in *"What happen" A Folk History of Costa Rica's Talamanca Coast* (2005), Jamaicans in Limón continued practicing cultural festivities as such up to the 1950s, such as Coronation Day, Easter Monday, Slavery Day, and Harvest.[44] Also, religious congregations that were alien to Costa Rican Catholicism were established in the province. Methodist, Baptist, Adventist, and Anglican congregations not only provided a religious system, but also gave way to the building and financing of English schools as early as the beginnings of the twentieth century.[45] Teachers were sent from Jamaica to promote a British-educational system and, as a consequence, Limón had one of the nation's highest percentages of literate people in the first decades of the twentieth century.[46] Parents, as well as the United Fruit Company financed these teachers, never an institutional organization nor a governmental initiative. The language of instruction of these schools was, coherently, English. Since the Costa Rican government didn't send Spanish teachers nor establish Spanish schools in Limón until 1920, a project which nonetheless only really took off after 1948 and represented assimilation instead of integration for Afrolimonenses, Afro-Caribbean integration was delayed.

On the other hand, representation of Shakespearian plays, literary activities like declamation of English classical writers, recitals, debates and rallies were part of a well-defined society that performed their identity as Jamaicans under the English crown.[47] As described by Mr. Paul Rodman,

> They had fraternal meetings and singings and all kind of thing. We had schools and churches that give concerts all the time, and educated people would come from Jamaica and they would have competition between the different villages in plays, Shakespeare, recitals and singing groups.[48]

Concerts were also an important part of everyday community life, with singing contests, dances, and musical performances. Mr. Sylvester Plummer explains how, "[y]ou have dance most times once every three months, a special dance. We bring in the musicians from Limón, have a really good dance."[49] Liberty Hall offered the space for such entertainment. "We had sacred concert and we had rag concert. Rag concert is a joke, just to make people laugh", recalls Miss Daisy Lewis.[50] Calypso music is also one of the most characteristic examples of Afro-Costa Rican culture, with Walter Ferguson as its main representative, who

---

44   Palmer, *What Happen*: 178. Regarding Coronation Day, see Rossi, "El Caribe perdido": 157f.
45   Palmer, *What Happen*: 168. See also Murillo, "Vaivén de arraigos y desarraigos": 192.
46   In comparison, only the provinces of Alajuela (3,5%) and Heredia (21,2%) had lower percentages of illiterate people than Limón (22,6%). The rest of the provinces presented higher rates: San José (28,1%), Cartago (37,2%), Guanacaste (41,6%) and Puntarenas (49,3%; Viales, *Después del enclave*: 52.)
47   See Rossi, "El Caribe perdido": 161–64.
48   Quoted in Palmer, *What Happen*: 178.
49   Quoted in ibid.: 190.
50   Quoted in ibid.: 174.

at his ninety-eight years of age was awarded the *Premio Nacional al Patrimonio Cultural Inmaterial Emilia Prieto 2017* for his long life contribution to Costa Rican cultural production through calypso music.

Sport contests – specially cricket in the 1920s and 1930s, later substituted by baseball (two uncommon sports among Costa Ricans), as well as horse racing – were a favorite among the communities: "for years every Sunday meant cricket and picnic in one community or another."[51] In addition, life and death were approached through non-Catholic nor western perspectives. Midwives and snake doctors were important medical figures in the community, as well as the formation of "Set Ups" (night of death) and "Nine Nights" (vigil at the home of the deceased) regarding mournful affairs. "These customs started from the real old-time Jamaican people", explained Miss Maivis Tyndal.[52]

Coupled with religion, education, leisure, and sport, Caribbeans in Limón also printed regional newspapers in English, such as *Limón Weekly* (1903–1906), *The Limón Times* (1910–1911), *The Times* (1912–1913), *The Search Light* (1929–1952), and *The Atlantic Post* (1949–1952), as documented by Anacristina Rossi (2005). These maintained connections with the homeland (Caribbean) and with Britain, as well as relating to Costa Rican national affairs. The editors were Afro-Caribbean leaders dedicated to voicing the social realities and economic needs of their transareal community. Because of this, Valeria Grinberg Pla (2012) affirms journalism was a fundamental platform for the Afro-Caribbean community's cultural life up to the second half of the twentieth century, by which the community's well-being was defended.[53] Coherently, Rossi had beforehand presumed that the *Limón Times* was forced to shut down most likely because of clashes with the United Fruit Company.[54] Philippe I. Bourgois (1989) explains this as the consequence of expressing "labor-oriented news [that] regularly attacked the transnational [i.e. UFCo.]."[55] Rossi sadly points out that from 1960 on these voices have remained silent.[56]

Regarding return-movements, Cohen affirms "Caribbean visionaries were at the forefront of the Back-to-Africa movements", where Marcus Garvey and the United Negro Improvement Association (UNIA, founded in Jamaica by Garvey in 1914) played a central role.[57] Limón was no exception. While Carmen Murillo (1999) underscores Afro-identity

---

[51] Palmer, *What Happen*: 186.

[52] "These customs started from the real old-time Jamaican people. If it's even a little baby die, they will have the Set Up in the house that night. They will bring the liquor, they will have different drinks, coffee, tea, chocolate, and they will bake their bread [...] They will sing and play their dominoes till morning light. After they go and bury the dead, nine days after they keep the Nine Night. They come also and they bring liquors and drinks, and the women serve soup and so forth until twelve o'clock, always twelve o'clock they serve black coffee, tea, chocolate. And they sing and play dominoes and cards until daylight. It's just a memorial, it show appreciation for the family, to cheer up the family" (Miss Maivis Tyndal quoted in Palmer, *What Happen*: 192). Claudia Fioretti Bongianino's dissertation on the relationship between ethnicity and religion in *Nain Nait* rituals among the dwellers of the Caribbean community in Old Bank, Panama makes evident the transareal cultural continuum along the Central American Caribbean (Diss. title, *Deus e outros parentes invisíveis em Old Bank [Bocas del Toro, Panamá]* – Diss. Chapter read and discussed at the 2017 Mark Claster Mamolen Dissertation Workshop, May 12–13, at Harvard University.)

[53] Grinberg Pla, "Una mirada a las letras en los periódicos afroantillanos de Limón": 83.

[54] Rossi, "El Caribe perdido": 158.

[55] Bourgois, *Ethnicity at Work*: 106.

[56] Rossi, "El Caribe perdido": 161: "A partir de esta fecha [1960], las voces antillanas quedan en silencio."

[57] Cohen, *Global Diasporas* (1997): 144; (2008): 130.

in Limón was constructed firstly upon the Jamaican-British elements, she also affirms Marcus Garvey's impact in the region made Afro-Caribbeans established here turn their gaze away from Britain and rather towards Africa as a defining horizon.[58] From the 1920s onwards, the UNIA would play a crucial role through its subsidiary network facilities called Liberty Halls. These were built in Puerto Limón, Matina, Cahuita, and other littoral cities at the Costa Rican Atlantic province, where Caribbean people would meet for cultural and leisure activities. The author states Liberty Halls, particularly the Black Star Line in Puerto Limón, reconstructed and shifted Afro-identity from the Anglo-perspective towards Garvey's discourse on colonialism and the African victim diaspora as a call to acknowledge African roots first and foremost.[59] In fact, the Black Star Line shipping company had the intention of bringing Afro-Caribbeans back to Africa. Sadly, the Black Star Line in Puerto Limón, an important recognized site of Costa Rican National Patrimony that had not ceased to function ever since its establishment in 1922, burned down in April 2016. Fortunately, the *Ministerio de Cultura y Juventud* granted a substantial grant to the UNIA for its reconstruction, set to begin in September 2019 and whose first stone was set in August 31st, 2019.[60]

It must be furthermore underscored that a foreseen return to the insular Caribbean homeland was originally the desire of Jamaican laborers who arrived in Limón as migrant laborers, very much in accordance with Clifford's understanding of diaspora cultures as "not-here-to-stay".[61] In fact, because of their strong sense of identity as anglophone, British subjects, older Jamaicans refused to obtain Costa Rican citizenship, notwithstanding the decades they had already lived and worked in the country. The Black community that had developed steadily in the province of Limón since the 1870s only met its full political recognition in 1949 after the Civil War of 1948. Figueres, the victorious leader of the newly founded political party Partido Liberación Nacional (PLN 1948), is "the man credited with bringing people of African descent into the political process" of Costa Rica.[62] One of the most significant outcomes of Figueres' leadership is the elimination of the 1934 clause which banned the hiring of Black people at the Pacific headquarters of the United Fruit Company. Nonetheless, it was truly Alex Curling, first Afro-Costa Rican political figure, who advocated for this and who sent a letter to Figueres pleading for its elimination in 1948, which the latter eradicates in November of 1949.[63]

After naturalization of Blacks in 1949, the 1963 census documented little under two thousand Jamaicans living in Costa Rica (1,873), of whom the vast majority (1,812) were

---

58   Murillo, "Vaivén de arraigos y desarraigos": 193.

59   See Murillo, "Vaivén de arraigos y desarraigos": 195–198. On Marcus Garvey and the UNIA's role in Limón, see Harpelle, *The West Indians of Costa Rica*: 53–63; Chomsky, *West Indian Workers*: 202–206; and Purcell, *Banana Fallout*: 37.

60   See the newspapers articles retrievable online from Méndez/Cascante, "Incendio consume edificio Black Star Line en Limón" (April 29, 2016); Villalobos Saborío, "Reconstrucción del Black Star Line de Limón iniciará en abril" (March 4, 2019); Melissa González, "Reconstrucción del Black Star Line iniciará este mes" (September 1, 2019), and Astorga, "Con la colocación de la primera piedra" (August 31, 2019).

61   Clifford, *Routes*: 254.

62   Harpelle, *The West Indians of Costa Rica*: 167.

63   Cf. ibid., 175–78. Purcell has underlined that Figueres also eliminated racial distinctions from the country's census, an action that for Purcell helped silence and thus make Afro-Caribbean presence in Costa Rica invisible (*Banana Fallout*: 84).

born in Jamaica. From this quantity, Olien refers 1,584 had "lived in Costa Rican for fourteen years or more". The author interprets these numbers as suggesting it was "primarily the older blacks who [had] not obtained citizenship", acknowledging additionally that the younger generations had more to gain with official integration.[64] Harpelle mentions how achieving Costa Rican citizenship was a gateway for social and economic mobility among younger Afro-Costa Rican generations, but it was however also seen as a "divisive issue because it alienated many young West Indians from their community". Hence, despite the fact that the year 1945 documented the highest number of solicitations for naturalization, "thousands of people still did not heed the call to become citizens".[65]

Lastly, Cohen mentions "*attitudes* (emphasis added), migration patterns and social conduct" as intrinsic to the behavior of cultural/deterritorialized diasporan people.[66] Trevor Purcell's documentation of an "ideology of superiority" in *Banana Fallout* (1993) regarding Afro-Caribbean attitudes opposite Costa Rican customs confirms Cohen's premise. For Purcell, this feeling of superiority stood as one of the central reasons concerning Afro-Caribbean reluctance to integrate to Costa Rican culture. It found its motivations in a varied array of cultural differences. Not only through language and British citizenship, but also in relation to everyday costumes like eating patterns, house construction, body odor, personal and domestic hygiene, attire.[67] Bourgois states furthermore that the feeling of superiority acted as a defense mechanism against anti-Black sentiments in the region.[68] While Harpelle refers to the fact that identification with the British crown provided a sentiment of national pride for Jamaicans, which looked down upon the Costa Ricans with whom they came in contact within the plantation system: uneducated peasants of the low socio-economic stratum. Moreover, Carlos Meléndez (1978) had asserted beforehand that Caribbean attitude towards Costa Ricans was for a long time one of complete absence of interest,[69] and according to Purcell this was so due to their prejudice against their incivility, rudeness, and bad manners:

> Dey looks to me laik dey were barberians, laik dey wud kil an' iit piiple, datz di wey dey looks. Deze piiple wur illiterate an' ignorant an wii wuz ahlwyes afreeid av dem. If yu goin along de striit an yu si dem yu waak on di odder sa'id. Dey always kiari dier kutlas wid dem.
>
> An elderly Black woman's impressions of Latinos in Limón[70]

This ideology of superiority was not the only cause that slowed their integration to the host land's cultural, socioeconomic, and political structures. The imagination of Cost Rica as a racially homogeneous people by its leaders, played a fundamental part in this process as well. As a consequence, Limón came to constitute the borderland of the Costa Rican

---

[64] Olien, "West Indian Blacks in Costa Rica": 148.
[65] Harpelle, *The West Indians of Costa Rica*: 158 and 161, respectively.
[66] Cohen, *Global Diasporas* (1997): 144.
[67] Purcell, *Banana Fallout*: 37.
[68] Bourgois, *Ethnicity at Work*: 93f.
[69] Meléndez, "Aspectos sobre la inmigración jamaicana": 89: "la actitud del negro respecto a Costa Rica, fue por mucho tiempo de total ausencia de interés".
[70] Purcell, *Conformity and Dissension*: 79; quoted in Bourgois, *Ethnicity at Work*: 66.

imagined community at the first half of the twentieth century, when mestizo Costa Ricans and Black Caribbeans came in contact within the plantation system of the United Fruit Company and where the dialectics of race and nation unfolded.

The Dialectics of Race and Nation

> The violation [of excluding blacks] is so flagrant that we cannot but think that you have fallen into the serious error of believing that all people of color residing in the country are foreigners, and that there are no native Costa Ricans of color. [...] Have the mentalities of our country forgotten the singular abnegation with which our ancestors gave themselves in their intrepid adventures, bearing enormous trials and paying with their lives for the construction of the Costa Rica Railroad, in order to give us what today we call the Atlantic Zone.
>
> Petition on behalf of Afro-Costa Ricans
> to Juan E. Romagosa and Virgilio Chaverri
> (Limón deputies in Congress)
> December 1st, 1934[1]

As seen in the opening discussion of *Becoming Afro-Costa Rican*, the self-defining process of the Costa Rican imagined community firstly referred cultural values (such as being poor, laborious, and harmonious) and other functional substitutes (such as political structures like democracy or peace) as particular characteristics of the country's inhabitants. With the arrival of liberalism in 1870 and until the first half of the twentieth century, these attributes were masked by racial criteria until racial homogeneity became one of the fundamental features. Gudmunson keenly takes note of how this allowed a "self-exaltation" to take place, which permitted Costa Rican intellectuals to claim a "more pure Spanish racial background than its Central and Latin American neighbors".[2] As argued by Jiménez, this became the key factor that consolidated and justified the Costa Rican exemplary difference by intertwining such positive features with the idea of a predominantly white society as the fundamental cause for it. The foundational myth of whiteness/racial homogeneity explained the source of social harmony, as well as of morality, peace, and democracy in the Costa Rican nation-building process.

Thus, in the process of settling the traits of the imagined community, the differentiation of the Costa Rican people took a racial form. The symbols of the nation were grounded, largely dependent on, and constructed by an imagined white people. This process refers precisely to what Robert Miles (1987) summarizes when addressing the issue of nationalism and its correlation to that of race. According to the author, both ideologies overlap each other so that "the idea of 'race' [serves] simultaneously as a criterion of inclusion/exclusion so that the boundary of the claimed nation is also equally a boundary of 'race'."[3] Otherwise put, the construction of the us~them dialectic, or more appropriately, of the Other, is the main element in fictionalizing a specific national mythology along the lines of an ethnic principle of nationality, which serves as the discursive boundary when delimiting the imagined community. On the subject, Gilroy explains the conflict of racializing nationality in England as a discourse of 'race' closely aligned "with the idea of national belonging", so

---

[1]   Quoted in Chomsky, *West Indian Workers*: 250f.
[2]   Gudmunson, "'Black' into 'White'": 44.
[3]   Miles, "Recent Marxist Theories of Nationalism and the Issue of Racism": 41.

that Blackness and English nationality "appeared suddenly to be mutually exclusive attributes".[4] Which is why it makes sense that Anderson defines the imagined community "as simultaneously open and closed".[5] That is, inclusive of those that pertain to national community, while excluding the Other through the category of (racial) difference. In this process of differentiation, an *us* outlines the distinguishing characteristics that help define simultaneously the existence of a *them* who lack those specific attributes, states Miles.[6] The rhetoric of the 'Costa Rican difference' based upon the myth of a white people functioned in fact as *the* "inclusive categorization, which necessarily had exclusive implications" for the Black Caribbean diaspora that with time settled in the country and became Costa Rican.[7]

Even if Paula Palmer situates the beginning of the settlement of the Talamanca Coast in 1828 with turtle fishermen that arrived during the eighteenth and nineteenth centuries,[8] it is the development of busy communities in Puerto Viejo and Cahuita through the banana-boom-production of the twentieth century to which the definite settlement of Afro-Caribbeans in Limón is intrinsically linked. Beforehand, the construction of the railroad to the Atlantic had opened up the routes of displacement from the insular to the continental Caribbean. Afterwards, the United Fruit Company (UFCo.) would determine new settlements, which was established in 1899 when Minor Keith merged his Tropical Trading and Transport Company with the Boston Fruit Company. Olien affirms that Keith had begun with the mono-cultivation of a commercial banana in the Caribbean, the Gros Michel, in order to finance the construction of the railroad system, which "began to provide freight for the railway as easily as 1880."[9] The desire to modernize and make of Costa Rica an export economy through the construction of the iron horse inevitably led to the creation and establishment of the United Fruit Company as the consolidation of postcolonial capitalist enterprises, furthermore transnationally sustained with Black workers from the Caribbean islands and, with time, with Central Valley Costa Ricans that had migrated to Limón in search of work. Moreover, with the inauguration of the banana transregional economy, Afro-Caribbeans were in constant movement springing from one Central American nation to the other in search of job opportunities, while the Central American nations converted into "banana republics" were trying to deal with the massive immigrations.[10]

As a result, the region was developed under what Kepner and Soothill appropriately named Minor Keith's *Banana Empire*. With Costa Rica as the starting point of operations, the Company grew into a Central American-based, extremely profitable banana-industry, whereby Limón developed a modality of dependent capitalism due to the enclave economic

---

4   Gilroy, *The Black Atlantic*: 10.

5   Anderson, *Imagined Communities*: 146.

6   Miles, "Recent Marxist Theories of Nationalism and the Issue of Racism": 27.

7   Ibid.: 33.

8   Palmer, *What Happen*: 21.

9   Olien, "The Adaptation of West Indian Blacks": 139.

10   Regarding the term "banana republics", see Henry, "The Admiral" (1904), a literary account of a fictitious place called Anchuria. Described as a "small, maritime banana republic" (p. 132), the fictional setting recalls to a great extent the Central American nations converted into United Fruit Company neocolonial enclaves (cf. Pérez-Brignoli, *Historia global de América Latina*: 452–455).

structure.[11] As defined by Bryce-Laporte and Purcell, this structure functioned as "a bureaucratic asymmetrical relationship [...] among [a] alien subordinate capital and technology, [b] native natural resources or territory and [c] subordinate alien or native labor".[12] Hence, [a] Minor Keith and his bondholders provided the capital and technology for [b] the mono cultivation of banana in the Costa Rican Atlantic/Caribbean seacoast. The operation opted for [c] an alien Afro-Caribbean workforce instead of indigenous or mestizo Costa Rican population, one of the main reasons being that Afro-Caribbeans spoke English, as did the North American managers. The United States economy, furthermore, acted as its metropolitan center. That is, as Costa Rica's main buyer. The small country reached its peak export figures during the first decades of the twentieth century. Contrary to the 420,000 stems that had been exported in 1884, three million bunches were sent to the U.S. in 1900, four million in 1902, and so much as ten million in 1908. As a result, Costa Rica became the world leader exporter of bananas in the first decade of the twentieth century, with little more that eleven million banana stems being shipped out towards North America between in 1912–1913.[13]

Though Keith controlled 75% of the country's exports through a well-installed monopoly by 1912, banana production started declining from 1913 onwards due firstly to soil exhaustion, secondly to a pronounced drop in the 1920s caused by Panama plant disease, followed by the North American economy crash. Even though a substantial 48% of the value of Costa Rica's exports was accomplished through the UFCo. in 1929, scarce four million bananas were exported in 1932. This resulted in severe cases of unemployment and of poverty in Limón. Moreover, the UFCo. had acted aggressively upon a weak Costa Rican economy throughout the years due to the enclave production and the transnational capitalistic export system. Harpelle documents how its extended presence in the Atlantic region had hard felt consequences for the Costa Rican national economy, causing public debt, high rates of inflation, and deficit spending.[14] The economic crisis that took place during the 1920s and 1930s led not only to a decrease in banana export, but mainly to a consequent increase in unemployment in the region along with reduction in wage levels.[15] Furthermore, when banana production fell in 1934 in Limón due to land erosion and plant disease, the UFCo. was given complete control over the banana industry at the Pacific coast in return for their investment in the country. This meant that the telegraph lines, rails, and bridges that Keith had installed in Limón during the years his banana monarchy grew, ceased to function when it relocated towards new ground. As affirmed by Harpelle, the Company "simply abandoned the community that it had helped to create."[16] The UFCo.

---

[11] Viales, *Después del enclave*: 25.
[12] Bryce-Laporte/Purcell, "A Lesser Known Chapter": 220.
[13] The banana export data and the following drop during these years can be confronted in Kepner/Soothill, *The Banana Empire*: 51f.; Harpelle, *The West Indians of Costa Rica*: 19–25; and Bryce-Laporte/Purcell, "A Lesser-Known Chapter": 228–230. To be noticed is the fact that the authors differ with respect to the years of Costa Rica's banana-peak export numbers (1907/1908/1912/1913).
[14] Harpelle, *The West Indians of Costa Rica*: 69.
[15] Senior, *Ciudadanía afrocostarricense*: 37; Harpelle, *The West Indians of Costa Rica*: 76.
[16] Harpelle, *The West Indians of Costa Rica*: 88.

gradually moved its operations to the southern Pacific coast and from 1940 onwards Limón fell into a state of decadence and political negligence.[17]

Before this, however, Afro-Caribbeans were able to mobilize upward in the labor hierarchy. As a consequence, a sort of middle class conformed by Afro-Caribbeans emerged,[18] which in turn caused Costa Ricans to become hostile to their counterparts. At this time, internal migration from the country's metropolitan area had led to a significant increase of Central Valley Costa Ricans now living in Limón, while the Caribbean population had simultaneously decreased since it had begun emigrating either back home or to work at the Panamá Canal.[19] Consequently, wage workers were continuously struggling against each other in the search for upward mobility in the socioeconomic hierarchy of a capitalist economy that was sinking.

As a modern multinational corporation in the midst of a socioeconomic displacement, the UFCo. conformed a hierarchy of productive forces that gave way to the formation of an enclave society determined by race relations largely determined by the role of the economical. Afro-Caribbeans, North Americans, and Costa Ricans became part of an economic structure adjusted to ethnicity, which inevitably led to their conscious and unconscious class confrontation. This transformed itself into race relations given that socioeconomic "relationships of exploitation, domination and violence" were carried out and signified through the notion of 'race'.[20] As a result, the socioeconomic stratification of the banana enclaves was imposed by an occupational hierarchy. Its social and productive force was structured upon labor organization, in turn modeled upon *nationality,* which mirrored simultaneously *race*. With time, racial relations came to mirror citizenship and were structured, as Bourgois has specified it, into an "ethnic occupational hierarchy"[21] – understood perhaps best in Du Bois's words. That is, structured across "the problem of the color-line."[22] The color-line acted in fact as a surrogate for both cultural and national identity, while class antagonism was assimilated and internalized parallely. The result was the establishment of a stratified enclave society that "reflected divisions of race and class".[23] Furthermore, racial and class segregation allowed North American managers to control and manipulate their workers to avoid labor union and thus benefit economically from a divided workforce. Racial segregation upon tasks and housing facilities also enabled the UFCo. to capitalize on rivalries and favor community divisions.[24]

According to Purcell, "the practice of cultural, class, and color domination"[25] by the UFCo. was its most important defining element, with social inequality at its backbone. As a result, Costa Rican laborers voiced their concern over the "disadvantageous position they

---

17 See Putnam, "Ideología racial": 172, where she too refers to the abandonment of the Limón province after the region was no longer useful to the export economy.

18 Chomsky, *West Indian Workers*: 238.

19 Harpelle, *The West Indians of Costa Rica*: 144–147.

20 Cf. Guillaumin, "The idea of race": 52.

21 Bourgois, *Ethnicity at Work*: 66 and 74: "According to elderly informants an ethnically based division of labor had emerged by the 1920s".

22 Du Bois, *The Souls of Black Folks*: 17.

23 Harpelle, *The West Indians of Costa Rica*: 93.

24 Purcell, *Banana Fallout*: 31; cf. Harpelle, *The West Indians of Costa Rica*: 26.

25 Purcell, *Banana Fallout*: 12.

felt themselves to be in with respect to blacks" and complained about "the predominance of workers of the coloured race, to the detriment of the creole worker."[26] Anti-Black feelings heightened among Costa Ricans who felt their national interests were being undermined regarding those of Afro-immigrants living in Limón. The racialisation, that is, "the attribution of race"[27] to social and economic significants gave way to a conflictive relation between Costa Rican and Afro-Caribbean wage workers and, as pointed out by Chomsky, "the tightening economic situation exacerbated tensions between [them]."[28] Finally, this led to feelings of enmity toward Black migrant laborers on behalf of the Costa Rican working class, as well as by the country's intellectuals.

Costa Ricans Speak Out… and Against

Costa Rican national racism toward Afro-Caribbean migrant workers emerged at its fullest precisely during the difficult economic situation of the 1920s and 30s. As affirmed by Bourgois, the "society surrounding the United Fruit Company's operations in Panamá and Costa Rica through the 1930s was profoundly racist."[29] Mainly because poverty and class formation within labor organization led to the flourishing of racist ideologies due to historically specific conditions. These coincided with the mid-1920s crash of the Costa Rican export economy, the 1930s Great Depression, and the difficulties mestizo Costa Ricans encountered in achieving upward mobility during this time. This socioeconomic context led to the intertwinement of class divisions and ethnonational differentiations within the banana enclaves to become blurred and indistinguishable. The self-differentiation of Costa Ricans from the Other labor immigrants through the category of *race* became a mask that hid and disguised the real economic causes that generated the inequality, i.e. the enclave society, the ethnic occupational hierarchy, world economic crisis, and crash of the export economy.[30] Ultimately, racism became a systemic component of socioeconomic relationships, where ethnonational divisions and class positioning were interdependent and furthermore structured upon Costa Rica's imagined racial homogeneity.

Elite Racism

The association of anti-imperialist discourses with racist propositions constituted a first wave of official anti-Black feelings promoted mainly by conservative and nationalist

---

[26] Chomsky, *West Indian Workers*: 235.
[27] Guilllaumin, "The idea of race": 49. As defined by Miles (1995), 'racialisation' is installed "by the signification of human biological characteristics in such a way as to define and contract differentiated social collectivities" (*Racism*: 75).
[28] Chomsky, *West Indian Workers*: 221.
[29] Bourgois, *Ethnicity at Work*: 88.
[30] As stated by Guillaumin, "The idea of race": 53: "behind 'race' relationships lies a whole historical and ideological development."

intellectuals that manifested themselves with anti-imperialist premises against the UFCo. With the purpose of discrediting the company's monopoly in Limón and thus seeking to favor national production at the hands of Costa Ricans, liberal elites of the coffee oligarchy argued that the presence of Afro-Caribbean laborers represented possible threats to national health, as well as the possibility of becoming an 'Africanized' country. Chomsky defines such anti-Black feelings as "elite racism".[31]

Much like Afro-Caribbean migrants were considered "panic migrants" in the United Kingdom and in the Netherlands in the 1950s and 1960s,[32] Jiménez locates too the origins of "social panic" concerning Black immigration in the country among certain groups of power who were concerned with matters of public and social health in Costa Rica. Even though Black immigration was tolerated as the necessary evil ("mal necesario") because it represented a key economic and labor force during the construction of the modern nation,[33] intellectuals problematized the presence of Caribbean workers hired by the United Fruit Company as a public, national, and hygienic threat from the 1920s onwards. Issues such as health and hygiene policies would in fact have repercussions on Black wage workers due to anti-Black legislation, which sought to hinder what Costa Rican politicians and leaders referred to as the blackening of the country's racial cartography.[34]

Drawing on the 1927 census, the director of the National Census Office, José Guerrero, expressed concern regarding the Caribbean population that had settled in the Limón province in his article "Cómo se quiere que sea Costa Rica, blanca o negra?" (1930). In it he referred to Caribbean immigration as a "Black injection" introduced into the white population of Costa Rica, naming it a "Negro invasion". Guerrero made a direct connection between the United Fruit Company's operations in Limón and the 'black injection' it functioned upon, claiming that "[t]he Negro is the shadow of the banana".[35] His main objective was to 'expose' the danger of a further 'Africanization' of the nation if the UFCo. was given freedom to continue acting according to its own interests. Likewise, the *Sociedad Económica de Amigos del País*, a nationalistic group whose president was Joaquín García Monge,[36] was an important intellectual circle that expressed an anti-imperialist ideology while overtly speaking against the presence of Black laborers from the 1920s onwards. Acting out on anti-imperialist sentiments against the United Fruit Company in Costa Rica, the *Sociedad* lastly reproduced an anti-Black discourse by "spreading the perception that

---

[31] See Chomsky, *West Indian Workers*: 236–238.

[32] Cohen, *Global Diasporas* (1997): 141.

[33] Alvarenga Venútolo, "La inmigración extranjera en la historia costarricense": 4.

[34] Jiménez, *El imposible país de los filósofos*: 200. For further reading on the subject of hygiene and health policies in Costa Rica, see Putnam, "Ideología racial" (1999) and Palmer, "Hacia la 'auto-inmigración'" (1995).

[35] Quoted in Putnam, *The Company They Kept*: 73. Cf. Guerrero, "¿Cómo se quiere que sea Costa Rica?": 149: "inyección negra (o negra inyección)" and "[e]l negro es la sombra del banano." On the subject, see also Pakkasvirta, "Particularidad nacional en una revista continental": 96.

[36] Joaquín García Monge is one of Costa Rica's most important and influential twentieth-century writer, educator, and intellectual. His book *El Moto* (1900) is considered a groundbreaking work in national literary history and is part of the national educational curriculum. He was also the editor of *Repertorio Americano*, a Costa Rican journal read throughout Latin America. Furthermore, he participated in the foundation of the *Partido Alianza de Obreros, Campesinos e Intelectuales* in 1929. García Monge was a pillar of the Costa Rican elite intellectual scenery at the beginning of the twentieth century.

people of African descent threatened the nation."[37] It presented furthermore a report based on their study of the banana industry in 1926 in which Monge stated:

> We must not omit to mention at least the issues relative to the merely racial question of immigration that this company principally stimulates: the black, who, it is known, has a greater disposition to sicknesses such as tuberculosis, leprosy, syphilis and insanity, creating a higher mortality quotient among these elements than among whites, for example.[38]

General Secretary of State Marco Aurelio Zumbado also spoke overtly against Black immigration in 1926 when referring to the subject of social hygiene in Costa Rica. For him, Afro-Caribbean immigration was unattractive and illogical for the country's well-being, for Blacks were fatal to the nation's social order. Zumbado defined Black migrant workers as depraved and generally of criminal nature in November 1926, which is why their immigration represented a national threat.[39] A threat that Clodomiro Picado, a prominent microbiologist and serologist in charge of the laboratories of the Hospital San Juan de Dios at the first half of the twentieth century, underscored as a problem of miscegenation and degradation of the Costa Rican people. In his letter (1939) to historian Ricardo Fernández Guardia, then director of the National Archive, Picado justifies anti-Black sentiments through science with the purpose of proving the present menace 'white' Costa Ricans were facing. By carrying out a series of blood experiments which he explains in the letter, Picado determined the hematologic constitution of Costa Ricans as pertaining in preponderance to the European type, with more or less twenty-five percent of Indo-American blood. However, due to recent waves of immigration that occurred at the turn of the century, Picado attested that the sanguineous formula of the nation's people "has had an addition of ten percent African blood." This provoked alarming concern in Picado and concludes the letter with fatalistic previsions: "OUR BLOOD IS BLACKENING! And if we continue like this, it will not be a nugget of gold that comes out of the crucible, but rather a piece of charcoal."[40]

Working-Class Racism

Animosity was not only expressed by elite intellectuals, but also by the Costa Rican working class. Chomsky questions whether workers' racist confrontation against Caribbean Blacks was but an echo of elite racism. Anti-Black sentiments among the working class were due mainly to the "job-seeking anxiety of average Hispanic Costa Ricans" because of labor shortage.[41] Bourgois highlights this as a central cause for Costa Rican racial hostility, stating that "during these economic crises, Hispanic workers viewed black West Indians as

[37]   Harpelle, *The West Indians of Costa Rica*: 70.
[38]   "Cuestión bananera: contratos celebrados entre el gobierno de Costa Rica, Mr. Marsh y la UFCO respectivamente", submitted to Congress, January 6, 1927; quoted in Chomsky, *West Indian Workers*: 222.
[39]   Quoted in Putnam, "Ideología racial": 168.
[40]   Picado, "Our Blood is Blackening": 244.
[41]   Palmer/Molina, *The Costa Rica Reader*: 245.

competitors for scarce jobs".[42] In *Racism*, Robert Miles (1995) refers similarly to how socioeconomic panic in Britain expanded when Caribbean and Indian migrants became a competing Other once they arrived and settled in the country during the decline of capitalist production. Their presence posed a threat and meant first and foremost competition for the British working-class regarding housing accommodations, social services, and employment.[43] Following Miles, it can be noticed how, parallel to elite racism, Costa Ricans also voiced a "working-class racism" mainly because of the "economic and social changes accompanying industrial and urban decline [as] experienced by sections of the working class."[44]

At the heightened peak of the banana crisis, a petition was presented to Congress (1925) by several Spanish-speaking workers of the banana industry soliciting that Blacks didn't hold places as supervisors, nor as office clerks nor vendors, nor hold any similar functions within the Company.[45] Another petition was signed a year later by over five hundred non-Black Limón residents. In it, the Caribbean community was attacked as undesired intruders of the nation and as rivals to the morally superior 'white' Costa Rican values. Thanks to an efficient official nationalism, Costa Ricans complained in the letter of being in a "humiliating situation in [their] own Fatherland", for "a race inferior to [their] own" has "a situation of privilege" in the United Fruit Company.[46]

Newspapers in general did not fall back either on reporting the "Black problem" that Limón represented for the nation and functioned as a national platform for publicly expressing such postulates. They too participated in spreading the idea that "Blacks had become the owners of the Atlantic region", which meant none other than 'Black danger was invading the country' (*La Prensa Libre* 1914).[47] Readers also took part in the discussion. One of them commented (1935) on how the men and women of color were all considered as vagabonds.[48] A year earlier, *La Tribuna* published an editorial regarding the UFCo.'s opening of business at the Pacific Coast, whose author stated:

> The people of color of the Atlantic are going to invade the Pacific with grave consequences ... which we must confront. For me there is only one fatherland: Costa Rica, a fatherland which I will defend forever... We must not permit the doors of the Pacific Zone to be opened to an avalanche of the races of color. I detest them...[49]

Furthermore, the *Comité Pro-Costarricense Blancos*, conformed by a small number of workers and which appeared in the 1930s, placed public announcements against the railroad enterprise's hiring preferences in national newspapers, criticizing Afro-Caribbean presence.[50]

---

42   Bourgois, *Ethnicity at Work*: 89.
43   Miles, *Racism*: 81.
44   Ibid.
45   Senior, *Ciudadanía afrocostarricense*: 39.
46   Quoted in Chomsky, *West Indian Workers*: 237.
47   Quoted in Soto-Quiros, "Desarrollo, etnia y marginalización": "los negros se han adueñado de la toda la región Atlántica del país [...] el peligro negro nos invade."
48   Quoted in Putnam, "Ideología racial": 170.
49   *La Tribuna*, December 8, 1934, quoted in Bourgois, *Ethnicity at Work*: 89.
50   Harpelle, *The West Indians of Costa Rica*: 131f.

The work situation for Caribbeans became even more complicated when soil erosion and banana plant disease in the region provoked the UFCo.'s gradual abandonment of the province towards the Pacific coast. With respect to hiring policies there, a "Companion Law" required that 60% of the UFCo.'s employers had to be Costa Rican.[51] Since Afro-Caribbeans had been obtaining Costa Rican citizenship, the UFCo. was able to dodge the law. An angry Costa Rican speaks out against this anonymously:

> The UFCO, to evade the law that obliges them to have a certain number of Costa Rican workers, is instructing its black employees to become naturalized and it facilitates them all possible means to achieve this as soon as possible so that when this requirement is demanded of them they will be able to present all of the niggers [*negrada*] that work for them as Costa Rican [...].[52]

The comment reflects precisely how access to citizenship by Costa Rican-born Caribbean-descendants meant potential upward mobility for these, causing, as Harpelle underscored it, "class division within the community [to be] intensified by national sentiments".[53] Attempting to correct this, the new banana contract drafted in 1934 (the Cortés-Chittenden Treaty) explicitly prohibited the hiring of colored people in the banana industry settled at the Pacific region.[54] Consequently, "in 1940 skin colour became a major determinant in the decision to terminate a worker's employment with the company."[55]

The result of such antipathy vis à vis Black presence in Limón was crystallized as the reluctance of the Costa Rican government to invest in infrastructure, public health, or education in Limón once the region was no longer relevant to the national economy.[56] Unlike the early agrarian interests in the region, which led to the construction of the railroad, the country's leaders were no longer interested in maintaining the Caribbean province as an economical center. Jiménez refers to this taking-of-action on behalf of the Costa Rican government as the manifestation of nationalism based upon ethnonational considerations that considered migrant Black laborers to be a threat to national concerns.[57]

---

[51] Chomsky, *West Indian Workers*: 250; Harpelle, *The West Indians of Costa Rica*: 85.

[52] This pertains to an anonymous letter presented in 1932, quoted and translated in Chomsky, *West Indian Workers*: 236: "[...] if the Company wanted to help the country in confronting the problem of the unemployed, this would not exist in the Atlantic coast region if they only gave preference to our own; but they only give preference to the blacks [...] The Congress should begin to pay attention to this Jamaican race that is not only the owners [sic] of Atlantic region but is also invading the interior of the country without anyone concerning themselves with the fact, and when they do begin to pay attention to it, it will be too late. Blacks, Chinese, Polacks, [Eastern European Jews], Coolies [South Asians], and all manner of undesirable scum who get thrown out of other countries or are kept out enter and exit our border like it's nothing without the authorities showing any interest, and this has worsened the agonizing situation of workers like us."

[53] Harpelle, *The West Indians of Costa Rica*: 157.

[54] Quoted in Senior, *Ciudadanía afrocostarricense*: 67: "Queda prohibido el empleo, en la zona Pacífica, de la gente de color en dichos trabajos."

[55] Harpelle, *The West Indians of Costa Rica*: 134.

[56] Jiménez, *El imposible país*: 199. "Así como el Estado estuvo presente y se expandió desde principios de siglo en la provincia de Limón, así también renunció al gasto público para la infraestructura, la salud pública, el crédito agrícola y la educación, a partir del momento en que la producción regional ya no formaba parte importante de la economía de exportación."

[57] Ibid.: "Cuando la Compañía Bananera abandona la zona y se discuten las condiciones laborales en las nuevas plantaciones del Pacífico Sur, se apela a un nacionalismo étnico y los negros son visto como una amenaza sanitaria pública."

This had as a consequence the marginalization of the Caribbean province, hindering the possibilities of upward mobility for Afro-Costa Ricans for years to come. Drawing on the 1973 census, Purcell (1993) referred that at that time Limón was the province with the lowest percentage of university students (65% below the national average), with only 0,2% of Afro-Costa Ricans going to university. Also, it presented the lowest salary scale in comparison with the other provinces. A general lack of Afro-limonense-owned business was also to be noted, along with high rates of unemployment. Moreover, Afro-Costa Ricans did not generally hold positions of political power.[58] Bryce-LaPorte and Purcell (1982) also affirm racial discrimination presented Afro-Costa Ricans with obstacles not only by stripping farmers from their untitled land, but lack of access to cultivable land, nepotism in access to jobs, unemployment, and restricted access to higher education played a crucial part in limiting the overcoming of inequality.[59] Though the 2000 census portrayed signs of an overall socioeconomic betterment among the Afro-Costa Rican minority, Lara Putnam (2004) refers critically to the data and instead suggests the census captured wealth, unemployment, and labor market indexes disproportionately.[60] The 2013 PNUD report on the socioeconomic realities of the Afro-Costa Rican minority does not provide contradictory evidence on the subject.

It cannot be overlooked that the nineteenth and twentieth century imagination of Costa Rica explains the ideological background of heightened anti-Black sentiments in the country from 1920s onwards. Because of complicated economic conditions, racial differentiations were underscored in the context of class confrontations, where elite and working-class racisms acted as integral components of Costa Rican nationalism. Finally, *race* was utilized in an instrumental way on behalf of the country's elite groups in order to exclude and segregate Blacks in favor of the national worker and for the sake of protecting racial homogeneity. The working class, instead, echoed such precepts when demanding their interests not be undermined opposite the 'non'-Costa Rican Black workforce.

It must then be acknowledged that Harpelle's assertion is quite accurate, "the interplay between class and ethnicity is the central feature of the West Indian experience in Costa Rica". As he asserts it, "nowhere [was] the contrast between the 'real' and the 'other' more evident than in the province of Limón".[61] For as Putnam declares it, the Caribbean represented one of the boundaries of Costa Rican whiteness.[62] Its unnatural border was both racial as geographical, linguistic as religious, economic, national and diasporic. Consequently, the cultural constellations particular to the deterritorialized diaspora settled in Limón and the precepts which imagined Costa Rica as a white, exemplary country in Central America led to the establishment of a *borderland* at the Caribbean province. Not only this, but mutual confrontation due to class and racialized relations was also key to the consolidation of this borderland as a cultural hinterland. In its being remote and dependent on the Central Valley – the ideological and hegemonic center enforcing what Anzaldúa calls

---

58   Purcell, *Banana Fallout*: 97 and 102. See Bryce-Laporte/Purcell, "A Lesser-Known Chapter": 228–231.
59   Bryce-Laporte/Purcell, "A Lesser-Known Chapter": 231–235.
60   Putnam, "La población afrocostarricense según los datos del censo de 2000": 387f.
61   Harpelle, *The West Indians of Costa Rica*: xvi and xiv, respectively.
62   Putnam, "Ideología racial": 141: "Para ilustrar la construcción y el impacto de la raza en la historia de Costa Rica, analizamos una de las fronteras de la 'blanquedad' costarricense, la zona del Caribe, a través del auge y el declive de la producción bananera."

"cultural tyranny"[63] –, Limón experienced cultural, economic, and social marginalization in the country.[64] As a consequence, *Afro*-Costa Ricans occupied a peripheral, i.e. ex-centric position in the country's historical imagination.

And so, as a way of concluding I would like to recall that what was mentioned at the beginning of these pages. Diaspora/s, with their complex nexus of local and translocal connectivity through mobility and displacement, make evident the outdated conceptualization of homogenous nations and instead participate actively in creating a new template across the nation~diaspora dynamic/s. Across it, each *sense of belonging* is constituted, as defined by Tölölyan in the Preface of the first edition of the *Diaspora* journal (1991), "as a heterogeneous and disequilibrated site of production, appropriation, and consumption, of negotiated identity and affect".[65] Hence, Caribbean settlement in Costa Rican territory and the particular economic conditions here outlined gave way to the creation of what Anzaldúa considers *borderlands* represent: "the lifeblood of two worlds merging to form a third country – a border culture."[66] Born out of the dialectics of race and nation and of displacement through travelling cultures, a "deterritorialization of social identity" took place, where this border culture challenged "an exclusive citizenship" by shifting towards "overlapping, permeable, and multiple forms of identification", as explained by Cohen.[67] Nowadays, the residue of this original borderland is carried upon the historical imagination that remains in the individual and collective memory of Afro/Costa Ricans.

Next, Part III – *The Following is a Story of the Past*, explores Afra-Costa Rican poetry with the purpose of analyzing how therein recoils a rhizomorphic structure mapped across diverse cultural and historical affiliations that are set between the translocal and the inter/transnational, instead of tied down by two incompatible fond feelings of attachment. Its fractal nature frames the spatial, ethnonational, and linguistic characteristics of Black Costa Ricans within a wider "story of hybridization and intermixture"[68] regarding the nation~diaspora dynamic/s, from which pluricentrical belonging emerges.

---

[63]   Anzaldúa, *Borderlands*: 38.
[64]   Glissant, "Cross-Cultural Poetics": 102.
[65]   Tölölyan, "The Nation-State and its Others": 6.
[66]   Anzaldúa, *Borderlands*: 25.
[67]   Cohen, *Global Diasporas* (1997): 157.
[68]   Gilroy, *The Black Atlantic*: 199.

Part III

The Following is a Story of the Past

Dlia McDonald – This Train is Bound to Glory

> I do not practice the economy of the meadow, I do not share the serenity of spring.
>
> Édouard Glissant, *Caribbean Discourse*

The story of *Black Costa Rica* starts here with diaspora/s. At the departure harbor of the ensuing literary analysis lay necessarily dislocation, movement, and travelling cultures. Industrial capitalism, competing economies, and processes of Modernity represent both the causes and the outcomes of diaspora/s caused by neo/colonialism. All brought into being by the *ship*, termed by Glissant in *Poétique de la Relation* (1990) as "the open boat" and defined by him as a *multilayered abyss*. The ship represents for the author a "womb abyss", for the boat is paradoxically "pregnant with as many dead as living under sentence of death".[1] The depths of the sea represent an *infinite abyss* as well, since thousands of slaves were thrown overboard with chains and balls to sink away once the ships needed to sail lighter and faster, never reaching any true destiny except death. An imagery that Aimé Césaire represents in *Et les chiens se taisent* (1946) as "the vomit of slave ships".[2] Marlene NourbeSe Philip's poetic account of the eighteenth-century massacre of slaves upon the British ship Zong recreates this in a unique manner (*Zong!* 2008). The third abyss Glissant refers to has to do with the loss of African historical memory and tradition, since their cultural codes were forced into oblivion. That is, it signals a *cultural death abyss* turned into the "absolute unknown". Glissant claims that it was the open boat and this triple-faced ordeal that which "quickened into this continuous/discontinuous thing" that colonialism inaugurated. The clash of cultures in new territories that gave way to the consolidation of the Caribbean as a location of "limitless *métissage*" within the Plantation site, defined by Glissant as "one of the focal points for the development of present-day modes of Relation."[3]

The ship bears a fundamental importance in the diasporic memory of the Black circum-Atlantic with uprooting at its core. Bob Marley's "Redemption Song" (*Uprising* 1980) recalls how "Old pirates, yes, they rob I / sold I to the merchant ships / minutes after they took I / from the bottomless pit." Likewise Nalo Hopkinson's futuristic *Midnight robber* (2000), where a hat crafted specially for the little girl Tan-Tan's choir recital is given to her in the form of a *rocket ship*. This "nation ship" named "Marryshow Corporation: Black Star Line II" represents a futuristic allegory for the *sea ship*, where "them black people inside woulda been lying pack-up head to toe in they own shit, with chains round them ankles", explains her the craftsman.[4] Or Amir Baraka's theatrical piece *Sea Ship: A Historical Pageant* (1967), where the slave ships are symbolic of the oppressed condition of African Americans.[5] The

---

[1] Glissant, *Poetics of Relation*: 5 and 6, respectively.
[2] Césaire quoted in Condé, "The Stealers of Fire": 156.
[3] Glissant, *Poetics of Relation*: 8, 7, 34, and 65, respectively.
[4] Hopkinson, *Midnight Robber*: 20 and 21, respectively.
[5] Kumar, "Form as a Site of Contest": 46. For literary representations of the slave ship in African American literature, see Pittman, *"Force. Spirit. Feeling:" Rewriting the Slave Ship in Contemporary African American Literature* (2014).

list is quite vertiginous and surpasses the literary genre, as Cheryl Finley's book *Committed to Memory. The Art of the Slave Ship Icon* (2018) demonstrates it.

It makes thus sense that Paul Gilroy also addresses the discontinuous histories regarding colonialism and diaspora through the imagery of the naval machine. The Middle Passage, the slave trade, and their relationship to industrialization and modernization of the western world are approached by Gilroy by way of the ship's symbolism as inherent to the Black Atlantic, which he defines as the 'counterculture of Modernity'.[6] For the author, ships become highly significant when considering how Blacks are linked both to revolutionary transformations and to the intellectual heritage of the West ever since Enlightenment.[7] Firstly because ships gave life to the Black Atlantic, where Modernity and slavery became indissoluble concepts. Secondly, because its imagery permits the author to define the Black Atlantic as an alternative understanding of the sociohistorical, cultural, and political processes that define Modernity. Specifically because of the ship's potential in creating de-territorialized, hybrid imaginings of belonging, thus standing as a symbol of both rootedness and multiplicity. As a result, Gilroy explains the nature of the Black Atlantic as "a system of cultural exchanges" due to the circulation of people thanks to the ships' interoceanic maritime voyages linking Europe, Africa, the Caribbean, and the Americas across time.[8] The ensuing pages contend that Gilroy's system of cultural exchanges is recreated in Central America via the *train* as it was first brought about at the Caribbean archipelago with the *ship*.

Regarding the Central America-Caribbean-islands diasporic movement, the railway system represents the modernized medium of routes compounded into plural roots. In fact, the decision to build a railroad to the Atlantic on behalf of Costa Rican leaders, which led to the installment of the United Fruit Company in the country and in the region, brought people of different parts of the globe together in a complex racial, social, and economical multilingual economy – just like slavery and colonialism had done beforehand with the naval machine. Therefore, the purpose of the following pages is to deploy a first layer in the stor(y)ing of Costa Rica's recent past through the imagery of the train and its relationship to a specific story of the past as a poetic manner of joining the national and the diasporan in the articulation of a pluricentrical sense of belonging. Not through territorialized imaginings, but rather through the transhistorical dimension behind them.

The discussion focuses here on Dlia McDonald's representation of Caribbean nature together with Limón's urbanized spaces in *...la lluvia es una piel...* (1999).[9] When Professor Werner Mackenbach asked "where does the Caribbean lie?" at the closing Round Table

---

[6] See Bauman, "The Left as the Counter-Culture of Modernity" (1986), where the author defines the Left as the "counter-culture of capitalism" (p. 81) while arguing it should be better understood as the "counter-culture of modernism" (p. 86). Gilroy specifically mentions Bauman as the source for his Black Atlantic thesis (*The Black Atlantic*: 36). See also Habermas, "Modernity: An Unfinished Project" (1997), where the author engages "the project of Modernity" by dialoging with the concepts of the modern and the postmodern, and with Enlightenment ideas and aesthetic claims concerning cultural modernity as "the unfulfilled promise of modernity's Enlightenment project" (Gilroy, *The Black Atlantic*: 46).

[7] Gilroy, *The Black Atlantic*: 2.

[8] Ibid.: 14.

[9] Following McDonald's desire to have the original version quoted here, all poems correspond to the 1999 first edition. The second edition was reprinted in 2010.

"Escribir sobre/en/desde/por los Caribes" (2015) with writers Quince Duncan, Anacristina Rossi, Sekou, and Dlia McDonald participating in it, the latter refers to herself as exclusively "valle centralina".[10] McDonald was born in 1965 in Colón, Panama but moved with her Costa Rican parents back to San José when she was five years old, where she grew up, carried out her studies, and resides since then.[11] Hence, born and raised in the capital, McDonald recognizes herself first and foremost as a Central Valley Costa Rican, opposed to the idea that all Black Costa Ricans come from the Caribbean province. Nonetheless, childhood memories are accentuated by trips to visit the family in Limón, which are given poetic form in Part II of *...la lluvia es una piel...* This representation is one of the mediums by which the reader comes in contact with Black Costa Rica in the book, together with the depiction of her family as one of the markers of her ethnic identity, and racism as she lived it at the Central Valley capital. On another note, diverse poems claim her poetic and mystical existence as *la bruja poeta*, a persistent *Selbstbild* found across her poetic œuvre.[12]

Her first compilation was published a couple of years earlier under the title *El séptimo círculo del obelisco* (1994), a twenty-eight free-verse poem anthology where she most strongly reaffirms her *négritude*, as affirmed by Christian Marcelo in the prologue.[13] Correctly perceived by Mosby, this collection expresses a "diaspora consciousness that transcends Costa Rica's borders",[14] for in their brevity the poems refer to her Blackness both in an individual as in a transnational manner.[15] Also, they poetize love experiences and convert nature into a fundamental aesthetic tool. In 1995 McDonald presented *Sangre de madera* where her ethnic identity is however not a central issue as in the aforementioned books, though minor references to Jamaica as the black island of her origins (III.6f: "desciendo / de una isla negra") and to African roots are present (three poems within a total of thirty-three). Instead, the poems are divided in two major thematic groups. Her *bruja* identity is strongly reiterated, while love poems, erotism, and absence of the lover guide the reader across the compilation. McDonald also refers to the power of her creative writing, in some cases linked to her *bruja* nature, in others as the only means for naming her feelings regarding the absent one. She denounces furthermore planetary indifference condemning human apathy opposite planet Earth, and, just like in her other anthologies, nature is always an indispensable artistic tool appealing to a complex imagery of diverse abstractions. The

---

[10] The Round Table took place at the international symposium *Convergencias Transculturales Caribe. Literatura, arte, cultura, historia, comunicación* as the closing discussion (November 18–21, 2015 in San José/Limón, Costa Rica). I took part in the symposium with a presentation entitled "'Lo que la historia nos debe': La construcción de una memoria ex–céntrica en las poetas afro-costarricenses." The Round Table is available in its entirety at https://www.youtube.com/watch?v=wJq5huaKQi8.

[11] Cf. Duncan, "Corrientes literarias Afro Limonenses": 77; Mosby, *Place, Language, and Identity in Afro-Costa Rican Literature*: 209, and Meza, "Memoria, identidad y utopía": 137.

[12] In her own words: "Yo soy una cimarrona. Las brujas en realidad eran cimarronas, eran mujeres rebeldes que crearon su mundo y se enfrentaron a los hombres. El mal que hicieron esas mujeres fue rebelarse, no ser igual a las otras, negarse a aceptar sus verdades, y como se negaron, murieron ahorcadas o quemadas en las fincas. ¿Cuántas brujas son las que se enfrentan día a día para sacar adelante a sus familias? Ésa [sic] es la magia y el poder" (quoted in Meza, "Memoria, identidad y utopía": 140).

[13] Marcelo, "Prólogo": 4.

[14] Mosby, *Place, Language, and Identity in Afro-Costa Rican Literature*: 210.

[15] The first poem "Entre las páginas" as well as "Digo negro" refer to Nicolás Guillén as a 'brother in Blackness'. Other poems include "Nací negra", "Soy una mujer negra", "Porque soy", "Desde siempre", "Ante el tiempo". (The titles of the poems correspond to the first verses of each individual poem.)

sea and her 'sailor-witch' presence are recurrent sites of meaning, together with seagulls, the horizon, the sun, the moon, and the rain. She has also compiled diverse anthologies: *Pregoneros de la memoria* (2006), *Instinto tribal. Antología poética* (2006, reuniting poems from *Sangre de madera*, *El séptimo círculo*, and *...la lluvia es una piel...*), and *Palabras indelebles de poetas negras* (2011), co-authored with Shirley Campbell in the context of the *Año Internacional de los Afrodescendientes*. In 2014, Silvia Solano referred to this compilation as being casted away into silence by literary critics in the country.[16]

In 2012 McDonald published *Todas las voces que canta el mar*. This book is a majestic appropriation of the foundational Greek myths exposed by Homer in the *Iliad* and in the *Odyssey*, where the main theme guiding her book is the pain of love. The book is divided in three sections ("Helenísticas", "Mitominotáuricas", and "Náuticas") with short free-versed poems entitled *Cantos* or *Corifeos* expressed by characters like Helene, Menelaus, Ulysses, Penelope, Cyclopes, Tiresias, Calypso, Aphrodite, the Oracle, and the female tripartite personification of destiny, the *Parcae* sisters, Clotho, Atropos, and Lachesis. Each individual voice sets a dialogue with the plurality of the other voices – hence the title – which mourn love, solitude, and abandonment across each section accordingly with the original myths. To be emphasized is the polyphony the book withholds, for it speaks the suffered voices of all the victims of love in Homer, including Menelaus. The sea and its waves, the ships and docks, the tides and their foam, as well as the moon and the sea birds recreate the maritime scenery proper to Homer's Hellenic landscape, which are nonetheless recurrent in McDonald's poetry and that, coupled with her sailor-witch identity, stand as expressions of Benítez-Rojo's definition of the Caribbean populations as "People of the Sea".[17] References to Minotaur, Daedalus, Icarus, Hades, *deux ex machina* or to Ulysses's faithful dog and the Golden Fleece make *Todas las voces que canta el mar* an ingenious poetic palimpsest concerning a classical work of literature, which focuses creatively on the subject of solitude and the existential pain caused by the absence of the loved one.

Of special interest is McDonald's personal blog, "La Coleccionista de Espejos", where one can find some of her early poems written in English under the entry title "Strange Language".[18] Article contributions by diverse people referring to her poetic work and to other authors are also retrievable here, as are a wider range of literary and cultural curiosities. She is currently working on a series of short stories called *¿Y quién ha visto un payaso negro?* and has recently published her first prose work, a novel entitled *La cofradía cimarrona* (2018), which the author claims is not written in "Costa Rican".[19] While Quince Duncan is the major Afro-Costa Rican prose writer nowadays, McDonald's novel represents a landmark in the literary historiography of the country, for it is the first one written and published by a Black woman in Costa Rica. Lastly, as reported by Mosby,[20] McDonald is fairly visible in the capital's literary scene by carrying out public readings, as

---

[16]   Solano, "El giro identitario": 372: "El silencio de la crítica literaria costarricense, en el caso particular de *Palabras indelebles de poetas negras* puede deberse a lo reciente de su publicación."

[17]   Benítez-Rojo, *The Repeating Island*: 26.

[18]   See https://themirrorcollector.blogspot.com/2011/05/strange-language.html. As reported by Meza, at McDonald's home Spanish was not spoken, but a mixture of Creole and English ("Memoria, identidad y utopía": 137).

[19]   Personal interview in San José (CR) on December 12, 2015.

[20]   Mosby, *Place, Language, and Identity in Afro-Costa Rican Literature*: 209.

for example in *Noches de poesía en el farolito* at the Centro Cultural de España, which dedicated the month of April 2007 to Afro-Costa Rican poets.[21] As well as by having previously directed the poetry workshop *Taller de Poesía Francisco Zúñiga*, an important literary space where ex-centric poets, i.e. those outside the national canon, could reunite and discuss their writing. McDonald refers to this as her "experience from within the war field".[22]

Despite the varied themes McDonald's poetizes, scholars have mainly focused on poems in which she refers to her ethnic identity and how she relates it to her Costa Rican-ness. In this sense, literary critics have approached her written production mainly with the purpose of making visible her poetic treatment of her local and transnational 'Blackness'. On the one hand, both Duncan and Mosby have correctly noted how McDonald has claimed her ethnic difference from the capital's location, furthermore coherent with the new Afro-Costa Rican generations born outside Limón who grew up and were schooled in San José, like Shirley Campbell. On the other hand, whereas Duncan's (2012) appreciation of McDonald's poetry as representing an important break with 'exile literature' (e.g. diasporan) is quite accurate, his conception of her poetry as a notable expression of a literature of *protest* and *denunciation*[23] (emphasis added) may be considered short-sighted when her œuvre is analyzed in an all-embracing view. Especially if we are to take into consideration her focus on the thematic of love and solitude both in *Sangre de madera* as in *Todas las voces que canta el mar*, the highlighting of her *bruja* poet identity across her œuvres, or even her refined aesthetic language as object of study *per se*. On the other hand, Mosby carries out an analysis of the poems of *...la lluvia es una piel...* by focusing specifically on those that develop the issues of identity from a place of isolation and marginalization as a consequence of the "experience of being the only black child in a school with a staff burdened with stereotypes of blacks and blackness".[24] Similarly, Meza passes on McDonald's words by stating how with *...la lluvia es una piel...* the poet undertook the challenge of writing an autobiography in verse, which spoke of the discrimination and marginalization she experienced as a primary school student.[25]

It cannot be denied that McDonald has engaged in her poetry the subject of her ethnic identity as well as the confrontations born out of it as a Black Costa Rican. Nevertheless, the purpose of the following section is to add an appreciation of the poetic richness of McDonald's aestheticized language by relating her poetic imagery to a strictly historical content regarding Costa Rica and Benítez-Rojo's *repeating island*. Mosby adds how in *...la lluvia es una piel...* McDonald carries out an important poetic connection with Limón from her own lived place as a Central Valley Costa Rican.[26] It is precisely this connection that the present

---

[21] See Piedra, *Noches de poesía en el farolito: una mirada a la poesía costarricense en el 2007* (2007).

[22] Personal interview, December 12, 2015. Cf. "Poemas del Taller Francisco Zúñiga" in *IMAGO* (Ministerio de Cultura, Juventud y Deportes, October 2000). A short introduction explains Francisco Zúñiga's Poetry Workshop as a place that gave a voice to those writers that had not been able to enter the national literary scenery (p. 43). McDonald appears in this compilation with a poem not published in any other of her compilations (p. 45).

[23] Duncan, "Corrientes literarias afrolimonenses": 76.

[24] Mosby, *Place, Language, and Identity in Afro-Costa Rican Literature*: 220.

[25] Meza, "Memoria, identidad y utopía": 141.

[26] Cf. Mosby, *Place, Language, and Identity in Afro-Costa Rican Literature*: 218ff. and 226.

pages depart from and upon which a hermeneutical close reading is centered. By carrying out a philological analysis of the poetic language portraying the Limón province in ...*la lluvia es una piel...*, the following pages present another interpretation of McDonald's poetry. In so doing, the discussion focuses upon the glocal representations of historical references concerning the colonial economy of the Caribbean and the neocolonial transnational enterprises in the Central American region.

The aim here is to engage a historical content that transcends both the structure of the nation-state *and* the constraints of the ethnonational specificity, as proposed by Gilroy,[27] reuniting them by way of their pluricentrical historical dimensions, i.e. ex-centric and outernational. Since the general subject of the present book is concerned with the reevaluation of Costa Rica's recent story of the past from the perspective that acknowledges its belongingness to the broader Black Atlantic, McDonald's thematization of love, erotism, or her *bruja* identity will not be approached here. Instead, the first part of the ensuing discussion focuses specifically in Part II of ...*la lluvia es una piel...* because the reader encounters a series of poems whose creative imageries rely on the intertwining of the train, the landscape, and the urban spaces of the Caribbean province. These will be approached hermeneutically as markers of a local ex-centric history that reflect the outcome of an outer/transnational one (diasporic). The poems in Part II are relevant to the discussion of pluricentrical belonging because, on the one hand, they re-present a translocal territorial identification through a complex semiotic from which, on the other hand, we can extract a historical content pertaining to the recent past of Black Costa Rica, furthermore connected to the *repeating island* that Antonio Benítez-Rojo has defined as the essence of the Caribbean meta-archipelago.

The poems will be analyzed according to three main sites of historical meaning, which together generate a *modernized-nature oxymoron*. The first I call Sites of Dwelling, represented in the poems as churches, long-legged houses, the grocery store, the park or the marketplace. These are, in turn, a subdivision comprised by the all-encompassing Sites of Modernization that refer to the poetic portrayal of cities and towns, the dock, the train station or the cutwater, and which are named as such for they represent the outcome of human action over nature towards urbanity and 'civilization'. By "modernization" I mean specifically a "*process* of structural *transformation* that is undergone by societies" (emphasis added), where urban development, that is, the development of cities and their respective infrastructure, is crucial.[28] Their counterpart is nature, fundamentally a *non-place*. This must not be confused with Marc Augé's concept of *non-lieu* (*Non-lieux* 1992), which the author defines as supermodernity spaces where the human being remains anonymous, like in a highway or in a waiting room at the airport. Instead, nature is defined here as a Non-Site because it is everywhere and nowhere *simultaneously*. It exists between *and* across *place and placelessness*. McDonald depicts it in the sand and in the stones, at the sea and among corals; through the wind and in the rain; as fireflies, crabs, palm trees, and coconut groves; at dawn or at the afternoon. Hence, the Non-Site of Nature corresponds principally to the *non-human world*. The train, itself a fundamental Site of Transportation – quintessential

---

27   Gilroy, *The Black Atlantic*: 19.
28   Whimster, "The Nation-State, the Protestant Ethic and Modernization": 61.

symbol of modernization, withholds a fundamental place in the sites of historical meaning to be analyzed next.

This poetics of landscape is explored through the oxymoronic image that places *nature* adjacent *modernization* and together as one single entity. The Oxford English Dictionary defines oxymoron as "a figure of speech in which a pair of opposed or markedly contradictory terms are placed in conjunction for emphasis." Like the Latin expression *contradictio in terminis* implies it, oxymoron refers to an apparent paradox created by placing opposites directly next to each other. The effect is the accentuation of such contraries, which together generate a new meaning, such as *colorful whiteness*.[29] The oxymoronic relation in McDonald's poetry lies upon the fact that *nature*, a non-human landscape, engorges urban development through an aestheticized imagery that recreates *urbanization* as one and the same entity with nature, itself transformed into a habitable, civilized space. Modernization is linked to processes of urban change opposite rural wilderness because of discourses on progress towards civilization. In Costa Rica, this liberal frame of thought led to the internal colonization of the Caribbean province in accordance with the political purposes of the country's leaders based at the Central Valley. In this sense, even though the modernized-nature oxymoron may appear at first sight an absurd enunciation, in contains actually a concealed reality. It points to an outernational, ex-centric story of the past of Limón/Costa Rica.

Following Glissant's claim that the Caribbean literary landscape does not reproduce the physical nature of a territory as following the techniques of European Realism, for the Caribbean landscape promotes other sceneries and the Caribbean writer refers to other realities through it,[30] McDonald's short poems are not approached here as the poetic reproduction of the environment as a faithful copy thereof. Neither is it approached as the literary representation of a country's landscape that appeals to the national community through the deployment of a familiar scenery with which s/he identifies as a citizen of a shared land (although this may nonetheless occur).[31] Rather, I focus on how McDonald's aestheticized language grants the non-human world a particular vivacity that, precisely in the merger of the Non-Sites of Nature with those of Modernization/Dwelling and the Train, results in a poetics of landscape *sensu* Glissant. As he defines it, the

> landscape in the work stops being merely decorative or supportive and emerges as a full character. Describing the land is not enough. The individual, the communities, the land are inextricable in the process of creating history. Landscape is a character in this process. Its deepest meanings need to be understood.[32]

---

[29] Metaphor is mine. Definitions taken from: *Oxford English Dictionary* [OED] online edition, s. v. "oxymoron", retrieved from http://www.oed.com/view/Entry/135679?redirectedFrom=oxymoron#eid; Lewis/Short, *A Latin Dictionary* online edition, s. v. "oxymorus", retrieved from http://www.perseus.tufts.edu/hopper/text?-doc=Perseus:text:1999.04.0059:entry=oxymorus; and from *Diccionario de la Real Academia Española* [DRAE] online edition, s. v. "oxímoron", retrieved from http://dle.rae.es/?id=RNRzJK5 (4.07.2017). See also Jordaan, *Ancient Greek Inside Out*: 171.

[30] Glissant, "Cross-Cultural Poetics": 146.

[31] Cf. Ovares et al, *La casa paterna*: 191.

[32] Glissant, "Cross-Cultural Poetics": 105f.

In addition, the author differentiates the "poetics of landscape" and the "physical nature of the country" as two different spaces. The latter is transformed into the former through an economy of expressive forms, specifically, through a polyphony of poetic phenomena.[33] In this manner, the landscape becomes *aestheticized*, as it will be demonstrated in the ensuing analysis.

For Mosby, McDonald's poems consist of short yet "hermetic" texts of "well-worked dense verses that imitate the precision of haiku."[34] Her perception is quite exact. The imagery that McDonald re-creates through her aestheticized language is in fact rich with abstraction and with punctual and precise naming of Limón's ecosystem, while depicting urban spaces intertwined with the exuberant nature that is everywhere and nowhere at once. She accomplishes this furthermore across a short number of verses, making her poetic language poignant. So that, as Glissant has noted, "[t]he landscape has its [own] language".[35] Wilson Harris also refers to this language-landscape relationship in the Preface to his book *The Palace of the Peacock* (1960), where he acknowledges his own poetic process as a literary "artifice rooted in nature" and as an orchestration of non-human elements.[36] In his "Author's Note", the Guyanese writer explains to the readership the motivations for "the particular variant of 'music'" and "rhythm" the book withholds.[37] Being haunted by legendary kingdoms of time past, Harris mentions El Dorado as an entity of "place and placelessness" orchestrated within nature – from which I draw in order to understand McDonald's Non-Sites of Nature – and from which Harris intuits "rhythmus to riverscapes, landscapes, skyscapes". These rhythms allow him to create a poetic "music of time".[38] McDonald's representation of nature develops in a similar manner its own language by which, much like Harris through his own poetic 'density of a rhythmic veil',[39] a semiotic of dislocated worlds confluence into shared and simultaneous presences of multiple forces and histories.

Therein lies, hence, a poetics of landscape that is not a site of immediate depiction of the physical environment, but a *character* that has been mediatized by language and as such represents a metaphorical dimension which has transformed *place* into *space*. Glissant defines this dimension as being "historical". In his opinion, the poetics of landscape "contains a historical dimension (of not obvious history)" in which "the memory of time past" is retained.[40] Let's recall that concerning the literary landscape, the francophone author claims that *its deepest meanings need to be understood*. Hence, this 'time past' in McDonald will be scrutinized in the following pages through the merger of Sites of Nature and of Modernization together with that of the Train, and as the symbolic ruins representing Costa Rica's *irruption into Modernity*.[41] By exploring McDonald's poetry against

---

33 Cf. Glissant, "Cross-Cultural Poetics": 150.
34 Mosby, *Place, Language, and Identity in Afro-Costa Rican Literature*: 209 and 210, respectively.
35 Glissant, "Cross-Cultural Poetics": 146.
36 Harris, *Palace of the Peacock*: 12.
37 Ibid.: 7, 8, and 9, respectively.
38 Ibid.: 10.
39 Cf. Ibid.: 11.
40 Glissant, "Cross-Cultural Poetics": 105 and 150.
41 This is an irruption that "is sudden and not sustained or 'evolved'", states Glissant ("Cross-Cultural Poetics": 146 and 149). On the subject, García Canclini problematizes "whether Latin America is a modern continent"

the historical backdrop regarding the liberal state-projects that came to be under the discourse of progress and modernization, her poetics of landscape *needs to be understood* as the result of postcolonial transnational capitalist enterprises. That is, McDonald's poetics of landscape withholds the memory of time past (specifically, of 'not obvious history') concerning the building of the railroad to the Atlantic by Minor Keith and the subsequent establishment of the United Fruit Company in the region as the events which brought about the urbanization of Limón towards a habitable, i.e. civilized, space.

Antonio Benítez-Rojo's argument, which defines the Caribbean as a repeating island, becomes under such considerations central to the ensuing stor(y)ing of Black Costa Rica's recent past. On the one hand, the analysis of McDonald's harmonic depiction of opposite spaces can only be comprehended against the historical backdrop that refers to "a space" which, following Benítez-Rojo's understanding of the Caribbean sociocultural region, "can only be intuited through the poetic, since it always puts forth an area of chaos."[42] This *area of chaos*, on the other hand, becomes clear when comprehended against Glissant's keen-sighted explanation of the landscape's historical dimension. According to the Martinican writer, the poetics of landscape

> is not saturated with a single History but effervescent with intermingled histories, spread around, rushing to fuse without destroying or reducing each other.[43]

Otherwise put, instead of a single, unilateral History concerning the circum-Caribbean, the poetics of landscape deploys *effervescent and intermingled histories* that, as argued by Benítez-Rojo, repeat themselves across a spatio-temporal continuum under new conditions and as echoed ripples of a recurrent past.

"Within the sociocultural fluidity that the Caribbean archipelago" represents, states the author, "one can sense the features of an island that 'repeats' itself". This *repeating island* unfolds and bifurcates itself through dynamics and processes "that show themselves within the marginal, the regional, the incoherent, [and] the heterogeneous" as regularities that reappear *globally* and *across time*.[44] Similar to Hall's (1990) claim, for whom the Caribbean exists within a continuum of *sameness* expressed however along the repetition of *difference/s*, the Cuban author considers that "there are common dynamics that express themselves in a more or less regular way within the chaos",[45] since the interplay of differences (cultural, linguistic, historical) occur nonetheless across dynamic regularities that break off as shared features *transhistorically*. These regularities, underscores the author, are dependent mainly on "changes in economic discourse"[46] and as such explain the causes for the Caribbean archipelago always *flowing* into another shape.

(*Hybrid Cultures*: xxxv). As explained by Renato Rosaldo, García Canclini's book explores "the tensions […] between modernization and democratization in Latin American nation-states", which consider themselves to be caught in a moment between traditions and a "modernity that has not yet arrived" ("Foreword: xi).

[42] Benítez-Rojo, *The Repeating Island*: 17.
[43] Glissant, "Cross-Cultural Poetics": 154. Glissant goes on to name Caribbean writers Naipaul, Carpentier, and Roumain as exemplary writers of this historical dimension.
[44] Benítez-Rojo, *The Repeating Island*: 3.
[45] Ibid.: 24.
[46] Ibid.: 5.

It is the aim of the ensuing pages to demonstrate how the poems of Part II from *...la lluvia es una piel...* give form to the *repeating island* in Afra-Costa Rican lyrical historical imagination. This specifically through the presence of the train and its aesthetic intertwinement with the urban and non-human spaces in the portrayal of a poetics of landscape. A philological close reading of it will elaborate on a story of the past routed through the modernized-nature oxymoron which, echoing Harris, "brings a pregnant apparition into the silences of space that have neither a beginning nor an ending."[47]

A Literary Introduction to Limón

When Costa Rica achieved its independence shortly after the beginning of the nineteenth century (1821), the country was imagined and discursively identified as the territory circumscribed within the Central Valley highlands (*meseta central*), which became the center of economic, political, and cultural power in the country. Literature played a central role in establishing this territorial identification, for it went hand in hand with what literary critic Álvaro Quesada (2002) has explained as the project of unifying and centralizing the many-sided faces of power around the agricultural hegemonic elite in charge of the international export of coffee.[48] The author also explains how the exclusion of other geographies in the literary spatial identification of the nation facilitated the oligarchic association with the European culture and strengthened the stereotype of Costa Rican racial and cultural homogeneity following the precepts of an occidental civilized nation.[49] In other words, the process of consolidating the nation was indivisible of the imagination of the country's racial cartography *and* of its territorial correlative.[50] *El Olimpo*, the first generation of national (all male) writers, [51] played a fundamental part in this process, for it established a model of national culture accordingly with the nation-building project the liberal oligarchy had been conceptualizing since the early decades of the nineteenth century, as explained by Rojas and Ovares (1995).[52]

---

[47] Harris, *Palace of the Peacock*: 12.

[48] Quesada, *Unos y los otros*: 17. Also noted by Rojas and Ovares in *Cien años de literatura costarricense*: 28.

[49] Quesada, *Unos y los otros*: 41. See also Quesada, *La formación de la narrativa nacional costarricense* (1995); Rojas/Ovares, *Cien años de literatura costarricense* (1995); Duncan et al, *Historia crítica de la narrativa costarricense* (1995), Ovares et al, *La casa paterna* (1993).

[50] Ovares et al, *La casa paterna*: 27f. See "La arcadia tropical": 21–107. Jose Luis Vega has named the indivisible elements that constituted the imagined community as (1) the geographical limitation of the nation with the Central Valley, as well as with (2) the growth of the coffee economy, and (3) the consolidation of the oligarchical hegemonic class. Costa Rica's territorial identification was brought together with a political space *and* an economic project, so that in this process a *class* project was established as of *national* interest (Vega, *Orden y progreso*: 155).

[51] The *Olimpo* men correspond to those who did not take part in the coffee industry, but however took charge of the ideological and literary imagination of Costa Rica. The writers of the *Olimpo* generation were born between 1850–1860 and wrote during the last decades of the nineteenth century. They represent the foundational writers of Costa Rican national literature, which are of obligatory reading in primary and secondary school (Quesada, *Unos y los otros*: 35ff.).

[52] Rojas/Ovares, *Cien años de literatura costarricense*: 32. Cf. Ovares et al, *La casa paterna*: "La arcadia tropical": 21–107.

Literary critics point out how throughout the nineteenth century an idyllic imagination of Costa Rica was recreated around the *labriegos* (peasants) and the land-owning oligarchs of the meseta central as a harmonic entity whose individual parts could prosper economically in an egalitarian fashion thanks to the Central Valley 'austere' coffee agriculture. This led to the establishment of an idealization of Costa Rica as *la arcadia tropical*, what Cortés (2003) affirms corresponds largely to Carlos Monge's "social democracy" and to which closer attention will be paid in the last segment dedicated to Bernard.[53] The authors of *La casa paterna* (1993) expose la arcadia tropical in early Costa Rican literature and explain it following Sergio Ramírez's (1983) topos of the orchard country (*país vergel*), for whom the topos functions as a rhetorical tool for attracting international investment and tourism in Central America. According to Ramírez, the region's territories have been idealized as the "feliz vergel donde se recogen frutos de sobremesa (cacao, café, y azúcar y después bananos)" due to its particular fertility.[54] The authors of *La casa paterna* affirm that in the Costa Rican case, the topos of *la arcadia tropical* mimics the *país vergel* insofar it represents the country as a natural, highly fertile, and versified orchard whose goods are cultivated without major effort or work by humble peasants who are eager to work and do not suffer from harvesting the land given that the land produces out of its own exuberant fertility.[55]

Moreover, the authors argue that the representation of Costa Rica's landscape at the origins of its national literature did not refer to the environment as a particular territorial reality. Instead, the sceneries reflect rather *a literary tradition*, where the imagery of the "Suiza centroamericana" was fundamental, its boundaries being the mountains circum-scribing the highlands of the central plateau.[56] Because of it, more than half of the country's land was excluded from the territorial identification, as signaled by the authors, and in this process diverse communities living in these regions were made invisible and consequently erased from the national imagery.[57] In fact, it was until 1856 that the Caribbean region was included in the territorial-cartographic representation of Costa Rica's geographical limits, even if inaccurate, for as Ronald Harpelle points out, the territory extended beyond its boundaries into Panamá.[58] This geographical innovation mirrored the nation-state's leaders' interest in the region as a potential economic pivot, which led to the inspection of the territory for the building of the railroad, as discussed in Part II. As Viales has indicated, the reports on the topography of the Atlantic province legitimated the economical projects in the region and ignored the presence of native people who inhabited it.[59] In fact, when Minor Keith first arrived in Costa Rica in 1872 for the building of the railway, his impressions were of "Limón and all the country between it and the cultivated portions of the interior [as] a dense wilderness. With the exception of the little village of Mantina [sic] [...], not one individual was settled anywhere on the line."[60] Such a perception made

---

[53] Cf. Cortés, "La invención de un país imaginario": 27–29.
[54] Ramírez, "Balcanes y volcanes": 36.
[55] Ovares et al, *La casa paterna*: 32f.
[56] Ibid.: 194.
[57] Ibid.: 7.
[58] Harpelle, *The West Indians of Costa Rica*: 11.
[59] Cf. Viales, "La segunda colonización": 91 and 121.
[60] Keith's letter to the Costa Rica Bondholders (1886), quoted in Chomsky, *West Indian Workers*: 20.

possible the internal colonization of the Atlantic/Caribbean region as though it were uninhabited and therefore waiting for it to be developed by the Central Valley Costa Rican. This consolidated the center-periphery dichotomy and reinforced the idea of Limón as a peripheral region regarding the territorial identification of the Costa Rican imagined community. That is, as an *ex-centric* territory.

Considering that the *Suiza centroamericana* was an epithet given by a foreign European traveler by explicitly naming it as the presence of the Old Continent in the New one, it makes sense that Quesada (1994) argues that the nation-building process led to the conformation of an alienated collective national identity. It was consolidated according to elite's interests, which corresponded furthermore to the foreign perspectives and motivations of the capitalist metropolis.[61] In this sense, San José-based intellectuals affirm their country's identity by looking towards Europe from the locality of the *Suiza centroamericana*, a.k.a. the Central Valley.[62] McDonald's poetry, together with fellow Afro-Costa Rican writers, become in this context refreshing, for they represent the Black voices that have given life to a new episode in national literary historiography since the beginning of the twentieth century, as Mosby's study has rescued it. The present section addresses and simultaneously goes beyond Costa Rican national literature by demonstrating rather how McDonald's oxymoronic poetic elements are bound to a global historical landscape in an outernational manner.

From Heaven to Hell

While in the first decades of the twentieth century Costa Rican geography is idealized as a placid rural reality without social conflict, this idealization disappears from the 1930s onwards. It shall be specifically with the *Generación del 40* that literature moves for the first time towards marginal regions such as the banana plantations, the Caribbean and Pacific seaside as well as into the jungle, breaking thus with the silence that had been imposed over these ex-centric regions, as noted in *La casa paterna*.[63] The Caribbean and the subaltern enter the national literary scene because of the political and economic crisis the country was going through, where the United Fruit Company was attacked as the threatening capitalist pivot. As a result of this political atmosphere, new geographies and communities were incorporated into the literary and territorial imagery of Costa Rica. These confronted the *Olimpo*'s *idyllic* Costa Rica from an anti-imperialist and communist perspective, based furthermore outside the meseta central.

The first literary work regarding the subject is Carmen Lyra's (1888–1949) compilation of five short stories under the title "Bananos y hombres" (1931), followed by the internationally acclaimed *Mamita Yunai* (1941) from Carlos Luis Fallas (1909–1966) and

---

[61]   Quesada, "Nación y enajenación": 116: "La dependencia económica del financiamiento externo y del mercado capitalista internacional determinó desde un principio el carácter precario de una identidad nacional que na-cía bajo el signo de la enajenación: la identificación de las necesidades *propias* de la incipiente república con los intereses *ajenos* de las metrópolis capitalistas."

[62]   Ovares et al, *La casa paterna*: 7.

[63]   Ibid.: 200; Rojas/Ovares, *Cien años de literatura costarricense*: 135.

Joaquín Gutiérrez's (1918–2000) *Puerto Limón* (1950), to name just three exemplary cases.[64] Together, these are representative of a *spatial turn* directly linked to the Caribbean province and regarding the country's literary territorial representation. Taking into consideration that the literary historiography reinforced this center-periphery dichotomy by excluding the Caribbean from the country's territorial identification, their literature constitutes a renewed literary imagining of Costa Rica from the ex-centric province of Limón, even if still determined by the perspective of the Central Valley mestizo Costa Rican.

Of specific interest here is their representation of nature as a hostile entity subordinated to the thematic of social issues, as noted by the authors of *La casa paterna*.[65] In Lyra's short stories, the banana plantations stand as expressions of inhumane existential conditions. Social inequality is depicted together with unfortunate stories of misery and nature-caused deaths, protesting how bananas hold more value than human life. *Mamita Yunai* also recreates nature through the harsh climate conditions, drawn between fierce hotness ("clima ardiente") and rain so cold as ice-needles ("agujitas de hielo"), topped with tropical downpours and the blistering heat plus the venomous serpents that awaited silently for their victims, hidden in the mountains that crumbled down upon the workers. By describing a destructive nature that acted aggressively against laborers, Fallas deploys the Caribbean environment as one of the many violent agents determining the workers' suffered experience at the Limón province.[66] Gutiérrez's *Puerto Limón* also represents sickness, social injustice, and death as consequences of the UFCo.'s banana fields, against which the first national strike was wagered in 1934 and which is also the novel's context – unlike Fallas's testimonial novel, which is set before the strike. Heavy showers are a recurrent topos in the book and an endless tropical downpour brings the novel, and the main character's uncle's life, to a climatic end. Hence, as the authors of *La casa paterna* keenly take note of it, with the *Generación del 40* Costa Rica's idyllic image of la arcadia tropical is on the one hand finally abandoned, while on the other ex-centric territories and their inhabitants are recognized. They conclude that regarding the image of nature in Costa Rican literature, its depiction travelled in a period of about thirty years from heaven to hell.[67]

This is relevant to McDonald's poetry insofar their literature is exemplary of the primordial antecedents regarding the literary representation of Limón, which lastly led to the integration of the region in the territorial imagination of Costa Rica thanks to the Central Valley proletarian class struggle at the Caribbean province (i.e. the 1934 strike against the United Fruit Company). These novels, specifically Fallas's testimonial novel, are groundbreaking concerning the imagination of Costa Rica for, as exposed by Grinberg Pla and Mackenbach (2006), they (re)define national identity *desde abajo*, i.e. from the

---

[64] Other exemplary novels are *El jaul* from Max Jiménez (1937), Adolfo Herrera's *Juan Varela* (1939), and Fabián Dobles *El sitio de las abras* (1950), in which an idealized version of nature has been substituted by its opposite, overwhelmed by social injustice. *Manglar* (1947) and *Murámonos Federico* (1973) from Joaquín Gutiérrez also take part in this process. In the former, the Pacific province of Guanacaste reenacts the scenery, while in the latter the Caribbean sets the territorial stage (Ovares et al, *La casa paterna*: "El lugar ameno": 196–202; Ovares/Rojas, *Cien años de literatura costarricense*, Chapter 4, "De la montaña a la costa": 116–142).

[65] Ovares et al, *La casa paterna*: 204.

[66] Fallas, *Mamita Yunai*: 146 and 168. Cf. Ravasio, "El caso de Mamita Yunai": 2f.

[67] Ovares et al, *La casa paterna*: 201: "La literatura ha viajado, en treinta años, del paraíso al infierno, en cuanto a la imagen de la naturaleza se refiere."

perspective of a new social subject. That of the working-class and rural proletariat who confront the oligarchical nation-building projects.[68] McDonald's poetry differentiates itself necessarily from such representations for diverse reasons. On the one hand, the poems of Part II are representative of a carefully crafted imagery of natural spaces imagined into being through a sensibly manipulated aesthetic language that intertwines nature with urban and industrialized spaces as a *poetics of landscape.* Second, McDonald's poems depict powerful frames of nature positively charged with exuberant and pulsating existence. Her poetic production is therefore not linked to the social and proletarian issues that impregnated the region at the first half of the twentieth century. Lastly, McDonald's poems engage the *modernized-natural* scenery because of her personal attempt to connect with her roots in Limón as a "valle centralina", as signaled by herself and explained by Mosby. That is, her personal past provides an intimate relationship with Limón. These poems represent, as Mosby draws attention to it, "an important cultural space and site of memory" for McDonald, for whom San José represents otherwise her *home.*[69] Unlike the Afro-Costa Rican protagonist in Quince Duncan's *Los cuatro espejos* (1973),[70] McDonald does not relate to the location of Limón as the original 'home' but instead as a vacationing destiny, made possible by the train which linked these regions through terrestrial journey. Therefore, unlike the depiction of nature at the first half of the twentieth century, and different to Duncan's approach to Limón through an identity crisis, the Train, the Non-Sites of Nature, and those of Dwelling and Modernization become instead a poetic inspiration for a personal memory of the past. One that however expands on the collective historical memory of the Black circum-Atlantic.

Therefore, the series of poems analyzed next express an outernational historical imagination since it traces Limón's paradoxical ex-centric position in the early twentieth century as "Costa Rica's window on the world".[71] And yet, as we shall see next, McDonald's poetics of landscape does not represent solely a Costa Rican literary landscape, but mainly a historical dimension that amplifies itself beyond terrestrial and maritime dimensions into Caribbean imaginings of time past.

---

[68]   Grinberg Pla/Mackenbach, "*Banana novel resiv(it)ed*": 162 and 164.

[69]   Mosby, *Place, Language, and Identity in Afro-Costa Rican Literature*: 230.

[70]   The main character's afro-alterity within and opposite Costa Rican society is built as the phenomenon of double consciousness across a psychological crisis in Quince Duncan's *Los cuatro espejos* (1973). The story begins when Afro-Costa Rican Charles McForbes wakes up one morning after attending a conference on ethnic minorities in San José and cannot see his own reflection when he stands in front of the mirror. By the third time he sees himself into the mirror, his face has blackened. The novel sets from this moment after on a sort of urban odyssey, whose protagonist wanders about in delirium trying to relocate his sanity, or otherwise put, his *identity*. Charles's mental well-being, an Afro-Costa Rican from Limón, aggressively disintegrates until he travels back to his hometown Estrada in the Caribbean province to cure his psychosis. Two elements are fundamental in the novel, the mirror and the representation of space. For complementary discussion on *Los cuatro espejos*, see Martin-Ogunsola, "Invisibility, Double Consciousness, and the Crisis of Identity in *Los cuatro espejos*" (1987); Persico, "Quince Duncan's *Los cuatro espejos*: Time, History, and a New Novel" (1991). Regarding *Los cuatro espejos* as a "narrative of passing" see Smith, "Reading the Intersection of Race and Gender in Narratives of Passing" (1994). See also Mosby, *Place, Language, and Identity in Afro-Costa Rican Literature*: Ch. 3 "Quince Duncan and the Development of Afro-Costa Rican Identity": 135–145; and *Quince Duncan. Writing Afro-Costa Rican and Caribbean Identity*: Ch. 2 "Novels of Identity: *Hombres curtidos* and *Los cuatro espejos*": 50–103.

[71]   Harpelle, *The West Indians of Costa Rica*: xiv.

"En vacaciones íbamos a Limón"

The poetic travel we are about to undertake withholds a personal narrative. As McDonald defines it, ...*la lluvia es una piel...* was "un trabajo de memoria" with the purpose of coming closer to her memories of Limón during her childhood years.[72] In an interview with Consuelo Meza (2015), McDonald tells her how these memories helped her understand her own personal story of the past, as well as her identity as an Afra-Costa Rican:

> Yo nunca tuve mayor vínculo con Limón y mis raíces afro, mis vínculos, se limitaban a ir, a veces, dos o tres semanas de vacaciones a las fincas de los abuelos o de los tíos, pero cuando murieron yo dejé de ir. Es en estos años, en los que he vuelto una o dos veces, que he ido recuperando ese sentido. Este despertar nace un día en el que me preguntaba por qué yo era como era.[73]

Thematically, Part II corresponds largely to a short story told in verse and in subsequent short poems whose main theme is the portrayal of vacationing at the Caribbean province, mimicking, as affirmed by Michel de Certeau (1988), how "[e]very story is a travel story – a spatial practice."[74] In McDonald's case, the series of movements she inscribes in her travel poetry recalls her personal voyages, revealing simultaneously a space intertwined with the dynamics of the past. As it shall be approached next, this 'spatial practice of travel' is revealed in ...*la lluvia es una piel...* as a historical imagination portraying the transformation of the peripheral province of Limón into a habitable space.

The first poem is programmatic, since it states the journey the readership is about to undertake: "En vacaciones íbamos a Limón" (Poem 29: vv. 1f.).[75] That is, while Bernard travels translocally from Limón to San José to study as a young child and later on to undertake the project of inaugurating the first Chair of Black Studies at the University of Costa Rica in 1981,[76] McDonald's movement is in the other direction, and in the context of leisure. A series of just over thirty poems follow this introductory poem, which participate broadly speaking in a positively charged re-presentation of the Costa Rican Caribbean through an oxymoronic relationship that binds together modernization and nature in an indivisible imagery. In it, two incongruent spaces are entangled with one another.

As Poem 42 of ...*la lluvia es una piel...* portrays it, McDonald's haikus describe Limón's ecosystem through a precise and brief, yet pregnant imagery: "el mar / no tiene color, / es el cielo / al revés."[77] Through her unornamented and direct language, the similitude between the sea and heaven is pictured as one single place of opposite spaces and as reflected images of one another – one ouranic, the other aquatic. This four-versed poem allows the reader to visualize the Caribbean Sea's transparent, light-blue water as a mirrored reflection of the sky. The sea is one of McDonald's frequents Site of Nature, which became known to her

---

[72] Personal interview, December 12, 2015 in San José (CR).
[73] Meza, "Memoria, identidad y utopía": 142f.
[74] De Certeau, *The Practice of Everyday Life*: 115.
[75] McDonald, *la lluvia es una piel*: 49.
[76] See "Eulalia Bernard" at http://www.editorialcostarica.com/escritores.cfm?detalle=1338, where it is stated she inaugurated Afro-American Studies (11.04.2016). See also Meza, "Memoria, identidad y utopía": 123f., who states Bernard was responsible for the Chair of Afro-Costa Rican Studies at the University of Costa Rica.
[77] McDonald, *la lluvia es una piel*: 65.

when she (or the sea) was only a child walking on its rocks (Poem 53, vv. 1–3: "Conocí / al mar cuando / todavía caminaba sobre las piedras"). In the closing verses of Poem 53, an austere language delivers a profoundly ambiguous reality, through which she personifies the immensity of the endless Caribbean Sea as held by a snail between its teeth (vv. 4f.: "lo llevaba un caracol / entre los dientes").[78]

Throughout the poems of Part II, McDonald's language witnesses a surreal representation of Nature by which it is given a powerful presence. Its immateriality is made tangible through visual imaginations that detail a *personified* particularity, like Poem 62 depicts the sea.

1	En la tarde,
2	el sol rompe rítmicamente
3	las caderas del mar.
4	Y cosidas al velorio de las olas
5	retumban las primeras
6	jorobas danzantes
7	cubiertas de encaje y sal.

II.62, ...*la lluvia es una piel*... (p. 86)

Here, nature is spatialized at the afternoon, with the sun over the sea and its waves, and finally in the sea's salt. The body of water is moreover given human form with hips struck by the sun (vv. 2f.), while its waves are dancing humps that rise lively and fall into death (v. 4: "velorio de las olas"). They are furthermore covered in salt whose whiteness resembles laced garments (v. 7: "encaje"). The consequence is the representation of the movement of the sea at an ontological level, that is, in the profound ever-passing moment of existence.

Like in Poems 42 and 62, the lively existence of nature is evoked also in Poem 35 by McDonald's poetic language. It grants it human qualities and *rhythms* (*sensu* Harris), conjuring movement through the 'mountain that repeats the moon's steps' (v. 2), or by giving it human feelings like the jungle with *moans* of rain (v. 8). Thickness and density of greenery (v. 6: "maleza") couples with the smell of wet earth (v. 7), while between and through these personifications of nature, *the train rides on* (v. 3).

1	La montaña,
2	repite los pasos de la luna,
3	el tren,
4	lleva ritmo
5	de triquitraque,
6	feria de maleza,
7	olor a tierra húmeda,
8	selva con quejas de lluvia.

II.35, ...*la lluvia es una piel*... (p. 56)

The train's presence can be found all along Part II as a relevant marker of an individual memory. It deploys McDonald's memories of travel, puzzles that she exteriorizes as part of her interior remembrances. Nonetheless, the train's poetization withholds symbolic content concerning the region's economic story of the past. Rojas and Ovares emphasize the

---

[78] McDonald, *la lluvia es una piel*: 76.

importance the train had in the liberal nation-building project as the aggressive symbol of industry, prosperity, and economical and cultural well-being in order to enter the grand narrative of civilization and progress.[79] When comprehended against the backdrop of the transareal criss-crossings between the insular and Central American Caribbean in the nineteenth and twentieth centuries, the lyrical portrayal of the train functions as the symbolic remains of Costa Rican liberalism par excellence.

As stated previously, the historical dimension withheld by McDonald's poetics of landscape rests upon a modernized-nature oxymoron that portrays two incompatible entities harmonically fashioned into a single image. Its 'deep structures' support, on the one hand, discourses of progress and civilization, while it poetically re-presents the ruins of modernization and internal colonization regarding the once peripheral wildness, on the other. The *contradictio in terminis* (industrial sites of historical meaning – nature) yields a site of historical reference which tacitly underscores the urban transformation of Limón. The oxymoron is constructed across Part II by a subtle yet cultivated language that conjures a lively depiction of the region's landscape through its fusion with diverse Sites of Modernization – here specifically with the train. Aesthetically, the iron horse functions as an in-between-element creating the oxymoronic image. It welds Nature, upon which Modernization operates in order to transform it into a civilized milieu, with Limón's habitable urban spaces and infrastructure. A historical close reading brings to the fore how McDonald's poetics of landscape tacitly reveals an economic story of the past, as poem 32 portrays it:

1   El tren,
2   es un eclipse laaaargo
3   y negro,
4   que viene recortando las nubes
5   para guardarse
6   un espacio
7   entre el cielo y la tierra.
                    II.32, ...*la lluvia es una piel*... (p. 52)

In her poems mentioned previously, the sun and the train are travel accomplices whereas in this specific case the train is represented as the counterpart of the sun through the simile of an eclipse (vv. 1f.) that blocks and obstructs its light. Because of this, the train is given the color *black* (v. 3), just like the skin of the wageworkers that built it. It is furthermore 'loooong' (v. 2: "laaaargo"), whose length stretches along the reduplication of five vowel sounds, making visible the sound of its measurement – roughly 160 km. Lastly, it is depicted as a single entity with nature upon which it imposes itself, finding its place between the sky and the earth, cutting across the clouds (vv. 4–7).

Poem 33 grants the readership a similar image of travel, where the ecosystem is occupied by the railway system. Yhe tunnels embrace the train's movement across space and time, slowly welcoming dawn (v. 4) by opening out onto the 'wide' sun (v. 1). These two opposite spaces are fused together by McDonald's poetic vain into an*other* entity which cannot be separated into its components, yielding the modernized-nature oxymoron.

---

[79]   Rojas/Ovares, *Cien años de literatura costarricense*: 20f.

```
1    Todo el ancho del Sol
2    con nosotros viajaba,
3    y en los túneles
4    nos amanecía despacio.
                II.33, ...la lluvia es una piel... (p. 53)
```

The train's journey is reiterated throughout the poems, as for example in the programmatic opening, which poeticizes its travel not only by referring to the 'low curves' (Poem 29: v. 6) specific to a railway closing in on the mountain's roundness, cut across furthermore by the tunnels, but principally by the aestheticization of the environment which is traversed by the journey itself:

```
1    En vacaciones íbamos a Limón,
2    en medio,
3    una algarabía de colores;
4    y el sol,
5    con un sombrero de cocoteros,
6    nos alcanzaba en las curvas bajas.
                II.29, ...la lluvia es una piel... (p. 49)
```

The sun appears again as a travelling escort between the departure and the arrival city (v. 1: "Limón"), while the confusing shouts of numerous people conversing simultaneously (v. 3: "algarabía") are metaphorically described as of a versicolor appearance ("de colores"). These verses introduce the train as a vibrant machine, where the compounded imagery of the natural environment and the iron vehicle reflects the pulsating colors of nature intersected by the people gliding within it. In this semiotic context, the train re-presents a Site of Transportation in the form "a place without a place", as Michel Foucault describes the ship in his discussion of heterotopias in "Of Other Spaces" ("Des Espaces Autres" 1967/1984). Like the ship, the train as a Site of Transportation represents too "a floating piece of space, a place without a place, that exists by itself, that is closed in on itself and at the same time is given over to the infinity of the sea".[80] Complementary, McDonald's poetization of the train is as well *given over to the interior land*. Poem 55 imagines this grandiose *placesslessness in motion*:

```
1    El sol
2    es una ventana grande,
3    infinita y sencilla
4    por donde entran
5    los árboles y la gente,
6    las cosas e imágenes
7    que van pasando,
8    todo sale y se mete en el tren
```

---

[80]   Foucault, "Of Other Spaces": 27. Originally presented as "Des espaces autres", the text corresponds to a lecture dictated on March 14, 1967. It was first published in 1984 in *Dits et écrits*.

9   con la infinita
10 facilidad
11 del sueño.
        II.55, ...*la lluvia es una piel...* (p. 78)

The voyage is represented by McDonald as the reunion of the train under the sun, which is defined as a big, infinite, and humble window (vv. 2f.). This solar opening refers symbolically to the train's picture window through which one enters the 'easiness of a dream' (vv. 10f.) by observing everything through it as it projects itself inwards and outwards (v. 8) into travelling images (like the trees and the people, v. 5). The iron machine voyages as a mobile place without a fixed abode. In its journeying movement, images traverse its mobility across the windows and from the perspective of the traveler, who by sitting motionless inside the iron horse is able to displace herself across nature.

It is in these Non-Sites of Nature, captured as frames of travel, that McDonald brings into being Glissant's poetics of landscape. Glissant had emphasized how this poetics must not be reduced to a static tableau of spaces that supersede each other as fixed or static backgrounds. Instead, the writer affirms that the Caribbean literary landscape is a mobile structure that bursts into life continuously. Like the Caribbean *jungle* that is McDonald's landscape, Glissant affirms "the language of my landscape is primarily that of the forest, which unceasingly bursts with life."[81] The picture window that captures the trees, the people, things and images that McDonald refers to reproduce all together this explosive dimension of life. An assessment furthermore also expressed by Octavio Paz in "Paisaje y novela en México" (1967), who affirms the literary landscape does not correspond to a mere description, it does not appear either as a stage nor as the background upon which a story is told. Instead, the Mexican author describes the literary landscape as something *vivant* that assumes a thousand forms. Paz asserts that it is not self-referential, but instead *reveals* something that lies behind its physical appearances, so that a landscape never refers to itself but to something else, to a *further away.*[82] In McDonald's poetry, this *further away* has to do mainly with "architectures of time past" (echoing Harris again),[83] brought to the forefront precisely by the journeying iron horse.

Beyond the train's function as a means of transportation it must be recalled now that the building of the railroad meant necessarily the relocation of thousands of Black Caribbeans at the Costa Rican Atlantic Seaside (see "Dwelling in Displacement", Part II). Because of Caribbean routes transformed into Afro-Costa Rican roots, the iron horse in McDonald's poetry not only conjures the economic ideology of liberalism, but it represents fundamentally the origins of *Afro-Costa Ricans*. As Mosby details it, the train is of great importance "in Afro-Costa Rican history and culture because of its connection to the movement of people and their dreams."[84] A travelling culture as described by James Clifford (1992), where "people leave home and return, enacting differently centered worlds, interconnected cosmopolitanisms" and who, after existing and surviving as a cultural/-

---

[81] Glissant, "Cross-Cultural Poetics": 146.
[82] Paz, "Paisaje y novel en México": 17.
[83] Harris, *Palace of the Peacock:* 10.
[84] Mosby, *Place, Language, and Identity in Afro-Costa Rican Literature*: 228.

deterritorialized diaspora, *became* 'Costa Rican'.[85] From this context emerges pluricentrical belonging, embedded within a network of cultural interchanges. The semiotic potential of the train is therefore approached here following Gilroy's premise, that is, as withholding "a wider applicability in cultural history and politics precisely because [it] offer[s] an alternative to the nationalist focus which dominates cultural criticism".[86] The lyrical representation of the train leads the way to a coinciding relationship between *roots* and *multiplicity* as "an alternative to the nationalistic focus", for it brings into discussion the nation~diaspora dynamic/s extended beyond national borders across the Central American Caribbean, and beyond it to the broader circum-Atlantic region.

In this frame of thought, the train becomes analogous to the ship. In *The Black Atlantic*, Gilroy settles on the image of *ships in motion* as the key aspect representing mobile points of juncture between the fixed places they connected across the Atlantic world.[87] As a result, the Black Atlantic articulates for Gilroy a "travelling culture" between European ports and the worldwide interfaces they connected to. The train, in this case, functions analogously in the story of the recent past of Costa Rica since because of it, insular Caribbean people set themselves in motion through the sea towards the continental Caribbean as migrant workers, settling afterwards in Costa Rica. The train in McDonald's poetics of landscape actualizes pluricentrical belonging by re-presenting the cause for displacement and the subsequent birth of twentieth century Afro-Costa Ricans. In its symbolic potential, it is able to link discontinuous diasporic histories lodged between the local and the global in one single territory so that a pluricentrical sense of belonging develops within an open, infinitely connected world.

Poem 37 is approached by both Meza and Mosby as McDonald's poetic attempt to bring together her cultural and familiar roots with the province of Limón.[88] Beyond their assessments, I argue that Poem 37 reenacts best the *intercultural positionality* the train withholds by being lodged between the local (Limón) and the global (Caribbean islands) in a similar manner that the ship holds the place of junction in Gilroy's Black Atlantic. And still, McDonald's depiction of the train here goes beyond the local/global couple by simultaneously uniting the 'center' and the 'ex-centric' by voyaging translocally between San José and Limón. She recreates the translocal journey by depicting a train stop where Black vendors sell food to the "negros chepines" (v. 2; Black Costa Ricans from the capital).[89] Even though McDonald does not specify that the vendors are Black, this is implied in the manner they speak Spanish, since they do not conjugate the verbs and instead use the

---

85 Clifford, "Travelling Cultures": 103. Problematizing twentieth century ethnography towards "an ideal type of mid-twentieth-century disciplinary anthropology" (p. 97), the author refers to "culture *as* travel" (p. 103). He underscores how "Anthropological 'culture' is not what it used to be" (p. 101) and thus underscores "the need to focus on the hybrid, cosmopolitan experiences as much as on the rooted, native ones" (ibid.). He therefore directs his gaze towards the "emergent culture-as-travel-relations" (p. 102) to analyze in a comparatively manner the dynamics of *dwelling* with that of *traveling*.

86 Gilroy, *The Black Atlantic*: 6.

87 Ibid.

88 See Mosby, *Place, Language, and Identity in Afro-Costa Rican Literature*: 229, and Meza, "Memoria, identidad y utopía": 142.

89 "Chepines" is derived from "Chepe", a substitute name for the city of San Jose, also noted by Mosby, *Place, Language, and Identity in Afro-Costa Rican Literature*: 228.

infinitive form (v. 9: "usted comer" in lieu of "usted *come*" or in v. 10: "no haber mejor" instead of "no *hay* mejor"):

> 7 "pan bon... pan boon, llevalleva pan bon...
> 8 pescao, ... pescao fresco... pescao y rondon...
> 9 15 cents y usted comer el mejor rondon del puerto...
> 10 15 cents y no haber mejor...bacalao, bacalao con akee y por donde entran
> 11 aceite de coco, ...bacalao... fruta e' pan...
> 12 ¿llevar fruta e'pan? asao... o frita... ¿pati? patipatipati..."
> [...]
>
> II.37, *...la lluvia es una piel...* (p. 58)

In just six verses, McDonald brings together all points of contact regarding the system of cultural exchanges, specifically through the foods she writes into the poem and the broken Spanish. The products sold by the vendors to the Black Central Valley travelers in the train are, as noted by Mosby, associated mainly with the Jamaican culinary tradition, such as *pan bon, rondón, akee, patí*, and which are circumscribed to the culinary tradition of Limón.[90] These foods are the link between the "negro chepines" and cultural and familiar roots in Limón, and further *over to the infinity of the sea* with the Caribbean islands, specifically Jamaica. In its intercultural positionality, the train represents the site of historical meaning where the reunion of the diasporic and the national is made evident as a rhizomatic plateau connecting San José with Limón, and Limón with the Caribbean archipelago.

As seen with the poems analyzed above, the iron horse that McDonald poetizes withholds in its symbolic essence the tacit remembrance of *movement* and *displacement*. For Mosby, the train in McDonald's poetry "portrays a sense of immensity and power, as well as nostalgia."[91] Whereas its immensity and power is irrefutable – manifested through the complex intertwinement of spatial and industrial metaphors into one single imagination – the train as a symbol of nostalgia does not pertain so much to McDonald, as it does to Campbell's and Bernard's poetization of it. In "El conductor invisible" (*Ciénaga/Marsh* 2001), Bernard depicts the railway as a death-ghost embodied in empty wagons and in drivers that do not exist anymore. The poet portrays an absent train gliding upon iron and blood, riding furthermore towards no true destiny.

> 1 Sobre hierro y sangre,
> 2 los coches vacíos
> 3 se deslizan.
> 4 El conductor invisible me pregunta:
> 5 ¿Vuestro destino...?
> 6 No entiendo la inquisición
> 7 respondí.
>
> Bernard, "El conductor invisible" (*Ciénaga/Marsh*: 51)

---

[90] Mosby, *Place, Language, and Identity in Afro-Costa Rican Literature*: 229. In Mosby's words: "*pan bon* (a sweet bun), fish, *rondon* (a derivation of the Jamaican dish run down [...]), *bacalao* (dried, salted cod fish), akee (a Jamaican fruit), coconut oil, breadfruit (a starchy fruit that resembles bread when baked, common in the West Indies, and *pati* (Jamaican patties, baked turnovers with a spicy meat filling)."

[91] Ibid.: 227.

The lyrical-I's incapacity to understand the ghost-driver's inquisition regarding the traveler's destiny (vv. 5f.) implies an obsolete dream that has perished upon the abandoned railway. Bernard's coupling of it with blood (v. 1) and an invisible operator (v. 4) grants it a nostalgic feeling of absentness and of pain, which Shirley Campbell reveals instead in the form of frustrated dreams.

1	El tren
2	el mismo que vistió de luto
3	recorriendo navidades sin regalos
4	el que se marco [sic] el rastro
5	carado [sic] de rotas manos
6	y sueños despedazados
7	el que se parece al mar
8	en lo humano
9	en las palabras calladas
10	y en los ojos con que mira
11	en los ojos con que llora
12	y en las palabras dolidas.
13	El tren
14	el mismo
15	el de la espalda danzante
16	de la espalda con hambre
17	esta [sic] aquí
18	no se ha marchado.

Campbell, "El tren" (*Naciendo*: 25)

According to Mosby, Campbell's representation of the train in *Naciendo* is a "melancholic poem that relates the hopes of the Limonese who left the province for the Central Valley but who return home".[92] My reading instead approaches the train-poem considering mobility from the Caribbean islands to Limón and whose depiction shares with Bernard's poem those dark symbolisms of death and absence. Campbell speaks of a mournful train (v. 2: "vistió de luto") that carries the memory of hurt, of sobs, and of hard work. In Campbell's portrayal of the iron horse, the dark metaphors can be understood as referring to the thousands of lives that perished because of the construction of the railroad. Which is why those expectations that brought thousands of Caribbean people to Central America are described by Campbell as shattered dreams (v. 6: "sueños despedazados"). The train itself has hands that are broken (v. 5), it sees with crying eyes (vv. 10f.), and it speaks words of hurt (v. 12). If the train stands as the means of transportation enabling the journey towards a better life, then Campbell poeticizes the result of its mobilities in the tearful eyes of those that cut open their hands in the hope of fulfilling new dreams. The Afra-Costa Rican poet creates in the last verses an analogy between Black men and the railroad they built (vv. 13–18). This Black man/railroad, the one with the dancing/hungry back (vv. 15f.), the one that was central to the modernization of Costa Rica, is still there, in the melancholic ruins of a construction left to rust away.

---

[92] Mosby, *Place, Language, and Identity in Afro-Costa Rican Literature*: 227.

Whereas my reading of Campbell's poem focuses on the train as the source of the Caribbean diaspora, Mosby's interpretation is not unfounded. Concerning its inherent mobile dynamic in creating multiple roots and routes, the author correctly addresses how "the train [also] represents the new series of migrations of their descendants from their old home, the coastal province, to their new home, Central Valley". In a return movement, it becomes too the link to family and cultural roots at the Limón province,[93] as for example in McDonald's case. Both readings are hence not exclusive of one another, but complementary when understanding the translocal movements of Afro-Costa Ricans within the country, as well as the transregional (across Central America) and transareal ones (isthmus/islands) that make visible the circum-Atlantic's travelling culture extended in continental Caribbean land.

Contrarily to her fellow Afra-Costa Rican poets, and as it has been analyzed so far, McDonald's *ars poetica* carries another expression. While Campbell and Bernard refer critically to the train as a melancholic symbol of transareal and translocal frustrated dreams, McDonald, on the other hand, unites the train and its irruption into nature as indissoluble beings through a merged imagery that is blind to such imaginations. As deployed exemplarily by Poem 35, McDonald's poetics of landscape depicts the iron machine fused with the Caribbean tropical jungle, with its thick uncultivated land, and with wild weeds cumbering the ground which overwhelm the growth of its own vegetation. It is also merged with its wet soil, bathed by the incessant tropical rain, and with the mountains upon which it travels and through which the tunnels converge. In such a manner, she conjures a *modernized-nature oxymoron* that depicts not only her remembrances of past travels, but, when approached by a hermeneutical close reading, it uncovers simultaneously the story of the past concerning Costa Rica's irruption into Modernity. The train-nature couple depicts a complex palimpsest, where her *cadres de la nature* act as protagonists of the poems, setting the railroad tracks upon which McDonald's memories voyage, where Campbell grieves death, and where Bernard finds ghosts of time past.

The lyrical depiction of the train is therefore an important symbol conveying historical meaning. One that necessarily symbolizes a national, simultaneously *ex-centric* past regarding the origins of the Afro-minority in Costa Rica. As an intercultural entity lodged between the local and the global, as outlined with Poem 37, the train withholds a wider applicability in cultural criticism for it approaches cultural history and politics with a gaze that overcomes a nationalistic focus. The train, as the ship, functions as the quintessential emblem of a diasporic origin regarding an outernational historical imagination inherently connected to the Black circum-Atlantic. So that beyond the local traces of Black Costa Rica's past, the train is hence highly useful in understanding Central American and Caribbean transhistorical cultural history. For it brings to the forefront transnational enterprises concerning Costa Rica's own modernization process at the hands of a North American concession (the Keith-Soto Act), which was physically carried out by Afro-Caribbean agency. It is therefore possible to intertwine the train's historical dimension with yet another ship analogy, that regarding the history of capitalist enterprises in the region.

---

[93] Mosby, *Place, Language, and Identity in Afro-Costa Rican Literature*: 228.

The Eternal Recurrence

The train by itself, in all its potentiality as a symbol of the past, makes evident an eternal recurrence proper to the region, a premise taken from Benítez-Rojo's *The Repeating Island*. In it, the author contends that the Caribbean represents fundamentally a *repeating island* since the meta-archipelago withholds an essence of chaos characterized by an inherent natural movement towards endless change. Its transformative nature reconstitutes itself once and again throughout time in similar patterns, for it "sketches in an 'other' shape that keeps changing [across] change, transit, return, fluxes".[94] The author goes on to explain that this eternal recurrence is necessarily linked to the historical layers that the region has sedimented across time since its discovery, which are furthermore highly determined by the economical discourses by which western powers have approached the region. The meta-archipelago that is the Caribbean symbolizes for the Cuban author "one of the main strands in the history of capitalism"[95] and whose beginning starts with colonialism. We may name its replicated layers according to its epochs, to which the *ship* is a primal feature. Its first strand was casted with the ocean ripples caused by European ships that sailed the seas bringing Africa to America, and America in contact with Europe.

Whereas Glissant understands the *open boat* as the means which permitted limitless métissage in the Caribbean to unfold in all its rhizomatic potential alongside the poetics of relation, Foucault asserts in "Of Other Spaces" that the boat has been since the sixteenth century and until present times "the great instrument of economic development" for western civilization.[96] Benítez-Rojo focuses on this reality and explains the emergence of the Caribbean as the outcome of a complex, multiple-levelled machine at the service of European colonialism.[97] Fundamental to its hegemony was the fleet system (*la flota*). That is, the convoys that "twice a year entered the Caribbean to come back to Seville with the great riches of America."[98] He portrays the fleet system as

> a machine made up of a naval machine, a military machine, a bureaucratic machine, a commercial machine, an extractive machine, a political machine, a legal machine, a religious machine, that is, an entire huge assemblage of machines […].[99]

La flota was organized therefore with a clear objective. It was furthermore made up not only of multiple ships, but of the necessary bureaucratic, military, and religious dimensions intrinsic to the whole. He defines the *flota* as a multipart system with an arboreal form branching out into diverse purposes and effects. Above all, he underscores how the coordination of various machines reinforced by the convoys' sea-journeys created a "machine installed in the Caribbean Sea and coupled to the Atlantic and the Pacific."[100]

---

[94] Benítez-Rojo, *The Repeating Island*: 4.
[95] Ibid.: 5.
[96] Foucault, "Of Other Spaces": 27.
[97] Benítez-Rojo details the relationship between the ship and economic development concerning the Caribbean region departing from Guattari and Deleuze's concept of the 'desiring machine' – what Benítez-Rojo refers to as "the machine machine machine" (*The Repeating Island*: 6).
[98] Ibid.: 8.
[99] Ibid.: 7.
[100] Ibid.

Hence, a further undulating strand in the history of capitalism was tied upon the various ships belonging to *la flota*, which perfected the original journeys through a system that not only transported slaves west, but took the discovered riches safely back east to Europe, drafting new maritime routes upon the old ones and, with them, yielding with time the leap "from the so-called Mercantilist Revolution to the Industrial Revolution".[101] An aspect to which Roach also refers to as the revolutionary change "that transformed the world economy and financed the industrial revolution".[102] We are talking about shipments of gold, raw, and human materials by which, according to Fanon, the Third World *literally* created Europe.[103] Coherent with these authors, Fanon had already claimed in an indignant tone how

> European opulence is literally a scandal for it was built on the backs of slaves, it fed on the blood of slaves, and owes its very existence to the soil and subsoil of the underdeveloped world.[104]

This was made possible mainly because of the "Atlantic triangle comprising the Americas (raw materials), Europe (manufactured goods), and Africa (human beings)",[105] made real by the ship's interoceanic voyages.

If for Benítez-Rojo "the Antilles are an island bridge connecting, in 'another way', North and South America" and this 'another way' refers to the character of an archipelago as a "discontinuous conjunction [of] regularities that repeat themselves globally",[106] then McDonald's poetization of the train makes evident another layer of the region's role in the history of capitalism in its local and rooted reality in Costa Rica. For the lyrical portrayal of the iron horse brings to the surface the historical content that the Costa Rican Caribbean province shares with the essence of this endless self-repeating island by way of a vertiginous repetition of economic histories – this time in continental land. The train and the ship function analogously in the history of the Black Atlantic and in the Central American Caribbean because they are both fundamental Sites of Transportation giving presence to salient patterns of continuity and discontinuity in the region's economic history/ies. Both Sites of Transportation represent a mobile entity that has overstepped the rigid boundaries of territorial and ethnonational identification caused by diasporic displacement/s that actualize the *repeating island*'s rhizomorphic and transcultural formation. The train, thus, adds a new historical layer to the downward spiral of western capitalism: the consolidation of the Banana Empire in Central America. A third underlying historic constituent shall be scrutinized next and thus added to McDonald's transhistorical poetics of landscape. One that has to do with the modernization of Limón and the industrialization of the country as a result of the United Fruit Company's presence in the region.

---

[101] Benítez-Rojo, *The Repeating Island*: 5.
[102] Roach, *Cities of the Dead*: 4.
[103] Fanon, *The Wretched of the Earth*: 58: "Europe is literally the creation of the Third World."
[104] Ibid.: 53.
[105] Roach, *Cities of the Dead*: 8.
[106] Benítez-Rojo, *The Repeating Island*: 2.

Spatializing Time Past

> What does travel ultimately produce if it is not, by a sort of reversal, 'an exploration of the deserted places of my memory', the return to nearby exoticism by way of a detour through distant places, and the 'discovery' of relics and legends...?
>
> Michel de Certeau, *The Practice of Everyday Life*

In the previous pages, I referred to a fundamental strand in the history of capitalism as casted by the slave ships that brought thousands of Africans to the New Continent, where the colonial *open boat* signified for Glissant the African uprooting that gave way to the Caribbean cultural rhizome, while for Gilroy the *ship* yielded the system of cultural interchanges intrinsic to the Black Atlantic. A series of threads were then redrawn upon old routes with Benítez-Rojo's description of the *fleet system* and its incessant looting, plundering, and pillaging of the American continent, taking back its riches to Europe.

The ship, the fleet system, and the *train* are elements within a historical dynamic where various layers of sociohistorical realities reiterate themselves through strands that have a marked resemblance, tying back to each other endlessly. Extending itself beyond the semiotic aquatic depth of the ship, the symbolic importance of the train represents in an analogous manner another filament intrinsic to the effervescent and intermingled stories of the Caribbean. If Glissant's open boat speaks of deterritorialization and reterritorialization like the train later meant for volunteer Caribbean wageworkers, and Gilroy's ship is replaced by the train as the new means of transportation that led the way towards a system of cultural exchanges between "voluntarily" uprooted Caribbean people who re-rooted throughout Central America in the twentieth century, then regarding the spatial/aquatic configuration of the Caribbean, the train plays within this argument its own terrestrial part as a wave that has backlashed from a first maritime impulse.[107] This time however connecting the Caribbean islands with the Americas. Firstly, through the construction of a railway system whose purpose was to journey the Central American isthmus along curves and within tunnels towards progress. Secondly, with the installment of the United Fruit Company's banana enclaves towards modernization and urbanization. In fact, to the multiple coupling of several machines that have given life to the meta-archipelago, Benítez-Rojo furthermore recognizes the need of adding Caribbean ports, sea walls, storehouses, as well as taverns, plazas, churches, streets, and roads, to name a few, as intrinsic elements of the Caribbean machine itself, whose strands stretch out from the maritime womb into the

---

[107] I claim here "voluntarily" for poverty is not a circumstantial reality, but a product of a colonial and capitalist system where racial and national differentiations play an important part, specially within the historic legacy of the plantation system. Gilroy's positive take on the "restlessness" intrinsic to the peoples/cultures of the Black Atlantic as the repossession, reconstruction, and affirmation of a travel culture is, in fact, "forged out of the experiences of racial subordination" (Gilroy, *The Black Atlantic*: 111). On the other hand, the travelling culture that Gilroy speaks of is defined by Benítez-Rojo as the Caribbean People of the Sea. That is, Caribbean people are described by the author as impelled to travel and to explore the world outside their insularity towards maritime journeys, "constituting one of our century's most notable migratory flows" (*The Repeating Island*: 25). Accordingly, Gilroy suggests that together with journeys, displacement and migrations "constitute these black cultures' special condition of existence" (*The Black Atlantic*: 111).

terrestrial dimension in the form of urbanized infrastructure.[108] In other words, the meta-archipelago unfolds and deploys itself not only through the maritime scenery that Gilroy rescues as a central site of historical meaning for the Black Atlantic, but also in the Sites of Dwelling and Sites of Modernization themselves.

Urbanization has to do with human action that imposes itself over nature in the effort of conquering it and transforming its wild hostility into urban reconstitutions. These actions yield 'civilized life' (e.g. markets, electrification) and help develop the economy and its structures so as to participate in the world capitalist system (e.g. export economy, banks). As mentioned in *Becoming Afro-Costa Rican*, liberal purposes in the region from approximately 1870 to the 1930s dominated actions and decision-making over the Caribbean province with the aim of integrating the region to the national economy by colonizing it.[109] It had become of crucial importance to develop a region that because of its isolation posed an obstacle to the nation's commerce and development. The building of the railroad to the Atlantic was undertaken with this objective, which led to the development of civil infrastructure like ports, bridges, and streets that established new roads of communication across the country and with the rest of the world. Purcell mentions how, by acquiring other governmental contracts, Keith built markets, established electrification, and even set up his own banks in San José and in Limón.[110]

McDonald's poetics of landscape make visible this history of modernization and urbanization in Limón by portraying diverse spaces of Limón as Sites of Dwelling and of Modernization across her modernized-nature oxymoron. Sites of Dwelling represent locations where people reside and inhabit as bodies occupying a space in a social manner, living within and across them. While the Sites of Modernization refer to the outcome of human activity over nature with the purpose of creating 'civilized' spaces. Fundamental sites in this last process are, for example, docks and harbors where ships arrive to load and unload people and merchandise; the cutwater that separates the sea from the land to create an urban difference from the flow of nature; the boats and the train that permit people to travel to and fro and, most importantly, *cities.*

Dwelling Sites are represented throughout Part II in the form of marketplaces, grocery stores, the church or the houses where people live. Poem 60 depicts the marketplace in three short verses as one of these Dwelling Sites, where the non-site of Nature defines it by the imagery of fruit, their lively colors, and the shining sun: "El mercado tiene / tatuajes de colores / y sol entre la fruta." Poem 50 paints the landscape in the form of a Saturday church, which the poet describes as dancing upon its old stilts (vv. 3f.). The forest and the train express a 'religious happiness' (vv. 5f.) next to the house built with a wooden corridor and double doors that receive the morning (vv. 7–12).[111]

---

[108]   Benítez-Rojo, *The Repeating Island*: 8: "The fleet system was itself a machine of ports, anchorages, sea walls, lookouts, fortresses, garrisons, militias, shipyards, storehouses, depots, offices, workshops, hospitals, inns, taverns, plazas, churches, palaces, streets, and roads [...]".

[109]   Cf. Viales, *Los Liberales y la Colonización de las Áreas de Frontera no Cafetaleras*: 109.

[110]   Purcell, *Banana Fallout*: 30.

[111]   McDonald, *la lluvia es una piel*: 84; for Poem 50, see p. 73.

Nature is always essential to the depiction of such sites. It finds its own place across placelessness, as conjured by Poem 41 in the representation of diverse locations like boats, the train, and the dock.

1	Del sur
2	baja el mar.
3	Los barcos están grabados
4	en la arena
5	y hay rumor de olas,
6	el tren gritando
7	y el muelle:
8	llora cangrejos
9	sobre las piedras…

II.41, ...*la lluvia es una piel...* (p.64)

Here, Sites of Modernization and Nature are poetized into a single entity through figures of personification. The ships are *engraved* in the sand (vv. 3f.), the dock is personified by *weeping* crabs upon the rocks (vv. 7–9), and the train by *screaming* (v. 6) as it rides upon the rails. Behind these sites, the murmur of the sea waves accompanies them (v. 5). Both the Non-Sites of Nature and the Sites of Modernization are intersected, cut across, and traversed by the rhythm of the train riding as one with(in) Nature. Their tripartite coupling re-presents poetically the diverse outcomes concerning the processes of urbanization which came to be firstly by the building of the railroad and completed finally by the United Fruit Company, which took on this task to consolidate its Banana Empire in the country and region.

The Octopus

The reunion of Nature and the Train with the Sites of Modernization and Dwelling reenact a landscape from which it is possible to extract the underlying history of the Costa Rican Caribbean. If we recall Benítez-Rojo assertion that the Caribbean expresses itself as a centripetal force resembling a galaxy tending outward, infinitely repeating itself along diverse filaments of history, we must now add that this *repeating island* has a paradigmatic space complementary to the maritime routes across which the meta-archipelago came to be by means of the ship. That is, the Plantation system. Édouard Glissant acknowledges their indivisible juncture: "[w]ithin the ship's space the cry of those deported was stifled, as it would be in the realm of the Plantations."[112] He furthermore acknowledges the Plantation system was installed in a similar manner across the multiplex Caribbean, creating "a rhythm of economic production" with a pyramidal-organization who could only function upon a slave structure. Similarly for Gilroy, plantation slavery is nothing else than "capitalism with its clothes off", and yet much more than "a system of labour and a distinct mode of racial domination".[113] For plantation slavery is what laid the foundations for a complex network

---

[112] Glissant, *Poetics of Relation*: 5 and 63f., respectively.
[113] Gilroy, *The Black Atlantic*: 15 and 54f., respectively.

of power relations to develop – social, economic, political, and discursive. Which is why Glissant affirms "the Plantation is one of the focal points for the development of present-day modes of Relation" and why Gilroy asserts that the Plantation and its slave-based economy is central "in the historical memories of the black Atlantic."[114] In an extended manner, this is also true regarding the Central American Caribbean and, specifically, *Black Costa Rica*.

For Benítez-Rojo, the Plantation space is another manifestation of the machine that has given a particular sociocultural and historic substance to the Caribbean and that, as claimed by Gilroy, is not significant solely to this region, but significant as well to Europe, Africa, and North America, to which it is necessary to add here the Black Americas as a whole.[115] Elegantly defined by Glissant as "one of the bellies of the world",[116] it is of paramount importance here to add twentieth-century Central America to the discussion of Plantation economy/ies. Benítez-Rojo traces the history of the Plantation machine in the French, English, Dutch, and Spanish colonies in the Caribbean so as to stretch out the differences particular to each hegemony, which were however born out of a shared system that contributed to the conformation of the sameness/difference continuum that the Caribbean represents. Along the chapter entitled "From the plantation to the Plantation", the author traces the history of the diverse Plantation systems to demonstrate his main argument, i.e. that "many factors come in to play [...] to differentiate one island from another", although he believes that these "differences that existed among the Caribbean colonies, and even the differences that we now perceive, were created in large part by the epoch in which the Plantation took over within each."[117] He furthermore rescues Sidney W. Mintz's (1966) argument that the phenomenon of the colonial plantation system led the way to the establishment of parallel socioeconomic structures between the region's diverse nations,[118] while adding himself that "it is only in the Caribbean region that [the plantation dynamics] produce a kind of socioeconomic instability whose morphology is repeated, becoming more or less ascendant from colonial times until the present."[119] This becomes highly accurate when considering the United Fruit Company's banana enclaves in Central America as the most recent filament in the history of capitalism embodied by the *repeating island* in continental land. Poem 49 conjures this doubly composed repeating history by reuniting the *train* (vv. 1f: "En el sueño, / dibujo un tren colorado) with its nocturnal cargo of *bananas* (v. 12: "con su carga nocturna / de bananos y sonidos…").[120]

These verses evoke the fact that, just like the ship led to the installment of a plantation system ruled by slavery, the decision to build a railroad to the Atlantic on behalf of Costa Rican politicians consequently determined the installment of a postcolonial banana plantation system at the Central and South American Atlantic coastline. Benítez-Rojo

---

[114] Glissant, *Poetics of Relation*: 65; Gilroy, *The Black Atlantic*: 55.
[115] Gilroy, *The Black Atlantic*: 15. For transdisciplinary dialogues and hemispheric perspectives regarding the Black Americas, see The Black Americas Research Network at https://www.uni-bielefeld.de/cias/blackamericas/index.html.
[116] Glissant, *Poetics of Relation*: 75.
[117] Benítez-Rojo, *The Repeating Island*: 68 and 63.
[118] See Mintz, "The Caribbean as a Socio-Cultural Area" (1966).
[119] Benítez-Rojo, *The Repeating Island*: 38.
[120] McDonald, *la lluvia es una piel*: 72.

claims that the colonial Plantation machine was so powerful as to systematically shape to its own convenience "the political, economic, social, and cultural spheres of the country that nourishes it until that country is changed into a *sugar island*."[121] Costa Rica was changed not into a *sugar island*, but into an enclave of the Banana Empire under the rule of the United Fruit Company. For Keith had managed to create a broad plantation system in the country that had allowed him to reinvest its earnings quickly and project his enterprise in neighboring Central and South American nations. Once his vast banana enterprise in Costa Rica had taken off, Keith "used the existing land and transport facilities as collateral to finance the expansion of his holdings into other parts of Latin America and the Caribbean."[122] Kepner and Soothill have remarked the reversing of roles: banana trade assumed first place and the railroad became an adjunct to it.[123]

And so, the 1899 merger which meant the establishment of the United Fruit Company redirected the future of the coast's productivity towards the establishment of *banana republics*. Their monopolistic character expressed itself as the absolute control of the productive factors of the banana and of its commercialization, as well as total ownership of its earnings. The enclave became furthermore an island of foreign power,[124] which, because it was largely exempted from domestic control, determined what historian Ronny Viales has named an imperialistic regional exploitation.[125] This unequal economic structure recalls Glissant's definition of the colonial Plantations as entities that were "dependent, by nature, on somewhere else."[126] The Banana Empire was built in fact upon a North American concession which transformed Costa Rica's economy into a banana enclave dependent on the U.S. market. In view of these unilateral economic relations, Purcell considers this economic model set "the basic conditions for the establishment of a banana plantation colony".[127]

Moreover, Glissant explains how in the Plantations of colonial times and specifically in "their practice of importing and exporting, the established politics [was] not decided from within."[128] The same is repeated with the Caribbean enclaves in continental land. The UFCo.'s banana plantations were like the former sugar slave plantations in that both were, in the words of Frederick Douglass, "a little nation of its own, having its own language, its own rules, regulations and customs."[129] From this sociohistorical context emerged the testimonial writings of the *Generación del 40* mentioned in the first part of this section, crucial to the left-wing and anti-imperialist movements in the country. Also intrinsic to this reality lies the outer-national story of the Caribbean archipelago's past. Much like the colonial past of the sugar islands, the monopoly of the United Fruit Company both in Costa Rica as in the Central American region adds its own part to the history of capitalism in the circum-Caribbean. It stretches in a spiral manner along historical strands that fold upon

---

[121] Benítez-Rojo, *The Repeating Island*: 72.
[122] Harpelle, *The West Indians of Costa Rica*: 16.
[123] Kepner and Soothill, *The Banana Empire*: 49.
[124] Hojman quoted in Viales, *Después del enclave*: 27.
[125] Viales, *Después del enclave*: 30.
[126] Glissant, *Poetics of Relation*: 67.
[127] Purcell, *Banana Fallout*: 25.
[128] Glissant, *Poetics of Relation*: 67.
[129] Frederick Douglass, *My Bondage and My Freedom* (1855), quoted in Gilroy, *The Black Atlantic*: 59.

each other, repeating themselves chaotically under new economic and social conditions. Be it the *colonial plantations* of sugar cane, coffee or cacao, or the *postcolonial banana plantations* of the twentieth century, the plantation system is lastly an "extraordinary machine" that "repeats itself continuously."[130] A Machine first brought upon in the Caribbean by the interoceanic ship travels, later repeated in Central America with the train.

As scholars have documented it, not only did the Company control the transportation system, labor supply, and the distribution of land tenure, provide housing accommodation, health care, and travel arrangements for their laborers, but as Chomsky adds, the *commissary stores* were central to the internal enclave economy.[131] Even though McDonald's poetry does not refer to this economic reality explicitly from Douglass's point of view, her poetry however re-presents the ruins thereof. Poem 45 is highly symbolic of the UFCo.'s unforgotten remains, for it portrays *el comisariato del chino* as one of its main Sites of Dwelling.

1   Junto a la cerca que el río
2   trajo con el invierno,
3   nos dejó el tren.
4   Más allá,
5   el comisariato del chino,
6   sus galeotes de pulpería y cantina
7   me recuerdan que hoy es domingo.
8   Sobre el sol,
9   la iglesia;
10   con silencios de semana larga.
            II.45, ...*la lluvia es una piel...* (p. 68)

The poem develops beyond the domain of nature (v. 1: río; v. 2: invierno) and past the train (v. 3) by delineating the urban constitution through a plurality of Dwelling Sites that one encounters when stepping off the train. Beyond the fence lies the church (v. 10), as well as the *pulpería* (v. 6) – what in Costa Rica corresponds to a small grocery store – and the *cantina* (v. 6), a tavern or bar for drinking alcohol.[132] Once again, McDonald's poetic of landscape reveals a historical dimension that can only be understood when reflecting upon the process of urbanization in Limón, the once empty, ex-centric region, to which the UFCo.'s *commissary store* (v. 5) was central. These stores were key to the internal enclave economy since they offered the workforce food and medicine through a coupon and deduction system directly tied to their wages, causing the laborers to re-invest their salary in the Company.[133] Chomsky explains these represented the UFCo.'s attempt to turn the enclave economy workers into consumers, given that these stores functioned as the central market place for the laboring population to acquire goods in an uninhabited, peripheral region. As a result, the twenty-four commissaries that operated in 1927 made more than

[130]   Benítez-Rojo, *The Repeating Island*: 8.
[131]   Chomsky, *West Indian Workers*: 55–59. See Purcell, *Banana Fallout*: 28f.; Bryce-Laporte/Purcell, "A Lesser-Known Chapter": 225. Cf. Kepner/Soothill, *The Banana Empire*: 52.
[132]   García Valverde, *Vocabulario básico y cotidiano abreviado del castellano y costarriqueñismos*: 99 and 23, respectively.
[133]   See Chomsky, *West Indian Workers*: 55–59.

one million dollars that year,[134] while its laborers remained poor and unable to abandon the plantation system so as to search for better job opportunities. As one of the official UFCo.'s historians wrote concerning the *comisariatos*:

> In some instances, they refused to employ native storekeepers, imported the necessary merchandise, in many instances duty free, and sold the goods at outrageous prices to the workers – all too frequently on credit, making charges against wages not yet earned. Such business was a straight road to peonage.[135]

Chomsky furthermore documents the Company's desire to inculcate consumerism in the work population as a "psychological motivation for the labor force to work", where the capitalist ideology of "purchasing power" could be cultivated as illusive collateral for upward mobility, thus incrementing the UFCo.'s profit to the fullest.[136] As Chomsky underlines it, this was not just inculcated in Limón, but functioned transregionally in the banana enclaves throughout Central America. No wonder that "in its banana days in Limón the company was indisputably monopolistic, totalitarian and imperialistic",[137] and was referred to throughout Central America as *the octopus*. By 1926, the UFCo. was present in nine Central American countries with 70,000 workers under their payroll; 1,834,000 acres of land for banana, sugar cane, coconut and cacao production. It owned 31,000 head of cattle; controlled 1,541 miles of railway and 722 miles of tramways; had furthermore 187 locomotives, 22 tram trains, 5,230 railway cars, and 1,859 tramcars.[138]

Not only the *comisariato* withholds a local and simultaneously transregional story of the past. By expressing custody through a possessive pronoun, the following verse ambiguously implies that the *pulpería* and *cantina* are run by "sus galeotes" (v. 6). The word means galley slave and refers to the person that was condemned to row in the underground galleries of the (slave) ships – the Black Atlantic's unequivocal Site of Transportation that acted as an uprooting bridge between Africa, the Caribbean, and the Americas. The ship later became the mobile element that transported the Caribbean people to Central America to build the railroad – the new Site of Transportation for the Black Atlantic's expansion into Central America, which led to the settlement of the largest ethnic minority in Costa Rica. Hence, by not expressing Blackness through a direct reference to skin color but instead implying it with *galeote*, McDonald is able to conjure the local presence of the Black minority in Costa Rica, originally located in Limón, by indicating in a tacit manner its historic liaison with the Black Atlantic.

This link reveals how the UFCo. enclaves acted very much like a ripple that expanded through space and time from a far-away first maritime impulse, even if under independent and separate socio-historic conditions. Let us not forget that coherent with the exponential growth that the Banana Empire meant in Costa Rica, by 1927 almost eighty percent of the population in Limón was Black. This migration flow echoes to a certain extent the slavery-based western economy of colonial times in that it cannot be overlooked how, because of similar processes – specifically a dependent-transnational economy based on a foreign

---

[134] Chomsky, *West Indian Workers*: 58.
[135] Quoted in ibid.: 56.
[136] Ibid.: 57.
[137] Bryce-Laporte/Purcell, "A Lesser-Known Chapter": 227.
[138] Harpelle, *The West Indians of Costa Rica*: 68.

workforce (one *enslaved*, the other *proletarian*) – "the West Indian population of Costa Rica developed into the largest ethnic minority in the country".[139] That is, just like slavery led to the rapid expansion of the Plantation machine across the Caribbean islands and therefore to the intense increment of the African population in them – as for example in Jamaica, where by 1800 eighty-eight percent of its population was made up of African slaves –,[140] the exploitative economic system of the United Fruit Company had created a banana plantation colony of transnational nature across the Central American Caribbean with Afro-Caribbeans dispersed throughout the region. It cannot be stated enough that, ultimately, the island repeats itself in continental land.

McDonald poetizes the *comisariato* once again in Poem 56, a four-strophe text where the Anglican Church is its complementary Site of Dwelling and whose representation relies heavily on Nature. The third strophe describes a landscape from the *comisariato's* perspective, where Nature invades the modernized space with people that resemble a mountain blue dusk (Poem 56, str. 3, vv. 1–3: "los hombres son un crepúsculo / de montaña azul"); with sounds described as multicolor (str. 3., v. 6: "sonidos muticolores"); and with children that are playing the game of dirt (str. 3, v. 7: "niños jugando a la tierra"), while the church is occupied by Black people of all ages (str. 1, v. 1: "un racimo de negros"). Mosby calls attention to the word *racimo* (which she translates as "a bunch") and explains the choice of the word as a relation of the "fertility of the culture to its agricultural base [...] where bananas and cacao are grown."[141] In so doing, she underscores the interlaced relationship between the Site of Dwelling, the cultural background, and the agrarian economy in Limón. The first strophe recreates a Sunday church scene, with the town people singing gospels and alleluias alongside an organ, while the young girls are fashionably dressed in fancy hairdos and with ribbons in their hair. Instead, the second strophe depicts the town's women as colorfully and elegantly dressed (str. 2, vv. 2f.: "violentas de color y paisaje"), while the last strophe refers to life as a passing by (str. 4, vv. 1f.: "Al final / todo es un paso) which finishes in the *iglesia anglicana* before being buried (str. 4, vv. 6f.: "y luego / el horizontal del polvo").[142]

The Anglican Church is an emblematic Dwelling Site of the transnational cultural/de-territorialized diaspora in Limón. Mosby in fact asserts McDonald captures a repeated scene "in various parts of Afro-America on a Sunday", whereby the poem's lyrical-I is able to capture "some of the Afro-West Indian presence in the province."[143] Poem 50 also represents the Anglican church, described as "la iglesia sabatina" (v. 3). Together with the reeds (v. 2: "junco") and the Caribbean jungle, the church is part of the landscape and not the central protagonist of the text, as in Poem 56. It is nonetheless represented just as lively as in the latter. Like the alleluias and gospels sung together with the organ playing music inside, the Anglican church in Poem 50 dances upon its old stilts during its Saturday service (vv. 3f.: "la iglesia sabatina / está bailando sobre sus zancos viejos").[144]

---

[139] Harpelle, *The West Indians of Costa Rica*: 19.
[140] Benítez-Rojo, *The Repeating Island*: 67 and 63.
[141] Mosby, *Place, Language, and Identity in Afro-Costa Rican Literature*: 227.
[142] McDonald, *la lluvia es una piel*: 79f.
[143] Mosby, *Place, Language, and Identity in Afro-Costa Rican Literature*: 227.
[144] McDonald, *la lluvia es una piel*: 73.

As portrayed in her poetry through the Sites of Modernization, the process of urbanization in Limón not only created streets, bridges, or docks that allowed maritime and terrestrial communication roads to serve the economy, but long-legged houses, churches, the park, and the small grocery store exist in her poems as evidence thereof. Whereas the Sites of Dwelling like the iglesia, the comisariato, the pulpería, or the cantina re-present *inhabited* places in the Limón province, the Sites of Modernization instead are indicators of socioeconomic processes where a *place* like Nature was converted into a 'civilized' *space*. In this specific case, into *cities*.

Architecture of Time Past

At the beginning of this section, I quoted de Certeau's claim that "[e]very story is a travel story – a spatial practice."[145] According to the author, travel stories are structured upon places that are transformed by spatializing operations. While *place* refers for the author to "configurations of positions" and stability, *space* instead is "composed of intersections of mobile elements".[146] That is, between place and space lies mobility, movement, and displacement. De Certeau distinguishes between *place* and *space* with the opposition maps vs. tours, where the main difference is set upon *seeing* and *going* (i.e. acting, movement). Hence, a map represents a fixed tableau as the *knowledge of the order of places*, while the tour represents *paths of organized movements*. In fact, in McDonald's poetics of landscape the train constitutes the paths which organize the travelling movement between those fixed places, while together with the Non-Site of Nature (wind, sea, rain, crabs) they both organize *movement(s)* (along the curves, through the tunnels), *direction* (across the mountains, upon the railway, opening onto the sun), *velocities* and *time* (dawn, afternoon, morning). In McDonald's artistic language it is possible to witness how the nature-train couple recreates a series of intersections between elements brought together by mobility. Her poetics of landscape hence depicts a *space* which tells stories that organize places through displacement.[147] Because of this, Part II of *...la lluvia es una piel...* re-presents a travel which is essentially a *spatializing practice* concerning the history of the Limón province.

The intertwined paths of the train within Nature give shape and life to the cities of the Limón province by weaving them together through displacement, something made possible thanks to the construction of the railroad. Like the pedestrian movements that de Certeau speaks of as conforming the city as a *lived space*, the train ride poetized by McDonald recreates her travel to the cities in a such manner that, paraphrasing the French author, they are not localized, but instead they spatialize the region itself and its own history.[148] On the one hand, the tableaux of stable positions are recreated by the Sites of Modernization/Dwelling of which *cities* are exemplary, since they transform the once peripheral and empty province into an urbanized space. The *city* by itself is highly symbolic of Limón's

---

[145] De Certeau, *The Practice of Everyday Life*: 115.
[146] Ibid.: 118.
[147] Cf. ibid.: 116.
[148] Ibid.: 97.

irruption into Modernity since it is, as understood by de Certeau, "simultaneously the machinery and the hero of modernity."[149] Moreover, the train actualizes a relationship between procedures of modernization and ex-centric *places* turned into *spaces* in that "the city serves as a totalizing and almost mythical landmark for socioeconomic and political strategies".[150] This is true concerning the Costa Rican case, since towns and cities like Limón, Puerto Matina, and Puerto Viejo grew into important economic and cultural centers under the mantle of the discourse of progress, which brought about the arrival of the Caribbean proletarian diaspora to carry out such purposes. The massive migration in the region influenced necessarily the development of cities in the Atlantic Costa Rican province and towns like Puerto Limón and Matina grew from 1874 onwards. These last pages add to McDonald's poetics of landscape a historical dimension regarding the urbanization of the province and its transformation into a habitable space through the cities that the train travel binds together. It reads hence McDonald's modernized-nature oxymoron across a travelled journey from one city to the next.

The first city one encounters in the poetic train ride of Part II is Turrialba (Poem 34), which is reached by sailing along rivers of rust (v. 4: "ríos de herrumbre"). The city is intertwined with the Non-Site of Nature in an artistic language that deploys an imagery of poetic surrealism proper of McDonald's poetic vain. The first strophe finishes by depicting the landscape with a *visual sound*: "Atlántico violento de sonidos" (v. 5). In the following strophe, McDonald disrupts sense by painting a scenery where palm trees exhibit a color blue that holds in its essence the capacity of being clever, resembling a blue-sharp color (v. 6: "azulinteligente"). Whereas in the second strophe, hotel windows (v. 12), long-legged houses (v. 17), and hung out clothes that look like a peacock's feathers (v. 15) are described as memory images of urbanity. The travel journey furthermore recreates time as though it were running behind her memories in a stage of fright (v. 18), as the train rapidly cuts across the sky and the mountains.

8   En la estación
9   (dentro de mí)
10   una partida en desorden:
11   algo va multiplicándolo todo,
12   las ventanas del hotel,
13   las montañas,
14   ejerciendo su color de yerba,
15   el pavo real de la ropa tendida al sol
16   y... mis recuerdo (sic!) de niña
17   que pasan presurosas por las casas zancudas
18   tras el tiempo que corre asustado.
                 II.34, "Turrialba", *...la lluvia es una piel...* (p. 55)

Next stop, Limón (Poem 39). This Site is succinctly described in six verses and solely by Nature. Her memories are built by fragments of sand (v. 2), themselves traces of time past in the form of seashell and stone remains due to the effect of erosion and of the sea. In this flow of time, Limón's essence is constructed by the corals that lie where the horizon meets

---

149   De Certeau, *The Practice of Everyday Life*: 95.
150   Ibid.

the sea (v. 3: "Mar adentro"). The modernized-nature oxymoron is evident in so far it is not the architecture of urbanity that which constructs Limón, but that of the sea and its corals (vv. 4–6).

```
1    … te construyo lentamente
2    con fragmentos de arena.
3    Mar adentro
4    la arquitectura
5    del coral te construye
6    en definitiva…
```
II.39, "Limón", *…la lluvia es una piel…* (p. 61)

After Limón, comes the town of Puerto Viejo (Poem 40). McDonald's recalls it by pictures of the sea, but her first memory of it, she writes, is an old harbor (1f.). In fact, the harbor is as old as the first turtle settlements at the beginning of the nineteenth century, before even the building of the railroad had been thought of. Paula Palmer's conversation with the oldest settlers in Puerto Viejo revealed the "pirate days in that port, which takes its name from the fact that it served as a harbor for the old pirate boats."[151] In a three strophe, twenty-line free verse poem, Puerto Viejo is described by Modernization Sites like the harbor and the dock (v. 2 and v. 3). Its Non-Sites are represented in the corals (v. 4), at the sea (v. 6), by the wind and the rain (vv. 7f.), at the afternoon (v. 9), with the feasting ants (v. 10), the crickets and butterflies (vv. 14f.), and the wild horses running along the beach (vv. 18–20).

```
1    …mi primer recuerdo
2    es un puerto viejo,
3    y el muelle
4    sembrado de corales.
5    El segundo
6    es el mar,
7    golpeado por el viento,
8    y la lluvia
9    regada por la tarde
10   y de hormigas colonizando los vasos.
     […]
```
II.40, *…la lluvia es una piel…* (p. 62)

And like Puerto Viejo, Puerto Vargas is also as beautiful because of its existence within the time-strands of Nature (Poem 61). McDonald's poetic vain is once again capable of recreating an urban space indivisible of the Non-Sites of Nature that define it and by which a surreal reality comes alive. The park which traverses Puerto Vargas is described as a placeless space that curls up upon itself in the form of a snail (v. 1). It withholds ponds and stones whose colorful fish discover their aquatic place as though they were floating upon the sea breeze.

```
1    El parque
2    es un caracol
```

---

[151] Palmer, *What Happen*: 27.

3   con luz
4   de chinas
5   y un nido de columpios,
6   estanque de piedra verde
7   y pececillos
8   de colores
9   escondidos bajo el agua
10   que flota en el viento.
                    II.61, ...*la lluvia es una piel...* (p. 85)

From these poetic representations of cities, towns, and ports it must be underscored that the modernized-nature oxymoron transforms the Limón province into something else. That is, into a *spatial signifier of the past* whose fragments (i.e. Sites) bring together a 'here' and a 'there'; a 'now' and a 'then'; a 'before' and an 'after'. Her artistic language intertwines the non-human world with urbanity much like the train is depicted as an essential part of Nature. Otherwise put, the modernized-nature oxymoron and the train that re-present the Limón province recreate together a penetration of boundaries that shuffle spatio-temporal dimensions. The train not only reunites the territorial gaps set within a translocal spatial continuum, but it creates a temporal one as well, for it brings continuity between the peripheral, empty area, and the urbanized, civilized province of Limón. In so doing, it tells the story of the economic practices it simultaneously signified. Nature provides the embroidery for the scenes that, recalling Glissant, burst into life continuously, while the train grants a *mobile* order that brings together not only the Dwelling Sites but ultimately the cities as the exemplary Sites of Modernization. This tripartite composition, then, reproduces a historical dimension regarding an urban poeticized palimpsest from which one can read the outcome of a transnational network of capitalist enterprises in the circum-Caribbean region. These poems recreate a train ride through the cities that refer to and comprise urban agglomerations that are nothing else than a projection of Costa Rica's irruption into Modernity upon a readable text that creates a poetic fiction thereof.

Once again, Benítez-Rojo's thesis regarding the *repeating island* is here relevant. "The fleet system created all of the cities of the Spanish Caribbean", states the author,[152] just like the train created the cities and dwelling spaces of the Costa Rican Caribbean province – before an empty, peripheral area.

And Thus...

In conclusion, McDonald's poetics of landscape poetizes an oxymoronic conjunction of diverse historical sites through a *modernized-nature* imagery, which neutralizes, suspends, and inverts the boundary between them into an indivisible entity, while simultaneously deploying pluricentrical traces of the past. It delivers Glissant's economy of expressive forms through the effectiveness of the poet's haikus when aestheticizing the spatiality of Limón. Whereas the polyphonic phenomena of her aestheticized language yield the oxymoronic harmony between the non-human world and the process of Modernization in

---

[152]   Benítez-Rojo, *The Repeating Island*: 8.

Limón, which refers back to Costa Rican liberal ideology and the transnational Banana Empire's effects in the Central American region. In this manner, the train rides through *the transhistorical codes of Nature*,[153] representing the primordial cause for the proletarian maritime movement connecting transareally, -regionally and -locally diverse peoples, communities, and stories into *travelling cultures*, from which pluricentrical belonging emerges.

The Sites of Modernization and Dwelling re-present the consequence of an agricultural capitalism based on the export of coffee that towards the end of the nineteenth century had as a central objective the coming of age (i.e. modernization) of Costa Rica through the construction of a railway system. This *ex-centric* recent past is called upon by the train as the Site of Transportation that unifies these two incongruent spaces as the symbol par excellence of both the origins of Afro-Costa Ricans, as of the transformation of Limón into a habitable space by way of an export capitalist economy. Historically, they refer to the outernational story of the past regarding the Caribbean diaspora which settled in Limón and built these towns, cities, docks, and rails as 'non'-Costa Ricans. And thus, specifically through a historical backwards-looking, Dlia McDonald's modernized-nature oxymoron of Part II of *...la lluvia es una piel...* portrays the ruins of Costa Rica's irruption into Modernity thanks to the proletarian Caribbean diaspora.

---

[153]   Cf. Benítez-Rojo, *The Repeating Island*: 17.

Shirley Campbell – The Memory of Skin: Traces of People Without History

Prefiero guardar silencio	¿Soy acaso negra? – me dije (¡sí!)
como lo han hecho los grandes	¿qué cosa es ser negra? (¡Negra!)
e ir conquistando a tragos	y yo no sabía la triste verdad
lo que la historia nos debe.	que aquello escondía (¡Negra!).
Shirley Campbell	Victoria Santa Cruz
"Rotundamente negra"	"Me gritaron Negra"

In the previous section, Dlia McDonald's poetics of landscape was approached as an eloquent trace of the past concerning the participation of Costa Rica's Caribbean province within the wider dynamic of a cultural and historical webbed network, yielding pluricentrical belonging through transhistorical codes of time past. In her poetics of landscape, sites of Dwelling and of Modernization together with the representation of the train act together in a modernized-nature oxymoron to constitute an emblem of a diasporic origin. A first outernational layer has thus been laid upon the palimpsest of historical imaginations that structure *Black Costa Rica*, acknowledged through the pluricentrical figures of belonging that refer both to the local and to the global simultaneously. In the present section, a second layer concerning the stor(y)ing of Black Costa Rica's recent past will be deployed with Shirley Campbell's poetic approach to the subject of History. This layer adds to the spatio-temporal dimension of pluricentrical belonging a specific meta-historical one, which makes evident how the history of the Caribbean diaspora in Limón reproduces Gilroy's definition of Black Atlantic subjects as "people in but not necessarily of the modern, western world".[1] As Eulalia Bernard declaims it, Blacks in Costa Rica represented a key economic and labor force in the country's modernization: "Dock Workers! / The roughness of the sea / Has made you, … can't you see? / The backbone of your country."[2] They remained, however, paradoxically constricted to the *outernational* margins because of their diasporic background *and* their color of skin, thus struggling to belong to the nation they had helped build.

In the Preface to her first book *Naciendo* (1988), Shirley Campbell explains her attempt at combining a group of words into poetry as an obligation that wishes to correct the lack of something very particular, personal and collective. For this Afra-Costa Rican writer, her poetry is a responsibility that stems from the urgent need to keep going despite an everlasting struggle ("mi poesía solo nace de esta necesidad urgente de seguir andando […]").[3] A struggle that has to do with exclusion, oppression, and underrating of cultures and dignity of lives past and present of Afro-descendent populations throughout the globe. The paratextual element explains Campbell's work as an aesthetic struggle whose purpose is for history to justify itself opposite a tireless battle ("de esta necesidad de que la historia

---

[1]   Gilroy, *The Black Atlantic*: 29.
[2]   Bernard, "Dock Workers", *My Black King*: n.p. (vv. 5–8).
[3]   Campbell, *Naciendo*: 5.

se justifique ante nuestra incansable batalla").[4] She delimits this battle as '*our* tireless battle' ("nuestra"). That is, as pertaining to a collectivity which, as her œuvre reasserts it, has been historically placed at the margins. The preface is in fact programmatic regarding her treatment of the subject of History across the totality of her œuvre and functions thus as an eloquent foreword to her literary combat. A combat concerned primarily with the vindication of Black historical imagination/s through a *skin-history metonymy*.[5]

In the ensuing pages, Campbell's meta-historical poetry shall be closely read so as to bring to the fore how the content meaning of *historia* is denominated with the word *piel* [skin]. By an extended use in an approximating sense,[6] a "connection of reciprocal dependency"[7] between *piel* and *historia* is installed in which *skin* functions as an adjacent *vox* concerning uprooting, racism, and marginalization, which are the content meanings of Campbell's *historia*. Given this semantic relation of contiguity, one word is substituted by the other recurrently (*summutantur verba pro verbis*)[8] and in so doing, the skin-history metonymy identifies a particular story of the past as being determined by the color of a person's skin. This past has been defined by a western *Weltanschauung* that implemented colonial enterprises construed upon racial terror. Racism and colonialism, as Gilroy explains them, "work insidiously and consistently to deny both historicity and cultural integrity to the artistic and cultural fruits of black life."[9] Which is why the skin-history metonymy corresponds to a rhetorical figure by which the poet embarks herself, her readers, and her Afro-descendant community/ies on the journey towards the rectification of an oppressed and silenced historical imagination.

Susan Bock-Morss's (2000) enlightening work on the veiling of the Haitian Revolution by Hegel in his writings on the slave-master dialectic, together with Michel-Rolph Trouillot's (1995) processes of erasure and silencing regarding the Haitian Revolution, are exemplary in making visible the oppressed historical imaginations that Campbell aims to reclaim with her poetry. On the one hand, Trouillot underlines "the general silence that Western historiography has produced around the Haitian Revolution", both immediately after the Revolution broke out as in contemporary scholarship, perceptible in global history textbooks.[10] In them, rhetorical tropes that he terms "formulas of erasure" and "of banalization" act jointly to create the "powerful silencing" around the subject. The author underlines the "cumulative irrelevance of a heap of details" as the manner in which the

---

4   Campbell, *Naciendo*: 5.
5   Metonymy is here understood as defined in *Rhetorica ad Herennium*, a manuscript which authors Peter Koch (1999) and Andreas Blank (1999) have pointed out as withholding the first real definition of metonymy. Koch translates the Latin definition of metonymy as follows: "Denominatio [i.e. 'metonymy'] is a trope that takes its expression from near and close things and by which we can comprehend a thing that is not denominated by its proper word" (Koch, "Frame and Contiguity": 140f.).
6   Following Silk, "Metaphor and Metonymy": 132: "If you are faced with a deviant usage wherein each word is *literally* possible in an expanded context in a sense approximating to that of its given use, you have metonymy."
7   Blank, referring to modern rhetoric manuals, "Co-presence and Succession": 170.
8   Cicero, *Rhetorica*: 27.93. Retrieved from http://www.perseus.tufts.edu/hopper/text?doc=Cic.%20Orat.%2027.93&lang=original (14.02.2017).
9   Gilroy, *The Black Atlantic*: 188.
10   Trouillot, *Silencing the Past*: 9; see pp. 95–107.

trope of banalization is carried out, so that these narratives "sweeten the horror".[11] Acting together, the relevance of the Haitian revolution is either *erased* completely, or it has become *trivialized* to the point that its uniqueness is denied, thus being emptied out of is radical character and referred to as a mere "revolt" or "rebellion".[12] The motor force behind this, according to the author, is the fact that the Haitian Revolution was "unthinkable" in the West before it actually took place, and still after it broke out, mainly because it challenged slavery precisely from the precepts intrinsic to Enlightenment thought.[13]

Susan Bock-Morss explains this paradox by pointing to the fact that the practice of slavery represented a severe internal contradiction concerning the philosophical discourse on freedom and liberty proper to the epoch, principally because the "exploitation of millions of colonial slave laborers was accepted as part of the given world by the very thinkers who proclaimed freedom to be man's natural state and inalienable right."[14] She refers to Hobbes, Locke, and Rousseau as examples of eminent philosophers whose defense on liberty was rarely done on the grounds of racial equality. She furthermore affirms that even though they may have condemned slavery, none of them spoke against it on behalf of the humanity of Africans and hence did not appeal to *their* right to self-determination. Ultimately, slave forced labor represented the institutional framework that supported the French bourgeoisie, who paradoxically developed the ideas of *Liberté, Egalité, Fraternité*. The Haitian Revolution brought into reality the essence of these values, embodied nonetheless by Black slaves who, because of the articulation of European Modernity upon colonialism and slavery, had been denied the basic right to freedom. Consequently, the silencing of the importance and historical landmark that this revolution signified starts for Trouillot precisely with revolutionary France and its colonial past. Which is why, for example, public celebrations surrounding the Bicentennial of the French Revolution in 1989–1991 overlapped the Haitian Revolution by mainly celebrating "revolutionary France" to the point of near total erasure of the former because of slavery and of France's colonial past, states the author.[15]

Much like Bock-Morss and Trouillot's work on the Haitian Revolution, Campbell affirms that she writes with the purpose of overcoming Black historical invisibility, voicelessness, and misrepresentation. She underscores that her poetry establishes therefore proper expressions and interpretations of Afro-descendant realities – past, present, and future – given that Afro-descendant writers and poets are the spokespersons and activists of the Black cause. The poet thus pleads for the need of a collective vindication carried out through their own words and by their own cultural productions. "Estamos llamados a contar nuestra propia historia, hemos sido contados por otros", explains Campbell her interviewer Javier Bragado (2017). Her declaration makes evident how her poetry is in effect a conscious literary combat. In a foreword to a series of poems she published with *Revista*

---

[11]   Trouillot, *Silencing the Past*: 96. Trouillot also mentions how "erasure and banalization are not unique to the Haitian Revolution" since there are "structural similarities in global silences", as for example regarding slavery in the U.S. Affirmations such as "some U.S. slaves were better fed than British workers", or in the case of the Holocaust, "some Jews did survive", permit this trivialization (p. 97).

[12]   Ibid.: 99.

[13]   Ibid.: 87.

[14]   Bock-Morss, "Hegel and Haiti": 822.

[15]   Trouillot, *Silencing the Past*: 100.

Casa de la Mujer (2014), she states that creative writers hold a huge amount of responsibility and underscores in her interview with Bragado that she therefore carries out literary activism.[16] Campbell recognizes herself as spokesperson of her supranational community and her purpose as a Black poet is 'to acknowledge me and my people, and that we are the result of a history that must still be rewritten, healed, and liberated', she explains.[17]

Campbell's poetic œuvre is multifold. Her first poetry compilation *Naciendo* (1988) gathers poems on diverse subjects such as diaspora and history intertwined with the mention of skin, Blackness, and of blood as metaphors thereof, while love and erotism exist in close relationship with motherhood. A sense of poetic struggle can be noticed throughout her poems where hope, faith, and a sense of brother- and sisterhood ("hermandad") are outlined in the form of a literary combat. Furthermore, grandmothers and grandfathers are both poetized as bearers of the stories of the past. Her second compilation *Rotundamente negra* (RN 1994, 2006)[18] is composed of three parts (entitled "La tierra prometida", "Ahora que puedo gritarlos", and "Rotundamente negra"), where the triad Black-Woman-Motherhood can be read across each part and which will be discussed towards the end of the present section. While the first part connects the sense of Blackness and of *historia* with her own lived experience of motherhood, the second part delivers mostly poems dedicated to love, erotism, and the act of making love. The third segment returns to the Black-Woman-Mother triad and intertwines these aspects in the form of a literary combat, where motherhood, Blackness, and history are expressed as inherent elements in the enduring struggle for personal and collective acknowledgement.

While her last anthology *Rotundamente Negra y otros poemas* (RNOP 2013) presents several excerpts and slightly modified versions of poems from the original *Rotundamente negra* compilation and from *Palabras indelebles de poetas negras* (2011; edited by Dlia McDonald), the compilation also includes other new compositions divided in thematic sections.[19] The last section entitled "Historia develada" constitutes one of the focal points of the following pages, in which close attention is paid to the poems "Al llegar", "De frente", "Desde siempre", and "Nuestra Historia". By approaching Campbell's poetry as meta-historical poetics, the ensuing discussion outlines the equivocal meaning *historia* deploys across selected poems found in *Naciendo*, in *Rotundamente Negra*, in the section "Historia develada" (RNOP), and in the poem "El encuentro" found in *Palabras indelebles de poetas negras*. Their subject is a silenced and veiled story of the past, which the poet takes on to disclose and to retrieve from concealment.

---

16 Bragado, "No éramos negros" (11.02.2017): "Yo hago activismo a través de mi poesía."
17 Campbell, "Poemas": 174. "Es la tarea de reconocerme a mí misma y a mis pueblos, y reconocer que somos el resultado de una historia que todavía tiene que ser reescrita, reparada y liberada. Nosotros/as, escritores/as y poetas afrodescendientes somos voceros/as de nuestros pueblos y activistas de la causa negra. El oficio de la creación literaria lleva consigo una enorme responsabilidad."
18 The edition cited in the ensuing pages corresponds to the second edition (2006).
19 The first part, composed of six poems, is entitled "Declaración de principios", while the second reads "…de manos abiertas…". The compilation's third part is divided in two subsections, "Sueños en mujer" and "Entre cartas y de abuelas". The former approaches poetically what it means 'to become *woman*', while the latter holds three texts dedicated to her grandmothers. The fourth and last section is entitled "Historia develada", some of whose poems were published in *Palabras indelebles de poetas negras* (2011).

The reader must be forewarned that the analysis of Campbell's poems carried out here is not focused on poetic aspects *per se*. That is, her poetic vain is not approached through aesthetic criteria referring to formal aspects such as rhythm, rhyme, cadence or musicality. Mainly because Campbell's work is best described as prose poetry. Contrary to McDonald's haikus, her texts mostly correspond to long, free-versed poems along which an argument on the subject of *historia* is deployed. The interest lies therefore in *tracing the thread* of such arguments across her work. A meta-historical discourse is approached intertextually so as to examine the trans/national linkages yielding pluricentrical belonging, where a supranational historical imagination regarding racism and exclusion can be simultaneously pinpointed in Costa Rican national specificities.

In so doing, the present study enquires, how does Campbell contribute to *Black Costa Rica* through the subject of *historia*? What does *historia* mean in Campbell's poetry and how are its meanings deployed in her poetry? How does her poetization of it portray pluricentrical belonging? What are the arguments surrounding the semantic constellation of *historia* and how do they reflect a historical imagination? Of what nature is this historical imagination and how can it be related to a local story of the past?

The Skin-History Metonymy and the Marginalization of Blacks in Limón

1	Llenémonos de mañanas victoriosas
2	soñémonos hombres de piedra
3	y de fuego
4	acribillémonos de amor
5	y de luchas
6	descubrámonos la piel
7	y la historia
8	solo entonces
9	empecemos.

Naciendo (p.10)[20]

Campbell's above quoted poem shall serve as a lucid introduction to the ensuing discussion. She articulates here a war cry with a series of hopeful commands expressed in imperative verbal forms. A cry of war whose objectives are victorious mornings for men of stone and fire filled with love and struggles. The combat moves are conjugated in the first-person plural where the receivers of the battle accomplishments are the people carrying out the actions themselves. That is, 'let *us* fill *ourselves* with victorious mornings' (v. 1). 'Let *us* dream *ourselves* men of stone and fire' (vv. 2f). 'Let *us* fill *ourselves* with love and struggles' (vv. 4f.). The reference to victory, stone and fire, and struggle coupled with love symbolize triumph, endurance, fervour, strength. It implies something is sought after, attainable only

---

[20] For an English translation of this poem, see Mosby, *Place, Language, and Identity in Afro-Costa Rican Literature*: 176. Some of the poems here discussed are also treated by Mosby, for which she provides her own translations (see pp. 169–209). English versions of Campbell's poems hereafter correspond all to my own translations unless stated otherwise.

through perseverance and persistence. An outcome that when achieved will burn passionately in the fire of its own conquest without consuming itself. The verb *acribillar* (v. 4) means to bombard or to riddle a body with a long and rapid series of bullets, much like in armed warfare when the person is "pumped full with lead".[21] Used as it is in this verse, it portrays a passionate image that inspires the imagined reader in a rather intense and ardently manner to bring together love and the vivid will to fight. Together, these metaphors speak a militant voice that encourages a specific collectivity to take notice of a clear battle, which Mosby has defined in Campbell's literary activism as a "process of discovery and vindication".[22] Campbell then sets forth the feud she entitles to her Afro-community by asserting: 'let us discover our skin and history, only then shall we begin (vv. 6–9).

The closing verses have a clear militant tone. Primarily, they allow us to enter the ensuing discussion between memory and History in Campbell's poetry. Secondly, they explain the imperative form in the first-person plural ('let *us* discover *our* skin') as a conscious choice. A choice that delimits a Black collectivity as the one she is summoning with her rallying cry. That is, a poetic 'us' is defined through an *epidermal metonymy*. Campbell has outlined and empathically claimed an in-group membership through an 'us' based on the category of skin color, which, as it will be argued along these pages, is linked to an Afro-descendant supranational historical imagination. This racial binary is frequent in Campbell's treatment of *historia* and represents to a large extent the uprooting and scattering of African people due to the victim diaspora and European colonialism, which has meant the oppression of their descendants ever since. Consequently, the skin-history metonymy is approached here as representing an 'us' joined by the meaning that *skin* was given by Enlightenment thought, responsible for a particular history of oppression and of erasure of cultural dignity as consequences thereof. Uprooting, colonization, and racism stand as its defining features.

Columbus' fortuitous 'discovery' of the unknown continent while searching for India led to the installation of a complex system of social relationships in which a hierarchical domination on behalf of Europeans was imposed upon the people and places they had stumbled upon and of which they furthermore claimed ownership. As the Peruvian sociologist Aníbal Quijano (2000) takes note of it, these relations of domination signified a new historical and sociological world that had no previous antecedents and which fundamentally set a new pattern of global dominance, what he terms the coloniality of power (*colonialidad del poder*) and which he and other Latin American decolonial intellectuals consider has not ceased to exist.[23] Fundamentally because nowadays "the interrelation among modern forms of exploitation and domination" are still carried out between former metropolis and their once peripheries.[24] Beforehand, the newly learned territories and the people inhabiting them were structured into a system of control which maneuvered not only the resources and the products the new lands provided, but mainly

---

21 S.v. "riddle", *Collins English Dictionary*, definition n. 3, retrieved from https://www.collinsdictionary.com/dictionary/english/riddle (19.06.2016).

22 Mosby, *Place, Language, and Identity in Afro-Costa Rican Literature*: 176.

23 Cf. Quijano, "Colonialidad del poder, eurocentrismo y América Latina": 204. See also Mignolo, "La colonialidad a lo largo y ancho" (2000); Castro-Gómez/Grosfoguel, *El giro decolonial* (2007); Maldonado-Torres, "Thinking through the Decolonial Turn" (2011); and Restrepo, *Intervenciones en Teoría Cultural* (2012).

24 Maldonado-Torres, "On the Coloniality of Being": 242.

the work force it used in order to retrieve the riches the continent held. To exponentially increase such assets and because forced labor had taken a toll on the autochthonous populations, Europeans colonizers dislocated thousands of individuals from their African homelands and transported them by ship to the New World, tearing their collectivities apart and forcing them into diaspora and slavery. As a consequence, a direct political, social, and cultural supremacy on behalf of European colonizers was forced upon the subalterns of the continents it looted.[25] The development of colonialism must be however comprehended as a consequence of Enlightenment thought, where the ideas of progress together with the installment of a scientific method and the supremacy of reason determined the origins of both occidental Modernity and of the African victim diaspora as collateral damage thereof.

In this context of encounter between three diverse groups of people – termed by Stuart Hall as *Présence Africaine, Présence Européenne,* and *Présence Américaine,* their union qualified by Benítez-Rojo as a *"supersyncretism"*[26] – the idea of 'race' became central in the conformation of a stratified social and economic scheme between colonizers and their colonized.[27] As a consequence, Modernity's colonial horizon was constituted, as stated by Quijano, as a Eurocentric hegemonic universe, which developed an anthropological categorization of humanity stratified in racial identities such as *white, indian, black,* and *mestizo* – a categorization that Gilroy (2004) qualifies as "the catastrophic power of race-thinking".[28] By way of the operatory category of race, Europeans legitimized the domination it imposed and justified its conquest based on biological criteria of the metaphysical kind, where the biological characteristics of a social group reflected the essence of their being. These racial identities were hierarchized and differentiated into colonial binaries such as superior/inferior, rational/irrational, and civilized/barbaric.[29] For Quijano (2007), the concept of *race* ultimately represented the foundation of the coloniality of power, which, as stated above, continues to legitimate capitalist relationships and the oppression of the formerly colonized nowadays.

Like Quijano, who considers 'race' to be none other than a mental construction, for Colette Guillaumin (1980) the social, political, and economical reality of the concepts of 'race' and 'race relations' were elevated to natural and legal status from the eighteenth century onwards, which is why the author affirms 'race' is in no way a material fact, but a concept, an idea.[30] Likewise, Miles considers 'race' and 'racism' correspond to "ideological

---

25 Cf. Quijano, "Colonialidad y modernidad/racionalidad": 11.
26 Hall states *"Présence Africaine* is the site of the repressed", while *"Présence Européenne* is about exclusion, imposition and appropriation". The author explains *Présence Américaine* as "The Third, 'New World' presence, [which] is not so much about power, as ground, place, territory" (Hall, "Cultural Identity and Diaspora": 398 and 400, respectively). Benítez-Rojo speaks on the other hand of the genesis of the plural forms of Caribbean culture as a "complex syncretism" (*The Repeating Island*: 12).
27 Quijano gives examples of this by stating that Indigenous people were confined to serfdom, although a minority of its noble class was exempted of it since they acted as cultural mediators. Whereas Africans were reduced to slavery and Europeans represented the hegemonic class (Quijano, "Colonialidad del poder, eurocentrismo y América Latina": 204f.).
28 Gilroy, "Foreword": xix.
29 Cf. Quijano, "Colonialidad del poder y clasificación social": 95.
30 For Guillaumin, "'race' is not a material fact which produces social consequences. It is an idea, a mental factor, and so a social fact in itself". See Guillaumin for a fairly complete history of the ideas of 'race', scientific racism, social darwinism, and somatic determinism from the eighteenth century up to the twentieth century. She

notions which are used to both construct and negotiate social relations",[31] while for Gilroy (2007) these represent a "virtual reality".[32] Like Miles, K. Anthony Appiah (1996) also underscores that 'races' do not exist and are instead conceptual consequences of the nineteenth century biological typology named *scientific racism*,[33] understood by Gilroy as a grand narrative of scientific reason and as "one of modernity's more durable intellectual products".[34] This discourse rested upon the idea that humans could be classified according to their phenotypic characteristics, which in turn determined moral, intellectual, and cultural qualities of the social group. Among the main postulates developed by nineteenth-century European biologists and anthropologists were (a) human species could be divided in discrete and fixed biological types which determined individual and cultural variation; from where (b) these differentiations classified as 'races' could be hierarchically ordered, determining certain were biologically and culturally superior. Thus, (c) a link was asserted between biology and cultural variation.[35] Consequently, 'race' was a "naturalist conception of social groups"[36] that justified endogenous characteristics, such as skin color, as a determining factor in cultural and moral behavior. It became "a category used to define psychological and social difference [based on] physical appearance", as Robert Miles underlines it in *Racism and Migrant Labour* (1982).[37] This justified the subjugation of peoples considered inferior, like for example Africans, who during the age of Enlightenment were defined as "bestial Others" by white, European thinkers.[38]

However, Trouillot is quick to underline that scientific racism has been wrongly attributed to the nineteenth century, otherwise sustaining that it "was already a feature of the ideological landscape of the Enlightenment".[39] On the subject, author Emmanuel Chukwudi Eze gathers in a controversial volume entitled *Race and the Enlightenment* (1997) a series of writings regarding the concept of race during the Enlightenment period, where he considers that an intertextuality among writers of the epoch signals the attribution of reason and civilization to white Europeans, while savagery and irrationality were attributed to non-white people located outside Europe. Paul B. Miller, who in his book *Elusive Origins* (2010) occupies himself with the historical imagination of Caribbean writers as a way of extricating themselves from the Enlightenment paradigms of binary relations like the ones mentioned above, quotes Kant's approach to "humanity" (*Menschheit*) as the ideological backdrop of Modernity, which makes evident Gilroy's assertion that before the consolidation of scientific racism, "the term 'race' was used very much in the way that the world 'culture' is used today".[40] For Kant,

---

refers to these as constructions developed parallel the evolution of modern science, the idea of determinism in Nature, and the emergence of a scientific spirit ("The idea of race": 37–68, quote p. 41).

31   Miles, *Racism*: 73.
32   Gilroy, *There Ain't no Black in the Union Jack*: xxii.
33   Appiah, "Race, Culture, Identity": 37f. See also Miles, *Racism and Migrant Labour*: 20.
34   Gilroy, *The Black Atlantic*: 44.
35   See Miles, "Recent Marxist Theories of Nationalism and the Issue of Racism": 28, and Guillaumin, "The idea of race": 52f, who explains that cultural and socio-mental characteristics were linked to physical ones.
36   Guillaumin, "The idea of race": 46.
37   Miles, *Racism and Migrant Labour*: 20.
38   Nick Nesbitt, *Universal Emancipation* (2008), quoted in Miller, *Elusive Origins*: 7.
39   Trouillot, *Silencing the Past*: 78.
40   Gilroy, *The Black Atlantic*: 8.

Humanity is at its greatest perfection in the race of whites. The yellow Indians do have a meagre talent. The Negroes are far below them and at the lowest point are a part of the American peoples.[41]

The reference to *piel* by Campbell implies to a large extent this historic conceptual framework, which led to Modernity's reified notion of race as a discourse justifying colonialism. As expressed by Campbell herself in her interview with Bragado, 'we weren't *Black* until we encountered *Europeans*, we were just people and once we came in contact we became Black, which acquired a negative connotation that to this day has not yet been cleansed' (emphasis added).[42] Because of this, the skin-history metonymy proves to be still relevant nowadays, as the following pages shall demonstrate it. In fact, the poet's metonymy echoes Gilroy's claim that "an embeddedness in Enlightenment assumptions continues despite the ostentatious gestures of disaffiliation."[43] Moreover, it makes evident Cohen's affirmation regarding Black diasporas:

> in the case of those of African descent skin colour normally remains a marker for two, three or more generations […] The deployment of skin colour in many societies as a signifier of status, power and opportunity, make it impossible for any people of African descent to avoid racial stigmatization.[44]

Let Us Discover Our Skin… and Our History

Poem XII of Part Three of *Rotundamente negra* deploys the skin-history metonymy in an exemplary manner. It is moreover representative of pluricentrical belonging because, as stated by Mosby (2012), the poem "reflects the tendency to articulate transnational Blackness through the local." While Mosby correctly addresses Campbell's poetic dialogue goes beyond Costa Rican borders "by connecting with transnational Blackness",[45] my analysis turns to the national. It aims to make visible the history of racism Afro-Costa Ricans underwent in the country during the first half of the twentieth century as a mirrored reality of the enduring marginalization of Afro-descendants. Even though Campbell engages the subject of racism as a global phenomenon by pointing to places like Africa, the U.S., and Haiti, a specific Costa Rican story of the past can also be pinpointed and specified through her poetry as a local reality regarding the supranational experience of racial discrimination. It is not gratuitous that she reiterates to Carlos – so that he doesn't forget it (v. 26: "y no lo olvides") – that there is inequality due to racial prejudice and discrimination *there* (v. 27: "allá"), *here* (v. 28: "y aquí"), and *everywhere* else (v. 29: "y en otras partes").

---

41 Quoted in Miller, *Elusive Origins*: 10.
42 Bragado, "No éramos negros" (11.02.2017): "No éramos negros hasta que entramos en contacto con los europeos, éramos solo personas y nos convertimos en negros al contacto con los europeos y tomó una significación negativa que hasta hoy no se ha limpiado."
43 Gilroy, *The Black Atlantic*: 53. Gilroy is referring to Patricia Hill Collins's arguments regarding western thought tradition and the effects of dualistic thinking (cf. p. 51ff.).
44 Cohen, *Global Diasporas* (1997): 144.
45 Mosby, "Roots and Routes": 10 and 14, respectively.

These adverbs of place are strategically used to make evident both a local reality *and* a global one as expressions of a supranational racialized experience.

As stated in the epigraphy, the poem is dedicated to her friend Carlos, who is beginning to understand ("*a Carlos... porque está empezando a entender*"). Carlos believes that there are no laws that suppress life (vv. 1–3: "Tengo un amigo que dice / que no hay leyes / que repriman la vida").[46] This is the central allegation that guides the development of the poem, a total of eighty-three free verses, which progresses along the lyrical voice's explanations of why he is wrong. Here, Campbell reenacts the skin-history metonymy by taking careful notice of specifying otherness in a concrete manner.

In the previous poem, an in-group membership regarding the skin-history metonymy was underlined with the first-person plural ('let *us*...'). Here, however, the emphasis of otherness is accomplished by the explicit us~them ethnoracial binary that has been recreated in an intimate discursive level – between a *me* and a *you*.[47] It is here enacted using singular possessive pronouns (*mi*/my, *tuyo*/yours) which are strongly expressive when outlining the following historical opposition:

13	Quiero que recuerdes
14	ante todo
15	que mi piel
16	es distinta
17	que la tuya
18	quiero que no olvides
19	que mi historia
20	tiene manchas grandes
21	y tristes
22	y bellas
23	y eternas
24	distintas que las tuyas.
	[...]

III.XII, *Rotundamente negra* (p. 86)

The conversation is set between a lyrical-I and a lyrical-you, which defines what is proper to the first and therefore extrinsic to that someone else. She speaks of '*my* skin' (v. 15) and opposes it to his, i.e. '*yours*' (v. 17: "la tuya"). Campbell kindly asks Carlos to remember that her skin is distinct from his so that she can shortly thereafter deepen the us-them binary by beseeching Carlos to not forget that '*my* history has great, and sad, and beautiful, and eternal stains, which are distinct from *yours*' (vv. 19–24). It must not be overseen that Campbell invokes the stains of her epidermally-determined history as *eternal*. They are ineradicable not only because of the ever-present remembrance of past traumas like slavery and the Middle Passage – which are big and great and sad –, but also because of

---

[46] Campbell, *Rotundamente negra*: 86.

[47] Mosby also refers to this intimate sphere, affirming the "ethnic, historic, and cultural borders are clearly drawn with the use of the possessives *mi*/my and *tuyo*/yours in this local, intimate, and personal debate between Costa Ricans of different ethno-cultural backgrounds: the Black identified voice and non-Black Carlos" ("Roots and Routes": 14).

the on-going reality of marginalized Black communities throughout the globe due to racism.

She furthermore claims they are *beautiful* stains (v. 22), an adjective that becomes highly significant since it grants value to her own Blackness. Even though the whole thematic of the poem wishes to make evident for Carlos why Blackness constitutes to a large extent Frantz Fanon's definition of it as "the burden of [this] corporeal malediction",[48] in this concrete case, Campbell goes beyond Fanon and grants Blackness a refreshing, positive identification. By claiming its *beauty*, her skin-history metonymy fulfills its semantic content against the racist considerations that Fanon summarizes as intrinsic to the color Black: "the Negro is an animal, the Negro is bad, the Negro is mean, the Negro is ugly".[49]

She does this as well in her famous poem "Rotundamente negra" (III.XIII, *RN*). The poet is overwhelmed by the distances the poem has crossed, as by how it has been appropriated by women around the world. In her interview with Bragado, Campbell tells him women have appropriated it ("[l]as mujeres lo tomaron como propio"), something that grants her a great sense of pride.[50] As the last text of *Rotundamente negra*, Campbell's poem concludes the book eloquently by asserting the beauty of her Blackness. She rejects emphatically the denial of her voice, her blood, and her skin (vv. 1–3: "me niego rotundamente / a negar mi voz / mi sangre y mi piel"). And takes to emphasizing the beauty of her big mouth (v. 9: "rotundamente grande"), of her lovely nose (v. 11: "rotundamente hermosa"), of her white teeth (v. 13: "rotundamente blancos"), and of her brave, black skin (v. 15: "valientemente negra").[51] Campbell is dialoging not just with Lacan's *stade de miroir*, referred to by Fanon as the internal process yielding the pathological neurosis of the alienated Black wo/man,[52] but she is also overturning Glissant's claim, who turns as well to the *mirror* as a means of addressing a "successful Colonialism". Glissant states the Black person "is upset to see himself so good in this mirror",[53] because, as Fanon explained it, "it is in his corporeality that the Negro [has been historically] attacked."[54] As a way of healing the psycho-existential complex these authors have theorized, Campbell emphasizes *categorically* that she *outright refuses* to deny her Blackness when she looks at herself in the mirror (v. 7: "cuando miro mi rostro en el espejo"). The repetition of adverbs like *rotundamente*, *categóricamente*, and *absolutamente* (vv. 1, 4, 16, 19) adds strength to and underscores her literary combat. Campbell's "Black is Beautiful" poetic scheme grants an

---

48 Fanon, *Black Skin, White Masks*: 84.
49 Ibid.: 86.
50 Bragado, "No éramos negros" (11.02.2017): "Es maravilloso y muy emotivo ver cómo está en camisetas, bolsos, en los emblemas de las asociaciones de afrodescendientes [sic], en telenovelas populares... está aquí mismo en España en catalán en un proyecto con mujeres dominicanas. En Brasil, que es una lengua diferente, lo corean. [...] Yo he ido a comunidades remotas en Ecuador y me dicen: 'Guau, usted es la del poema.'"
51 Campbell, *Rotundamente negra*: 89.
52 Fanon elaborates on the ontological subalterity of the colonized Black wo/man by quoting Lacan's approach to the consolidation of the child's identity during the *mirror period*. "The subject's recognition of his image in the mirror", Fanon quotes Lacan, is useful in understanding the psycho-existential complex he speaks of. In the author's words, "it is in white terms that one perceives one's fellows." For Fanon, "every Antillean expects all the others to perceive him in terms of the essence of the white man" (Fanon, *Black Skin, White Masks*: 124–126, n. 25).
53 Glissant, "History–Histories–Stories": 89.
54 Fanon, *Black Skin, White Masks*: 126.

empowering force to the meaning her skin holds for her and, as a consequence, she fights *words on* to overturn such embodied denigration. A metaphor that she reproduces in another one of *Naciendo*'s poems by stating that her skin has a *beautiful shadow*, which gives her the strength to continue living.[55]

Her own poetic combat is reproduced by other Afra-Central American poets, such as Nicaraguan Creole poet Carmen Andira Watson (*1977), who names one of her poems with the same title – "Rotundamente negra" – and dedicates it to "la poeta Shirley Campbell Barr". Watson's poem echoes Campbell's by stating "Soy como vos Shirley / *Rotundamente negra*" (vv. 1f.) and flows from Spanish into English while describing her own Afro-identity as inspired by Campbell's prerogative. A description of Caribbean foods (vv. 5–7: "*rice and beans, / green banana, / bread fruit*"), her place of origin (v. 3: Managua), and the mention of the color of her skin (vv. 10f.: "La gente me ve blanca / pero yo me siento negra") build up the poem's content until she closes her ethnic assertiveness with "aunque todos me miren blanca / soy rotundamente negra / Como vos Shirley / como vos" (vv. 22–25).[56]

Nevertheless, Campbell is not blind to the historical scheme of Blackness, which is why she goes on to explain to Carlos why there is such a thing as racism, oppression, and unequal living conditions everywhere:

```
25   Quiero decirte
26   y no lo olvides
27   que allá
28   y aquí
29   y en otras partes
30   mis pueblos se desangran
31   por la vida
32   mis pueblos tienen
33   más hambre que los tuyos
34   y mis pueblos como los tuyos
35   sientan (sic!) y aman
36   y están muriendo
37   por la esperanza.
     [...]
```

III.XII, *Rotundamente negra* (p. 86f.)

She affirms that 'there and here and anywhere else' (vv. 27–29), '*my* people bleed to death' (v. 30) and '*my* people are hungrier than *yours*' (v. 33). Because of this, '*my* people are dying' (v. 36). With the reiteration of the singular first- and second-person possessive pronouns, the poet stresses two histories belonging to two different collectivities, explained through the epidermal element (*mi piel*). 'That there are no laws that oppress life?', she asks Carlos rhetorically (v. 38). Even though the poet recurrently expresses her desire to believe his ideals,[57] she demonstrates poetically why Carlos's argument is flawed, for he has a misleading notion of class and ethnic struggles that Campbell refutes by immediately

---

55   Campbell, *Naciendo*: 34: "mirarse la piel / con su hermosa sombra / y seguir viviendo" (vv. 19–21).
56   Reproduced in Meza, "Memoria, identidad y utopia": 157f.
57   Verses 4f.: "de verdad Carlos / quisiera creerte"; v. 39: "a veces lo creo"; vv. 46f.: "a veces lo creo / y a veces quiero creerlo"; 62f.: "A veces de verdad Carlos / quisiera creerte" (*Rotundamente negra*: 86, 87, and 88).

answering her rhetorical question (vv. 39–61). Her friend's unsound reasoning is corrected by referring to Mandela's freedom and to the presence of racism, hunger, and death in Africa, Haiti, the U.S., and in the world:

```
51    que me gritan
52    que Mandela es libre
53    pero su pueblo muere
54    que me dicen
55    que en África
56    y en Haití
57    y en Sur de los Estados Unidos
58    y en el mundo
59    hay hambre
60    y racismo
61    y muerte.
      [...]
```

III.XII, *Rotundamente negra* (p. 87f.)

As expressed here, discrimination, starvation, and mortality are the visible outcomes of racial oppression, exposed moreover in a transnational fashion. These are furthermore embodied in Mandela, who is described by Gilroy as "a black hero whose global significance lies beyond the limits of his partial South African citizenship and the impossible national identity which goes with it."[58] The African continent, the Caribbean insular and continental basin, Black North and Latin America are brought together under one symbolic paternal talisman figure in Campbell's skin-history metonymy.

Fanon calls attention to the fact that "[i]n America, Negroes are segregated. In South America, Negroes are whipped in the streets, and Negro strikers are cut down by machine-guns. In West Africa, the Negro is an animal."[59] Campbell echoes such considerations by symbolizing historical oppression based on ethnic criteria: *mi piel... mi historia*. She installs thus Du Bois's veil of race in a poetic manner by versifying that inequitable socio-economic realities affect her people in a prejudiced fashion because their skin is different from others'. The coupling of skin with history makes visible the deployment of different stories of the past due to the color of a wo/man's skin, where the veil acts as a symbolic demarcation regarding "the problem of the color-line, – the relation of the darker to the lighter races of men".[60] Campbell's skin-history metonymy marks this line explicitly. The ethnoracial element – made evident with *piel* – is for Campbell the reason why her history has stains of repression and of racism; why her people, unlike his – although both are equally human in their hopes and experiences (vv. 34f.) – go hungry and die.

---

[58]   Gilroy, *The Black Atlantic*: 95. Gilroy engages the figure of Mandela when arguing in his book that music is "the principal symbol of racial authenticity" in Black cultural production (p. 96). He refers to the song "Proud of Mandela" by Macka B as exemplary of how music production in London brought together Africa, America, Europe, and the Caribbean through a "process of fusion and of intermixture" regarding a vernacular music form transformed into reggae for the international market. Through this process, Mandela represents a "talisman that could suspend and refocus intraracial differences" (p. 95).

[59]   Fanon, *Black Skin, White Masks*: 85.

[60]   Du Bois, *The Souls of Black Folks*: 17.

Are There Truly No Laws That Oppress Life?

Even though Robert Miles (1995) warns caution before claiming that exclusionary practices on behalf of the state are based on racist terms,[61] Senior (2011) is sure to affirm that official discrimination politics existed against the Afro-Caribbean population on behalf of the Costa Rican government.[62] Like Senior, Harpelle (2001) affirms "legislation was combined with overt discrimination in an effort to contain the growth and spread of the West Indian community."[63] Olien (1977) also referred to the fact that Costa Ricans "exerted legal and nonlegal pressures to restrict blacks from settling in the highlands" because of multiple reasons. Firstly, because of their fear that they would upset the racial pattern of the country; secondly, because it was considered Afro-Caribbeans would spread diseases and immoral conducts; and thirdly, because they would compete with the national workforce if allowed to relocate with the UFCo.[64]

Miles accentuates that racial differentiations are created in the context of class differentiations, where concepts of race are socially and politically constructed with direct relation to the class structure. Therefore, even though racism may function as a "rational abstraction", it is in reality "a product of historical relations" and has sense only for and within those relations, as highlighted by Stuart Hall (1980).[65] Thus, *race* and *ethnicity* are but constructs that emerge from social inequality and from power structures between different social groups that take place in diverse historical moments within capitalist systems. Philip Bourgois, who carried out fieldwork in UFCo.'s plantations in Limón and Bocas del Toro in mid-1982, elucidated how ethnicity acted in these localities as "an ideological phenomenon: a set of symbolic markers that have been created – or have escalated – into a means of structuring power relations".[66] This explains why the presence of Caribbean Black wage workers during the first half of the twentieth century in Limón was firstly criticized by referring to *economic* factors, which were consequently explained through *ethnonational* considerations. This resulted in Costa Rican workers comprehending their economical marginalization in *national* terms, blaming the UFCo. for hiring 'too many Blacks' over of a national workforce, seeking hence protection under their government (see "The Dialectics of Race and Nation", Part I). The government, in turn, reacted by imposing anti-Black legislation.

The intertwining of race, class, and citizenship during the banana crisis defined and determined to a large extent Costa Rican racism towards Blacks in Limón so that the

---

[61]   See Miles, *Racism*: 50–61.

[62]   Senior, *Ciudadanía afrocostarricense*: 127.

[63]   Harpelle, *The West Indians of Costa Rica*: 143.

[64]   Olien, "The Adaptation of West Indians": 141f. and 145.

[65]   Hall, "Race, articulation, and societies": 337. Hall points out that "racial structures cannot be understood adequately outside the framework of quite specific sets of economic relations" (p. 308).

[66]   Bourgois understands ethnicity "in the context of unequal power relations in the production process both within and across classes" (Bourgois, *Ethnicity at Work*: x). Cf. Putnam, "Ideología racial": 141: "Pero los que teorizan sobre la construcción social de la raza, insisten que la raza surge de la desigualdad, no al revés. En suma, fueron las diferencias de poder propias de los encuentros históricos entre grupos sociales, las que dieron formación a las múltiples concepciones de la diferenciación 'natural' humana que agrupamos bajo la etiqueta de 'raza'."

struggle and the subsequent resolution of the predicament were thought of in racist terms: "the problems could be resolved by excluding the [Black] Other."[67] At issue was not the ethnic occupational hierarchy, nor the Depression that had caused the dependent capitalist economy to sink, not even the environmental factors that caused plant diseases, but the confusion between race/ethnicity and class led to a xenophobic attitude on behalf of working-class Costa Ricans, as of the nation's leaders and intellectuals. As a consequence of diffusing a strong and effective "national racist mythology", as termed by Gudmunson (1984),[68] the establishment of legislative means (institutionalized racism) excluded Caribbean immigrant laborers from the advantages of the Costa Rican economic and political structures.

President León Cortés's (1936–1940) response to the general discontent of the labor situation in Limón, for example, was to confine Black workers to the Caribbean province. A region which in turn had been abandoned and suffered severe negligence after it was no longer relevant to the export economy. This geographical 'confinement' was also founded upon an inexistent law which both Costa Ricans and Caribbean people took for real: Blacks were not to enter the capital. In fact, the railroad conductor that came from Limón was to change places with a national employer when arriving at Peralta (halfway between San José and Limón), so that a Costa Rican employee could continue to the Pacific station.[69] Even though no historian has found a law confirming the legality of such a prohibition, this was generally respected and few, almost no Blacks, travelled to San José. However, Senior refers to some, even if minimal, records of Afro-Caribbeans visiting the capital as tourists, musicians or performers.[70] Beyond the tacit idea that Blacks were not to enter the capital, Harpelle asserts President Cortés's mission was the suppression of the Afro-Caribbean community in Costa Rica, given that during his administration Blacks were systematically excluded and segregated in Limón.[71] They couldn't enter white hotels and were also prohibited to enter the newly established swimming pool and public baths. Movie theaters had segregated seating and Blacks were refused admittance in the country's only mental hospital.[72]

'That there are no laws that repress life?', asks Campbell her friend Carlos (v. 38: "Que no hay leyes que repriman la vida?"). The best example that confronts and dismantles Carlos fallacious supposition is the new banana contract drafted in 1934 (the Cortés-Chittenden Treaty), when the crisis in Limón finally caused the Company to leave the region in 1938. National fervor did not "permit the company to transfer its black workers there",[73] explicitly prohibiting the hiring of colored people in the banana industry at the Pacific region.[74] That is why Lara Putnam (1999) states, contrary to Steven Palmer, that

---

[67] Miles, *Racism*: 81.
[68] Gudmunson, "'Black' into 'White'": 44.
[69] Bourgois, *Ethnicity at Work*: 90.
[70] Senior, *Ciudadanía afrocostarricense*: 122.
[71] Harpelle, *The West Indians of Costa Rica*: 140.
[72] Palmer, *What Happen*: 208. Cf. Bourgois, *Ethnicity at Work*: 88: "Blacks were forbidden admission to the newly completed municipal swimming pool in Limón in 1936."
[73] Chomsky, *West Indian Workers*: 252.
[74] Quoted in Senior, *Ciudadanía afrocostarricense*: 67: "Queda prohibido el empleo, en la zona Pacífica, de la gente de color en dichos trabajos."

twentieth century Costa Rican racial ideology did not emerge solely from biological considerations, but instead arose greatly from unequal social and power relationships which were outlined along a rigid ethno-social hierarchy imposed under the UFCo.'s *shadow of the banana*.[75] Patricia Alvarenga Venútolo (2007) underscores furthermore that xenophobic reactions were not solely a consequence of labor shortage, but most strongly dependent on the racist discourses that the state had been systematically elaborating alongside its eugenic migration policies.[76] During this time, the dominant groups made use of racial criteria so as to ensure the isolation of those oppressed for, as claimed by Richard Delgado (1999), "[s]ociety enacts restrictive immigration laws and policies to keep foreigners – usually ones of darker coloration – out." And most importantly, "it enacts measurements aimed at making things difficult for those who are already here."[77] Such measurements 'for those who are already here' lead forcibly to marginalization and exclusion, and thus to social immobility.

Exclusionary practices like restrictive immigration laws and work impediments on Blacks settled at the Limón province promoted their subordination and marginalization as an outernational community, legitimating inequality between groups with assumed distinct origins on behalf of an imagined white community. The dynamics of race in the Caribbean region were intimately bounded to the power dynamic at a national level, as explained by Putnam, for the idea of race served political aims and needs.[78] It was used by the leaders of the country as a national political construct in the service of an exclusionary legislation which wished to protect its myth of ethnic homogeneity under a racial comprehension of the nation. Chomsky agrees with Putnam and points out that "the extreme polarization of race and class on [Costa Rica's] Atlantic Coast" provides a quite distinct history in regards with that of the rest of the country.[79] This story of the past is determined by relegation, for as Jiménez explains it, the government did not invest in infrastructure, neither in public health nor in education in the region once the banana/cacao economy of the Caribbean province stopped being relevant to the national economy.[80] This led to a state of total decadency in the province because racism had become an integral part of nationalism. Even though Anderson affirms "racism has its origins in ideologies of class, rather than in those of nation",[81] Costa Rican xenophobic reaction to the Afro-Caribbean community in Limón reenacts the intertwinement of the economical with the ethnonational.

So, let us repeat Campbell's prerogative, are there truly no laws that oppress life? The story of the marginalization of the Afro-Costa Rican minority begs to differ. As Campbell poetizes it to Carlos, her skin is different than his and thus holds her own stains, embodying a different story of the past. Like Campbell, Bernard also poetizes how skins determine

---

[75] Putnam, "Ideología racial": 173.
[76] Alvarenga Venútolo, "La inmigración extranjera en la historia costarricense": 17.
[77] Delgado, "Citizenship": 247.
[78] Putnam, "Ideología racial": 141: "Ya que queremos demostrar que la dinámica de la raza en la región del Caribe estaba íntimamente ligada a la dinámica del poder al nivel nacional, ubicamos nuestro análisis de la producción cotidiana de la raza en Limón, en el contexto del proyecto ideológico y la expansión institucional del Estado liberal."
[79] Chomsky, *West Indian Workers*: xi.
[80] Jiménez, *El imposible país*: 199.
[81] Anderson, *Imagined Communities*: 149.

specific histories of exclusion by referring to the denial of citizenship to Caribbean people because of their Blackness. In "Requiem a mi primo jamaiquino" (*Ritmohéroe* 1982), Bernard's lyrical-I details how her cousin never received Costa Rican citizenship, even though he had worked the land there for years. Instead, he suffered endless detours from *white* papers in *white* hands (vv. 14f.: "Rodeos y más rodeos tuvo / de blancos papeles de blancas manos"). The anaphora of "blancos/blancas" exemplifies to a full extent the denial of citizenship for Costa Rican-born Blacks due to ethnonational criteria. Bernard's final verses exemplify what the Caribbean diaspora lastly meant for the Costa Rican imagined community: a *black star* in the flag's splendid white, blue, and red coloring: "Soy una estrella negra / en el flamante blanco, azul y rojo / de nuestra bandera" (vv. 19–21).[82] As noticed by Mosby, the black star has violently imposed itself onto the national imagery, deployed throughout the poem with the mention of the flag, of the national anthem, the *cédula de identidad*, and lastly by an implicit reference to the national shield with the seven stars representing each province.[83] Hence, *la estrella negra* imposes itself as a foreign element and marks it from its place of difference, one that literally recalls the Black Star Line of Marcus Garvey. Just like Campbell, Bernard also claims her place of difference through an us~them binary, where the color of a wo/man's skin is decisive in the history of marginalization.

On the subject, Alvarenga Venútolo affirms the majority of the Caribbean population was considered "foreign" even though they had been born in the country.[84] A reality confirmed by linguist Elizabeth Winkler (2013), who carried out interviews while studying Limonese Creole in Costa Rica. As one of her informants explained her:

> B: Firs taym Costa Rica law, pipl fram outsayd wer der maada an faada baan, dat is yer nashunality.
> E: So even if you were born here you weren't Costa Rican?
> B: Afta 48 [1948] now yu baan ier, yu is Tico [Costa Rican]. But firs taym, if yu is baan outsayd yu av to tek da nashunality. If yu come fram Jamaica, yer Jamaican.[85]

Quince Duncan's biography, as reported by Mosby (2014), is evidence of this procedure. Born in San José in 1940 to a Panamanian father and a Limonese-born Caribbean-descendant mother, Duncan was not registered as a legitimate Costa Rican citizen since, at that time, "children born to women of West Indian descent were recorded as Jamaican in the birth registry."[86] An automatic procedure, hence. Moreover, Afro-American people born in the country had to carry out a special formality in order to acquire citizenship, having to pay for it.[87] These procedures make evident how the Costa Rican Caribbean participates in Gilroy's unrealized democracy because of denied citizenship due to cultural insiderism and ethnonational criteria. Campbell's poetic dialogue with Carlos calls upon this reality, while the metonymy points to a supranational imagination that gives content and form to pluricentrical belonging.

---

[82] Bernard, *Ritmohéroe*: 29.
[83] Mosby, *Place, Language, and Identity in Afro-Costa Rican Literature*: 81.
[84] Alvarenga Venútolo, "La inmigración extranjera en la historia costarricense": 10.
[85] Winkler, "Limonese Creole English": 207.
[86] Mosby, *Quince Duncan*: 5f.
[87] Alvarenga Venútolo, "La inmigración extranjera en la historia costarricense": 18.

The poet seeks to open up Carlos's close-mindedness by explaining to him:

66   vas a entender
67   que hay leyes
68   y razones
69   y hombres
70   que reprimen la vida
     [...]
          III.XII, *Rotundamente negra* (p. 88)

that only by sharing her history, i.e. her skin, he will understand that there are *laws* and reasons and men that oppress the life of others. Such as, for example, Costa Rican immigration policies throughout the twentieth century, which in 1904 sought to deny entrance to Arab, Turks, Armenians, and Gipsy populations.[88] Or the New Immigrations Law drafted by President Rafael Ángel Calderón in 1942, which attempted to prohibit entrance of people of African descent along with that of Chinese, Arabs, Turks, Syrians, and other non-white racial minorities. Among these were also the mentally ill, anarchists, gamblers, beggars, drug addicts, and smugglers, all of which were labeled as 'undesirable', 'inconvenient', 'harmful', or 'dangerous' people that could hinder the country's progress.[89] Another example is the Labor Code of 1943, which stated employers were required to have a 90% Costa Rican citizen workforce, posing even more labor difficulties for settled immigrants. Especially for Black Caribbean people that had settled in the province since their participation in the railroad construction and had refused to obtain Costa Rican citizenship, like Bernard's Jamaican cousin. Other cases are the 1930 "Immigrants Law", which required West Indians to pay $250 upon arrival, as well as requesting all resident foreigners to apply for permission when leaving the country temporarily. Furthermore, in 1934, the year the Cortés-Chittenden Treaty was signed, the government ordered that Black tourists were not to be granted green cards (*visas*).[90]

Campbell then concludes the poem by stating that human existence is not homogeneous, but instead is constituted by experiences that are tinged by skin color. Which is why Carlos cannot understand this, for he does not *embody* Blackness. If he could, then – and only then – could he understand,

77   solamente entonces Carlos
78   entenderás
79   que el tiempo es desigual
80   que las pieles tienen matices

---

[88]   Alvarenga Venútolo, "La inmigración extranjera en la historia costarricense": 13.
[89]   The New Immigrations Law justified the legal exclusion of these people by stating they are "personas inconvenientes, nocivas o peligrosas al orden o progreso de la República o a la conservación de la raza, ya sea por sus tendencias agitadoras, ya por sus escasos medios de subsistencia o por las características que predominen en ellas y sean de notoria desafinidad con la población nacional" (Jiménez, *El imposible país*: 196). See also Palmer, "Racismo intelectual": 118, and Murillo, "Vaivén de arraigos y desarraigos: 199. Cf. Harpelle, *The West Indians of Costa Rica*: 141.
[90]   Harpelle, *The West Indians of Costa Rica*: 134 and 140. Regarding *visas*, see Bourgois, *Ethnicity at Work*: 89.

81   y que el amanecer
82   pinta distinto
83   desde estos ojos.
        III.XII, *Rotundamente negra* (p. 88)

that time is not *homogeneous* nor *empty*, but erratic in its performance (79: "desigual"). It is inconsistent and does not follow a regular, harmonized pattern of progression, which homogenizes human experience above class struggle. Nor is it ethically just. Instead, it follows an irregular path of struggle for survival. Campbell gives precise examples of why it is not homogeneous nor void. It is dialectically filled with violence and battles against oppression; with deprivation and the will to eradicate hunger and life repression; as with the ongoing fight versus racism (vv. 52–61). This is why 'dawn colors differently from these eyes' (vv. 81–83), says the lyrical-I. For existential and historical conditions vary from one ('my') imagined community to the next ('yours'), whose overall differences are necessarily contingent on ethnicity and the story of the past because of it. Campbell seeks recognition through the skin-history metonymy in order to *discover* how the color of a wo/man's skin is inherently linked to her story of the past as to both the present and the future.

In conclusion, though Campbell does not refer explicitly to the story of Afro-Costa Rica, a close reading of the poem has coupled the poetic claims she makes with the sociohistorical marginalization that gave way to the Afro-Costa Rican borderland. In so doing, the skin-history metonymy goes beyond the nation, and yet the supranational experience her poetry declaims is simultaneously recognized in the national specificity of Limón, Costa Rica. The metonymy thus deploys pluricentrical belonging by underscoring an intrinsically glocal content.

"The Advocation of an InfraHistory" will next add depth to the equivocal meanings of historia by focusing on the dimension of historical writing as a complementary discourse constituting diaspora-consciousness. In the following section, Campbell's metonymy shall make visible Gilroy's assertion that the "distinctive historical experiences of this diaspora's populations have created a unique body of reflections on modernity and its discontents which is an enduring presence in the cultural and political struggles of their descendants today."[91] The Afra-Costa Rican's glocal poetry comprises in fact such reflections and echoes Gilroy's precepts by recognizing that her Afro-identity has been constructed by racist philosophies and colonial ideologies as fundamental discourses of Modernity. As Campbell herself acknowledges it,

> nuestra identidad afrodescendiente está cimentada en un andamiaje construido por filosofías e ideologías racistas y pensamientos eurocéntricos, la temática de mi poesía es solo el resultado de esa conciencia y la necesidad de manifestarlo.[92]

Her poetry thus responds to a personal process of consciousness, whereby she recognizes and undertakes the task of an ever-lasting struggle. One concerned with overturning with her poetry the long-term presence of such frames of thought. The ensuing pages engage Campbell's representation of History as constructed specifically through a *space of writing* that corresponds to the hegemonic discursive universe of the West.

---

[91]   Gilroy, *The Black Atlantic*: 45.
[92]   Campbell, "Poemas": 173f.

The Advocation of an InfraHistory

> There are at least two histories: that of collective memory and that of historians.
>
> Jacques LeGoff, *History and Memory*

It was Ernst Renan who took notice of how grief and suffering were of significant value when envisioning the historical imagination of a nation. Their power of cohesion becomes social capital when consolidating sentimental imaginings of attachment,[93] drawing people together as fellow members of a history that their antecessors suffered collectively. As seen in the previous pages, oppression and suffering function in the poetic dialogue with Carlos as the elements of unity and solidarity for those sharing Campbell's skin color and, hence, herstory. This historical memory is carried upon the *skin* as part of an ever-present reality which is why the metonymy converts *historia* into something other very particular. Mainly, into something that is necessarily recognized and experienced concretely through the body itself. That is, the skin-history metonymy corresponds to an *embodied* supranational historical imagination.[94]

Consequently, *historia* in Campbell has to do more with Maurice Halbwachs's (*La mémoire collective* 1950) consideration of *memory* as something that *dwells*, than with the scientific establishment of the past through documents, explanations thereof, and written re-construction of historical facts, as Paul Ricœur (2000) defines the historiographical operation. For Halbwachs, collective memory distinguishes itself from History in a precise manner. The former is a continuous trend of thought installed within a group and has no artificial aggregates, since it withholds a past that is still very much alive – "encore vivant ou capable de vivre" – in a group's self-consciousness. History, instead, is placed outside of the group and corresponds to the "besoin didactique de schematization".[95] Likewise, for Ricœur *only* memory can *re-present* the past with testimonies, images, and reminiscences, whereas History *re-establishes* it through a historiographical operation involving a documentary stage, an explicative one, and a writing phase. The author affirms the semantic difference between *representing* and *reconstructing* the past lies in the perspective of proximity or distance to it. The first is more immediate and subjective regarding remembrances, while the latter is distant and objectified.[96]

If History portrays "the reconstruction of the past without lacunae", says Pierre Nora,[97] then memory enacts its contrary for it is in perpetual deformation and transformation, periodically revived because it is tied to the eternal present of human beings. Unlike History, (collective/individual) memory is not sketched out along stationary limits, nor can it be

---

[93]   Renan, "What is a nation?": 19.

[94]   For an in-depth analysis of Shirley Campbell's representation of physical Blackness as withholding the intrinsic relationship between motherhood, Blackness, and culture, see Solano, "El giro identitario en la poesía de Shirley Campbell Barr" (2014). In her article, Solano approaches the importance of corporeal blackness in Campbell as a counterhegemonic manner of reaffirming her own identity, history, and culture through her own body.

[95]   Halbwachs, *La mémoire collective*: 46.

[96]   Ricœur, "L'écriture de l'histoire": 736f.

[97]   Nora, "Between Memory and History": 9.

abstracted into a historical period, for it has irregular, uncertain limits, and a regenerative nature too, as explained by Halbwachs. For the author, collective memory extends itself up to the point where it can be remembered, i.e. up to the groups' specific remembrances that constitute and give life to it. Because of this, it is in perpetual evolution, transforming itself ceaselessly according to the way its society changes so that it becomes a "histoire vivante".[98] This explains why Nora considers that "[m]emory is *life* (emphasis added), borne by living societies."[99] History, contrarily, is the science of a dead past, as defined by Miguel de Unamuno in 1895, for it follows a didactic need of schematization that separates the continuum of time into fixed periods and epochs. On the subject, Hayden White explains how Romanticism in Europe fostered a general interest in History during the second quarter of the nineteenth century and points out that its early thinkers were preoccupied with knowing "in what sense their own age constituted an advance over, or a decline from, the immediately preceding age."[100] The scholarly interest in understanding the natural laws that governed over historical events, which in turn determined social and cultural transformations, led to the establishment of History as a discipline that could construct historical fact and organize the actions of mankind into interrelated periods of time. This schematization is the result of the recollection and categorization of dates, biographies, events, and data, as de Unamuno points out. According to the author, History is a discipline that freezes the past into a dissected tradition as the science of a dead past which is buried forever in lifeless entities like books and papers, monuments and stones.[101] Almost a century later, Pierre Nora referred to this process as the crystallization of memory at the hands of History because of which infinite, everyday memories are materialized into an endless stock of events and occurrences that a society cannot remember alone by themselves. These *lieux de mémoire* exist for the author as evidence of modern memory, which corresponds to the veneration of the archive and its intrinsic traceability of the past.[102]

Taking into consideration the aforementioned reflections on the subject, the ensuing approach to Campbell's skin-history metonymy will reveal rather a very intimate experience of history, what Halbwachs differentiates from *histoire écrite* as *histoire vécue*.[103] It is here underscored as *intimate* and *vécue* precisely because of its identification with *piel*, thus referring to a specific kind of collective historical memory. One that exists necessarily *opposite* the discipline of western History. Hereafter I will examine how *historia* is deployed in "Nuestra Historia", "Desde Siempre", and "Al llegar" as pertaining to a supranational historical imagination withholding at its center forced diaspora and 'the torment of the absolute unknown'. The section comprising these poems in *Rotundamente Negra y otros poemas* is eloquently entitled "Historia develada", for *develada* is a past participle that means to 'un-veil' (*de-velar*). This makes explicit Campbell's purpose in revealing a mask (History) that conceals something behind it – what shall be defined in the ensuing pages as an *infrahistory*, i.e. an *undisciplined* historical memory. Moreover, the poems entitled "De

---

98   Halbwachs, *La mémoire collective*: 47 and 35: "La mémoire d'une société s'étend jusque-là où elle peut, c'est-à-dire jusqu'où atteint la mémoire des groups dont elle este composée."

99   Nora, "Between Memory and History": 8.

100   White, "Romanticism, Historicism, and Realism": 72.

101   See de Unamuno, "La tradición eterna": 110f. and 114f.

102   Nora, "Between Memory and History": 13.

103   Halbwachs, *La mémoire collective*: 38.

frente" ("Historia develada", *RNOP*) and "El encuentro" (*Palabras indelebles de poetas negras* 2011) will be woven into the discourse by analyzing how the lyrical violence portrayed in these poems carries out the un-veiling of a collective *postmemory*.

The Postmemory of a Nonhistory

Let us return to the Preface discussed at the beginning, which Campbell concludes by stating that her poetry is intended to settle in her people's memory:

> Pienso que es solo el principio de la poesía grande que deseo llegar a hacer, y es para mi gente, la que aun (sic) me mira con ojos extraños preguntándome con qué derecho escribo lo que no he vivido, a lo que respondo que mi poesía solo nace de esta necesidad urgente de seguir andando; de esta necesidad de que la historia se justifique ante nuestra incansable batalla.
>
> Es este mi trabajo que pretende instalarse en la memoria de este pueblo que no baja el rostro y sigue sonriendo.[104]

Campbell dedicates *Naciendo* and the whole of her poetry to '*my* people', which, as we have seen, is delimited by the skin-history metonymy. Despite her in-group membership, the poet states that her people still look at her with strange eyes, asking her how she dare write about what she has not experienced. She dissolves the protest aimed at her by specifying that her poetry is an aesthetic work utilized for vindicating a Black collective memory, not an individual one.

Postmemory

In "The Generation of Postmemory" (2008), Marianne Hirsch defines "postmemory" as the relationship of a second generation to powerful and traumatic experiences "that preceded their births but that were nevertheless transmitted to them so deeply as to seem to constitute memories in their own right".[105] In other words, postmemory has to do with the remembrance of traumatic past events by people who did not live the happenings themselves, but that however constitute an important content matter of their own memory. This is the case, for example, of the descendants of Holocaust survivors upon which Hirsch focuses her

---

[104] Campbell, *Naciendo*: 5. I provide next Mosby's translation: "I think that it is only the beginning of the great poetry that I desire to create, and it is for my people, who still look at me with strange eyes asking me what right do I have write about that which I have not lived, to which I respond that my poetry is only born of this urgent necessity to continue forward; of this necessity that history be justified before our untiring battle. It is this, my work, that seeks to settle in the memory of this people who do not lower their heads and who keep smiling" (*Place, Language, and Identity in Afro-Costa Rican Literature*: 174f.).

[105] Hirsch, "The Generation of Postmemory": 103. The idea of "postmemory" is found in other writers before Hirsch. In fact, she refers to other wordings of the concept before her as "absent memory", "inherited memory", "belated memory", "prosthetic memory", "mémoire trouée", "mémoire des cendres", "vicarious witnessing", or "received history" (p. 105f.). Hirsch discusses how these concepts deploy contradictory meanings that are intrinsic to the phenomenon of postmemory. On the one hand, memory that has not been lived can be somehow transmitted and interiorized as proper, yet on the other, this 'received memory' is different from what the actual witnesses/participants recall.

work. Following the author, who states that postmemory "is relevant to numerous other contexts of traumatic transfer",[106] the ensuing pages appropriate Hirsch's concept and explore the historical memory of the African victim diaspora in Campbell as a received history concerning colonialism, uprooting, and racism.

James Young defined the concept of "received history" In "Toward a Received History of the Holocaust" (1997) by describing it as a "double-stranded narrative that tells a survivor-historian's story and my own [generation's] relationship to it". He brings together the historian's narrative as well as the narratives "indelibly shaped by the survivors' stories" that a person born after the war has received. Together, they constitute what Young defines a "vicarious past": an indirect and delegated story of the past not personally lived but somehow reconstructed as part of the individual's own experience. Young focuses upon the effects of the tellings that are carried out across generations as a way of remembering history to subsequent generations. This act gives life to "another kind of history-telling" which in turn yields a specific kind of postmemory.[107] Campbell's poetry, specifically her skin-history metonymy and the poems dealing with the constitution of an alienating discipline of History, carry out this dynamic exemplary.

In her writing, *postmemory* distinguishes itself from *memory* precisely because of the "discontinuous subjective attachment to what one has *not* experienced [and which exists necessarily] in the mediation of generational distance", as Sandra So Hee Chi Kim (2007) explains postmemory.[108] Nonetheless, it does not refer to a belated or inherited memory that is ultimately and solely an *absent* memory. Instead, it has to do with an intimate memory carried upon the skin. Even though Campbell has not lived the trauma of enslavement and of uprooting herself, her skin-history metonymy holds the *embodied* remembrance of it. Her poetry represents thus a structure of transmission whose content regarding *historia* refers to a series of events that preceded her and that have been furthermore *so deeply* and *affectively* transmitted across time and generations "as to *seem* to constitute memories in their own right."[109] The received historical memory concerning the effects of colonialism comprises not only racism and oppression as the poet clarifies it to Carlos, but the traumatic experience of forced diaspora as well. Because of this, a dual-faced *historia* can be extracted from Campbell's meta-historical poetics. One has to do with the discipline of History, the other with the rupture and erasure of African origins due to forced uprooting and colonialism, constituting a *nonhistory*.

---

[106] Hirsch, "The Generation of Postmemory": 108. The author constantly refers to Eva Hoffman's writings concerning the Holocaust (*After Such Knowledge: Memory, History, and the Legacy of the Holocaust* 2004) and uses Art Spiegelmann's graphic novel *Maus* (1987) in an exemplary fashion to discuss the trope of maternal abandonment as manifestations of postmemory.

[107] Young, "Toward a Received History of the Holocaust": 23, 40, 42, and 41.

[108] Kim, "Redefining Diaspora": 339.

[109] Hirsch, "The Generation of Postmemory": 107.

Nonhistory

Regarding the history of the Black Caribbean – be it French-, Dutch-, English- or Spanish-speaking – Glissant affirms that it does not express itself through a continuum. Unlike European History, its people do not hold a collective consciousness that has been deposited gradually and continuously from its origins up to present times.[110] This is addressed in a similar manner by Frantz Fanon in *Peau noire, masques blancs*, where he states that the plural collectivities of Black people do not have a "long historical past" like Germans or Russians do.[111] Instead, as emphasized by Glissant, the true origins of Afro-descendants are essentially dislocated due to a single brutal rupture: the slave trade. The author emphasizes this rupture with the purpose of debating how Afro-descendants have no History and therefore their story of the past corresponds largely to what Glissant calls a "nonhistory" (*non-histoire*).[112]

When Susan Bock-Morss initiates her discussion on the veiling of slavery in the discourses of Enlightenment philosophers and of the silencing of the Haitian Revolution in Hegel, she defines the economic practice of slavery as "the systematic, highly sophisticated capitalist enslavement of *non*-Europeans as a labor force in the colonies."[113] This system led to the uprooting of Africans as slave subjects of Modernity, brought to new lands in order to endure forced labor and crimes of inhumanity for centuries. According to Glissant, this caused Afro-descendant collective consciousness to be detached of its original past and unaware of itself, "erasing […] collective memory".[114] If Michel de Certeau clarifies that the discipline of History "formally answers to questions on *beginnings*",[115] then given the forced dislocation of Africans and their loss of a proper cultural memory, it is understandable that for Glissant the past of Afro-descendants exists in its negative version. It is a *non*-history insofar it mirrors negatively the acquaintance of origins whose sediment lies instead in the "context of shock, contraction, painful negation, and explosive forces" that the slave trade implied, rather than in the memorial traces of their own sociohistorical conditions and cultural practices.[116] Mainly because the imaginations of the hegemonic Other did not know nor wished to know the cradle of the African civilization before its enslavement. As asserted by Du Bois, "the fond imaginings of the other world […] does not know and does not want to know our power".[117]

Because of the dislocation of a historical/memorial continuum, Glissant considers the story of the past of Afro-descendants to be a nonhistory, where the negating prefix *non-* emphasizes *absence, erasure, silence*. As a daughter of the diaspora, Campbell's poetization

---

[110] Glissant, "History–Histories–Stories": 61f.
[111] Fanon, *Black Skin, White Masks*: 21.
[112] Glissant, "History–Histories–Stories": 62. In the French version, "Histoire, histoires": 224.
[113] Buck-Morss, "Hegel and Haiti": 821.
[114] Glissant, "History–Histories–Stories": 62.
[115] De Certeau explains History's scientific methodology as taking place within a space of writing that wishes to "frame a linear succession which formally answers to questions on *beginnings* and to the need of *order*" – to which a linear conceptualization of time is key (*The Writing of History*: 12).
[116] Glissant, "History–Histories–Stories": 62.
[117] Du Bois, *The Souls of Black Folks*: 14.

of *historia* in "Historia develada" echoes to a large extent Glissant's nonhistory in the form of a supranational *muted* postmemory. As she poetizes it in "Nuestra Historia",

1   La nuestra no nos llegó en capítulos
2   ni de menor a mayor
3   como suele suceder
4   no nos llegó desde el principio
5   desde la cuna
6   desde los primeros días de escuela
7   no nos apareció en los libros
      [...]
      "Nuestra historia", *Rotundamente Negra y otros poemas* (p. 66)

an origin has been displaced and disarticulated, making impossible to carry out a telling of '*our* history' (v. 1: "la nuestra") from its beginnings (v. 4). Here, *historia* represents the story of the past that has no chapters (v. 1) nor sequences of epochs that gradually progress into perfected versions of another one (v. 2), as the principle of *perfectibility* would have it. In his *Vorlesungen über die Philosophie der Weltgeschichte* (1822/1830), Hegel explains the idea of 'men in time' as a progressive development, suggesting a gradation of epochs that "assumes successive forms which it successively transcends; and by this very process of transcending its earlier stages gains an affirmative, and, in fact, a richer and more concrete shape". In other words, History fixes humankind in a progressive succession of periods, in which each one is guided by an impulse of perfectibility, that is, by "an advance to something better, more perfect." Thus, World History is divided in eras named Antiquity, followed by the Middle Ages, then surmounted by the rebirth termed Renaissance, advanced by Modernity and (the debatable) Postmodernity. African history before enslavement and uprooting holds no position within this World History, which Hegel furthermore termed the "Unhistorical": "What we properly understand by Africa, is the Unhistorical, Undeveloped Spirit, still involved in the conditions of mere nature, and which had to be presented here only as on the threshold of the World's History."[118] This explains why Campbell versifies that "nuestra historia" does not have a beginning (v. 4) nor did it appear in history books (v. 7).

As a result, the lyrical-I is frantically looking for 'history' in "Al llegar", as though it had been misplaced:

1   Al llegar, sólo recuerdo haber corrido
2   por todos los rincones buscándola
3   ...tenía que encontrarla
4   ...debía estar en alguna parte.
5   Yo sólo llegué y empecé a buscarla
      [...]
      "Al llegar", *Rotundamente Negra y otros poemas* (p. 59)

The reiteration of frantically searching for it (vv. 2, 5, 24) by running to all corners of the world (vv. 1f., 23), for 'it had to be found, it had to be somewhere' (v. 3f.), mirrors Glissant's consideration that this dislocated past manifests itself as a *neurosis* in Black

---

[118]   Hegel, *The Philosophy of History*: 79, 70, and 117, respectively.

writers given "the torture of true origins" characterized by the "symptom of loss".[119] Therefore the anxiety and obsessive behavior with which the lyrical-I desperately (v. 25: "desesperadamente") searches for her history. The anxious act of looking for it manifests what Glissant specifically explains as the "longing for history" (*le désiré historique*), a yearning that craves that which is irrecoverable.[120] This desire translates itself into an obsession, which is why the lyrical-I is anxious to find something it can't retrieve, what Glissant terms "the primordial source", in other words, "the knowledge of origins, of the origin" before the slave trade.[121]

The "longing for history" that Glissant attributes to Afro-descendant collectivities is thus lived similar to when one carries an acute pain, states the lyrical-I in "Al llegar", a pain substantially located in the past (v. 27). If postmemory refers to, as stated by Kim, a "categorically different kind of memory"[122] that is fundamentally *detached* from the places of the original memories, then Campbell's 'pain situated in the past' represents this detachment.

> 23 Sólo recuerdo haber corrido por todos los rincones
> 24 ...buscándola
> 25 como quien desesperadamente
> 26 buscar reafirmar su existencia
> 27 como quien lleva un dolor agudo en el pasado
> 28 y se resiste a transmitirlo.
> [...]
> "Al llegar", *Rotundamente Negra y otros poemas* (p. 59f.)

The ellipsis used at the beginning of the verses (vv. 3, 4, 24) does not represent omission, but instead a frantic pause. The rhetorical effect is the building up of the despairing atmosphere, where she searches incessantly, running all over the place, pausing, then searching again in new corners. '...I had to find it / ...it had to be somewhere' (v. 4), she states, for even though it is absent, it *has* nonetheless *been*. As emphasized by Campbell, these origins exist but they have been torn away. Mainly stolen. 'But it *was* ours' (v. 28), states the lyrical-I in "Desde siempre", underscoring a stolen possession. The poet also underlines this aspect in her interview with Meza, where she explains why Black writers and poets are responsible for telling their own story of the past. She declaims that their *historia* goes beyond slavery and must be rescued beyond this unasked rupture, for, she underscores, 'we *have* history' (emphasis added).[123]

In *Naciendo*, Campbell stresses in a metaphorical manner that this nonhistory corresponds to a 'dusky past' ("pasado anochecido"), a verse that in turn echoes Glissant's "ob-

---

[119] "Would it be ridiculous to consider our lived history as a steadily advancing neurosis?" (Glissant, "History–Histories–Stories": 65).

[120] Ibid.: 83, n. 8. In the French version, "Histoire, histoires": 260, n. 1: "Le désiré historique, lancinement d'une trace primordiale [...]", and in p. 255 : "[...] le *désiré historique* est la marque de cette hantise."

[121] Glissant, "History–Histories–Stories": 79 and 80.

[122] Kim, "Redefining Diaspora": 339.

[123] Meza, "Memoria, identidad y utopía": 137: "[...] nuestra historia no empieza con la esclavitud, que nuestra historia va mucho más allá, y que antes de la esclavitud, que es un proceso terrible que nosotros no escogimos, nosotros tenemos una historia."

scured history" (*histoire obscurcie*).[124] By qualifying the past upon which nightfall has been casted upon – that is, darkened (from *anochecer*) –, the gloom and despairing character of unknown origins are symbolized through the metaphor of nightfall. A darkness that shades and conceals the object behind its dusk, converting it into the 'absolute unknown'. Coherently, Campbell's lyrical-I in "Al llegar" is searching for *historia* because it has been disarticulated and thus yearns a story of the past told from its beginnings and by its own agents–actors–subjects.[125] The motor force that fuels this longing is the need to re-affirm a proper existence (v. 26). Campbell's poetry implies to a large extent that the loss of a proper past is lived by its people as though they were – as I would like to explain it – *existential orphans*. As stated in "Desde siempre", to grow up without *historia* is the same as growing up *motherless* (v. 44). Even though she had *it*, she was ignorant of *her*. This converted the lyrical-I into an orphan child, alone and motherless, condemned to wander her life unprotected (v. 45: "a la intemperie").

```
41   La tenía
42   siempre la tuve
43   y crecí sin ella
44   igual que sin madre
45   a la intemperie
46   sola.
     [...]
```

"Desde siempre", *Rotundamente Negra y otros poemas* (p. 65)

Whereas in the previous discussion the metonymy made visible the local reality of marginalization and exclusion of Blacks in Costa Rica, in "Historia develada" Campbell transmits a postmemory regarding the loss of African origins because of forced displacement. Since these origins have been eradicated, her postmemory can only recall the rupture that has condemned her memory to a muted nonhistory, lacking a knowledge (memory) of its own origins. However, as we shall see next, her lyric elaborates the subject of enforced uprooting *beyond slavery* by focusing instead upon the *dimension of writing* specific to the discipline of western History. She charges *words on* against it and attacks primarily the alienating *Weltanschauung* imposed by it. Her purpose is to tell a proper story of the past. In order to re-appropriate herstory, lyrical violence is needed because, as demanded by Fanon, "decolonization is always a violent event."[126]

---

[124] Campbell, *Naciendo*: 13 (v. 13). Glissant, "History–Histories–Stories": 63; "Histoire, histoires": 225.

[125] According to Trouillot, "History, as a social process, involves peoples in three distinct capacities". The first one refers to *agents*, which he defines as "occupants of structural positions" such as "workers, slaves, mothers" who belong to a specific strata, class and status, and whose roles are determined according to these positions. As a second capacity, Trouillots defines *actors* by the "bundle of capacities that are specific" to the space-time circumstances of specific situations within the social process. Lastly, he defines *subjects* as the people whose subjective dimensions are "an integral part" of the social process *per se* (*Silencing the Past*: 23 and 24, respectively). In this sense, people are *agents* insofar they are positioned within the social structure undergoing transformation processes in a specific *role*. They are *actors* since they are caught within the spatio-temporal conditions that determine their actions within these processes. Finally, they are *subjects* because they do not undergo nor take part in social transformations in an objective fashion, rather they "define the very terms under which some situations can be described" (p. 23).

[126] Fanon, *The Wretched of the Earth*: 1.

De-Colonial Violence – "De frente" & "El encuentro"

> The argument chosen by the colonized was conveyed to them by the colonist, and by an ironic twist of fate it is now the colonized who state that it is the colonizer who only understands the language of force.
>
> Frantz Fanon, *The Wretched of the Earth*

In both "De frente" as in "El encuentro", Cambpell represents an encounter between two clearly personified entities. In my reading, one refers allegorically to History, which is defined following Glissant's premises. That is, History corresponds to "a highly functional fantasy of the West"[127] whose content of meaning, as he specifies it in *Poetics of Relation*, is tautologically determined by "the sense given by the West to this word".[128] In other words, as the only existing possibility of understanding the development of humankind through "a 'single' historical time",[129] that of western scholarship. The author criticizes the consolidation of the discipline of History as the knowledge of the past that has imposed itself on the collective and particular histories of the West's colonized subalterns like an operatory category through which, in Fanon's words, the colonized "has adopted the abstract, universal values of the colonizer".[130] In this sense, History is a practice (discipline) *and* a discourse (the knowledge of the past) exclusive to Occidental thought – furthermore highly representative of the story of the past through the lens, words, and discourses which have stemmed out of Europe. In fact, Michel de Certeau emphasizes that the knowledge of beginnings and the principle of order, which are inherent to the discipline of History, are "a uniquely Western trait".[131]

On the other hand, the discipline of History redeems itself face to face both in "De frente" and in "El encuentro" against a lyrical voice which I take to personifying Glissant's nonhistory. It is the 'pain situated in the past' from where the lyrical-I's violence emerges, as well as her craving for revenge. By staging lyrical confrontation through hostility, Cambpell's poetic vain carries out a critique of the West's colonizing space of writing parallel to the postmemory of enforced uprooting. In so doing, decolonial violence in Campbell's lyric represents fundamentally the plight between History and memory. The latter specifically representing a *postmemory of a nonhistory*.

If we recall the Preface of *Naciendo* mentioned at the beginning, where Campbell had defended her poetry as stemming out of the need for History to justify itself, in these poems, published over twenty years after *Naciendo*, Campbell's aesthetic vein has now turned to poetic fierceness with the purpose of necessary vindication. The allegorical entities – *History vs. postmemory* – stage hence a play following Fanon's definition of decolonization.

---

[127] Glissant, "History–Histories–Stories": 64.
[128] Glissant, *Poetics of Relation*: 25.
[129] Glissant, "History–Histories–Stories": 92.
[130] Fanon, *The Wretched of the Earth*: 9.
[131] De Certeau, *The Writing of History*: 4.

Decolonization is the encounter between two congenitally antagonistic forces that in fact owe their singularity to the kind of reification secreted and nurtured by the colonial situation.[132]

Campbell's lyrical decolonial violence performs thus what Jean-Paul Sartre noted in his preface to Fanon's *Les damnés de la terre*, where he states that nothing eliminates the marks of colonial violence, except violence itself on behalf of the colonized.[133] Decisively, Campbell's lyrical-I reclaims the recognition of stolen traditions, histories, and cultures subjugated by colonial imperialism from within aggression and it is from violence itself that she reaffirms her existence and cures her 'torment of the past'.

"El encuentro" is a long poem constituted by eighty-three verses divided in six long stanzas. It presents neither rhyme nor metrical structuring and it is composed, like the rest of her poems, as prose poetry. The first verses state that it was necessary to unmask History: "Después de todo era necesario / desenmascarar la historia" (vv. 1f.), a phrase that is reiterated three more times in the unfolding of the encounter (vv. 14, 45, 82). Rhetorically, it justifies the use of violence such as tearing her hair out in chunks (v. 46: "…le arranqué a pedazos trozos del cabello"); biting her face (v. 48: "…le mordí la cara"); or tearing her teeth out (v. 49: "…le arranqué los dientes"). Much like Fanon claims that "only after a murderous and decisive confrontation between the two protagonists" decolonization and liberation are possible,[134] the quarrelsome meeting in "El encuentro" becomes explicitly physical in order to 'make History talk' (vv. 4f.: "era necesario […] hacerla hablar"). In other words, to *un-veil History* signifies in this poem to 'make her spit the truth with blood' (v. 3: "hacerla escupir con sangre la verdad"). Slightly modified versions of this latter verse – sometimes with blood, sometimes with tears – are purposively placed near the former one in order to complement the vindication. Force and physical assaults are used in order to obtain answers concerning a nonhistory with the purpose of decolonizing the foreign Weltanschauung. Lastly, the discipline of History suffers not only because she has been taken down by fierce assaults, but also because she recognizes her mistakes and by regretting them, beseeches thus forgiveness. In stanza four, History discovers she made a mistake (v. 42: "descubre violentamente que se equivocó"), while in stanza five she begs for forgiveness and says she regrets her actions (v. 66: "imploró perdón / me dijo entre voces que se arrepentía").

After the first series of attacks, History in "El encuentro" acknowledges the theft and seizure of nonhistory's beginnings much like the lyrical-I in "Desde siempre" echoes that Blacks were the first to inhabit the Earth (v. 19):

17 Mis tiempos fueron los primeros tiempos
18 los tiempos de todos
19 fuimos los primeros en poblar la tierra.
        "Desde siempre", *Rotundamente Negra y otros poemas* (p. 64)

---

[132] Fanon, *The Wretched of the Earth*: 2.
[133] Sartre, "Preface": lv.: "I believe we once knew, and have since forgotten, the truth that no indulgence can erase the marks of colonial violence: violence alone can eliminate them. And the colonized are cured of colonial neurosis by driving the colonist by force."
[134] Fanon, *The Wretched of the Earth*: 3.

In an intertextual manner, History *screams* (v. 7) and *cries* (v. 9) in "El encuentro" when revealing where humanity began and whose voices were the first to inhabit Earth:

```
7    Me contó entre gritos sobre los primeros
8    las primeras voces en poblar la tierra
9    me contó llorando del principio humano
     [...]
12   y que la humanidad con certeza
13   empezó en África.
```
                        "El encuentro", *Palabras indelebles de poetas negras* (p. 43)

By referring precisely to how humankind's existence began in Africa (vv. 12f.), Campbell's poetic decolonial violence reenacts Fanon's affirmation concerning the search for African cultural dignity before the experience of colonialism. This longing corresponds to a "secret hope" that wants to discover a "magnificent and shining era that redeems us in our eyes and in the eyes of others" and in so doing goes "beyond the present wretchedness, beyond this self-hatred, this abdication and denial".[135] The lyrical-I in "Al llegar" furthermore acknowledges that her *longing for history* is not for *herself*, but for the children (vv. 7f. and 29f.). Hence, her poetic hostility is meant to cure the *ontological orphanness* I referred to previously by projecting its purpose into the future.

The bloody encounter develops along the strophes of "El encuentro" with the purpose of un-veiling History's crimes. In the poem's third stanza and after the first series of attacks – such as being tied down (v. 17: "…le amarré los brazos") and kicked in the womb (v. 19: "…la patee en el vientre") – History commences to talk about the *beginning*:

```
23   me habló del principio…
24   empezó balbuceando palabras casi inentendibles
25   acerca de inventos y civilizaciones lejanas
26   de mujeres negras armando su historia
27   de valiente hombres reinando por siglos
28   de inventos
29   de sueños
30   de escritos
31   de mapas
32   de revoluciones
33   y de evoluciones
34   de sueños
35   de muertes
36   de siembras
37   cosechas.
     [...]
```
                        "El encuentro", *Palabras indelebles de poetas negras* (p. 43f.)

She recalls (imagines) the lost origins that Glissant condemns as intrinsic to Modernity's slave economy and refers figuratively to (what could have been) the cultural and social practices of Africa's distant, yet forgotten civilizations. History begins telling, actually, *stutters* incomprehensible words (v. 24) regarding those kingdoms of brave men and those

---

[135] Fanon, *The Wretched of the Earth*: 148.

Black women who participated in the creation of their disremembered history (vv. 26f.). As well as of those inventions, writing, and maps pertaining to such reigns and histories (vv. 28–31) in which sowing and harvest times (vv. 36f.) were dislocated and obliterated. In the fifth stanza, moreover, History tells her to look in Africa for the truth (vv. 53–55: "me dijo entre súplicas / que buscara en África / toda la verdad").

Throughout the poem, Campbell echoes Fanon's considerations, who states "[t]he white Man was wrong", the European colonizer made a mistake. The Black collectivities it dislocated were not uncivilized nor deficient in humanity, but instead represented millenary civilizations: "I was not primitive, not even a half-man, I belonged to a race that had already been working in gold and silver two thousand years ago."[136] Gilroy also rescues this site of historical meaning from Frederick Douglass's *The Claims of the Negro Ethnologically Considered* (1854), where the author attacks the "hellenomaniacal excision of Africa from the narrative of civilisation's development."[137] As asserted by Gilroy, Douglass's intellectual interest in the ethnological queries regarding Africa "show that the path [of humankind] began in Africa rather than Greece",[138] an origin that Campbell poetizes in her poetry very much like Hall defined Africa as the imagined community for Afro-descendants. Campbell's poetization of an African cradle of civilization, however, suffers against Gilroy's critique. According to Gilroy, the imagination of an "anteriority of African civilisation to western civilisation" is not able to escape the linear time imposed by Modernity's conception of World History and instead becomes "subordinate" to the master narrative of "white supremacy's continuing power". In other words, Africa as an idealized homeland is imagined according to western concepts of tradition, civilization, and time.[139]

Campbell's poetization of Africa as the mythical origin nevertheless participates of the Black circum-Atlantic's intellectual and cultural past by referring to this site of historical meaning as a marker of a supranational historical imagination comprising the shared experience of forced diaspora. In so doing, it rescues the 'absolute unknown' from the shadows of its erasure and banalization. In "Al llegar", hence, Campbell finally finds herstory, which breaks her silence.

37   la encontramos
38   estaba escondida
39   en silencio
40   sola
41   pero finalmente habló…
    […]
"Al llegar", *Rotundamente Negra y otros poemas* (p. 60)

As claimed by Fanon, reclaiming this nonhistory by granting it a voice and the knowledge of displaced origins, *dis-covers* (un-covers, un-veils) the cultural dignity and rehabilitates the grandeur of colonized and eradicated cultures. This, as a consequence, "triggers a change of fundamental importance in the [subaltern's] psycho-effective

---

[136]   Fanon, *Black Skin, White Masks*: 99.
[137]   Gilroy, *The Black Atlantic*: 59.
[138]   Ibid.: 60; cf. p. 113.
[139]   Ibid.: 190f.

equilibrium."[140] Coherently, the lyrical-I in "Al llegar" concludes that they are no longer the same. Acceptance, empowerment and love now assert their existence with certainty (vv. 46–48).

44	… habló…
45	a partir de entonces
46	ya no somos los mismos
47	ahora podemos amarnos
48	sonreír
49	y vivir
50	con voces mucho más ciertas
51	con mucha más certeza.

"Al llegar", *Rotundamente Negra y otros poemas* (p. 60)

The Veil – "Nuestra Historia" & "Desde Siempre"

Lyrical violence as staged in "De frente" and "El encuentro" must be read against "Nuestra historia" and "Desde siempre" in order to comprehend thoroughly the process of de-colonization that Campbell is reenacting. If one the one hand lyrical violence has pointed the way to the vindication of the postmemory of a nonhistory, these poems instead comprise the particularity of *historia* within the making of History as circumscribed by the dimension of *writing*. For de Certeau, the making of History vacillates between two poles since it is both a *practice* as it is a closed intelligible *discourse*. That is, History refers both to a discipline carried out through a precise methodology, as well as to the product of content and meaning that it yields through the written dimension in the form of historical discourse. Fanon describes this discursive mechanism as intrinsic to colonialism, who "turns its attention to the past of the colonized people and distorts it, disfigures it, and destroys it [*l'anéantit*]."[141] It is against these dynamics of alienation, specifically developed by a space of writing, that Campbell's poetic hostility is aimed at. As Kim explains it, postmemory represents an "*imaginative* recollection of a(nother's) prior *reality*".[142] And in the case of Campbell's poetization of nonhistory, this *a(nother's) prior reality* has not only been uprooted and disarticulated. This story of the past has been mainly *veiled* (i.e. distorted, disfigured, destroyed) with disaffecting discourses.

Like Susan Buck-Morss has pointed out, "the sadness of Africans transported to the Indies that resulted in suicides, mutinies, and maroonings"[143] can only be heard among the silence that has repressed it. In an analogous manner, it has not been the Indigenous tribes conquered by Spaniards those who have *written* a story of their own past and of their cultural productions, nor of the brutal clash of civilizations that lastly signified colonialism. This instead has been done from the standpoint of the conquerors of their territories, of

---

[140] Fanon, *The Wretched of the Earth*: 148.
[141] Ibid.: 149. In the French version, "[l]e colonialisme […] s'oriente vers le passé du peuple opprimé, le distord, le défigure, l'anéantit" (*Les damnés de la terre*: 197).
[142] Kim, "Redefining Diaspora": 345.
[143] Buck-Morss, "Hegel and Haiti": 831.

their cultures, of their languages. No reconstruction of the past as History is done without the suppression of those lying prostrate to the emergent victors. Which is why "[t]here is no document of civilization which is not at the same time a document of barbarism", states Benjamin, since History conceals – *veils* – behind the accounts of the victors the "anonymous toil of their contemporaries."[144] Trouillot echoes this perspective in a clear manner: "[a]t best, history is a story about power, a story about those who won".[145] If historical progression does not correspond to *homogeneous, empty time,* for it is filled with the struggles of diverse collectivities, then it must be acknowledged that whoever has emerged victorious from these struggles participates directly in the wording and in the representation of such victories, largely influencing the re-telling of those historical accounts.

Under these considerations, the story of the past becomes a narrative drafted from a unilateral perspective, yielding the one-sided Historicity that Campbell is engaging in "Historia develada". In the attempt of overturning the silence and erasure that comprises nonhistory, Campbell poetizes how Black origins have not only become untraceable and its human dignity silenced, but their historical imagination has been claimed by others. It has been done anew by a practice of textual power carried out with symbolisms and discourses alien to it. Fundamentally, Campbell's poems confront the nineteenth-century systematization of the past that represents the discipline of History "as a European knowledge-building project", which created what Mary Louise Pratt termed a Eurocentric planetary consciousness.[146] In the second chapter of her book *Imperial Eyes,* Pratt (1997) discusses how the exploration of Nature by European scientists in the Americas during the eighteenth century led to establishment of a planetary consciousness that implemented itself as modern Eurocentrism. Her definition of the science of Natural History "as a European knowledge-building project" becomes extremely relevant when discussing History as the western discipline that imposes its understanding and narrativization of the past hegemonically by excluding the stories of Others. That is, as a European model for stor(y)ing the past that was imposed as a universal one upon all cultures and social groups it colonized, determining the historical imagination of those subjugated. As explained by Fanon, in "the Weltanschauung of a colonized people there is an impurity, a flaw that outlaws any ontological explanation."[147] The theft of the past by colonialism has turned the descendants of colonized slaves into parentless beings who miss a source of origins that can explain their own actuality (i.e. a *proper* collective memory). Instead, they carry the burden of a foreign *Weltanschauung* that has created the *sub-altern.* Which is why Quijano affirms that "eurocentrism" does not correspond exclusively to European thought or to the powerful of the capitalist world, but to those educated under their hegemony as well.[148] In this sense, Campbell's lyrical violence does not wish to claim a national culture specifically, but rather a supranational historical imagination which, following Fanon, aims "to pit an

---

144   Benjamin, "Theses on the Philosophy of History": 257.
145   Trouillot, *Silencing the Past*: 5.
146   Pratt, *Imperial Eyes*: 37.
147   Fanon, *Black Skin, White Masks*: 82.
148   Quijano, "Colonialidad del poder y clasificación social": 94: "El eurocentrismo, por lo tanto, no es la perspec-
     tiva cognitiva de los europeos exclusivamente, o sólo de los dominantes del capitalismo mundial, sino del
     conjunto de los educados bajo su hegemonía."

[...] African culture against the universal condemnation of the colonizer."[149] In "Nuestra historia", "Desde siempre", and "Al llegar", Campbell's meta-historical lyric declaims what Fanon so keenly took note of: "[i]t is the colonist who fabricated and continues to fabricate the colonized subject."[150]

In "Desde siempre", the lyrical-I states that 'she always had *it*', but it was somehow ignored by her (v. 32) because it had been deformed by 'others'. It is not until verse 31 that the lyrical-I affirms explicitly that 'I always had *historia*'. In fact, by avoiding the explicit mention of the poem's subject, she deploys other meaningful constructions of sense concerning nonhistory.

6	La tenía
7	siempre la tuve
8	sólo que yo y los míos no lo sabíamos
9	sólo que fueron unos cuantos
10	los que se la apropriaron
11	y la rescribieron
12	y la reinventaron
13	y la rebuscaron
14	y se la quedaron
15	pero la tenia
16	siempre la tuve.
	[...]

"Desde siempre", *Rotundamente Negra y otros poemas* (p. 64)

As a first textual strategy, a process of deformation is detailed in verses 10–14 through a series of actions related concretely to the *space of writing*. Above all, this space is enclosed within 'appropriation' as the starting point (v. 10: "se la apropiaron"), and 'possession' as its outcome (v. 14: "se la quedaron"). The actions that constitute the process between these poles are verbs that gather around the idea of manipulating historical imagination by 're-writing' (vv. 11: "rescribieron") and 're-inventing' (v. 12: "reinventaron") it. Campbell poetizes specifically this manipulative character in the above quoted cluster of verses by the alliteration of the *re-* prefix. It delivers the sense of transformation and of change, that is, to do anew after appropriation. This manipulation is done explicitly within *and* by the space of writing (*reescribieron = reinventaron*),[151] so that entity H becomes thereafter entity ~h. Nonetheless, it is in the skin-history metonymy that this nonhistory is rescued. It is not gratuitous that in "Desde el centro del alma" (*RNOP*) the lyrical-I expresses that she unlearned written history and in a reverse action took to understanding the meaning of her skin: "desaprendí la historia escrita / y me inventé la piel" (vv. 29f.).[152]

Campbell also uses plural versions of the personal pronouns to represent an *us* by 'me and my own' (v. 8: "yo y los míos") and a *them* as those who took possession of *historia*, who happen to be 'just a few' (v. 9: "unos cuantos"). In so doing, Campbell speaks of *historia*

---

[149] Fanon, *The Wretched of the Earth*: 152.

[150] Ibid.: 2.

[151] Recalling Ricœur, History *re-establishes* the past through a historiographical operation involving a documentary stage, an explicative one, and a writing phase, where the action of *re-presenting* and *re-constructing* the past lies at the center.

[152] Campbell, *Rotundamente Negra y otros poemas*: 46.

as an entity that has been first, claimed unrightfully by a few; second, manipulated through the act of writing into a different object; so that, finally, those carrying out this operation kept the discursive end-product for themselves. This process is echoed in verses 20–28:

20 La tenía
21 siempre la tuve
22 pero ellos llegaron y se la quedaron
23 la reconstruyeron
24 con sus propias voces
25 sus propias palabras
26 sus propios colores
27 sus mismas miradas
28 pero era nuestra
29 fuimos los primeros en poblar la tierra.
    […]

"Desde siempre", *Rotundamente Negra y otros poemas* (p. 64f.)

Here, the *space of writing* is exemplified by the verb 'reconstruct' (v. 23: "reconstruyeron"). It is furthermore coupled with nouns pertaining to the act of appropriation through language, giving it a new form with 'their own *voices*' (v. 24), 'their own *words*' (v. 25), and 'their same *views*' (v. 27: "miradas"). *Mirada* in Spanish means *gaze, a look*, and refers to the act of *observing*. Here, it is metaphorically used for worldview (*Weltanschauung*). Once again, the us-them binary is implemented using possessive pronouns (*sus propias*) to delineate a distinction between something proper and something Other, principally denoted by nouns pertaining to the dimension of language (voices, words, discourses).

Along the same line of thought, the poet specifies in "Nuestra historia" how exactly the act of writing at the hands of these 'few others' establishes a discourse that denies the possession of a proper story to those who lay prostrate to them, thus *veiling* it.

13 Ella nos llegó en lenguajes desconocidos
14 fragmentada
15 nos llegó interpretada por los enemigos
16 con sus rostros y sus verdades
17 se nos entregó sucia… vacía
18 hecha pedazos
19 nos llegó en harapos
20 descalza
21 acribillada
22 la recogimos humillada.
    […]

"Nuestra Historia", *Rotundamente Negra y otros poemas* (p. 66)

Campbell expresses here how their story of the past (v. 13: "ella") was not narrated in subsequent chapters nor from its formal beginnings, but was rather displaced and thus erased. It was kept hidden and after it had been interpreted by the enemies (v. 15) who had concealed it, it was delivered disguised with unknown languages (v. 13). This made it incomprehensible and hence in need of decoding. Above all, it was made foreign because it was interpreted with 'masks and truths' (v. 16) belonging to others. This is why, for

Campbell, '*our* history' cannot tell its beginnings 'from its crib, nor was it told in the first days of school, nor did it appear in books' ("Nuestra historia", vv. 4–7).

The Afra-Costa Rican poet reflects in both "Desde siempre" and in "Nuestra historia" upon a distorted interpretation of Black history (v. 1: "la nuestra"), whereby *nuestra historia* is constructed and imagined into reality by others' discourses. The semantic constellation surrounding *historia* in these poems echoes Fanon's critique of an ethnoracial historical alienation due to the discursive hegemony that colonial Modernity created regarding the racial identities it constructed within the economic structure of racial exploitation and slavery. He refers to this alienation as a "psychoexistential complex",[153] which led to the "formation and crystallization of an attitude and a way of thinking and of seeing [*une habitude de penser et de voir*] that are essentially" white constructions.[154] By referring to 'our history' as something that has been rewritten, reconstructed, and reinvented by a few others, Campbell specifies how precisely this *habitude de penser et de voir* was crystallized through a space of writing that installed the "coloniality of being", that is, the "ontological difference or sub-ontological difference" of the colonial subject. It is across "invisibility and dehumanization" that "the violation of the meaning of human alterity [is carried out] to the point where the alter-ego becomes a sub-alter" vis à vis the European colonizer. As defined by Maldonado-Torres (2007), the coloniality of being is "coextensive with the production of the color-line in its different expressions and dimensions".[155] Campbell locates this in the *written* dimension.

The consequence of this procedure is Du Bois's double consciousness "as two unreconciled strivings" caught between identities that are torn apart by the veil of race. Double consciousness reveals "no true self-consciousness" and instead a self-understanding is done only "through the revelation of the other world".[156] Campbell poetizes this 'other world' and this 'twoness' very much in tune with Du Bois's precepts and Fanon's *habitude de voir et de penser* by condemning that 'our history' has been 'clothed in unknown languages, fragmented, interpreted by the enemies with their masks and truths' ("Nuestra historia", vv. 13–16). '*Our* history', she states, has been desecrated by the imposition of a foreign system of thought and self-comprehension. The impossibility to recognize a proper past and a dignified humanity due to the negative connotation given to her *piel* by the discourses of the colonizer, determine Campbell's skin-history metonymy as a struggle

---

[153]   Fanon, *Black Skin, White Masks*: 5.

[154]   Ibid.: 114. In the French version: "le jeune Noir adopte subjectivement une attitude de Blanc. […] Peu à peu, on voit se former et cristalliser chez le jeune Antillais une attitude, une habitude de penser et de voir, qui sont essentiellement blanches" (*Peau noire, masques blancs*: 120).

[155]   Maldonado-Torres, "On the Coloniality of Being": 256, 257, and 242, respectively. In his article, Maldonado-Torres discusses the concept of the coloniality of Being as a conceptual project stemming from Decolonial intellectuals. He grants the concept's authorship to Walter Mignolo (*The Darker Side of the Renaissance* 1995), who takes Fanon as a departing source while elaborating on the subject by relating Heidegger's ontological philosophy (*Dasein*) and Descartes *Meditations* to "Fanonian mediations". This in order to explain the "sub-ontological difference" of the colonial subject as addressed by Fanon in *Peau noire, masques blancs*. For the author, the concept *per se* responds to "the effects of coloniality in lived experience" rather than exclusively on the mind (p. 242). Language has therefore a predominant importance. What I find valuable in the concept of the "coloniality of Being" is the emphasis it sheds upon the "dehumanization" of the person of color, which Campbell also reflects upon by poetically criticizing the re-writing of History at the hands of those in power.

[156]   Du Bois, *The Souls of Black Folks*: 7.

against the West's hegemonic *space of writing*. It furthermore justifies her use of violence in "El encuentro" and "De frente".

Bernabé, Chamoiseau and Confiant (1999) refer as well to this *twoness*, this incompatibility between two beings – one ontologically estranged, the other violently imposed – as an inherited *foreign gaze* (*regard extérieur*) dictated from an outsider's perspective in the form of "an exterior look [upon] our reality".[157] Campbell echoes the authors' claims with *sus propias voces, palabras, miradas* ("Desde siempre": vv. 24–27). Together with Fanon, the authors of *L'Éloge de la Créolité* affirm European colonialism has painted "our lives with the colors [*couleurs*] of Elsewhere"[158] – reiterated by Campbell in "Desde siempre" with "sus propios *colores*" (v. 26). Colonized collectivities and its descendants like (but not only) Afro-descendants were homogenized under the image of the colonizer/s, thus alienating their own understanding of their cultural productions that with time became forgotten ("Desde siempre", vv. 6–8: "La tenía / siempre la tuve / solo que yo y los míos no lo sabíamos"). This justifies lyrical decolonial violence as a need for healing such a *defilement* of Campbell's *historia*, which has been delivered dirty and empty, shred to pieces, in rags, barefoot, and gunned-down ("Nuestra historia": vv. 17–21). In a heartfelt image, the lyrical-I states in a warming tone how '*we* picked *her* [nuestra historia] up, crushed and humiliated' (v. 22).

History as an academic discipline of the West holds an exemplifying position in this dialectic of power. Campbell's poems in "Historia develada" dialogue thus with Glissant's claim, who defines nonhistory against History with a capital H as "a totality that excludes other histories that do not fit into that of the West".[159] While also implying the discursive hegemony from which double consciousness emerges. As explained by the Defenders of *Créolité*, this proceeds from two logics, "one monopolizing our minds submitted to its torture, the other living in our flesh ridden by its scars".[160] Campbell's skin-history metonymy withholds this opposed binary logic and explains simultaneously why she poetizes a hostile confrontation between History and nonhistory in order to *discover our skin... and our history*. For it is specifically through violence – "this violence rippling under the skin [*à fleur de peau*]", states Fanon[161] – that alienation and the longing for history can be cured.

If we recall Campbell's "El encuentro", the poet corrects nonhistory's 'torment of true origins' with the use of hostility, since a knowledge of her displaced beginnings has been granted thanks to it ("El encuentro": vv. 23–37). Even though this knowledge will never substitute what has been forever lost, the act of violence has brought upon the *naming* of what has been silenced, erased, and veiled. This is highly symbolic, for it is a performance that yields reappropriation together with redemption. As stated by Sartre, once violence

---

157 Bernabé/Chamoiseau/Confiant, *In Praise of Creoleness*: 87. In the French version: "[n]otre situation a été de porter un regard extérieur sur la réalité de nous-mêmes [...]" (*Éloge de la Créolité*: 25).

158 Bernabé/Chamoiseau/Confiant, *In Praise of Creoleness*: 80. In the French versión: "[l]'Assimilation, à travers ses pompes et ses œuvres d'Europe, s'acharnait à peindre notre vécu aux couleurs de l'Ailleurs" (*Éloge de la Créolité*: 18).

159 Glissant, "History–Histories–Stories": 75.

160 Bernabé/Chamoiseau/Confiant, *In Praise of Creoleness*: 80.

161 Fanon, *The Wretched of the Earth*: 31. In the French version: "[m]ais revenons à cette violence atmosphérique, à cette violence à fleur de peau" (*Les damnés de la terre*: 75).

"explodes, they [the colonized] recover their lost coherence, they experience self-knowledge through reconstruction of themselves".[162] In other words, through (symbolic) violence, the 'pain located in the past' is healed, liberating itself.

Campbell's *historia* (postmemory of a nonhistory) has seized what was rightfully hers by the forced surrendering of its adversary (the discipline of History). In so doing, her lyrical-I accomplishes Glissant's imperative command: "the repossession of the meaning of our history" is only possible "with the awareness of the real discontinuity that we no longer *passively* live through" (emphasis added).[163] Campbell's lyrical-I is not passive, instead she has made her opponent cry bloody tears in "El encuentro" (v. 61: "Ella estaba llorando / lloraba con sangre"), whereby she claims her responsibility in the ruptured discontinuity. And even though the lyrical-I feels sorry for the History she has shattered to pieces, she is quick to affirm that she deserved her violent death, for it was necessary: "… se lo merecía / era necesario desenmascararla" (vv. 81f.). Her own destructive behavior is thus justified. Following Fanon, Campbell's violent appropriation of a supranational collective postmemory has acted as "a cleansing force (*désintoxique*)" that aims to rid herstory of the inferiority complex and of a passive attitude while simultaneously restoring justice.[164] In fact, the lyrical-I in "De frente" states that the hostile confrontation between her and History was foreordained, for it was *written* (v. 1 and v. 2: "Estaba escrito") that the 'absolute unknown' would be vindicated by destroying her oppressor's face (v. 4: "le destrozaría la cara"). "De frente" moreover justifies violence as the only way to make History pay (v. 8) for her long-lasting *words* (v. 13) and *arguments* (v. 14):

```
5    Era necesario
6    alguien tenía que hacerlo
7    alguien tenía que enfrentarla
8    y hacerla pagar.
9    Alguien tenía que desbaratar su orgullo
10   devolviéndole lo que ella
11   durante siglos hizo.
12   Alguien tenía que obligarla
13   a tragarse sus palabras.
14   Alguien tenía que rebatir sus argumentos
15   con violencia.
     [...]
```
            "De frente", *Rotundamente Negra y otros poemas* (p. 63)

The Advocation

Campbell's meta-historical poetry engages the narrativization of the story of the past through History as an act of thievery. Searching for the origins of her nonhistory, she has

---

[162] Sartre, "Preface": lv.
[163] Glissant, "History–Histories–Stories": 92.
[164] Fanon, *The Wretched of the Earth*: 51. In the French version: "[a]u niveau des individus, la violence désintoxique. Elle débarrasse le colonisé de son complexe d'infériorité, de ses attitudes contemplatives ou désésperées. Elle le rend intrépide, le réhabilite à ses propres yeux" (*Les damnés de la terre*: 96).

declaimed the traces of its erasure and its subsequent veiling through a hegemonic space of writing. She has hence carried out her literary combat following Glissant's call to arms: "the duty of the writer is to explore this obsession". Her meta-historical poetry has the particularity of arching this obsession from the distant past towards actual times, in order "to show its relevance in a continuous fashion to the immediate presence."[165]

In so doing, another meaning of *historia* can be now added to the skin-history metonymy. The semantic constellations surrounding *historia* in "Historia develada" construct the opposition History/*infrahistory*, which deploys itself in a dual manner. The Latin prefix *infra* – meaning 'below', 'on the underside' – acts as a metaphor for the positioning of Campbell's *historia* as a *subordinated* historical imagination. On the one hand, the prefix qualifies *historia* as something that does not hold proper existence *by itself* because it exists only in relation to another story of the past upon which it is *dependent*. That proclaimed by History. Indeed, the confrontation in "De frente" and in "El encuentro" performs a significant appropriation and reversal of her subordinated position. On the other hand, the prefix indicates the position in which this *infrahistory* has been placed, i.e. under the mantle or under the authority of a hegemonic discourse. Because of its subordinate position, it has been inevitably distorted by it, as expressed in "Desde siempre" and "Nuestra historia". The reiteration of verbs and nouns pertaining to the space of writing makes this evident as the source of double consciousness, the psycho-existential complex, and the foreign gaze.

Because of this, Campbell's intertextual poetic discourse on *historia* across the here analyzed poems becomes a sort of oxymoron by which contradictory terms are placed in conjunction. The lexeme has a literal form (*historia*), whose figurative meaning points towards another semantic (postmemory). Of course, one could reproach me here why should the reader interpret literal *history* as figurative *memory* in Campbell's verses, being as they are in conflict? How could fundamental contraries be in such a close relationship that the mention of one could be understood as the other? The answer to this lies precisely in the identification of *historia* with *piel* and in its structures of transmission, which shall be explored next. For Campbell's *Black-Woman-Mother triad* rests upon the need to make new something old. Something that only memory can do.

The Black-Woman-Mother Triad

> What is at issue here is not how history can recover memory,
> but, rather, what memory will bequeath to history.
> Patrick Hutton, *History as an art of memory*

In the previous pages, the skin-history metonymy was addressed as representing a supranational historical imagination with two fundamental contents. Campbell under-scores her *skin* as the element that allows her not only to actualize her collectivity/ies' suffered experiences to Carlos on the one hand, but also to refer to the story of the past as a collective *postmemory* concerning an erased, silenced, and veiled *infrahistory*, on the other.

---

[165] Glissant, "History–Histories–Stories": 63f.

The ensuing discussion shall explore yet another semantic of *historia* by focusing on Black/s' invisibility in Costa Rican cultural memory. The following pages overturn this position by rescuing the Black-Woman-Motherhood triad from Campbell's poetry and its relationship to the skin-history metonymy as an expression of a new racial cartography of the Costa Rican imagined community.

If we recall Harpelle's claim which put in motion the present study – "the [Afro-Caribbean] community has remained a footnote in Costa Rican history and a forgotten part of the national heritage"[166] – Campbell's poetic deployment of *historia* as the imposition-inheritance-consolidation of double consciousness through the exclusion from and imposition of master narratives can also be identified in Costa Rican cultural memory. The skin-history metonymy can be grounded within the tension break between the Caribbean diaspora and the Costa Rican imagined community, for just as Afro-descendants represent the ignored and erased agents-actors-subjects of History, Afro-Costa Ricans as well were absent in, have been erased of, and finally were assimilated to Costa Rica's imagined community as people *in* but not *of* the country. Their story of the past in Costa Rica constitutes also an *infrahistory* of the (outdated) imagined community. Education and literature played a fundamental role in this process.

The Disappearance

In 1900, Ricardo Fernández Guardia affirmed before the readership of *El Heraldo de Costa Rica*, his incapacity to find literary inspiration in the Indigenous element. He argued against literary nationalists his incapacity to write ten lines in honor of, or even about, *una cholita* from Pacaca.[167] For he found far more interesting a Parisian woman or a *josefina* [from San José, the capital], than "the most tempting of those robust Indigenous women".[168] For him, it was obvious that an ancient Greek woman could inspire a Venus de Milo, but an Indigenous woman from Pacaca could only inspire another Indigenous woman from Pacaca.[169]

Fernandez's claims elaborate a hierarchy of female beauty where the European woman possesses the mythical throne, while the Costa Rican woman – specifically from the capital – holds second place by necessity. The Indigenous one instead is cast aside as not relevant, whereas Black women do not even form part at all of this hierarchy. In such a silent shadowing, in its not-being-mentioned-at-all, Fernández simultaneously denies and erases

---

[166] Harpelle, *The West Indians of Costa Rica*: 183.

[167] Fernández Guardia, "Nacionalismo literario" (November 10, 1900): "[…] incapacidad para escribir diez líneas en honor, o sobre una cholita de Pacaca" (cf. p. 336). All quotes are taken from Amer et al, "Polémica entre nacionalismo y literatura" (1984), which reunites the controversy regarding nationalism in literature in one single document. Retrieved from http://www.revistas.una.ac.cr/index.php/letras/article/viewFile/4396/4226 (12.07.2015).

[168] Fernández Guardia, "Nacionalismo literario" (*La República*, May 24, 1900): "[…] más interesante una parisiense o una [josefina], que la más apetitosa de esas robustas indígenas" (Amer et al, "Polémica": 310).

[169] Fernández Guardia, "El nacionalismo en literatura" (*El Heraldo de Costa Rica*, June 24, 1894): "se comprende sin esfuerzo que con una griega de la antigüedad […] se pudiera hacer una Venus de Milo. […] [pero] con una india de Pacaca sólo se puede hacer otra india de Pacaca" (Amer et al, "Polémica": 196f.).

the presence of Blackness in the conformation of the national population, making evident the ideological engineering of Costa Rica. Fernandez's comments are exemplary of what Ronald Soto-Quirós (1998) has researched as the "disappearance" of the Indigenous element in the ethnoracial perception of the Costa Rican population,[170] which applies likewise to the erasure of the Afro-American element in its racial cartography.

Like both Anderson and Hobsbawm have taken note, not only did modernization of the state lead to a homogenization and standardization of its inhabitants under the premise of ethnicity, but the education system was central to this purpose. In fact, print-media and institutionalization of primary education served official nationalism by transmitting its self-imageries and national metaphors to the people being imagined. Indeed, educational texts regarding the history, geography, and conformation of the Costa Rican community carried out precisely what Anderson has defined as central in the consolidation of an imagined community: print in the service of the young nation-state. It was the means for consolidating the feelings of communion and of belonging by allowing an imagery to be fixed and internalized by all members within the community through the written word, independent of their social or economic position. Not only that, it was a powerful ally in erasing the heritage common to all Latin American nations, i.e. mestizaje, while simultaneously inventing a common past that contradicted this reality.

In 1869 primary education had become free and obligatory in Costa Rica by Constitutional right and from 1880 onwards, liberals found in the educational system the strongest apparatus for disseminating the elite's ideals. In his study of "official nationalism" and "auto-immigration" policies in Costa Rica, Palmer (1995) lists a series of liberal textbooks as examples of how the narratives of whiteness and ethnic homogeneity were drafted and delivered to the popular social strata from the oligarchical perspective. Likewise, Jussi Pakkasvirta (1997) underscores how education was one of the strongest and most effective means of delivering sentimental imaginings of Costa Rica down vertically to the lower social strata,[171] where the creation of a common past and an ethnic principle of nationality were intertwined as foundational discourses of the imagined community. Costa Rican intellectuals eliminated the African and Indigenous heritage by discursively creating a direct lineage with Spaniards of colonial times. History books, for example, set a myth of national origin with the biography of Columbus as an introductory chapter to the history of Costa Rica (Francisco Montero Barrantes, *Elementos de la Historia de Costa Rica* 1892).[172] While geography textbooks described the Costa Rican racial cartography by stating that with almost insignificant difference, all of Costa Rica's inhabitants are white and constitute a homogeneous population (Barrantes as well, in *Geografía de Costa Rica* 1892).[173] Moreover, in what Pakkasvirta has defined as the first "national" work in Costa Rica, Joaquín Bernardo Calvo stated in *República de Costa Rica. Apuntamientos geográficos, estadísticos e históricos* (1887) that even though 'a primitive race' exists in Costa Rica, its quantity is meager and is completely separated from the civilized population, which he

---

[170] Soto-Quirós, "Desaparecidos de la Nación" (1998).
[171] Pakkasvirta, *¿Un continente, una nación?*: 115.
[172] Quoted in Palmer, "Hacia la 'auto-inmigración'": 78.
[173] Quoted in ibid. and in Palmer, "Racismo intelectual": 115: "[…] con poquísimo, casi insignificante todos los habitantes de Costa Rica pertenecen a la raza blanca. […] La población es homogénea […]".

characterizes as 'white, homogenous, healthy and robust'.[174] And still in the twentieth century (1909), it was stated that 'in only four of the Latin American republics predominates at present the white race; one of them is Costa Rica' (Ricardo Fernández Guardia, *Cartilla histórica de Costa Rica*).[175] What these textbooks have in common with each other is the denial of miscegenation in the country, which helped erase it (see "Imagining Costa Rica", Part I).

"It is good for everyone to know how to forget", states Renan.[176] But, *why* is this so exactly? Mainly because the elaboration of a common past is achieved by selecting certain memories over others, forgetting those unchosen and lastly erasing them. As claimed by Roach, "forgetting, like miscegenation, is an opportunistic tactic of whiteness. As a Yoruba proverb puts it: 'The white man who made the pencil also made the eraser.'"[177] Coherently, and as the textbooks make it evident, Costa Rica *forgot* its miscegenation. *Denied* its colonial heritage. *Imagined* pureness within mestizaje. *Disappeared* the Indigenous autochthonous populations. And *erased* Afro-American presence for the sake of the 'Costa Rican exceptional difference'. Campbell's skin-history metonymy confronts this.

Like in "Historia develada", the subject of a *silenced* (made invisible) *historia* appears in *Rotundamente negra* as well, where Campbell refers to it in a supra/national manner. Let's take for example poem VI of the third section:

```
46   Betty, Mishell o yo
47   hubiéramos dado cualquier cosa
48   por tener una palabra de consuelo
49   o una maestra
50   o una canción
51   o un cuento
52   en donde fuésemos nosotras las protagonistas
53   en donde nadie nos quitara el derecho
54   a ser dueñas de nuestra propia historia.
     [...]
```
III.VI, *Rotundamente negra* (p. 74)

In these verses, the lyrical-I nostalgically thinks about how she and others like her (v. 46: "Betty, Mishell o yo") would have done anything for their presence to be found in documents where they were the main figures (v. 52: "las protagonistas"). She regrets mostly that the right to own their proper history had been seized by others (vv. 53f.). Campbell echoes the same argument in Poem VIII of the first part, where she refers to how her son holds in his eyes images of a near Africa and next to those images lie those ignored, whose

---

[174] Quoted in Pakkasvirta, *¿Un continente, una nación?*: 116: "En Costa Rica, si bien existe la raza primitiva, su número es exiguo y está completamente separada de la población civilizada. Esta es blanca, homogénea, sana y robusta, y une a estas condiciones físicas las que son de un valor más estimable: su laboriosidad y afán por su cultura y prosperidad." Cf. Soto-Quirós, "La difusión del etnotipo costarricense" (2012).

[175] Quoted in Palmer, "Hacia la 'auto-inmigración': 19: "[...] solo en cuatro de las repúblicas hispanoamericanas predomina actualmente la raza blanca; una de ellas es Costa Rica." Fernández mentions Argentina, Chile, and Uruguay as the other three countries, which according to Palmer, represented the countries that the liberals wished to compare Costa Rica to.

[176] Renan, "What is a nation?": 16.

[177] Roach, *Cities of the Dead*: 6.

names do not appear in books (vv. 51–53: "al lado de los ignorados / al lado de los nombres / que no están en los libros").[178]

To be also underscored is the use of the feminine plural as the marker of the subject pronoun in Poem VI quoted above. By expressing the desire to possess themselves the story of their past, Campbell laments that she and other women like her would have done anything to be portrayed as *agents–actors–subjects* of times past and present, whereby they could have been the owners of their own representation. She furthermore specifically names *women* as protagonists and actors of herstory by consciously selecting the plural feminine form. Rather than choosing the masculine mark, traditionally used in Spanish to encompass all gender forms under one homogenous representation, Campbell writes in "nosotr**a**s las protagonist**a**s" (v. 52) and "dueñ**a**s" (v. 54). In so doing, she takes poetic action against what Anzaldúa has claimed, i.e. "[w]e are robbed of our female being by the masculine plural. Language is a male discourse."[179] Campbell thus overturns Black female voicelessness through the gender choice.

The purpose of her literary combat is indeed to place women at the center of her poetry as those un-represented historical agents. It is them who she characterizes in Poem VIII (Part I) of *Rotundamente negra* as *historia*'s ignored ones, who have 'sprinkled history with their Blackness' (vv. 30f.):

```
28   esas
29   las de la historia
30   las que rociaron de negrura y pasión
31   a la historia.
32   Me refiero a las mismas
33   las ignoradas.
     […]
```

I.VIII, *Rotundamente negra* (p. 27)

This supranational reality of Black invisibility in master narratives does not correspond solely to the duality of History/*infrahistory* because of colonialism, but it can also be denoted within the specific case of Costa Rica's cultural memory, as for example in the depiction of Blacks in national literature at the turn of the nineteenth and twentieth centuries. A few examples shall serve to prove this point so as to deepen the glocal aspects of Campbell's metonymy.[180]

"¡Mira mamá, un mono!"

The periodical publication of "El huerfanillo de Jericó" (1888) by Manuel Argüello Mora represents a first example of misrepresentation of Blacks in Costa Rican literature. In it, an orphan boy is manipulated into doing criminal deeds and keeping silent by a man named *el negro Phelps*, who is portrayed as evil-hearted, cruel, and murderous. "Yo soy muy bueno

---

178 Campbell, *Rotundamente negra*: 27.
179 Anzaldúa, *Borderlands*: 76.
180 I thank Silvia Solano Rivera and Jorge Ramírez Caro for pointing my way towards this literature while they were still in the process of editing *Racismo y antirracismo en literatura. Lectura etnocrítica* (2017).

y cuido mucho los chiquitos; pero si esos niños hablan o dicen lo que me ven hacer, los mato sin misericordia."[181] Another text that presents Blackness pejoratively is Carmen Lyra's short story "La negra y la rubia" (*Cuentos de mi tía Panchita* 1920), where the author opposes a beautiful white, blonde, good girl to a hideous, thick-lipped, bad and spoiled Black one. The short story, thus, reproduces colonial binaries of racial identities.[182] Beyond these negative stereotypes, national literature also *reinvented* the diasporan experience in Costa Rica by constructing and imagining it from an outsiders' perspective. On the one hand, the depiction of Caribbean workers in the region is carried out by Joaquín Gutiérrez in *Puerto Limón* (1950) through dialogues that express their being through broken Spanish and with Black characters that represent the hired help. On the other, Carlos Luis Fallas portrays in *Mamita Yunai* (1941) the United Fruit Company's Caribbean workers as those who enjoyed dance and rum, which sometimes led to violent fights between them. In his novel, the mestizo workers who watched this show exclaim, "¡[p]arecen congos!". That is, *howler monkeys*.[183]

Likewise Gutiérrez's *Cocorí* (1947), a story of a little Afro-Costa Rican boy who falls in love with a white girl who visits his home place by arriving on a ship. Upon their encounter, and in the original published version, the little girl tells her mother: 'look mom, a monkey!'[184] This phrase was later modified by the author – the single one – and in the following versions we read "[m]amá, ¡mira qué raro!"[185] Both exclamations reproduce the white girl's startled impression as if the Black boy were a cause of perplexity instead of another human being. In 2015, Epsy Campbell (Shirley Campbell's sister) and Maureen Clark, (the only) two Black politicians in the legislative assembly, petitioned for the definite removal of this children's book,[186] which was part of national primary school curricula since 1996. A petition already past in 2003 by the Minister of Education because of its racist overtone, itself a repeated claim firstly voiced by Quince Duncan and Lorein Powell in 1983 and that President Abel Pacheco "solved" in 2000 by substituting "the obligatory reading list for primary school with a list of suggested titles".[187]

Together with literary representation, intellectuals also drafted essays at the first half of the twentieth century where their depiction of Black people in Costa Rica followed the precepts of scientific racism. Luis Dobles Segreda, Secretary of Public Education during the 1930s, presented in 1927 a petition to Congress regarding the necessary preparation of Black teachers in order for them to teach Black students in Limón. In it, Segreda characterizes the psychology of the colored man as 'preferring to obey blindly than to

---

181 Argüello Mora, "El huerfanillo de Jericó": 123.
182 Lyra, "La rubia y la negra": 131f.
183 Fallas, *Mamita Yunai*: 153.
184 An original version is quoted in Bosch, *Clásicos de la literatura infantil-juvenil de América Latina y el Caribe*: 33: "¡Mamá, mira un monito!"
185 Gutiérrez, *Cocorí*: 14.
186 Regarding the Cocorí controversy, see Muñoz-Muñoz, "Nacionalismo blanco, presa e inversión de las víctimas durante la 'polémica Cocorí'" (2019); Murillo, "Un libro infantil agita el racismo en Costa Rica" (2015); Duncan, "Qué aprendí leyendo a Cocorí... En defensa de don Joaquín" (2015); Villanueva, "El libro infantil *Cocorí*, ¿una obra racista?" (2015); and Rodríguez Jiménez, "¿Hay elementos racistas en *Cocorí*? (2004).
187 González, *Resistance and Survival*: 64f.

comprehend with reason why he should obey.[188] Similarly, in "El negro, sentido de alegría" (1937), Yolanda Oreamuno claims that Blacks 'do not have a refined capacity for thought, are slow in thinking creatively, passionate like an animal in heat, and guided by instinct'.[189] Like Segreda and Lyra, Oreamuno reproduces colonial racial binaries of the superior/inferior, rational/irrational, barbaric/civilized kind by asserting that the 'white man' has pure thought because, quoting Oreamuno, 'he has accumulated centuries of civilization and of reflexive thinking', while the Black man is still in puberty. She goes on to explain that he is 'a boy whose mentality is still in diapers: reckless, obedient, and submissive.'[190] With these examples in mind, it makes sense then why Bourgois declares that Blacks in Limón were able to mobilize upwards "only with respect to class; [but] they remained oppressed *ideologically*" (emphasis added).[191]

If we recall the official textbooks of primary and secondary education mentioned above, it is then obvious why Campbell claims she would have done anything to be the protagonist of her own story. Blacks (and Indigenous people) were denied a proper re-presentation in the imagination of Costa Ricans, which is why, in an analogous manner, it is relevant to reiterate how the supranational historical imagination Campbell poetizes refers to a local specificity as well. In Poem VI (Part III), she tells of little Shamara's concerns about the future, which the lyrical-I quietens by referring to the children she will bear and to whom she will be able *tell a new story*: "contarles una nueva historia" (v. 10).[192] I have chosen to translate here *historia* as 'story' due to the composition of the verse, whose verb is *contar*, i.e. to tell, to narrate. Campbell refers to *historia* as a story of the past that is waiting to be told, which Mosby has recognized as one of the main motifs in *Rotundamente negra*, expressed as "[d]reams of a new day and a new world".[193] It represents thus an undisciplined history whose silenced stories are waiting to be voiced, just as the lyrical-I tells Shamara. For Bock-Morss, the exclusion and erasure of infrahistories in western scholarship is in fact "due to the construction of disciplinary discourses through which knowledge of the past has been inherited".[194] This hereditary character implies an acquired, handed-down understanding of the past that has been institutionalized within a structural framework regarding an official (western) intellectual history and whose Other alternatives are effectively silenced in a structural manner.[195] They remain, as Trouillot pronounces it, only

---

[188] Segreda, "El estado y la cultura de los hombres de color": 401: "La psicología del hombre de color es diferente, su carácter es más recio y opone mayor resistencia a la voz de la simpatía. Prefiere obedecer ciegamente a comprender la razón que le invita a la obediencia."

[189] Oreamuno, "El negro, sentido de la alegría": 110: "El negro es tosco de pensamiento y lento de imaginación, es apasionado como un animal en celo, pero se guía en esto por instinto, por una fuerza tan natural como la que mueve las piernas para caminar o hace abrir los ojos para ver […]".

[190] Ibid.: 111: "Un negro de veinticinco años es un niño al que le han crecido las desmesuradamente las piernas, y con su mentalidad en pañales, es irreflexivo, obediente, sumiso y alegre."

[191] Bourgois, *Ethnicity at Work*: 109.

[192] Campbell *Rotundamente negra*: 73.

[193] Mosby, *Place, Language, and Identity in Afro-Costa Rican Literature*: 204.

[194] Bock-Morss, "Hegel and Haiti": 845.

[195] Following White, "The Tasks of Intellectual History": 80: "As long as a dominant social group's way of viewing the world operates sufficiently well to contribute to the maintenance of the group's power, then other, subordinate or recessive groups' ideals and ideas will generally be perceived as mere curiosities, as outright errors, or as heresies to be suppressed – not as possible alternatives; and the intellectual leaders will be little inclined to treat them as objects of serious philosophical or historical investigation."

a footnote within a narrative of global domination,[196] much like Harpelle refers to Blacks in Costa Rican national heritage. This is why for Campbell 'our history', Afro-descendant *and* Afro-Costa Rican, cannot tell its beginnings from its crib, nor was it told in the first days of school, nor did it appear in books.

"What other silences would need to be broken? What *un*-disciplined stories would be told?", Bock-Morss asks her readers.[197] The following verses of Poem VI reveal how it will disclose and thus make known *other stories*, specifically those erased, silenced, and veiled. By telling a new story, Shamara may hope to offer her unborn children answers about her true name (vv. 13f.: "acerca de su nombre completo / el verdadero) in the hope of eliminating the trauma of the loss of identity imposed by the re-naming of slaves. This 'new story' may hopefully deliver answers about her place of origin as well (v. 15: "de su lugar de origen"), that place from where nonhistory stems out of darkness. That is, from the cultural death abyss Glissant referred to as the 'absolute unknown'. She goes on to state how 'we are all here' with a specific objective, or precisely because of something special, because they are making new something old: "haciendo fresca / una historia vieja" (vv. 26f.).[198] For Mosby, these verses "ensure the realization of this dream for a 'new day' and the control for the revitalization of history."[199]

This brings us back to the skin-history metonymy and the primordial premise in Campbell's literary combat: the need to *discover our skin... and our history*. Mosby correctly acknowledges that Campbell's *historia* "move[s] from a distant legend to living in the present day."[200] In so doing, the story of the past determined by the skin-history metonymy is still relevant, in a continuous manner, to the immediate. Fundamental to this process are the structures of transmission concerning this postmemory. Thus, the metonymy becomes powerful insofar it reinvests a memorial affective force to the story of the past that has been erased, silenced, and veiled through forced displacement, slavery, and the West's hegemonic discursive universe. It activates memorial structures by embodying them through the mention of *skin* and granting them simultaneously a *corporeal voice*. Kim affirms postmemory "is at once haunted by the collective and yet undeniably individual and private".[201] Which is why it is of no surprise that Campbell's skin-history metonymy is embedded within a web of individual *and* collective memories, for even though it speaks of an embodied collective nonhistory, *historia* in Campbell is also poetized as deep-rooted in individual memory and transmitted across a familial structure. In this sense, Campbell's reiterated poetic coupling of *piel* with *historia* across a Black-Woman-Mother triad confronts Afro-invisibility and overturns silence from a specifically Afra-perspective.

---

[196]   Trouillot, *Silencing the Past*: 107.
[197]   Bock-Morss, "Hegel and Haiti": 865.
[198]   Campbell, *Rotundamente negra*: 73.
[199]   Mosby, *Place, Language, and Identity in Afro-Costa Rican Literature*: 205.
[200]   Ibid.
[201]   Kim, "Redefining Diaspora": 344.

The Triad

The Black-Woman-Mother triad becomes of upmost relevance regarding the skin-history metonymy that Campbell reenacts in Poem VIII of the first part of *Rotundamente negra*, with which now I proceed to conclude the study on Campbell's meta-historical poetry. Poem VIII is an eighty-verse prose poem where she engages the relationship between skin and history through a triangular constellation that deploys the metonymy from a gendered perspective. Specifically, across a matrilineal structure of transmission. The poem starts by acknowledging that she now has two children, referred to constantly across the poem to affirm to the readership that it is through, and because of them, that she understands the meaningful memory of her skin. She loves her daughter, for she is the first one that forces her to understand that it is a 'daily art to have the skin of this color' (v. 40f.):

34 Amo a esta hija mía
35 porque de primera me está obligando
36 a volverme la piel
37 hasta la raíz
38 me está obligando
39 a entender
40 que es un arte diario
41 tener la piel de este color.
      [...]
           I.VIII, *Rotundamente negra* (p. 26f.)

Further on she claims that she loves her children because through them she understands that this skin 'must be beaten into love' (vv. 54–57: "Amo a mis hijos / porque con ellos entiendo / que esta piel / hay que amarla a golpes"). And finally, towards the end of the poem, she states that her black skin is aligned with an uproar felt in the womb: "[...] esta piel negra tiene que ver / con clamor que se siente desde el vientre" (vv. 67f.). That is why in Poem V of the last section, her lyrical-I declares herself mother and Black (v. 25: "a declararme madre y negra").[202] Campbell's embodied historical postmemory intertwines the categories of being Black, being Woman, and being Mother through a deeply introspective perspective. As Donald K. Gordon (2003) has pointed out, the "Black woman is central to Campbell's poetry and the nexus Black-woman-mother is an important theme in *Rotundamente negra*."[203]

By coupling *piel* and *historia* with her personal experience of motherhood, Campbell's verses make evident Hirsch's consideration that kinship structures reinforce "the *living* connection between the past and the present, between the generation of witnesses and survivors and the generations after".[204] Kim reaffirms this by considering the familial space "as a shared space of dwelling" that "becomes a crucial unit of transmission of an embodied form of memory".[205] On the subject, Beatriz Sarlo (2006) addresses in a problematic fashion the difference between history and postmemory by stating that the subjective dimension

---

202 Campbell, *Rotundamente negra*: 71.
203 Gordon, "Shirley Campbell's *Rotundamente negra*: Content and Technique": 437.
204 Hirsch, "The Generation of Postmemory": 125.
205 Kim, "Redefining Diaspora": 349 and 348.

implicit in the mediation act is what allows this type of memory to be understood as Hirsch's *postmemory*. Its content matter is transmitted through kinship structures and as a result it is cut across by the subjective dimension expressed in personal terms.[206] In fact, what is at stake for Hirsch is the way in which such memories are mediatized trans-generationally, and refers to two different modes of transmission, familial and affiliative. The first refers to an intergenerational *vertical* transmission of memory through a direct connection between the parents and their direct second generation (children). Whereas the latter refers to an intragenerational *horizontal* identification among the postgeneration as a whole, beyond the direct second generation. As stated by the author, the affiliative mode of transmission is broader enough to encompass a larger collectivity and creates an "organic web of transmission", while clarifying that the familial structure is the one that facilitates the affiliative mode of transmission.[207] In Campbell's skin-history metonymy, grandmothers, mothers, and her children become the structure that creates the organic web of transmission, connecting Campbell's *historia* to a supranational collective postmemory through the epidermal element. The skin-history metonymy is in fact exemplary of the relationship between a familial and an affiliative transmission of a postmemory, delineating a matrilineal heritage.

Moreover, the intertwined relationship between skin, history, and motherhood reflects the interplay between individual and collective memories. Philosophers and historians alike have described History as the counterpart of memory. For Nora, the former is objectified and represents the past as an object belonging to everyone and no-one, whence claiming universality. Memory contrarily "takes root in the concrete", which is why it is eternally tied to the present of human beings.[208] Nora goes on to add that collective memories are plural – and yet individual. A thesis he takes from Maurice Halbwachs, for whom memory acts as a Janus-faced sensibility that results from the intertextuality between individual and collective memories, as well as between real and imagined ones occurring at the intersection between remembrance and forgetfulness.[209] Ricœur resumes Halbwachs's considerations by stating that individual memory is but an *enclave* of collective memory.[210] Thus, personal memories, understood as the act of recalling past experiences, are never completely *individual*. Rather, they are installed within a social network upon which it simultaneously rests, so that both are concurrently influenced by one another. Neither one is independent of the other, rather they rely on each other for the fabrication of things-past and are engaged in a ludic relationship of individual and collective imaginations. As Halbwachs explains it: "nous ne sommes jamais seuls",[211] which is why we never remember alone. Or inversely, as Augusto Roa Bastos writes in his masterpiece *Yo, el supremo* (1974), "memoria de uno solo no sirve para nada".[212]

---

[206]   Cf. Sarlo, *Tiempo pasado*: 130f.
[207]   Hirsch, "The Generation of Postmemory": 114f.
[208]   Nora, "Between Memory and History": 9.
[209]   Halbwachs, *La mémoire collective*: 6f.
[210]   Ricœur, "L'écriture de l'histoire": 734: "la mémoire individuelle ne serait qu'un rejeton, une enclave, de la mémoire collective."
[211]   Halbwachs, *La mémoire collective*: 6.
[212]   Roa Bastos, *Yo, el supremo*: 9.

Throughout Campbell's verses, the interplay between the individual and the collective is made evident by installing an individual, intimate expression of Black postmemory by referring to her personal understanding of Blackness from a gendered perspective, focusing on motherhood as actualized through her two children (familial transmission). This in turn is linked intrinsically to the recognition of a supranational historical imagination as a daughter of diaspora and by the female generations before her (affiliative transmission), to which the skin-history metonymy is crucial. In poem VIII of *Rotundamente negra*, the lexemes *piel* and *historia* are not placed contiguous to one another and are instead deployed in an interdependent manner along the poem, until she declaims,

58	entiendo que esta piel
59	tuya
60	nuestra
61	se viene ensamblando
62	desde que no había historia
	[...]

I.VIII, *Rotundamente negra* (p. 27)

that her *piel* has become 'assembled' (v. 61: *ensamblarse*), that is, it has been gathering its own existence ever since before there was *historia* (v. 62). Here *historia* refers to the discipline of History as the established knowledge of the past, while *piel* acquires a memorial meaning. It represents a history that is alive, agreeing with Nora that *memory is life*.[213]

As acknowledged by Díaz-Diocaretz regarding Latin American women poets, Campbell too deploys a "strategic discursive consciousness" which speaks "through a woman's voice". This voice finds its sound and articulations across the Black-Mother-Woman triad. In so doing, she reveals "a woman-oriented position" from which she names and declaims *her-story*.[214] Accordingly, Campbell poetizes in Poem III of the first part of *Rotundamente negra* that she finds herself telling her daughter Tiffany that they are Black (vv. 44f.: "contándote de pronto / que somos negras").[215] Complementarily, the lyrical-I affirms in the ensuing Poem VIII that it is together with her daughter that she construes their every-day Blackness, just like their grandmothers and mothers before them (vv. 24–27: "Es junto a mi hija / que construyo esta cotidianidad (sic) nuestra / de ser negras como nuestras abuelas / y nuestras madres").[216] Grand/mothers are furthermore the women that she has characterized as *historia's ignored ones* (v. 33: "las ignoradas") and yet are fundamental in the lucid interplay of postmemory's transmission in the form of a skin-history metonymy. In fact, it is not only through her children that Campbell recognizes the meaning of her skin, but specifically through a matrilineal heritage that dictates her relationship to herstory, transmitting a transgenerational postmemory. Campbell's grandmothers are "revered as the repositories and dispenses of the truths of the past", as referred to by Janet Jones (1995), an element that she furthermore finds in African American poet Rita Dove. For Jones, each author "paints portraits of the older generation as the dignified custodians and transmitters of truths of

---

213 Nora, "Between Memory and History": 8.
214 Díaz-Diocaretz, "I will be a Scandal in your Boat": 91 and 92, respectively.
215 Campbell, *Rotundamente negra*: 17.
216 Ibid.: 26.

their heritage" and in so doing, they "convey common aspects of the world of the diasporan people of the Americas."[217]

In an intertextual manner, grandmothers hold a special place throughout Campbell's poetry. In *Rotundamente negra* she writes that in her own blood she recognizes a grandmother and a long row of singing women, which helped her understand herself woman and comprehend herself Black.[218] In *Naciendo*, the Afra-Costa Rican poet speaks of grandmothers that tell their grandchildren stories, transmitting them an ancient mourning.[219] Among these female characters, her grandfather is portrayed as a man of few words that did not kiss them when someone else remembered them the color of their skin.[220] A grandfather whose hands hold furthermore the untold story of the past.[221] In "A una abuela negra cualquiera", a two-part, six-stanza and forty-seven-free verse poem, Campbell presents an old proud Black woman who walks along the streets while recalling her dreams, her frustrations and pains, her loss and her joys.[222] And in *Rotundamente Negra y otros poemas*, Campbell consecrates three poem-letters to the grandmothers she did not meet in the section "Entre cartas y de abuelas", whose 'wrinkled hands were filled with stories (*historias*)'.[223]

Not only is the link Black-Woman-Mother fundamental in the transgenerational transmission of the skin-history metonymy and its glocal aspects regarding racism, exclusion, and misrepresentation, but most importantly in the need for *making new something old*. This corresponds to a postmemory recreated both *individually* through a gendered perspective regarding motherhood – something personal felt in the womb – as well as *collectively* through the grand/mothers before her. Hence, individual and collective memory correspond to two types of memories. One is interior, recalled from inward and whose souvenirs are specific, personal, autobiographical, and largely emerging from experiences lived within closed collectivities such as family, school or friends. Campbell's personal experience of motherhood reenacts this *interior* memory. The reference to grandmothers and mothers in her poetry instead represent an *external* memory, which corresponds to broader societal dynamics, translated into a collective memory by which the social construction of a group's *Selbstbild* is carried out.[224] Moreover, in Campbell's poetry *matrifocal* kinship structures identify skin with history within a familial, matrilineal structure of transmission, so that Campbell becomes poetically engaged in the declamation

---

[217] Jones, "Portraits of a Diasporan People": 37 and 34, respectively.

[218] Campbell, *Rotundamente negra*: 79: "descubrí en mi sangre / de pronto una abuela / a una hembra / y a una hilera larga / de mujeres cantando" (vv. 44–48) and later on: "me entendí mujer, me entendí negra" (vv. 56f.).

[219] Campbell, *Naciendo*: 23: "nos protegen de duras verdades / cargándonos las venas / de su antiguo luto" (vv. 30–32).

[220] This grandfather "ni nos besó la frente / cuando hubo quien / nos recordara el color de la piel" ("Abuelo", *Naciendo*: 42).

[221] Campbell, *Naciendo*: 24: "Nadie nos contó la historia / un día / detrás de la tarde la encontramos / vestidas de multitudes / en las manos de mi abuelo."

[222] Ibid.: 40f.

[223] Campbell, "Mi abuela a mí no me habló", *Rotundamente Negra y otros poemas*: 56: "No le alcanzó la vida / para preparar guisos de abuela / en ollas ennegrecidas de tanto uso y de tanto amor / guisos con sabor a manos de abuela / arrugadas y llenas de historias".

[224] Cf. Halbwachs, *La mémoire collective*: 26.

of her diasporan community's postmemory as something carried out by women.[225] It's therefore the *Mothers of the Diaspora* those who lay at the center of a supranational historical imagination.

In an interview with Consuelo Meza, the poet explains to her how a patriarchal society has led her to undertake the task of "giving new meanings to the history of women, since it is imperative to re-signify the role mothers, grandmothers, and great-grandmothers had in constructing who they are today." For Campbell, *Black women* are the ones called upon to do this:

> Efectivamente, es la tarea que tenemos nosotras de darle nuevos significados a esta historia de mujeres, a este papel que han tenido las madres y las abuelas y las bisabuelas en la construcción de lo que nosotras somos hoy, las mujeres somos las que tenemos que hacerlo.[226]

Her poetry attempts to correct how Black women have historically been placed at the bottom of society's structure: below the white man, the white woman, the Black man, and below the *cholita from Pacaca* too. Meza explains how Campbell represents grandmothers, mothers, and daughters as agents of social change, for it is in them that injustice and discrimination are synthesized.[227] As the poet tells Meza, her lyric is not (only) about an aesthetic struggle, but a feminist one as well whose most important motives are Black women and a literary combat as an "instrument of self-esteem" for her Afro-community.[228] Campbell recognizes the value of her poetry as an empowering act where a Black woman is writing and speaking *about* Black women: "Es importante mi poesía porque es importante que una mujer negra esté hablando de las mujeres negras."[229] Thus, Campbell's lyrical-I *speaks.*

---

[225] In a groundbreaking study, Henriques (1949) classified the Caribbean family in four types (Christian family, faithful family, maternal, or grandmother family, and keeper family). He argued that except in the Christian family, "the woman is quite often the dominant member of the family" ("West Indian Family Organization": 33). He furthermore affirmed the "Jamaican lower-class woman both in social and in family affairs has a prominence which is absent in the equivalent European society" (p. 36). As studied by sociologists and anthropologists in contemporary times, the Caribbean family has been acknowledged as *matrifocal* because it has a "'mother-centered' dynamic" where the "mother-child bond" is valorized above others (Ho, "Caribbean Transnationalism as a Gendered Process": 36). Joycelin Massiah (1983) defined "matrifocality" as "a concept denoting the role of the mother is structurally, culturally and effectively centered" (*Women as Heads of Household in the Caribbean*: 12). Christine Barrow (2001) claims the concept has been reinterpreted to imply "an adequate adaptive response to a particular set of circumstances", such as high rates of male unemployment ("Men, Women and the Family in the Caribbean": 421). She also affirms (1996) matrifocality refers to "the association of close and enduring family ties with the mother-child bond" (*Family in the Caribbean*: 170). These definitions agree upon R.T. Smith's (1973) original conceptualization of the term, for whom matrifocality refers to "a situation in which '*it is the women in their role as mothers* who come to be the *focus* of the relationships'" (quoted in Barrow, "Men, Women and the Family in the Caribbean": 423). See Smith, *West Indian Family Structure*: 216, who affirms "the importance of maternal grandmothers in the West Indian family organization has been greatly overemphasized."

[226] Meza, "Memoria, identidad y utopía": 135.

[227] Ibid.: 136.

[228] Ibid.: 132: "Y la causa que a mí me toca es la causa de las mujeres negras, la causa del pueblo afrodescendiente. El proyecto más grande que yo tengo es apoyar el movimiento afrodescendiente a través de mi poesía, como un instrumento de autoestima para los pueblos."

[229] Bragado, "No éramos negros" (11.02.2017).

Eulalia Bernard's portrayal of her mother as an interstitial cultural figure becomes here relevant to Campbell's triad, for it carries out as well an important matrilineal structure of cultural transmission. Bernard places her mother at the center of the knowledge she has of herself as a daughter of an Afro-cultural/deterritorialized diaspora in catholic Costa Rica. She expresses this knowledge by straddling cultural borders between Africa, the Caribbean, and Costa Rica. In "Mi madre y el tajamar" (*My Black King*), Bernard tells how it was at the cutwater (*tajamar*) that she learned from her mother's lips the solemn truth about her forefathers:

```
22   Desde ahí, del tajamar,
23   Aprendí de los labios de ella
24   La solemne verdad
25   Sobre mis antepasados
26   (En esta tierra abandonados.)
     [...]
```

She goes on to recreate the scene in which her mother tells her about her African forefathers, who are furthermore indifferent to Costa Rican identification cards, to a Christian God, and to a Holy Virgin.

```
34   "Ahí están", me decía
35   "Tus abuelos koromanti,
36   Tus abuelos fanti,
37   Que no saben nada
38   De cédulas de identidad, ni
39   De cristos crucificados
40   Sobre los rieles de los muelles, ni
41   De santos sordos, ni
42   de vírgenes pardas."
     [...]
```
Bernard, "Mi madre y el tajamar" (My Black King, n.p.)

Likewise, in "Invocarte Madre" (*Ciénaga/Marsh*), she appeals to her mother and identifies her remembrance as 'a walk towards wisdom between processions and carnivals, among calypsos and Holy-Maries, and lit up by electric organs and bongos':

```
1    Invocarte Madre
2    es revivir Domingos de fiesta
3    y diluvios de altares vistosos
4    y esa abundancia de pan y sol.
5    Invocarte Madre,
6    es escuchar coros de ilusiones,
7    en alborozos calipsos y avemarías
8    encendidos por órganos y bongos.
9    Invocarte Madre,
10   es una caminata, hacia la sabiduría
11   entre procesiones y carnavales;
     [...]
```
Bernard, "Invocarte Madre" (Ciénaga/Marsh, p. 35)

Bernard's mother holds thus an intermediate position between Costa Rican culture and her Afro-origins. On one side, bongos and calypsos lay next to her African ancestors, while on the other, electric organs and Holy-Maries play together under the image of a crucified Christ. Her mother is the one that permits Bernard to comprehend herself *and* the kaleidoscope of her multiple identities, granting her a fundamental role in the transmission of a supranational historical imagination. In her poetry, Bernard specifically addresses her rhizomatic pluricentrical belonging as a *Costa Rican* daughter of the diaspora.

Campbell and Bernard both counteract the myth of the 'white, national family' by portraying their families in their poetry. In so doing, they necessarily re-present a new racial cartography of the country's imagined population as *Afra*-Costa Ricans. Dlia McDonald's poetry also participates in this contestation by dedicating a series of poems to her family in Part I of *...la lluvia es una piel...* With them she recreates a humble portrait of the Caribbean community that outgrew their condition as immigrants and instead left their legacy beyond cities, docks, and harbors in the families that established themselves in Costa Rica. McDonald refers to her mother as 'an elegy of religious songs and ritual mystery' (I.19),[230] who tells her of her grandmother, a woman 'with white hair and annatto skin, wise and Jamaican' (I.18).[231] Her father instead was 'Black, tall as an eclipse, and with blue eyes' (I.21).[232] Her sister is depicted as a 'Black woman, serene like a palm tree, rhythmic as a dance of hungry rattlesnakes' (I.22).[233] While her brother is a 'Black man with the sounds of bamboo' (I.23).[234] McDonald's representation of her family extends itself to her aunts, who, 'like all Black women', knew who to sow (I.24).[235] And to her cousins as well, who when traveling in the train to Siquirres, held 'a wide smile in their eyes' (II.52).[236] In Poem 28 she states her 'tribe' is a song 'similar to a Black man who dances while walking'.[237] McDonald thus fixes in writing the representation of the Costa Rican Black family, whereas mothers are represented by both Campbell and Bernard as *the* "cultural guardians" of their collectivities.[238]

In conclusion, Afra-Costa Rican poetry has come a long way since Pío Víquez's "Marina" towards the end of the nineteenth century, where he homologs Limón to the mulatto woman, describing it as withholding kindness, seduction, and defiance. He goes on to describe Limón as a hot cacao-colored woman with lips that resemble thirsty flames,

---

[230] McDonald, *la lluvia es una piel*: 35; vv. 1–4: "Mi madre, ... / es una elegía / de canciones religiosas / y misterio ritual".

[231] Ibid. 34; vv. 10–14: "[...] y me habla de una mamá buena, / con cabello blanco y piel de achiote, / con ojos de canela, / sabia y jamaiquina, / sabia y señora."

[232] Ibid.: 38; vv. 2–5: "Pará era negro, / con estaturas de eclipses / cabeza brillante / y ojos azules".

[233] Ibid.: 39: "Mi hermana, / es una negra / serena y palmera; / rítmica y elaborada / como un baile / de cascabeles / con hambre."

[234] Ibid.: 40; vv. 1–4: "Mi hermano / es un negro / con los sonidos / del bambú."

[235] Ibid.: 41; vv. 1f.: "Como todas las negras, / mis tías saben coser."

[236] Ibid.: 75: "... / y mamá dijo: / 'Ahí van tus primos...' / Volví a ver, / y siempre, / recuerdo un vagón lleno de negros / que venían del colegio en Siquirres / y una sonrisa ancha / en los ojos de todos. / Después, / conocí a mis primos."

[237] Ibid.: 46; vv. 1–3: "Mi tribu / es una canción: / un negro que camina bailando [...]".

[238] Mosby, *Place, Language, and Identity in Afro-Costa Rican Literature*: 205.

exceptionally seductive high breasts, and thighs of intoxicating delight.[239] Afra-Costa Rican poetry has also declined the perception of the philosopher Constantino Láscaris in *El Costarricense* (1975), who, when speaking about young Afra-Costa Ricans in Limón, refers to them as 'those young ladies (the mature ones are usually very interesting as well) with hips like the bongo drum, firm breasts like sweet lemons, and wide lips where one could get lost for a whole day.'[240]

Traces of People with History

The skin-history metonymy reenacts pluricentrical belonging through a supranational historical imagination whose semantic content is threefold. On the one hand, the contiguity of *piel* with *historia* allows Campbell to poetize racial discrimination and marginalization as global dimensions of contemporary Blackness. A reality reproduced in the coming of age of the Afro-Costa Rican minority. Simultaneously, the metonymy defines an untold story of the past because this *historia* has been erased, silenced, and veiled by the written dimension of western History. This in turn yielded Campbell's *historia* in the form of *undisciplined infrahistories*, where for example she, little Shamara, and others like her would have done anything to be the protagonists of their own representations in the white-washed imaginations of her nation. Also, the skin-history metonymy underscores *historia* as an embodied *postmemory*, which is carried upon the skin in the form of a *nonhistory*. Campbell's lyrical combat advocates the need of acknowledging this. Finally, by expressing the metonymy as a gendered experience and from the perspective of the Black-Woman-Mother triad, the Mothers of the Diaspora represent the cultural agents and sources of *historia*, giving *piel* a meaning that goes beyond the racist ideologies inherited from European colonial Modernity. The intimate level of this triad is supported upon her two children and complemented with Bernard's and McDonald's poetization of their respective families. Together, their poetry carries out a new depiction of the country's racial cartography across individual, familial, and affiliative memories.

Campbell's skin-history metonymy grants Blackness a refreshing and empowering self-esteem that claims presence and visibility in Costa Rican cultural memory by way of a supranational historical imagination. Which is why I believe the most eloquent conclusion here is to let Campbell speak for herself by recalling the poem "Rotundamente Negra", where she refuses in a boastful manner to silence her voice, her skin, her Blackness. This complements the epigraph quoted at the beginning of this chapter from "Me gritaron negra" by Afro-Peruvian artist Victoria Santa Cruz (1922–2014).[241] Her majestic perfor-

---

[239] Quoted in Rojas/Ovares, *Cien años de literatura costarricense*: 20: "Los términos para describir esta tierra la detallan como una mujer: 'con su tez de cacao encendido como la sangre nueva; con su ubérrimo alto pecho, a las cuatro luces seductor, descubierto; con su muslo que tiembla avaro de embriagador deleite'."

[240] Láscaris, *El costarricense*: 98: "[…] las limonenses: esas jovencitas (las maduritas también suelen ser muy interesantes) de talle cimbreante, caderas como el bongó, pechos firmes como limones dulces y labios amplios para perderse un día entero."

[241] Cruz's personal explanation behind the lyrics of "Me dijeron negra" recalls to a large extent Du Bois's narration of the visiting-card episode when he was a little boy in school (cf. Du Bois, *The Souls of Black Folks*: 6.) See the documentary entitled *Retratos* (Part 3): https://www.youtube.com/watch?v=754QnDUW.

mance-poem[242] is echoed by Shirley Campbell with her Black lyrical activism, which stands as a beautiful vociferation that concludes the discussion of the skin-history metonymy in an articulated manner. In her reluctance to deny her Blackness, Campbell has *discovered her skin… and herstory.*

> Me niego rotundamente
> a negar mi voz
> mi sangre y mi piel
> y me niego rotundamente
> a dejar de ser yo
> a dejar de sentirme bien
> cuando miro mi rostro en el espejo
> con mi boca
> rotundamente grande
> mi nariz
> rotundamente Hermosa
> y mis dientes
> rotundamente blancos
> y mi piel
> valientemente negra.
> Y me niego categóricamente
> a dejar de hablar
> mi lengua, mi acento y mi historia
> y me niego absolutamente
> a ser de los que callan
> de los que temen
> de los que lloran
> porque
> me acepto
> rotundamente libre
> rotundamente negra
> rotundamente hermosa.

III.XIII, *Rotundamente negra* (p. 89)

---

[242] For Santa Cruz's performance of "Me dijeron negra", see https://www.youtube.com/watch?v=cHr8DTNRZdg.

Eulalia Bernard – The Telling of an InfraNational Linguistic History

> Ethnic identity is twin skin to linguistic identity – I am my language.
> Gloria Anzaldúa, *Borderlands*

As seen in the previous analysis of poetry by Dlia McDonald and Shirley Campbell, Gilroy's understanding of Black Atlantic subjects as people in but not necessarily of the modern, western world is highly relevant to the history of the Afro-Costa Rican minority. On the one hand, Campbell's skin-history metonymy speaks of marginality and racism in a global capitalist system, where Costa Rican Blacks stand as an eloquent example of this. They too were indispensable to Costa Rica because they helped develop the Costa Rican economy and the Caribbean province into a habitable space, as McDonald's poetics of landscape testifies it. On the other hand, by pinpointing Campbell's skin-history metonymy to Costa Rican specificities it was made visible how a metaphysical ethnonational racism hindered their right to belong both to the democratic nation, as to its imagined community. This closing section shall bring now to the fore the dynamics of assimilation and of marginalization of Blacks in Costa Rica. This time through an infranational story of the past told by, in, and through multilingualism as enacted by Bernard through code-switching (CS).

Born in 1935 to Jamaican immigrants in Limón, Eulalia Bernard is emblematic of the rhizomatic experience that holds no one-truer-identity as expression of her origins. To put it in Bryce-Laporte's words, Bernard pertains to the creole culture of Limón, "neither fully Costa Rican nor fully Jamaican any longer".[1] Dorothy Mosby qualifies her poetry as "doubly Creolized" since it "reflects a largely African-based culture from the West Indies, which has then been transformed by the Hispanic culture of Costa Rica."[2] As a writer, therefore, she is highly representative of the diffracted Caribbean-Central American cultural continuum. With specific relation to the Costa Rican scenario, she is paramount to the culture of resistance that historizes the Costa Rican Caribbean at the *linguistic* level. An aspect that makes this visible is her poetic multilingualism, the core thematic of the ensuing discussion.[3] Literary multilingualism, as will be approached in Bernard, refers to the use of two or more languages *within* a single individual poem, *between* poems pertaining to a single compilation, as well as across the entirety of her extensive cultural production. The languages across which she speaks are Spanish, English, and the other mother tongue of Afrolimonenses, Limon Creole.[4]

---

1. Bryce-Laporte, *Social Relations and Cultural Persistance*: 2.
2. Mosby, *Place, Language, and Identity in Afro-Costa Rican Literature*: 118.
3. "Die Terminologie ist […] wenig genormt", states Werner Helmich (2016) regarding the conceptual manifoldness of multilingualism in literary criticism. Helmich refers to diverse compilations to underline the various names given for the same subject. German Romance Philology speaks of *literarische Mehrsprachigkeit* or *Vielsprachigkeit*; while Italian Romanists refer to *plurilinguismo* (*letterario*), *poliglotismo* or *eteroglossia*. French scholars instead name it *hétérolinguisme* or *écritures métisses*, whereas other scholarly traditions refer to it by signaling its multiple nature: multililingual literature, multilingüísmo or multilinguisme (Helmich, *Ästhetik der Mehrsprachigkeit*: 14f.).
4. There are different terms for referring to the creole mother tongue of Afrolimonenses. The first linguist to

Coherent with the cultural atmosphere of the 1970s, when Black awareness had conceptualized Afro-Latin American cultural production in the form of what Richard L. Jackson (1979) called "literary blackness" (e.g. *Negrismo, Négritude, Harlem Renaissance, Antillanité, Créolité, Afrorealismo*),[5] Bernard recorded in 1976 and as a young woman a vinyl with declamations of poems in English, in Spanish, and in Limon Creole entitled *Negritud*, with which she went door to door trying to awaken engagement among Blacks of Limón, so remembers Shirley Campbell.[6] The vinyl, rather innovative because of its transmedial form and content, has remained *unheard* by literary critics who have approached Bernard's cultural production. Though her publications have in fact overshadowed the orality of her *Negritud*, studies by me (2020) and scholar Marianela Muñoz-Muñoz (2019) from the University of Costa Rica have rescued it from silence and are currently overturning its voicelessness. Nineteen ninety-one was the year that *My Black King (MBK)* was published in the United States of America by the World Peace University with many of these once vinyl-recorded poems. Recalling to a certain extent the vinyl composition itself, *MBK* is also divided in five acts plus two sections entitled "Special" and "Encore".[7] The majority are written in English, except for a few exceptions in Spanish. The poems in *MBK* exhort the Black wo/man to emancipate and call upon freedom and revolution in a racist world, while recurrent sites of meaning are Africa, Blackness, the mother-child relationship, as well as relating to Costa Rica through Limón's dock workers or bilingual campesinos. The section entitled "Creole Talk" is exemplary of Bernard's literary attempt of manifesting her rhizomatic identity through multilingualism. It intertwines English with Spanish, while nuances of Limon Creole color her poetics as she expressed it to Shirley Jackson (2003): "Creole language [...] is rich, rhythmical, and fascinating."[8] Almost a decade earlier, she had published the Spanish-written *Ritmohéroe (RH 1982)*, whose free-verse poems not only address her Jamaican origins and the conflict regarding Afro-Costa Rican assimilation, but also poetize Limón and the positive features

---

study the language, Anita Herzfeld, termed it "Limon Creole" in 1977, later writing a book entitled *Mekatelyu: la lengua criolla de Limón* (2002). "Mekatelyu" translates to "let me tell you something" in standard English (p. xvii). This nomenclature has been however discarded, as I once heard Afro-Costa Rican writer Quince Duncan reject it during the international symposium "Convergencias Transculturales en el Caribe. Literatura, arte, cultura, historia, comunicación" (November 18–21, 2015 in San José/Limón, Costa Rica). Besides "Limon Creole", Elizabeth Winkler refers to it as *Limonese Creole* (1998) or *Limonese Creole English* (2013), while Mario Portilla (2000) speaks of "inglés criollo" and Tanja Zimmer (2011) of "criollo limonense." Throughout these pages I use "Limon Creole" so as to underline that this language has a particular story of the past as a proper linguistic entity, yet however installed within a linguistic continuum comprising both English and Spanish.

5   Jackson, *Black Writers in Latin America*: 1–14 ("Introduction: The Problems of Literary Blackness in Latin America"). For discussions on literary blackness in the Spanish-speaking Caribbean, see also Jackson, *Black Writers and the Hispanic Canon* (1997); Watson, "Black in Spanish and Latin American Literature", 25–47 (in *Afro-Hispanic Literature* 1991), and Roberts, *Main Themes in Twentieth-Century Afro-Hispanic Caribbean Poetry* (2008).

6   Meza Márquez, "Memoria, identidad y utopia": 124: "Shirley recuerda a Eulalia Bernard tocando puertas, casa por casa, para vender su libro y un disco de acetato en el que leía sus poemas. La poeta, señala Campbell, es una mujer que nunca aceptó un 'no' por respuesta."

7   Act I – Recalling; Act II – Africa Soul; Act III – Creole Talk; Act IV – Freedom; Act V – Image.

8   Jackson, "Our Weapon is Strong Language": 125.

of cultural contact as well as condemning inequality. Poems that express her childhood memories also appear.

At the beginning of the twentieth century came *Ciénaga/Marsh* (*CM* 2001). This compilation, written the first part in Spanish and the second in English, as the title elegantly suggests it, takes part as well in delineating this multiple and fluid sense of pluricentrical belonging through multilingualism. In fact, it becomes exemplary of the literary combat that multilingualism in Bernard undergoes. Translanguaging in *Ciénaga/Marsh*, that means, writing a first part in Spanish and the second one in English,[9] lastly represents multilingualism in Bernard's œuvre as an *engagé* literary practice having the function of what Mandred Schmeling and Monika Schmitz-Emans (2002) define as an aesthetic resistance.[10] By representing her community's linguistic heritage, multilingualism shakes and shatters ("erschüttert") the symbolic cultural capital of Costa Rican monolingual foundations for, as Mosby points out, "Bernard's deployment of language is another challenge to the country's assertion that it is exclusively a Spanish-speaking society."[11] Following Elke Sturm-Trigonakis (2007), code-switching functions as the "Entkanonisierung" of a national literary historiography,[12] where Bernard's poetic choice to write multilingually overturns an exclusive monolingual national canon. It further practices a linguistic transgression of the hegemonic discourse of Costa Rica's imagined community, for the national is sacrificed in favor of the transnational and in the name of the cultural continuum, so that translingual pluralism can be acknowledged as a mirror of overlapping worlds born out of diaspora/s and transnational capitalism. Lastly, the multilingual poems selected for the ensuing analysis document first and foremost a struggle against linguistic assimilation and a protest against economic marginalization of multilingual Afro-Costa Ricans.

The main contention here is that Bernard's literary language mixture deploys Anzaldúa's *mestiza*-consciousness in an exemplary manner as a crossing of linguistic and cultural borderlands. In so doing, her multilingualism carries out a performance of pluricentrical belonging. On the one hand, Bernard is *tricultural*, since with her poetry she

---

9   The concept of "translanguaging" [Welsh *trawsieithu*] was first used by Cen Williams in the 1980s to name a pedagogical practice in bilingual classrooms. In it, language switches are done according to the learning activity being carried out, e.g. reading is done in one language, while writing or speaking in another (cf. Baker, *Foundations of Bilingual Education and Bilinguism* [2001]). Ofelia García (2009) draws on Williams and redefines translanguaging as representing "*multiple discursive practices* in which bilinguals engage in order to *make sense of their bilingual worlds*" (*Bilingual Education in the 21st Century*: 45; emphasis in the original). It is the manner in which bilingual individuals, families, and communities construct meaning multilingually in situations in which bilingual language contact take place (for example, minority children acting as translators for the elders). García extends on translanguaging as switching languages within the same *domain* (e.g. family, friendship, religion, employment or education). I reconfigure Ofelia García's definition of "translanguaging" to fit the literary context of the present analysis.

10   Schmeling/Schmitz-Emans, *Multilinguale Literatur*: 205.

11   Mosby, *Place, Language, and Identity in Afro-Costa Rican Literature*: 119.

12   Sturm-Trigonakis, *Global Playing in der Literatur*: 155f: "sich bewußt außerhalb einer kanonisierten Nationalliteratur zu verorten und andere Optionen aufzuzeigen [...]. Damit praktizieren die Texte eine Transgression des Hegemonialdiskurses; das Nationale, Eindeutige wird zugunsten des Transationalen und der Heterogenität geopfert, wobei zugleich ein emazipatorisher Vektor vorgegeben ist, weil durch den transtextuellen Pluralismus die Beschränkheit eines national ausgerichteten Literaturverständnisses offengelegt und attackiert wird."

claims *belongingness* to Costa Rica, to the Caribbean, and to Africa (in the form of Hall's idealized imagined community). On the other, she speaks *multilingually*, expressing herself by way of a *forked tongue* comprised by Spanish, English, and Limon Creole. Coherently, she lives "in a state of perpetual transition" between her cultures and through her tongues. In this manner, Bernard's *mestiza*-consciousness transcends double consciousness.[13] Her poetic code-switching makes the *mestiza*-consciousness thus perceptible, for it transcends exclusive *duality* towards inclusive *plural belongingness*. Here, an alternate historical imagination will be deployed across language switches that reenact a linguistic stor(y)ing of the nation~diaspora dynamic/s specific to Costa Rica.

While in the Spanish-written part of *CM* Bernard delineates her Blackness as an Afra-Central American on the one hand, and as an Afra-Costa Rican through references to Limón on the other, the English-written part instead pleads for recognition of Black culture in general through recurrent themes linked to Africa and to the Caribbean, as well as explicitly referring to the power of writing in the struggle for acknowledgement. Women also hold an important role in *CM*, and outcries against inequality and injustice can be found in both parts. As reported by Mosby, some of the poems in *CM* were published first in *Griot* (1997), engaged by Jackson in her interview with Bernard and which was published by the Seventh Day Adventist Youth Society of Costa Rica in recognition of Bernard's vindication of Black culture both in Costa Rica and the world.[14] The poems published in *Griot* furthermore refer to the fact that she was granted the Griot Award in 1996 by the American African Caribbean Council in Miami.[15] As she explained Jackson, "I have been fighting and writing about the importance of our African heritage. I am one of the first female poets in Latin America to do this", because of which she was declared the "Griot of the Americas".[16] *Tatuaje* (2011) is Bernard's last published work composed of seventy poems, of which only one is in English, entitled "Christmas Tree."[17] Bernard has also published an essay on political philosophy entitled *Nuevo ensayo sobre la existencia y la libertad política* (1981), where she engages themes like the master-slave relationship, social oppression, and political and existential freedom.

Although Bernard's poetic œuvre is thematically rich and withholds over two hundred poems overall that "shift from references to places and figures from Africa, Africa-America [to] the Caribbean" as noted by Kitzie McKinney (1996),[18] the following pages focus nevertheless on three cautiously selected poems where multilingualism is clearly manipulated as a poetic formality and where the content is crucial regarding Bernard's

---

13 Anzaldúa, *Borderlands*: 100. Cf. 102: "The work of the *mestiza*-consciousness is to break down the subject-object duality that keeps her a prisoner and to show in the flesh and through the images in her work how duality is transcended."

14 Bernard, *Griot*: 5: "Dr. Eulalia Bernard, has been a providential instrument of the Lord for the vindication of the black race, culture and history, not only in Costa Rica but in the world. She is a true griot."

15 Mosby, *Place, Language, and Identity in Afro-Costa Rican Literature*: 109. In *Griot,* Bernard writes "Premio Griot 1996" or "Griot Awardee 1996" as an epigraph to her poems.

16 Jackson, "Our Weapon is Strong Language": 122.

17 For a study on *Tatuaje*, see Gallego, "On Both Sides of the Atlantic" (2012), who analyzes Bernard's last book together with Agnès Agboton and Mónica Carrillo's Spanish-written poetry in a comparative manner and as spokeswomen of the "Spanish-Speaking Diaspora."

18 McKinney, "Costa Rica's Black Body": 16.

contribution to *Black Costa Rica* from an *infranational* perspective. Code-switching in Bernard does not refer to a random manifestation of language switches in literature. It represents instead a specific literary practice regarding the conjunction of the global circum-Atlantic and the local Costa Rican-ness. The picture I want to draw here hinges on how Bernard's languages constitute a poetic imagining withholding a pluricentrical sense of belonging which unravels – in a *literal* fashion (from lat. *littera*) – a story of the past concerning relations of linguistic domination in Costa Rica on the one hand, and of economic marginalization in the second half of the twentieth century on the other. Through an interpretative historical, linguistic, and literary critical approach, I attempt to show why code-switching in Bernard can be read as both a linguistic strategy *and* a rhetorical language play that brings to the forefront an ethnolinguistic infranational history of the Afro-Costa Rican minority. That is, a story of the past representing the marginalization and assimilation of the anglophone Afro-Costa Rican community as second-class citizens.

Taking into consideration the sociolinguistic background of the province of Limón, to which I will refer firstly, Bernard's lyrical multilingualism is instrumental in challenging the hegemonic culture by creatively and strategically exploiting the linguistic resources available to her. Her poetic code-switching is not only a a performance of literary and linguistic resistance, but mainly a bringing together of cultural discrepancies into a transformed pluricentrical identification. Much like McDonald's modernized-nature oxymoron and Campbell's skin-history metonymy, poetic multilingualism in Bernard is a counter-hegemonic strategy because it captures the lived experience of the Black working class in Limón. Her manipulation of language has the aesthetic potential of representing, at a linguistic and discursive level, a peculiar dynamic of struggle that Costa Rican-born Caribbean descendants underwent in the country. On the one hand, multilingualism draws tacitly on the linguistic history of the Afro-Costa Rican minority, while simultaneously conjuring the resistance to total assimilation to Costa Rican culture by claiming *belonging-ness* to the supranational Black Atlantic *linguistically*. In this sense, Bernard's code mixing introduces the circum-Atlantic's inherent movement of intercultural and transnational connections into the monolingual, Spanish-speaking imagined community.

Language mixture has been traditionally studied in conversational interaction by sociolinguists, where it acts as a verbal strategy for achieving conversational goals in specific domains. It prevails as a speech behavior and a language practice that arises as a language contact phenomenon.[19] In this sense, it emerges in an interactional moment and is a product of social communication between speakers of, for example, linguistic borderlands like those of large immigrant populations or diasporan communities (as were Jamaicans and other Afro-Caribbean immigrants) within their host country (in Limón, Costa Rica). If on the one hand Sociolinguistics focuses on the social outcome of *spontaneous spoken language* concerning "what people gain or lose by using language in certain ways in certain interactions",[20] my focus pertains on the other hand solely on the manipulation of written poetic language. That is, on the "conscious reflection [and] inherent correction, editing, and

---

[19]   Cf. Thomason, who provides an introductory study on the subject in *Language Contact* (2001), where she details other phenomena such as transference, interference, borrowing, and codemixing as examples of language contact phenomena.

[20]   Heller, "Introduction": 13.

rewriting process that accompanies any act of writing".[21] Therefore, code-switching in spoken conversation – exclusively a verbal skill (Poplack 1980) of sub-conscious and automatic linguistic selection (Gumperz 1982) that functions according to syntactic constraints which preserve the syntactic integrity of the languages involved (Timm 1975) – must be necessarily differentiated from language mixture in literature, the latter a product of a self-conscious act wanting to achieve a particular literary effect (Lipski 1982). Hence, multilingual code-switching in literature refers to the simultaneous conjunction of morphemes, graphemes, and phonemes from two or more linguistic varieties as a *deliberate aesthetic choice*.

My study of Bernard's selected poems is strictly historical and language-based. The focus lies primarily in analyzing the *meaningful* role language mixture has in Bernard's poetry as a "discourse phenomenon" that yields an infranational historical imagination.[22] It is centered on the aesthetic relevance that multilingualism has as a rhetorical device concerned with style and effect, *but also* with the meaning produced by and through it. Therefore, I will approach three of Bernard's multilingual poems from a formal analysis, while simultaneously carrying out a literary analysis of these formalities in order to categorize code-switching into diverse aesthetic functions according to the role they undertake within the text, both rhetorical as argumentative. Preferring to express her poetry in two (or more) languages throughout the same poem or within a single compilation becomes a strategy by which Bernard says some*thing* without saying *it*. It is not only a question of *what is being said*, but mainly of *how it is being said*.

Ian Smart has referred to other Central American writers of Afro-Caribbean-descent (all men except for Bernard) that used literary bilingualism as markers of their socio-historical realities at the second half of the twentieth century. His groundbreaking work *Central American Writers of West Indian Origin* (1984) devoted chapter two to "The Language of the New West Indian Literature", where he refers to the question of biculturalism in writers like Afro-Panamanians Carlos Guillermo Wilson ("Cubena" *1941)

---

[21]   Lispki, "Spanish-English Language Switching": 192. Tatiana Bisanti (2006) formulates the hypothesis that only in very few cases can literary multilingualism refer to an unconscious and spontaneous phenomenon, since it responds to "una precisa intenzione dell'autore [che] assolve a determinate funzioni" (Bisanti, "Retorica e plurilinguismo letterario": 266).

[22]   As expressed by John Gumperz in *Discourse Strategies* (1982), CS in social situations plays an important role in conveying a specific meaning, where *persuasion* and *rhetorical* effectiveness take part in communicating it (p. 99). The author affirms that switching languages within a single enunciation does not correspond to random language mixture, nor does it reflect insufficient knowledge of either one of the languages being switched, as opposed to the "ideal bilingual" defined in the 1950s. He emphasized against this that code-switching's main concern was with the *communicative effect* of what was being said through it (p. 61). For Gumperz, motivation behind conversational language switches seemed to be a sub-conscious *stylistic* phenomenon (p. 90) and underlined the fact that the *style* of communication (i.e. switching between languages) affects the interpretation of what the speaker tends to communicate (p. 65), determining CS as a pragmatic function that has an important role in both delivering a message (on behalf of the speaker), as in its understanding (by the interlocutor). In this sense, CS becomes a useful stylistic and rhetorical choice for transmitting a certain message in a determined context. It might come useful in accomplishing a specific conversational goal, such as highlighting new or important information, emphasizing a specific attitude regarding the message, provoking a particular response, or simply getting the message through in the most effective manner. Hence, code-switching has mainly and primarily an *expressive*, *communicative* function. From these considerations he concludes: "code switching is a discourse phenomenon" (p. 97).

and Gerardo Maloney (*1945), as well as in Afro-Costa Ricans Quince Duncan and Eulalia Bernard.[23] According to Smart, authentic biculturalism gave way to the creation of a "literary language" that emerged as "an artistic 'West Indian' Spanish".[24] Even if he is pointing towards the right direction by naming the writers' manipulation of Spanish as an "artistic bilingualism" that surpasses the Costa Rican precursors Carlos Luis Fallas's (*Mamita Yunai* 1941), Joaquin Gutiérrez's (*Puerto Limón* 1950), and Panamanian Joaquín Beleño's (*Curundú* 1963) attempt in depicting the Caribbean communities through their language, Smart's analysis is nonetheless limited, for he concentrates mostly on individual lexical terms and isolated expressions as markers of Afro-Caribbean-ness and of Black experience, life, and culture in Central America. Moreover, Smart mistakenly defines Bernard's written work in 1984 as "understandably fully Hispanic".[25] Most likely because he was not able to acquire a copy of her *Negritud* album, but mainly because her literary multilingualism would appear in published compilations in the forthcoming decades.

On the other hand, Mosby's groundbreaking study of Afro-Costa Rican literature, being the first to outline a historiography of Afro-Costa Rican literature in the nation, does pay attention to this aspect. She refers to Bernard's code-switching poems as a mirror of the language in the region, "an example of the cultural adaptation among the second and third generations of Costa Ricans of West Indian descent" and, rightly asserted, she categorizes the intertwinement of multiple languages in Bernard as "markers of cultural memory and identity" that defy monolingualism in Costa Rica.[26] Notwithstanding her title (*Place, Language, and Identity in Afro-Costa Rican Literature*), Mosby however does not extend a philological analysis of code mixing in Bernard. Thus, like Smart, her analysis misses to fully grasp the linguistic component of the culture of resistance she attributes to Bernard by focusing solely on the content, which lacks a more specific treatment of the sociolinguistic background.

Finally, Consuelo Meza carries out a transareal/regional analysis of Afro-Central American women poets, where she superficially mentions the development of a hybrid writing as a shared literary feature between these female writers, characterized by the incursions of words in English, Spanish, and/or Creole versions, as well as a mixture of these.[27] She mentions Eulalia Bernard as the first woman writer to inaugurate this literary tradition, whose multilingual poetry reflects, according to Meza, the processes of identity construction and negotiation as an Afro-Caribbean / Afro-Costa Rican.[28] Nevertheless, her transregional analysis does not permit her to carry out an extensive, in-depth analysis that couples the linguistic form with the historical and social changes that Bernard's trifold poetic register re-presents. Lastly, Silvia Solano Rivera and Jorge Ramírez Caro (2016) criticize Central Valley literary scholars for focusing solely on literary work written in Spanish and leaving out literature written in Costa Rica in English or with a bilingual format.[29] In an effort to rescue these voices, M.Sc. Karla Araya (University of Costa Rica) is

---

[23] Smart, *Central American Writers of West Indian Origin*: 31–50.
[24] Ibid.: 50.
[25] Ibid.
[26] Mosby, *Place, Language, and Identity in Afro-Costa Rican Literature*: 109.
[27] Meza Márquez, "Memoria, identidad y utopía": 123.
[28] Ibid.: 125.
[29] Solano/Ramírez, "Poética de la liberación en Shirley Campbell Barr": 156.

currently compiling the first anthology of Afro-Costa Rican anglophone poetry from the first half twentieth century.[30] Considering the present *status quæstionis* on the subject, the ensuing study on Bernard's multilingualism becomes innovative.

The close reading of "What fi do?" (*MBK*), "Bilingual Campesinos Speak Out" (*MBK*), and "Bilingual Economy" (*Griot*) will attempt on the one hand to make visible the linguistic intertwinement of plural belongingness while focusing, on the other, on how multilingualism is a poetic strategy with a precise historical function making visible the multidimensionality of institutionalized oppressions concerning Blacks in Costa Rica. It adds to McDonald's outernational/ex-centric first layer and to Campbell's supranational meta-historical stratum, a third infranational and (for the time being) final layer stor(y)ing Black Costa Rica's recent story of the past. The questions from which this last stretch of the voyage departs from ponder about the role multilingualism has in Bernard's poetry: what kind of reading practice does it require?

Since I do not intend to signal the author's intention for implementing code-switching, I investigate rather what is the impact multilingualism has in the reader. What can s/he learn from the code-switched text itself?[31] How does this literary act narrate an*other* story of the past? What political, colonial, and cultural histories are summoned by/with/through it? What does it tell us about *Black Costa Rica*? Which rhetorical tools make Bernard's language mixture a discursive practice? What content/s is multilingualism portraying and how does it speak of assimilation and of marginalization? Why is it a linguistic strategy expressing cultural resistance? Is code-switching only a border tongue or something beyond it? How does it portray relations of power and how does it transcend borderlands?

The answers to these questions shall demonstrate why multilingualism in Bernard enacts a glocal performance of pluricentrical belonging.

"Limón on the Raw": The Sociolinguistic Background of Bernard's Multilingualism

Along the ensuing pages, Bernard's poem "What fi do?" (hereafter WFD) will be used in order to tell the history of the languages of her multilingual poetic vain. Here, special attention will be paid to English and to Limon Creole, while the next segment will deal specifically with the implementation of Spanish in schools in the Caribbean province. In so doing, Bernard's rhizomatic sense of belonging can be mapped out across the Afro-Costa Rican linguistic story of the past.

---

[30] Personal e-mail communication (4.02.2016). At that time, Araya was the director of the *Bachillerato y Licenciatura en la Enseñanza del Inglés* at the University of Costa Rica (Sede de Occidente). She is currently carrying out her doctoral investigation at the *Romanisches Seminar – Leibniz Universität Hannover* as a DAAD scholarship holder. For references to bilingual Afro-Costa Rican writers, see Mosby, *Place, Language and Identity in Afro-Costa Rican Literature*: Ch. 1 "Roots and Routes. Foundations of Black Literature in Costa Rica" and Duncan, "Corrientes literarias afrolimonenses" (2012).

[31] Following Helmich, *Ästhetik der Mehrsprachigkeit*: 33.

What fi do?

1   What a molote (*hubbub*)!
2   Look like a viaje (*trip*) to the moon,
3   This paseo (*picnic*) to Portete (*beach in Limón, Costa Rica*),
4   Mary you ready ya?
5   The rice and beans ya está (*Is it ready yet?*)?
6   No forget the crocus bag; …you hear?
7   Fi pick up the basura (*garbage*),
8   You understand?... after
9   The pachanga (*'live it up' time*) done.
10   Hie – jie… What a basilón! (*hell of a good time*)
11   Me can't wait fi the time to come.
12   I hope the camión (*bus*) no broke down
13   And lef' we pan the ground.
14   That would be a big tirada. (*nuisance*)
15   No sa! … What fi do?...
16   We going have a real basilón
17   Camion or no camion, …and done!
My Black King (n.p.)

Portete is a beach at the Limón province, where the seawater is crystal blue, the jungle green, and the air wet. Code-switching occurs here largely at a lexical level, where nouns are switched from a matrix language, here Standard English (hereafter SE), both to Spanish (Spa) and to Limon Creole (LC). To be underlined is the short glossary given at the bottom of the poem for the words in Spa, which I have transcribed next to the Spanish lexemes in the poem reproduced above. The glossary extends an important interpretative tool for the readership. It is clearly not written for the Afro-Costa Rican community itself but for readers anywhere else in the world, who are unaware of the multilingualism of the Afro-Costa Rican community. It is thus a direct manner of portraying the linguistic reality in Limón, made accessible to the monolingual SE reader thanks to the translated Spa words. As an explanation to the glossary, it is also stated in the original print version that "In Limón, Costa Rica the people are bilingual and the language is a mixture of English and Spanish".[32]

In "What fi do?", switching occurs at the intra-verse level, i.e. as a mid-sentence switch, deploying Bernard's trifold linguistic repertoire. The trip to the beach unfolds colorfully thanks to the irruption of Spanish and to the switch to Limon Creole within the base language of the LC lexifier, English. The reason I identify WFD as manifesting a *trifold* linguistic repertoire with SE as the base language – instead of a *bilingual* LC/Spa poem – is based on Anita Herzfeld's and Elizabeth Winkler's claim that Limon Creole does not represent a homogeneous linguistic entity. Instead, as Herzfeld defined it, "LC can be best described as a linguistic continuum that stretches from a West Indian English-based Creole to Standard Limonese English (SLE) […]".[33] She affirms that LC is not used by all in the same manner, for "no one speaker uses exclusively standard features all the time, or creole

---

[32]   Bernard, *My Black King*: n.p.
[33]   Herzfeld, "Language and Identity": 118f.

features all the time".[34] Instead, the speaker moves along the SE-LC continuum depending on the social circumstances and on her linguistic ability. Therefore, recalling that *written* (literary) code-switching corresponds to a self-conscious act of language manipulation by the writer, I consider that multilingualism in WFD moves along the linguistic continuum with Standard English as the acrolect form of LC while also playing with basilect and mesolect LC linguistic variables, which are made evident either by phonemic orthography or by linguistic structures proper to the Creole language.[35] Spanish must be furthermore added to this continuum given the contact between all three linguistic systems in Limón, thus expanding the continuum. This reading, furthermore, draws on Edward Kamau Brathwaite's consideration of *nation language* (*History of the Voice* 1984) in that Bernard's multilingualism represents a Caribbean aesthetic strategy that rescues the submerged cultural and linguistic heritage of the circum-Atlantic, performing pluricentrical belonging by poetizing in multiple languages.[36]

The elements alternated in almost every verse are nouns in Spa. The fact that a Spa noun is switched routinely in almost every verse in Bernard's "What fi do?" provides evidence that we are not dealing with single and fortuitous lexeme incorporations, but rather with a conscious switching of words along the linguistic continuum and as an aesthetic multilingual strategy.[37] As Carol Myers-Scotton notes in *Duelling Languages* (1993), "codeswitching of languages offers bilinguals a way to increase their flexibility of expression, going beyond the style-switching of monolinguals" and being Bernard trilingual, it can be deduced that noun-switching in her poetry does not refer to a monolingual literary device, but to a more complex intertwining of her linguistic capacities. It exemplifies the *mestiza*-consciousness Anzaldúa speaks of, performing her pluricentrical belonging *linguistically*. As explained by Anzaldúa, the switch between languages influences the readership to perceive how "ideas and information [are being transferred] from one culture to another" as a shifting movement between plural and varied worlds.[38] Anzaldúa's own bilingual prose defining the

---

[34] Ibid.: 128. Cf. also Herzfeld, *Mekaytelyuw*: xxi; xxv: "Una vez más, vale la pena recalcar que la variación es la característica más sobresaliente de esta lengua: todos sus hablantes no emplean necesariamente el mismo sistema fonémico, y aún el mismo hablante no siempre se adhiere a una exclusiva realización fonética."

[35] The Creole continuum refers to a spectrum of linguistic varieties between a creole and the standard form of its lexifier. In this sense, the LC Continuum is composed of (a) an acrolect, being the form closest to SE (the lexifier); (b) the basilect, at the other extreme of the continuum being the form most distant of SE; and in between lies (c) the mesolect (Winkler, *Limonese Creole*: 190).

[36] Cf. Brathwaite, *History of the Voice*: 5-8.

[37] Whether a single noun-switch can qualify as 'true' CS has been debatable, even though large percentage of spoken code-switching material has been documented as occurring mostly between lexemes, both in empiric research as in literature (Myers-Scotton, *Duelling Languages*: 180f.). Single lexeme switches have been understood by sociolinguists "to be part of the speaker's monolingual style" (Poplack, "Sometimes I'll start a sentence in Spanish": 181), where lexical substitutions of words from one language (L2) are implanted in another (L1). In fact, lexeme switches can even be found in total absence of bilingualism (Thomason, *Language Contact*: 72), "while 'code-switching' implies some degree of competence in two languages" (Pfaff, "Constraints on Language Mixing": 295f.). Under these considerations, and acting as simple lexical substitutions, these noun-switches do not constitute true code alternations, for they do no function as syntactically congruent shifts (Lipski, "Spanish-English Language Switching"). They are rather switched either due to the "lack of an exact equivalent in the other language/culture [or due to] a momentary gap in the lexicon of the individual" (Montes-Alcalá, "Code-switching in US Latino literature": 274). In Bernard's poetry, however, this is not the case, for as it will be discussed, she switches for aesthetic reasons that reinforce the poetic argument.

[38] Anzaldúa, *Borderlands*: 107.

mestiza-consciousness provides a fairly exact image of Bernard's code-switching as a performance of her pluricentrical belonging:

> Because I, a *mestiza*,
> continually walk out of one culture
> and into another,
> because I am in all cultures at the same time,
> *alma entre dos mundos, tres, cuatro,*
> *me zumba la cabeza con lo contradictorio.*
> *Estoy norteada por todas las voces que me hablan*
> *simultáneamente.*[39]

Following the author, Bernard's poetic vain is polyphonic. It enters one world while simultaneously exiting another one, stor(y)ing multiple versions of her belongingness. Her code-switched poetry unravels the multilingual background of the Spanish-speaking Black Costa Rican community as culturally, historically, and linguistically connected to the insular anglophone Caribbean and by historical and cultural extension to the Black Atlantic and Africa too. In fact, Winkler and Obeng (2000) have linked Limon Creole to the Akan of Ghana, tracing thus LC's linguistic heritage to West Africa.[40] Bernard's linguistic identity, hence, is embodied across a *mestiza*-consciousness that, as defined by Anzaldúa, "develop[s] a tolerance for contradictions, a tolerance for ambiguities."[41] In Bernard's multilingual poetry, national (Spa), outernational (SE), and infranational (LC) languages carry out a play of contradictions that however coexist across pluricentrical belonging. This is her paradigm for stor(y)ing the past.

Let's proceed now to the Costa Rican linguistic particularity that exists across the continuum of sameness that is the Central American Caribbean, Limon Creole. A *creole*[42] language surfaces when a *pidgin* (that is, a marginal language that acquired a *lingua franca* function in the context of restricted communication needs between people who shared no common language) becomes the mother tongue of a speech community.[43] In this sense, both a pidgin and a creole come to be due the interaction between communities of diverse origins speaking different languages and coexisting in a shared new location that is not the native

---

[39] Ibid.: 99.

[40] See Winkler/Obeng, "West Africanisms in Limonese Creole English" (2000).

[41] Anzaldúa, *Borderlands*: 101.

[42] The term *creole* has an interesting etymology. It is derived from the Portuguese *crioulo*, via Spanish and French, and originally meant a white person of European descent who was born and raised in a tropical colony. It was later extended to mean indigenous natives and others of non-European origin (e.g. African slaves), and finally was used to name certain languages spoken by 'creoles' in the colonized Caribbean and in Africa (Decamp, "Introduction": 15).

[43] Todd, *Pidgins and Creoles*: 1–3. For an interesting and problematizing discussion on the concept of "mother tongue" as an ambiguous technical and legislative term, cf. Romaine, *Language in Society*: 36–39. She draws on various examples from Canada, the United States, India, and Britain in order to compare and contrast how the term is not univocal and how considerations on "mother tongues" are also influenced by political debates regarding immigrants, ethnicity, national census drawings, patriarchal vs. matriarchal societies, language used for religious affairs, minority groups within a country, and the colonial past of imperial nations. She also refers to complications when defining mother tongues as languages or as dialects, as for example, regarding "members of some minority groups, such as West Indians in Britain, [who] would like to claim that varieties of West Indian Creole constitute a language and that this language therefore deserves recognition as their mother tongue" (p. 39).

one. However, a creole is different from a pidgin in that the former develops into a first language for its speakers, while the latter remains a bridge or vehicular contact language with a limited life span. Nonetheless, "both are marginal, in the circumstances of their origin" and in the fact that they exist "at the margins of historical consciousness".[44] Such is the case, for example, of creole languages born out of trade ships and plantations systems of colonial times in the Greater Caribbean, which surfaced as sociohistorical phenomena of the subaltern type. In other words, French-, English-, Spanish-, Portuguese-, and Dutch-based creoles arose in the Antilles due to language contact between European and West African languages during colonialism.[45]

Referred to with McDonald's poetics of landscape, the Plantation system of the twentieth century becomes again "the economic, racial, historical, and cultural structure [...] that made possible and even imposed a particular form of cultural transformation" in Limón, Costa Rica by way of the train.[46] This time again in the form of language contact yielding *creolization*. As defined by Martínez-San Miguel in *Coloniality of Diasporas* (2014), creolization is the outcome of simultaneous processes of "linguistic and other cultural contacts that produce a new language, a new identity."[47] Her words recall Anzaldúa's affirmation, which was quoted as an eloquent epigraphy at the beginning of this section and for whom "[e]thnic identity is twin skin to linguistic identity."[48] By referring to the precepts proposed in *Éloge de la Créolité*, Martínez-San Miguel states "creolization" constitutes a theoretical shift in the study of Caribbean Postcolonial Studies, where "[l]anguages in contact – instead of races in contact – become the new paradigm for theorizing the configuration of identities" between borderlands.[49] Hence, we are about to voyage across Bernard's poetic multilingualism as an alternative cultural identity paradigm that articulates pluricentrical belonging. One where lyric and linguistics can reveal a historical imagination concerning the nation~diaspora dynamic/s between border languages. One that speaks furthermore from the infranational perspective because it was deemed non-Costa Rican, leading hence to marginalization and assimilation of the Black minority.

In "What fi do?", the presence of various languages symbolize the collective property of the multilingual Afro-Costa Rican speech community.[50] Bernard is engaging different languages so that their varieties correspond to an extra-textual oral reality that makes visible the "translocality from which [her] border languages emerge".[51] That is, from the location of the Caribbean province/diaspora in contact with the official state language and

---

44 Hymes, "Preface": 3 and 5.
45 John Holm (1983) explains English-based creoles as having a language system that is African in its structural origin and European at the lexical level, for preverbal tense and aspect markers, for example, function semantically and syntactically like those of the African languages, while European English lexeme are borrowed and integrated into the new linguistic system (*Central American English*: 16). See Martínez-San Miguel, *Coloniality of Diasporas*: 133f., where she discusses McWhorter's "AfroGenesis Hypothesis" ("The Scarcity of Spanish-based Creoles Explained" 1995), "which explains how creoles emerged from a Portuguese- or English-based pidgin developed in the West Coast of Africa by the European countries with trading posts in this area."
46 Martínez-San Miguel, *Coloniality of Diasporas*: 127.
47 Ibid.: 128.
48 Anzaldúa, *Borderlands*: 81.
49 Martínez-San Miguel, *Coloniality of Diasporas*: 127.
50 Cf. Sebba, "Writing Switching in British Creole": 7.
51 Martínez-San Miguel, *Coloniality of Diasporas*: 129.

simultaneously with the language of the banana enclave structure. In 1977, the linguist Anita Herzfeld termed "Limon creole" when studying the oral language of anglophone Costa Rican-born Caribbean descendants in the Atlantic province.[52] As defined by Tanja Zimmer (2011), it is an English-based creole that developed exclusively in Limón throughout the twentieth century due to the Caribbean proletarian diaspora, where Standard American English and Jamaican Creole (JC) underwent intense language contact.[53] The local creole originated from and then became a separate linguistic identity regarding JC, which was the language for communicating in family and in communal life between the workers.[54] The 1927 national census documented that 91% of the Afro-Caribbeans in Limón were Jamaican, from which Zimmer deduces that the vast majority was thus familiar with Jamaican Creole. An aspect she asserts allowed LC to develop and be installed as the language of the Afro-Costa Rican community. It has since then become the mother tongue of the Black minority in Costa Rica and during the first decades of its flourishing coming to be, it was confined to linguistic isolation in Limón.[55] Nonetheless, this situation was overturned in the second half of the twentieth century, when LC came into intense contact with Spanish.

Back in 1977 Herzfeld correctly asserted that Limon Creole had not yet "acquired other channels than the verbal",[56] Bernard's *Negritud* vinyl being an exceptional cultural product thereof. Hence, Bernard's poetry collections represent the first irruptions of it into the written medium. Nowadays, Queen Nzinga takes Limon Creole poetry to the spoken word performativity level, and Marcia Reid's *Nátral Filingz* bilingual poetic compilation in Limon Creole and English awaits publishing.[57] Before Bernard, however, the Costa Rican-born Dolores William Joseph Montout's (1904–1990) award-winning three-short story collection entitled *Tres relatos del Caribe costarricense* (1982) must not be precluded. The short stories were presented in 1982 as part of a literary contest organized by the Ministerio de Cultura y Juventud on the Costa Rican Caribbean. Written in English, Montout's short stories intertwine a well-written English of high-register literality with LC as a stylistic technique portraying the people of Limón.[58] The first short story of the collection, "Limon on the raw", brings out, as the author affirms,

> the mode of speaking, the everyday expressions of man and woman of everyday life, the peculiarities, etc., etc. [which] bring forward the different moods of the average people, the different expressions, the moods, the various accents, some typically Jamaican, some, Barbadians, others descendants of the smaller island groups, Trinidad, St. Lucia, Antigua, St. Kitts, Nevis, Guadalupe, Martinique, and even the

---

52 Herzfeld, "Second Language Acrolect": 194.
53 Zimmer, *El español hablado por los afrocostarricenses*: 32.
54 Herzfeld, *Mekaytelyuw*: 31; "Language and Identity": 127.
55 Zimmer, *El español hablado por los afrocostarricenses*: 132f.
56 Herzfeld, "Second Language Acrolect": 195.
57 Cf. Queen Nzinga, *Afrokon* (2012) and her recorded demos at soundcloud: https://soundcloud.com/nzinga-maxwell. Some of Reid's poems have been published in *Káñina, Revista de Artes y Letras* (2010), as in *Sargasso. Linguistic Explorations of Gender and Sexuality* (2008–2009).
58 For more on Montout's contribution to Afro-Costa Rican literary history, see Gordon, "Expressions of the Costa Rican Black Experience" (1991); Mosby, *Place, Language, and Identity in Afro-Costa Rican Literature*: Ch. 1; and Karla Araya's Master thesis (University of Costa Rica), *Anglophone Afro-Costa Rican Literature: Texts and counter-discourses in the unpublished literary work of Dolores Joseph Montout* (2015).

people from Curazao [sic], not to leave out the people hailing from Bluefields, Nicaragua and British Honduras.

Group of people from Grand and Lesser Cayman, St. Andres and Providence and a straggling of the people from Bocas del Toro, make this story, LIMON ON THE RAW.[59]

Montout's introductory remark mirrors the cosmopolitan character of the Limón province during the first half of the twentieth century and pinpoints the plurilinguistic atmosphere that impregnated life in the city. Limon Creole is but a coherent outcome of this sociolinguistic context.

If Bernard's poetry re-presents her multilingual community through written poetry, it must be nevertheless underlined that these speech acts do not exist in isolation, that is, as a unique case of language creolization. Instead, Limon Creole is simultaneously and historically connected to African heritage due to slavery; to the clash of European, African, and autochthonous cultures through colonialism; to the multilingual Caribbean that came to be as the outcome of Modernity; as well as to the North American transnational capitalist enterprises in the Central American region in the nineteenth and twentieth centuries. By installing LC, Bernard is able to covertly poetize a historical backdrop that renders visible a pluricentrical belonging determined economically across time, as seen with the transhistorical analysis of McDonald's modernized-nature oxymoron. In fact, the Creole insertions function as a linguistic permanence of her Afro-history for, in a tacit and allegorical manner, "it carries the traces of the many other languages, cultural traditions, and displaced subjectivities that coincided in the context of the insular Caribbean."[60]

On the one hand, Limon Creole can be detected at the grammatical,[61] morphosyntactical,[62] and phonological[63] level, reproducing the verbal structure of English-based Creole languages. Holm extends on the African verb structures that were incorporated into the English-based Creoles of Central America, where he brings attention to the zero or no form [$\emptyset$] mark of the progressive action that eliminates the conjugated "to be" verb.[64] Thus, SE *we are going* is spoken in LC as Bernard poetizes it: "*We going have* a real basilón" (v. 16). On the other hand, Herzfeld's description of the negation system in the Limon Creole Continuum shares linguistic features with Guyanese Creole. While Herzfeld notes that

---

[59] Montout, *Tres relatos*: 15.

[60] Martínez-San Miguel, *Coloniality of Diasporas*: 138. See p. 137f., where she refers to Brathwaite's *History of the Voice* as concerned with "how and when 'national language'" or Caribbean versions of European languages become apt for creating "national literature" (p. 139).

[61] As for example with *fi* instead of 'to, for' (Sebba, "Writing Switching in British Creole": 98; *Dictionary of Caribbean English Usage*: 229).

[62] Regarding the morphosyntactical level, SE *I* is replaced LC *me* as the subject marker (v. 13 and v. 15). These correspond to pronoun markers in English-based Creole languages, as dictionaries confirm it (see Cassidy/Le Page, *Dictionary of Jamaican English* 1980 and Allsopp, *Dictionary of Caribbean English* 1996). In some cases, the switches occur syntactically. That is, between a non-complete sentence due to the elision of the verb ("Mary, you ready") and an adverb ("ya?"; v. 4); between a noun phrase ("The rice and beans") and a verb phrase ("ya está?"; v. 5); or between a verb phrase ("Fi pick up") and a noun phrase functioning as the direct object ("the basura"; v. 7).

[63] That is, "pan" (v. 13) and "No sa!" (v. 15) reproduce literally the speech sound of "upon" and "No sir" in spoken LC.

[64] Holm, *Central American English*: 17.

"didn(t)" is more frequently a mesolect marker for indicating negation in past or anterior tenses, she notes that the basilect markers for negation are "no", "duon" (SE *don't*), and "neba" (SE *never*).[65] Hence, she explains the LC basilectal Negative Rule as similar to the Guyanese Creole rule formulated by Derek Bickerton in 1975. At the basilect level, the form "no" is used for past/non-past tense negations instead of SE "don't", following the structure Subj + NEG + unmarked Verb.[66] So, instead of **I don't go*, the LC negative structure expresses itself either as 'a duon gow' or as 'a no gow'[67] – as verse six of "What fi do" mimics it: "*No forget* the crocus bag".

Moreover, since Limon Creole has not (yet) been standardized, which according to Marlis Hellinger (1986) relies on "linguistic descriptions and the availability of grammars, dictionaries and a writing system",[68] there are no agreed spelling norms for LC, being thus dependent of the SE writing system for its written manifestation. Consequently, Mark Sebba (2012) affirms "everything that is written in Creole, whether in Britain or the Caribbean" – *also applicable to the Central American Caribbean* – "uses a modified Standard English orthography".[69] Much like other Creole writers of the Caribbean, Bernard applies a phonemic orthography when writing in LC, that is, an orthography whose graphemes correspond to the sound of phonemes.[70] Bernard's *fi* for *to/for* (vv. 7, 11, 15), *pan* for *upon* (v. 13), and *sa* for *sir* (v. 15) are but examples of this. Through the phonemic incorporation of written Limon Creole, Bernard creates a symbolic distance between the two languages, as well as a simultaneous polarization of codes, so that the switches are much more explicit within the linguistic continuum of the poem.[71]

Spanish switches in "What fi do?" are on the other hand not gratuitous at all, since they convey the main foregrounding element of the poem by applying stylistic variation upon standard language. The term 'foregrounding' refers to Jan Mukařovský's concept *aktualisace*, which he explains in "Standard Language and Poetic Language" (1932).[72] In it, the author states language becomes poetic by the intentional, consistent, and deliberate violation of the norm of standard language, drawing attention to it. The effect is brought about by the interrelationship of diverse components in the whole text so that by manipulating elements like tone, syntax, word order, among others, foregrounding colors the text differently. Like Brathwaite's nation language, which corresponds to "the process

---

[65] Herzfeld, "Towards the Description of a Creole": 106.
[66] Ibid.: 110.
[67] Herzfeld affirms *duon* is used as an alternate form of *no* and points out these forms are used at times indistinctly (ibid.: 107f., see transcriptions 22.2.15 and 30.2.29.)
[68] Hellinger, "On Writing English-related Creoles in the Caribbean": 54.
[69] Sebba, "Writing Switching in British Creole": 91.
[70] In fact, Dolores Joseph also introduces "pan" and "fi" in his portrayal of Limonese speech, whose depiction of spoken language in Limón also reproduces oral code-switching. This is however not a literary skill exclusive to Caribbean writers, but a general aesthetic tool. For example, Tolstoy also applies a phonemic orthography when he reproduces French at the mouth of Waniuscha in *The Cossaks*, using the Cyrillic alphabet to reproduce French sounds (Horn, "Ästhetische Funktionen der Sprachmischung": 228f.).
[71] Cf. Sebba, "Writing Switching in British Creole": 89 and 96f.
[72] Mukařovský (1891–1975) was a Czech theorist who belonged to the Prague Linguistic Circle (Prague School) and published during the first half of the twentieth century on style and aesthetics. In "Standard Language and Poetic Language" (1932), the author questions what is the relationship of the first type of language to the second, which he defines as two dissimilar forms, each with specific functions.

of using English in a different way from the 'norm'", foregrounding in Bernard's multilingual poetry sets itself against the normative background and is thus perceived as the conscious, poetic distortion of various standard languages (i.e. English and Spanish).[73] I take multilingualism to be the dynamic unit and the dominant component of foregrounding in Bernard, whose nation language spans all of her tongues along her linguistic continuum, going beyond a monolingual linguistic performativity. Therefore, even though Mosby affirms that in WFD "Bernard demonstrates the borrowings from Spanish displayed in Limonese Creole and the code mixing that occurs as a *natural* development in the language"[74] (emphasis added), I argue that Spanish switches in WFD are rather emphasized so as to achieve fundamentally an *aesthetic* purpose. That is, they install rhyme and rhythm, cadence and musicality – aspects that Brathwaite highlighted as fundamental to nation language.[75]

In general, the poem does not present regular rhyme along its verses, and rhythm does not seem to be determined by a rigid verse-number structure. Instead, rhyme is installed by *bilingual* vocal tail rhymes, while the single noun switches from SE to Spa enact the acoustic play among vocals and consonants, adding cadence by lengthening the verses. Let's take for example verses 10–13, where the switch from *come* to *camión* reunites [k], [m], and dissimilar vowel sounds between SE [kom] and Spa [kam], while simultaneously lengthening the verse with the disyllable *camión*, thus adding cadence. *Basilón* couples with *camión* at [a] and [on] sounds, and with lightly dissimilar vocal sounds between SE [kom] (*come*) and Spa [lon] (*basilón*). LC incursions (*fi, pan*) add a distinctive orality by playing with a differentiated pronunciation of standardized English. Hence, rhyme and rhythm in the poem are created *by the very act of straddling the linguistic continuum*. Due to the interaction between English, Limon Creole, and Spanish in Bernard's poem, the main feature being aestheticized is the fact of multilingualism itself.[76] The composition of similar but yet simultaneously dissimilar sounds through noun-switches is precisely what foregrounds the poem, which when read orally, acquires another tone: joyful. (Please read out loud.)

10   Hie – jie… What a basilón!
11   Me can't wait fi the time to come.
12   I hope the camión no broke down
13   And lef' we pan the ground.

Some of the Spa lexeme install furthermore "cultural alternatives" because they refer to a Spanish-speaking cultural domain.[77] Words like "molote" (v. 1: 'hubbub'), "vacilón" (v. 10: 'hell of a good time'), or "tirada" (v. 14: 'nuisance') are particular to Costa Rican regionalisms and reflect linguistic particularity, some of them shared furthermore by

---

[73]   Brathwaite, *History of the Voice*: 5. Cf. Mukařovský, "Standard Language and Poetic Language": 50.

[74]   Mosby, *Place, Language, and Identity in Afro-Costa Rican Literature*: 108.

[75]   Brathwaite, *History of the Voice*: 13: "English it may be in terms of some of its lexical features. But in its contours, its rhythm and timbre, its sound explosions, it is not English, even though the words, as you hear them, might be English to a greater or lesser degree."

[76]   Cf. Lipski, "Spanish-English Language Switching": 195: "the prime feature being foregrounded is the fact of bilingualism."

[77]   Cf. Valdes-Fallis, "Code-Switching in Bilingual Chicano Poetry": 880.

neighboring countries.[78] Contrariwise, "viaje" (v. 2: 'trip'), "paseo" (v. 3: 'picnic'), and "camión" (v. 17: 'truck') do not carry any suggestive nuance, nor do they add a particular cultural meaning, as for example *"rice and beans"* does (v. 5). This is defined in the glossary as a "typical dish" and marks a cultural domain specific to the culinary tradition of the Costa Rican Caribbean. Lorena Madrigal (2006) correctly refers to the fact that "the food of the Afro-Limonenses differs from that of most Costa Ricans in its reliance on coconut products".[79] In fact, *rice and beans* is not at all like the traditional *gallo pinto*, a mixture of rice and beans eaten across the Costa Rican territory at breakfast, a dish furthermore shared with Nicaraguan cuisine. The main ingredient that differentiates them is the use of coconut milk in the former's preparation. In this case, it is not code-switching that which adds a semantic specificity, but the glossary itself. Therefore, Spa lexeme switches perform multilingualism principally for the sake of poetic composition, which have an aesthetic function directly related to orality: rhythm, rhyme, and cadence, as well as to mimicked multilingualism. Together, these aspects create a specific effect: the setting of a cheerful tone, coherent with the content of the poem. That is, the excitement of taking a trip to the beach.

Within the whole of the code-switched poem, the linguistic repertoire claims Bernard's belongingness to Spanish-speaking Costa Rica, while simultaneously reuniting this linguistic identity with her transnational connection to the insular anglophone Caribbean, taking root furthermore in the specific Creole language of Limón, Costa Rica. In this manner, the largest ethno-linguistic minority in the country is made visible by poetic multilingualism. Moreover, Bernard's aesthetic decision to write in a plurality of languages becomes highly significant in the context of linguistic relations of power in the country. When Anita Herzfeld conducted her fieldwork in Limón with the purpose of studying the LC grammar system (1973–1978),[80] she tells of how Limon Creole speakers were critical of their own language, considered by some as a "second-class language", which in turn mirrored their position as second-class citizens in Costa Rica. She summarizes their prejudices by stating that "they believed [LC] should be replaced in most situations by 'correct' English or Spanish. LC speakers were apologetic (saying their language was 'bad' English), and Jamaican-educated grandparents abhorred the creole spoken by their 'grands.'"[81] Herzfeld explains this negatively charged emotional attitude towards LC as a consequence of it being associated with a "deprecatory self-image", for it was linked with "lack of education, primitive ways, superstitious beliefs, poverty, slavery, and a general inadequacy for acquiring a high social status."[82] This linguistic attitude was determined by

---

[78]   García Valverde's *Vocabulario básico y cotidiano abreviado del castellano y costarriqueñismos* (2010) consists of a carefully elaborated trilingual Costa Rican/Pan-Hispanic/English dictionary that permits the anglophone and Spanish-speaking reader to visualize the particularity of Costa Rican words within a larger spectrum of Pan-Hispanic Spanish in a comparative fashion. The author signals *molote* in Costa Rica as corresponding to "tumulto" in Standard Spanish and to "bunch, crowd" in English (p. 77). Costa Rican *vacilón* means "celebración, fiesta" ("celebration, party"; 126), while the entry *qué tirada* denotes its exclamatory character in expressing "¡qué calamidad!, ¡qué desgracia!" ("what a problem!"; p. 118). Cf. the lexeme entries in *DRAE*, where the regionalisms are also indicated.

[79]   Madrigal, *Human Biology of Afro-Caribbean Populations*: 174.

[80]   See Herzfeld, *Mekaytelyuw* (2002), specifically the Introduction.

[81]   Herzfeld, "Language and Identity": 129 and 131.

[82]   Ibid.: 129.

the marginalized position Blacks had in the country because they were considered 'non'-Costa Rican and who, as a consequence, negatively correlated their infranational position with linguistic variety.

In an intimate remembrance, Gloria Anzaldúa recalls how her mother used to tell her: "*Pa'hallar un buen trabajo tienes que saber hablar el inglés bien.*"[83] Substitute *inglés* for *Spanish* and both Afro-Costa Ricans as Chicanos are caught between equivalent borderland dynamics. It is no coincidence that Anzaldúa's claims match perfectly Afro-Costa Ricans' ethnolinguistic infranational reality, for "Chicanos and other people of color suffer economically for not acculturating".[84] "Acculturating" means in this context to adopt the language of the dominant culture. The *infranational* character of Bernard's historical imagination is therefore best understood by relating it to the backdrop her trifold linguistic repertoire holds, specifically Limon Creole. A border language that reflects the reality of integration turned into *assimilation* through the linguistic element, where English and Limon Creole were relegated to the sidelines as 'non'-Costa Rican languages.

The situation is not particular to the Costa Rican Caribbean linguistic minority, but common of contact and resistance dynamics between cultural, racial, and linguistic borderlands across the globe. In marginalized contexts, contact languages like Limon Creole are "considered inferior by the same communities that use and communicate them", explains the author of *Coloniality of Diasporas*.[85] Anzaldúa's approach to Chicano Spanish as a border tongue in the United States ("How to Tame a Wild Tongue", *Borderlands*) is a perfect example of this. She explains Chicano Spanish is considered "poor Spanish" and an "illegitimate" language. Specifically, a "bastard language", even for the people who speak it.[86] This reality, in fact, is another aspect of the meta-archipelagic *repeating island*, traceable to colonialism and creoles born out it. As Martínez-San Miguel refers to it, creole speakers of the insular Caribbean also deemed their own languages as substandard, for they "linked them with slavery or lack of education and deemed their creoles as inferior to the European and metropolitan languages of their former colonizers".[87] Mainly because its speakers have *internalized* "how our language has been used against us by the dominant culture", as explained by Anzaldúa.[88] Afro-Costa Rican emotional attitudes towards LC as registered by Herzfeld reflect a mirrored – if not identical – process of such "linguistic terrorism", as keenly termed by the Chicana writer.[89]

Bernard's insertion of Limon Creole in her poetry, as well as her poetic code-switching in general, correspond in this manner to a performative act against such repudiations. As analyzed by Martínez-San Miguel in Edward Kamau Brathwaite (*History of the Voice* 1984), the *Éloge de la Créolité* defenders (1989), and in Ana Celia Zentella (*Growing up Bilingual* 1997), Bernard's *creole talk* also transforms her languages "from a place of inferiority and shame into a poetics, and a source of celebration for the creativity and agency" that her

---

[83]   Anzaldúa, *Borderlands*: 75.
[84]   Ibid.: 85.
[85]   Martínez-San Miguel, *Coloniality of Diasporas*: 132.
[86]   Anzaldúa, *Borderlands*: 80.
[87]   Martínez-San Miguel, *Coloniality of Diasporas*: 132.
[88]   Anzaldúa, *Borderlands*: 80.
[89]   Ibid.

infranational language constitutes.[90] Recalling Bernard's assertion: "Creole language, which is the oldest and newest thing we have, is rich, rhythmical, and fascinating."[91] Her multilingual poetry *legitimizes* her linguistic identity by "recovering the local and cultural inflections of the [Costa Rican Caribbean] landscape"[92] and in so doing claims its importance in the history of Costa Rica. Her code-switching performs hence her *mestiza-consciousness* linguistically, which flows from one cultural identity to the next, while simultaneously resisting unequal relations of power between her languages.

Unequal Languages

"Central American English is one of the Western Hemisphere's best-kept secrets", affirms John Holm (1983), for it can be found all along the Central American Caribbean coast, from Belize down to Panamá.[93] Holm traces the appearance of English in the New Continent to European colonialism, when Britain and Spain fought each other over the new territories. Jamaica, Barbados, St. Kitts, among other islands that had become British property, became thus anglophone colonies. This is relevant to Limón's history since it was from these islands that the vast number of volunteer workers migrated to Costa Rica, especially from Jamaica. As a consequence of the anglophone Afro-Caribbean diaspora, Limón became a linguistic borderland composed by an ethnolinguistic minority whose language (SE) simultaneously defined ethnic and class divisions among the workforce in Limón, yielding the elite and working-class racism (see "The Dialectics of Race and Nation" and "The Skin-History Metonymy and the Marginalization of Blacks in Limón").

The linguistic element functioned not only as a symbol of identification with British culture, but also as the basic vehicle for obtaining higher-ranking jobs within the United Fruit Company. Workers could communicate directly with the North Americans in charge and thus had an advantage with regards to Costa Rican Spanish-speaking laborers. Bourgois's research has documented that "blacks in the 1920s averaged higher wages than Hispanics and occupied the more prestigious positions."[94] Preferential employment allowed Afro-Caribbeans to fill low-level management positions as mechanics, supervisors, or watchmen in diverse UFCo.'s divisions such as the Electricity, the Transport, the Engineering, the Maintenance, or the Railroad Departments.[95] North Americans were replaced by Afro-Caribbeans in diverse positions in the Railway enterprise, though with lower paid salaries. These salaries were nonetheless higher than those of the Spanish-speaking laborers between 1920 and 1925.[96] Afro-Caribbeans earned fifteen cents an hour

---

[90] Martínez-San Miguel, *Coloniality of Diasporas*: 137.
[91] Jackson, "Our Weapon is Strong Language": 125.
[92] Martínez-San Miguel, *Coloniality of Diasporas*: 143.
[93] Holm, *Central American English*: 7. See also Zimmer, *El español hablado por los afrocostarricenses*: 25–30, where the author refers to the creoles of Belize, Guatemala, Nicaragua, and Panamá, as well as to the Bay Islands (Honduras), to the islands of San Andrés and Providence (Colombia), and to other minority languages spoken in these territories.
[94] Bourgois, *Ethnicity at Work*: 75.
[95] Ibid.: 82.
[96] Senior, *Ciudadanía afrocostarricense*: 39.

working night shifts on the docks, while Costa Ricans were paid twelve and one-half cents for the same work. The former received ten cents an hour for daily shifts, while the latter earned eight and a-half cents.[97] Likewise, Chomsky calls attention to the fact that "the most prestigious high-paying jobs, those with the railroad, were predominantly in the hands of blacks", while most Costa Ricans were working under the rain and under the sun in the open fields.[98]

Costa Ricans reacted to this by making use of the state's legal system to impose Spanish in the working sphere as the norm language, which would favor citizens first and foremost. That is why the first of state regulations to be passed in favor of Costa Ricans and against Black Caribbeans was the Law of Railways in 1927. It stated that a quota of Costa Ricans had to be hired as part of the workforce, and that all workers should speak, read, and write Spanish.[99] The Law of Railways sought to overturn the advantage that Afro-Caribbeans had opposite Costa Ricans by forcing the UFCo. to hire Costa Rican laborers. 'That there are no laws that oppress life?', asks Campbell. Once again, nation~diaspora dynamic/s in Costa Rica tend to differ. Speaking English was a decisive factor in upward (or no) mobility within the United Fruit Company in Limón. Hence, English was not only an element of cultural difference, but also of economic opportunity: "[it] was the single most important criterion of status allocation, as it was of image formation".[100] Indeed, as long as the United Fruit Company would remain in Limón, it would be the official enclave language given that over half the population in the region was anglophone, as stated by the 1927 Census.[101] This is why language standardization in the region was one of the state's most important projects when the UFCo. moved its operations to the Pacific coast after 1934.

Once the Company abandoned the region and Caribbean descendants acquired Costa Rican citizenship, English lost prestige and Spanish became the dominant language. It became fundamental to learn the latter to avoid being marginalized both in the political as in the economical domains. Consequently, the linguistic isolation that the Afro-Costa Rican community had experienced until then had finally been broken. Regarding the linguistic repertoire of Black Costa Ricans, Herzfeld (1983) rightly points to how Limón's generational divisions at the beginning of the 1980s still reproduced Bryce-Laporte's observations (1962). The oldest generations are Jamaica-oriented and speak English. The next generation, to which Bernard pertains, is bilingual, since it speaks English and Spanish, while for "the youngest generation, which identifies with Costa Rica, Spanish is the language of prestige". Herzfeld however notes that "the mother tongue continues to be Limonese Creole".[102] Nonetheless, Winkler documented in 2013 that "although most young Blacks understand LC, some either do not want to speak it or cannot".[103] She sadly affirms that the current number of LC speakers is most likely smaller than that suggested by Herzfeld at the end of the 1970s (thirty to forty thousand) and by the Ethnologue website in 1986 (fifty-five

---

97 Olien, "The Adapation of West Indian Blacks": 154, n. 9.
98 Chomsky, *West Indian Workers*: 49.
99 Harpelle, *The West Indians of Costa Rica*: 70.
100 Purcell, *Banana Fallout*: 6.
101 According to the 1927 census, Spanish was the second most spoken language in the region (36,5%), while indigenous languages were spoken by 6,5% of the population in Limón (Viales, *Después del enclave*: 51).
102 Herzfeld, "The Creoles of Costa Rica and Panama": 134.
103 Winkler, "Limonese Creole English": 209.

thousand) "due to the almost complete loss of the monolingual LC community over the last 20 years as well as the shift of many young Blacks to Spanish".[104]

As a result, LC has been shadowed to a certain extent due to the naturalization of Blacks in Costa Rica and to substitution of English by Spanish as the new language of power. In fact, when a project was launched by the Ministry of Education in 1974 with the aim of reincorporating English in primary education in Limón, students' fluency in LC was to be used so as to permit a quick transition to English. Paula Palmer writes the Plan encouraged "students and teachers in Limón to investigate the values and strengths of the Limón culture which are rooted in the experience of the Afro-Caribbean settlers."[105] Nevertheless, Herzfeld tells how "strong negative reactions from parents and teachers" were expressed against the project, for integration to Costa Rica's mainstream society would be compromised by teaching and learning English through Limon Creole. The project was consequently aborted. Eulalia Bernard coordinated this *Plan Educativo de Limón* and directed the teacher training seminars.[106]

Both Winkler and Herzfeld have argued that the reconfiguration of the population in Limón at the second half of the twentieth century due to internal migration to the Atlantic seaside in search of better work opportunities in the second half of the twentieth century – facilitated by new means of transportation connecting the capital of San José with the Limón province and port – have led, among other reasons, to a process of *decreolization*. Referring to postcolonial situations, Martínez-San Miguel explains decreolization in the Caribbean occurs when creole "speakers adopt lexicon and structures from coexisting European or metropolitan languages that are deemed to be more prestigious."[107] In the case of Black Costa Rica, the metropolitan language corresponds to the country's official state language, which reenacts the same structures of linguistic relations of power in an analogous manner. On the one hand, Herzfeld asserts that creole features are being replaced by Spanish ones due to the intense contact between these languages.[108] On the other, Winkler explains that since Spanish has acquired a greater importance and predominance in the region since the last decades of the twentieth century, code-switching and borrowing Spa lexemes habitually take place, Spanish being introduced into an English-based matrix grammar more frequently than the other way around.[109] In fact, back in 2000 she affirmed that it was rare in Limón to hear people speaking English or Limon Creole in their pure forms, without Spanish borrowings.[110]

Under such considerations, the Spa switches which foreground the poem "What fi do?" can be best understood as a linguistic practice that mirrors the increase of Spanish use in everyday conversation, as signaled by Winkler and Mosby. Beyond this explanation, however, and as explained by Anzaldúa, both Limon Creole *and* code-switching in Bernard's poetry correspond largely to "border tongue[s] which developed naturally" into what she calls a "forked tongue", a variation of two [or more] languages". This *forked tongue*

[104] Winkler, "Limonese Creole English": 212.
[105] Palmer, *What Happen*: 14.
[106] Herzfeld, "Language and Identity": 129.
[107] Martínez-San Miguel, *Coloniality of Diasporas*: 131.
[108] Herzfeld, "Language and Identity": 129.
[109] Winkler, "Cambio de códigos": 191.
[110] Ibid.: 196.

is a language which reflects the borderland conflict and corresponds to *"un modo de vivir* [...] a living language" that Bernard has appropriated to serve her poetics. Winkler's affirmations concerning Spa irruptions in LC as occurring *habitually* sustain Anzaldúa's cultural perception of the *forked tongue*. It is an entity that is kept alive by its speakers in the form of an ethnic identity, switching to and fro, straddling the linguistic borderlands of their national~diasporan past. Bernard's poetic *forked tongue* has become itself, in fact, a "homeland" where the poet's linguistic identity corresponds largely to her ethnic identity.[111] Nonetheless, as we shall see next, the poet's *forked tongue* represents also a political aesthetic because it is "capable of communicating the realities" of the people who speak it.[112] That is, the economical marginalization of Black campesinos and their enforced linguistic assimilation. The decision of the Costa Rican government to pass a law in 1953 prohibiting English schools in Limón,[113] together with the educational reforms that went hand in hand with the nationalizing campaign in the province, were central in carrying out a re-accommodation of linguistic power relations in the region. The ensuing discussion focuses on the assimilation of Afro-Costa Ricans through monolingual education as read through the poet's bilingual claims, while the concluding pages argue Bernard's code-switching functions as a literary combat aimed at demystifying Costa Rica's social democracy.

---

[111] Anzaldúa, *Borderlands*: 77.
[112] Ibid.: 77, cf. p. 81.
[113] Winkler, "Limonese Creole English": 210. Herzfeld, "Language and Identity": 129.

On the Path Towards Language

"BILINGUAL CAMPESINOS SPEAK OUT"

1   "Bull Shit," said the Pueblo
2   And vomited.
3   "Bull Shit," said the Pueblo
4   And Spat.
5   "A la mierda with Eso…,"
6   Said the intelligent Pueblo
7   And Aborted.
8   Rubbish, shit; pura paja…
9   Not one inch of that carajada…
10 We don't quiere…
11 We won't have it.
12 Boring whores,
13 Damn pendejos…
14 Come from lejos, to rajar to us;
15 What the hell!…;
16 They think we were born ayer?
17 That's the error que tienen…,
18 Los que vienen, …talking
19 About alfabetización,…
20 Middle técnico;
21 Want you leave your rancho
22 And go to hell, …or México, and,
23 De ahí become a "wet back or Chicano"
24 Stick your… whatever in your
25 "Ah no" end up I am not
26 In no aula de mierda to get
27 A damn doctorado in…
28 "Hombre desocupado."

My Black King (n.p.)
First recorded in *Negritud* (1976)

In "Bilingual Campesinos Speak Out" (hereafter BCSO), Bernard carries out an act of "radical bilingualism" that challenges "both Spanish and English monolingual expectations"[114] since the poem can best be grasped by a bilingual audience. Critics refer to this particular aspect of bilingual literature as a challenge imposed on the monolingual readership, who either feels compelled to interact with and engage the multilingual text so as to comprehend its meaning, or is discouraged by non-comprehension and probably sets the text aside.[115] Bernard's choice not to facilitate the understanding of the poem for the monolingual readership by glossing words as she did in WFD can be thus read as a "political

---

[114]   Torres, "In the Contact-Zone": 86.
[115]   Cf. Ch'ien, *Weird English* (2004) and Torres, "In the Contact-Zone" (2007).

act", as understood by Ashcroft, Griffiths, and Tifflin (1989) when referring to glossaries and the translations of foreign words in postcolonial literature.[116] She is not giving primacy to the monolingual reader, but instead reenacting a powerful literary practice that furthermore "captures the author's bicultural reality and her transnational experiences living in an 'in between' place".[117]

If we are to pose the question, who is Bernard writing for when she code-switches?, the answer must probably would have to remain open so as to grasp how this 'in-between place' is best explained by Anzaldúa, who underscores the importance of asserting one's ethnic and cultural identity through the linguistic entity. That is, by understanding code-switching as a performative act that reveals a borderland *per se*. She affirms:

> Until I am free to write bilingually and to switch codes without having always to translate […] and as long as I have to accommodate the English speakers rather than having them accommodate me, my tongue will be illegitimate.[118]

Bernard's reluctance to include a glossary as she did in WFD reveals a consciousness that is linked to the purpose of transgressing linguistic and ethnic borderlands without having to apologize, i.e. *explain* herself, hence legitimizing all of her tongues. Through this lens, then, Bernard's multilingualism gives precedence to her rhizomatic belonging, expressed linguistically in the form of anglophone Caribbean-ness and Spanish-speaking Central American-ness coupled with Limon Creole's inherent code mixing. Code-switching brings together and reunites these cultural identities in a linguistic continuum by what Gary Keller (1979) terms a "secondary language system".[119] That is, a language that expresses itself by means of two grammars. A sort of "bilingual talk", as defined by Leonora Timm (1975).[120]

Throughout the poem there is a poly-competence that interrelates these languages, even if English is clearly the language that sets the stage. According to Myers-Scotton's (1993) Matrix Language-Frame Model (MLF), English can be identified as the Matrix Language (ML), that is, "the language that provides the grammatical structure", while Spanish is the Embedded Language (EL), i.e. the lesser role language that contributes fewer morphemes to the speech enunciation.[121] Following the MLF Model, the poem evidences three types of constituents. The reader encounters (a) [ML + EL] verses, where the internal dependency between SE and Spa is grammatically governed by English, as the opening verses demonstrate it (vv. 1, 3, 5, 6). Also, the poem presents (b) verses written solely in the Matrix Language (ML islands), such as verses 11–12: "We won't have it / Boring whores". Here, no code-switching occurs. The third type of constituent, (c) EL islands, are however not an active-developing element of the poem, the only exception being the final verse "Hombre desocupado" (v. 28), to which I will come back soon enough. Nevertheless, the constant [ML → EL] intra/interverse switch is the poem's stylistic variation par excellence. Through it, a playful structure is maintained across the poem and installs what Lipski referred to as

---

[116] Ashcroft/Griffiths/Tifflin, *The Empire Strikes Back*: 61.
[117] Torres, "In the Contact-Zone": 88f.
[118] Anzaldúa, *Borderlands*: 91.
[119] Keller, "The Literary Stratagems Available to the Bilingual Chicano Writer": 275.
[120] Timm, "Spanish-English code-switching": 473.
[121] Callahan, *Spanish/English Codeswitching*: 11.

the interplay between the base language and the embedded language as a "bilingual grammar". As he explains it, the speaker makes use of two essentially distinct grammars integrating them fully to the point that a bilingual structural composition is noticeable.[122] This does not correspond to the existence of a third grammar, as Pfaff states, but instead both grammars are "meshed", they are entangled and have become interlocked according to a number of functional, structural, and semantic constraints.[123] In fact, contrary to what sociolinguists describe as an automatic and unconscious mechanism, written code-switching represents the poet's literary awareness, who plays with linguistic behavior and with bilingual meaning through supposed ungrammaticality, as for example in verse 10: "We don't quiere".

A short digression is here necessary in order to underscore Bernard's code-switching as a literary combat regarding linguistic assimilation. "We don't quiere" is a counterexample of code-switching restraints that occurs purposively for stylistic reasons, as defined by Laura Callahan (2004).[124] Traditionally, and specifically regarding English/Spanish CS, a switch between the auxiliary and its verb – like in *(I) don't quiero – would be unacceptable in spoken conversation,[125] since it is a risky shift that may compromise the grammaticality of the enunciation.[126] When disobeyed, such a switch "generates pidgin-like utterances, which strike [...] as nothing less than bizarre".[127] These sociolinguistic theoretical precepts are overturned by Anzaldúa's comprehension of the *forked-tongue* as "neither *español ni inglés*".[128] If on the one hand sociolinguistic theory defines such code-switching as 'incorrect' and hence a "mutilation of Spanish" (as the Chicana author refers to the comments her own multilingual writing has received), then Bernard's poetic multilingual-ism, itself a conscious manipulation of language, performs a *forked tongue* insofar, in Anzaldúa's words, it is not held back by the *reglas de la academia*.[129] She is rather playing with ungrammaticality in order to express a particular tone and a specific attitude regarding the content matter against which she is protesting. An ironic tone, for that matter. The poem flows from one language to the other in such a way that both systems are integrated in a balanced fashion, even when 'ungrammatically', which projects instead *irony*.

The switches to Spa in BCSO, like in the previous poem, allow the verses to rhyme. A perfect rhyme is produced between verses 13 and 14 (*pendejos, lejos*), while there is a perfect vocal rhyme at distinct [a] sounds between verses 8 and 9 (*pura paja, carajada*). Moreover, the clauses in Spa fit in perfectly in the SE structure and through the language switch, rhyme is created monolingually between *tienen* & (*los que*) *vienen* (v. 17f.).

---

[122] Lipski, "Spanish-English Language Switching": 198.

[123] Pfaff, "Constraints on Language Mixing": 314.

[124] Callahan, *Spanish/English Codeswitching*: 14f.

[125] Timm states such a switch would not be predictable, for negating elements must correspond in code to the verbs undergoing negation ("Spanish-English code-switching": 479). Thus, as a rule, switching should be avoided in negative constructions, as well as between pronouns and their verbs (we + quiere).

[126] This corresponds to the equivalence constraint (Poplack, "Sometimes I'll start a sentence in Spanish" 1980) that governs code-switching at the spoken level. That is, switches will occur at points where a violation of syntactic rules of either language does not occur, so that their structures map onto each other.

[127] Timm, "Spanish-English code-switching": 479. A switch like *(I) don't quiero is inadmissible because it vio-lates a simple and unequivocal language constraint rule.

[128] Anzaldúa, *Borderlands*: 77.

[129] Ibid.: 77 and 76: "They would hold us back with their bag of *reglas de academia*" (emphasis in original).

Alliteration is however reproduced multilingually in verses 16–18 between *They* / *That's the* / *tienen* / *talking*. It must be noted that "error" (v. 17) is a Spanish word, for BCSO was recorded in the 1976 *Negritud* album and Bernard's pronunciation of the word is clearly Spanish. This is relevant to the whole of the poem since the Spa code-switch creates a break in the English language flow and gives the verse a particular cadence with broken tempo. Accent is stressed on the final syllable by 'e/rrór', with special emphasis on the <rr> sound realized as the alveolar trill [r] in Spa, very different to the alveolar tap sound [ɾ] in SE. Further, "error" shares with "ayer" a similar production of the [ɾ] sound at the end of the word.[130] And Spa lexeme (*ayer* / *error* / *vienen* / *tienen*) add cadence to the verses by lengthening them. These characteristics are but evidence of how language switch is not arbitrary, nor evidence of a less-than-ideal bilingual, but a deliberate poetic choice.[131]

Linguistic Terrorism

Bernard's bilingual talk does not refer solely to the rhetorical manipulation of language in function of style and effect. The content being expressed by it simultaneously deploys a particular argument regarding a specific situation withholding infranational historical content. It cannot be stressed enough that stylistic switching acts as a strategic device that transgresses linguistic borderlands. Their borders have to do in part with social and cultural identities, but in part as well with the linguistic relations of power that came to be as a consequence of borderland dynamics in Limón.

With time and having obtained Costa Rican citizenship, linguistic assimilation of Blacks born in the country gradually took place. This led to English and Limon Creole spoken by Afro-Costa Ricans to suffer linguistic domination on behalf of the Costa Rican state apparatus as an effect of internal colonialism, defined by Suzanne Romaine (1994) as the "marginalization of the languages and cultures of minority peoples".[132] It is currently discussed if because of the interference of Spanish in Limon Creole the latter could disappear, what in sociolinguistic terms is called a "language shift". In fact, Limon Creole receives so many interferences from Spanish by code-switching and borrowing, that Herzfeld (2011), as well as Portilla (2000) and Winkler (1998 and 2000), problematize if a

---

[130] I thank my colleague Dr. Robert Hesselbach for his help in the linguistic transcription of my literary analysis.

[131] Uriel Weinreich (*Languages in Contact* 1953) stated that the "*ideal bilingual* switches from one language to another according to appropriate changes in the speech situation […], but not in an unchanged speech situation, *and certainly not within a single sentence*" (p. 73; emphasis added). According to Weinreich, intrasentential code-switching was evidence of a lack of competence in either one of the languages, for switching meant the need to appeal to another system to fill in a linguistic gap. Poplack's study had already addressed this prejudice against CS, observing that code switching is indeed a rule-governed verbal skill that acts as an indicator of bilingual competence. Dismantling Weinreich's statement, Blom and Gumperz ("Social meaning in linguistic structure: code-switching in Norway" 1972) conceptualized "situational" and "metaphorical switching" to make evident how conversational CS enacts particular social relationships between speakers, where the spoken utterances in one or the other language are but units of social meaning within social interaction (p. 127f.).

[132] Romaine, *Language in Society*: 35.

language shift is taking place, i.e. language death.[133] According to these authors, Limon Creole suffers a much more significant influence from Spanish than the other way around due to the intense and asymmetrical language contact between them, which leads to the Creole speaker reconstituting her set of linguistic rules and incorporating Spanish more frequently into the LC grammatical system. Among the reasons for such a heavy influence the authors refer to the fact that Spa has become the language of prestige in the region, being the official state language, and thus directly tied to national, educational, political, social, and economical aspects.

In other words, linguistic relations of power exist in Bernard's (and the Afro-community she belongs to) trifold linguistic repertoire, which for Susan Gal (1988) refer to unequal relations between dominant and minority groups within the state.[134] Which is why according to Ofelia García's understanding of multilingualism in scenarios of language contact, "the languages of an individual are rarely socially equal, having different power and prestige".[135] She goes on to clarify that because of this, the speaker has diverse and unequal experiences with each of the languages. Herzfeld (1994) also refers to this complex relationship by affirming that multilingual speakers do not experience language contact situations "under neutral emotional conditions", but instead the situation "involves some kind of dominance of one group over the other, thus always producing significant attitudinal reactions."[136] As it will be unfolded in the ensuing pages, code-switching in "Bilingual Campesinos Speak Out" makes visible the linguistic relations of power that each of Bernard's languages hold in relation to one another. I consider that swear words, together with irony and sarcasm deployed by CS in BCSO transmit sociohistorical information in the form of *social protest* concerning the monolingual educational reforms that took place in Limón towards the second half of the twentieth century. In this manner, Bernard's manipulation of various languages in a single text constitute a resistance literature.

The key switch that unravels the infranational character of Bernard's code-switched stor(y)ing is specifically verse nineteen, where she switches to Spa with "*alfabetización*" ["literacy campaign"]. Choosing to express this word in Spanish permits us to extract a particular historical imagination regarding *linguistic terrorism* in Limón. Born in 1935, Eulalia Bernard lived the multilingual reality of 'Limón in the raw' when growing up as a child until she moved to the capital to carry out her primary studies, returning later to Limón once again for her secondary education.[137] An English/Creole-speaking ethnolinguistic minority much like the one to which she belongs to is not particular solely to the Costa Rican Caribbean coast, as is not the uneasy relationship that the Spanish-speaking governments had with assimilating the English-speaking Black minorities on the Honduran, Nicaraguan, and Panamanian Caribbean coast.[138] Throughout the area, English

---

[133] Herzfeld, "Una evaluación de la vitalidad lingüística del inglés criollo de Limón: su vigencia o su desplazamiento" (2011); Winkler, *Limonense Creole: A Case of Contact-Induced Language Change* (1998) and "Cambio de códigos en el criollo limonense" (2000); and Portilla, "Hispanismos en el diccionario de inglés criollo de Costa Rica" (2000).

[134] Cf. Gal, "The political economy of code choice" (1988).

[135] García, *Bilingual Education in the 21st Century*: 45.

[136] Herzfeld, "Language and Identity": 116.

[137] De Costa-Willis, *Daughters of the Diaspora*: 117f.

[138] Holm, *Central American English*: 7ff.

represented a threat to the national unity of the officially self-declared Spanish-speaking states, Belize being the sole exception. Let us not forget that back in 1927, the newly appointed Law of Railway limited the hiring of anglophone laborers in order to favor the Costa Rican worker. That same year, the educator and diplomat Luis Dobles Segreda (1889–1956) had referred to the complicated circumstances regarding anglophone Blacks in Limón within the Costa Rican Spanish-speaking educational system. He however confused the situation as a problem of ethnicity. Segreda considered that white teachers could not educate Black children because of ethnocultural differences and therefore pleaded for the training of Black teachers along the lines of the national educational program, so that these could in turn teach Black children ("Es preciso [...] preparar maestros de color para que eduquen a los niños de color"). Furthermore, Spanish spoken by the Black community impoverished the student-teacher communication because it was slow and dim according to Segreda ("torpe"), as well as imperfectly developed ("rudimentario").[139]

It is once again noticeable how Anzaldúa's consideration of Chicano Spanish as a border tongue applies to the linguistic reality in Limón, caught between a trifold repertoire creating a linguistic ethno/infranational borderland. "In childhood we are told that our language is wrong", affirms Anzaldúa, just like Segreda judged Spanish spoken by Afro-Costa Ricans to be *rudimentario y torpe*. "*Somos del español deficiente*" explains Anzaldúa, much like Segreda advocated the urgent need of bringing Spanish into Limón classrooms so as to perfect it. "Because we speak with tongues of fire we are culturally crucified", she goes on to state,[140] which mirrors as well Segreda's plea for a nationalized curriculum in Limón's schools with the purpose of assimilating Black Costa Ricans to the hegemonic culture.[141] Hence, what Bernard poetically accomplishes is fundamentally a transgression of cultural and ethnic boundaries by crossing border tongues in a performative manner through code-switching. And in so doing she declaims symbolically the oppressive character of glocal *alfabetización* programs that crucify the cultural dignity of minority groups through linguistic assimilation.

Even though Segreda's considerations were not accomplished as proposed under his racist ideology, educational policies during the first half of the twentieth century, especially from 1940 onwards, did address Segreda's concerns. These became according to Olien a "successful acculturating force" that took charge of molding Limón's Caribbean cultural and linguistic heritage to a hegemonic/homogenous and monolithic Costa Rican identity.[142] The imposition of Spanish was its most efficient tool. These policies were concerned with assimilating Blacks through monolingualism, rather than integrating or including them into the Costa Rican imagined community. Since the beginning of the twentieth century, teachers had been sent from Jamaica to promote a British-educational system and, as a consequence, Limón was one of the top three provinces with the highest literacy

---

[139] Segreda, "El estado y la cultura de los hombres de color: 402.

[140] Anzaldúa, *Borderlands*: 80.

[141] Segreda, "El estado y la cultura de los hombres de color: 402: "Llevémosle un maestro de su raza [...] Si ese maestro conoce bien la lengua castellana y le exigimos que le enseñe siempre y la haga practicar en todos los ejercicios; le pedimos que enseñe geografía patria y llame a simpatía por nuestra historia y por nuestro porvenir; que enseñe las normas generales de nuestra organización social y de nuestra legislación, habremos conseguido mucho."

[142] Olien, "The Adaptation of West Indian Blacks": 148.

percentages among its inhabitants, as recorded by the 1927 census (See "Dwelling in Displacement", Part I). In the 1930s, at least thirty-three private English-speaking schools outnumbered the eleven Spanish-speaking governmental public schools based at the Limón province,[143] of which some were only at the primary level. As Mrs. Pearl Cunningham confirms it:

> Oh, yes, yes, we have Spanish school from I was small, from I have sense. But only two grades, first grade, second grade, first grade, second grade, first grade, second grade, like so. How long you can keep going first grade, second grade? So just a few people send their childen [sic] there. Everybody was English school, English school.[144]

Consequently, when President Rafael Angel Guardia Calderón was elected into office (1940–1944) and having the United Fruit Company abandoned its operations in Limón, the government pushed forward a program of educational reforms that sought to nationalize, standardize, and regulate instruction in the country under the official language and as part of a nationalized curriculum, pressuring, according to Olien, Caribbean families to send their children to Spanish-speaking public schools.[145] After the civil revolution of 1948 and the legal clearance for the naturalization of all Costa Rican-born Caribbean descendants under the newly appointed President Figueres, forty-seven schools were built in Limón. By 1963, Puerto Limón had eighty-two elementary public schools and two high schools.[146]

The imposition of the state language through education policies corresponded to a political and ideological mobilization on behalf of the nation's government. Limón's English schools were put under scrutiny,[147] for politicians in the 1940s like Secretary of State Ricardo Fournier saw in private English schools the tendency to "denationalize" the ideals and sentiments of Costa Rica.[148] Non-Black Costa Ricans living in the Caribbean province also saw the need for similar educational measures in favor of nationalizing the 'foreign' Caribbean workers, that is, in order to "españolizar la raza de color", as a resident of Siquirres expressed himself in the Limón-based newspaper *La voz del Atlántico* (1940).[149] For the 1945 school year, the government expected that Spanish be a prerequisite for attendance in all schools and, wishing to impose a Spanish-based education on Black children, threatened to close down all English schools. A threat that it had to abandon since it could not enforce it.[150] Curiously enough, in 1900 Nicaragua *did* impose overnight the

---

[143] Harpelle, *The West Indians of Costa Rica*: 210, n. 18. Michael Olien, however, writes in 1977 that prior to 1951 only six public schools were based in Limón ("The Adaptation of West Indian Blacks": 147).

[144] Quoted in Palmer, *What Happen*: 171.

[145] Olien, "The Adaptation of West Indian Blacks": 146.

[146] Rosario, *Identidades de la población de origen jamaiquino*: 265. Cf. Olien, "The Adaptation of West Indian Blacks": 147.

[147] For example, the National Educators Association certified only a small number of the private schools as legally authorized schools. Those that had not been certified became thus illegal centers of instruction (Harpelle, *The West Indians of Costa Rica*: 128f.).

[148] Ibid.: 125.

[149] The editorial was printed on November 16, 1940. The author pleaded for stricter regulations regarding instruction in the region. He considered this was the most effective way to assimilate Costa Rican-born Caribbean descendants. An obliged instruction in Spanish was, according to him, the best way to 'to *hispanize* the colored race' (Guevara, "Las escuelas particulares de la zona Atlántica": 5).

[150] Harpelle, *The West Indians of Costa Rica*: 128.

banning of English in schools as part of their educational reforms, which in 1981 was overturned through literacy campaigns in English.[151] Nonetheless, as a consequence of these procedures in Costa Rica, Black children attended both public and private schools. During the late afternoon and on weekends they went to private schools,[152] where they went over the same material covered in public institutions but in English.[153] This however did not help them succeed in the national institutions and still in 1965, almost fifty percent of Black children (46%) had to repeat one or more grades because of language difficulties in public schools.[154]

Bernard's switch to "alfabetización" (v. 19) does not occur in semantic isolation. Instead, it is embedded in the whole of the poem through an upbeat enthusiastic tone,[155] which, due to the taboo word switches (swear words) occurring at virtually every verse, an annoyed and outraged lyrical attitude is emphasized concerning the *alfabetización* process she claims to be an *error*. The language switches between English and Spanish in Bernard, coupled with the content of what is being said, sets a sarcastic voice that expresses itself against what a literacy campaign means.[156] In this case, and as the poet herself emphasizes it by swearing, it signifies "Rubbish, shit; *pura paja…*" (v. 8). Swear words are particularly sense-creating in BCSO.[157] They in fact open up the poem (vv. 1–4) and determine its thematic and formal development. The lyrical voice expresses disbelief on behalf of the *Pueblo* by saying 'to hell with that' (v. 5: "A la mierda with Eso"). She goes on to reiterate what a bad idea that *carajada* ('thing', in this specific case 'situation') is, i.e. the literacy campaign, which she considers to be nonsense. "Rubbish, shit" is reiterated in Spa with "pura paja" in order to amplify and emphasize the message she is trying to communicate, typical of conversational code-switching as categorized by Gumperz.[158] *Pura paja* pertains to a Costa Rican linguistic domain reflected by linguistic particularity. In Central American Spanish "paja" metaphorically refers to lies.[159] Adding "pura" (in this context, 'simply') emphasizes the trickery Bernard is protesting.[160]

---

[151]   Holm, *Central American English*: 11.

[152]   Harpelle, *The West Indians of Costa Rica*: 127.

[153]   Olien, "The Adaptation of West Indian Blacks": 148.

[154]   Ibid.: 151.

[155]   According to Keller, code-switching acts as a function of style, by which the *tone* of the poem is set ("The Literary Stratagems Available to the Bilingual Chicano Writer": 302–310).

[156]   Cf. Horn, "Ästhetische Funktionen der Sprachmischung in der Literatur": 232.

[157]   Herzfeld in fact had pointed to the fact that code alternations in Limon Creole speakers acted as a rhetorical device concerning taboo words (Herzfeld, "Una evaluación de la vitalidad lingüística del inglés criollo de Limón": 116).

[158]   Gumperz, *Discourse Strategies*: 78.

[159]   Definition n. 13 provided by the *DRAE* states that "paja" is in El Salvador, Guatemala, Honduras, and Nicaragua used interchangeably for 'lies'. It is also employed as such in Costa Rica. Definition n. 10 states that in El Salvador "paja" means "tontería" – 'foolishness', which is also appropriate in the poem's context. Retrieved from http://dle.rae.es/?id=RTGhL0f. For *carajada*, see http://dle.rae.es/?id=7P9iw0o. Cf. García Valverde, *Vocabulario básico y cotidiano abreviado del castellano y costarriqueñismos*: 24.

[160]   *Pura paja* functions semantically as in English-based Chicano poetry, where a single word in Spa may mark a shift to, or an emphasis of the specific Mexican cultural domain, adding cultural alternative to the text. As Valdés-Fallis explains it, the "Mexican tradition is thought and referred to [linguistically]" by switching to Spa while being contrasted against the anglophone background (Valdes-Fallis, "Code-Switching in Bilingual Chicano Poetry": 880).

Furthermore, by switching to "alfabetización" Bernard installs mainly what Sturm-Trigonakis has called an "Alteritäts-Effekt" because it signals *un-identical spaces*.[161] Verse 14 ("Come from *lejos* [...]") makes explicit the physical distance between these spaces by incorporating the idea of 'a faraway' with respect to the location of Bernard's *Pueblo*, the bilingual campesinos of Limón. These un-identical places contrast the anglophone culture and its English schools with the official state language and its educational reforms dictated from the San José capital. Let us remember that English schools in Limón were run by Protestant, Baptist, Adventist, and Anglican congregations.[162] They were financed by the Afro-Caribbean communities and the parents themselves, by Garvey's United Negro Improvement Association (UNIA), as well as by the North American transnational Banana Empire which benefited from having an educated workforce who spoke their language (see "Dwelling in Displacement", Part I). In contrast, the written Spa switch to *alfabetización* recalls Calderón's educational reforms when he took office in the 1940s, reinforced with the subsequent school construction-boom that took off with Figueres after 1949 and that in the long run meant nonetheless educational failure for Black children. This corresponds to a reality shared in a supranational manner by similar outernational communities, as documented by Romaine. She mentions that in Great Britain West-Indian children tend to do worse than British ones. In the United States, Hispanic students are about three and a half years behind in school achievement. In Denmark, not a single student of Turkish or Pakistani origin finished high school between 1975 and 1978. And non-English-speaking immigrant children in Toronto performed worse academically than Canadian-born students in the years from 1969 to 1975.[163]

Considering that education is one of society's main integrating instruments, schools have a powerful role in assimilating, not integrating, minorities into the state and its imagined community. According to Romaine, who in her book *Language in Society* carries out a study of the interdependent relationship of language and society, linguistic problems transform themselves into societal problems, one of them being educational failure (see Chapter 7). The author claims that children of ethnic minority background are likely to experience conflict in school because of language problems. In fact, language deficiency has been cited as "the main cause for the greater rate of school failure among minority children".[164] Olien's observation that 46% of Black children were held back in 1965 because of their limited Spanish capacities supports Romaine's affirmation. She also lists a series of factors that could be accounted for such educational failure. On the one hand, "linguistic/cultural mismatch between home and school" could limit the student when it came to learn and use Spanish, since its presence was confined to the state schools. Whereas at home, English and a form of Creole was probably spoken, as well as on the streets. As a second factor, Romaine asserts that "attitudes of the majority to the minorities and viceversa" restrict a better development of the linguistic capacities due to a series of cultural and ethnonational prejudices.[165] The attitude of the Costa Rican majority was characterized

---

161   Sturm-Trigonakis, *Global Playing in der Literatur*: 149.
162   Palmer, *What Happen*: 168.
163   Romaine, *Language in Society*: 192.
164   Ibid.: 191.
165   Ibid.: 194.

by racist sentiments that had gained strength from the 1920s (see "The Dialectics of Race and Nation", Part I) whereas Caribbean attitude towards Costa Rican culture and society, characterized by Purcell as an *ideology of superiority*, must have obstructed as well the entrance into monolingualism (see "Dwelling in Displacement", Part I). It makes sense to consider that Spanish public schools must have not been received openly in Limón but viewed as the forced intrusion of the state's official language and culture through the institutional and legal apparatus.

For these reasons, the *Pueblo* is not gullible: "They think we were born ayer?" (v. 16). Instead, the *Pueblo* is mad, will not stand for it, and calls those who come to convince them otherwise "boring whores" and damn fools ("pendejos"; vv. 12f.). In the final verses, Bernard defines the literacy campaign as taking place in a worthless and good-for-nothing schoolroom (v. 26: "aula de mierda"), since in the long run, not even a "damn" PhD title (v. 27) will make a significant difference in acquiring a job.

> 25   "Ah no" end up I am not
> 26   In no aula de mierda to get
> 27   A damn doctorado in...
> 28   "Hombre desocupado."

The above quoted verses make evident how code-switching allows Bernard to play with various levels of swearing, harmonically and poetically fashioned along a linguistic continuum. Taboo noun-switches act together with what is another stylistic effect of code-switching, *gradatio*. According to Keller, it is through CS that a "progressive advance is made from one sentence to the other, until a climax is achieved".[166] Accordingly, the taboo-noun-switches reinforce the enraged poetic tone and the climax is achieved with a sarcastic overtone at the final verse, "Hombre desocupado". On the one hand, the climax is ironically presented in Spa (EL island), while on the other, this *litteral/argumentative* couple reflects what Horn has referred to as code-switching's ludic dominance ("Dominanz des Spielerisches") and whose purpose is to install sarcasm. By it, incongruence ("Inkongruenz") and dissonance ("Disparatheit") lead the content *ad absurdum*,[167] for it is a parody and simply contradictory to think one needs a PhD degree to become an expert in being jobless.[168] In effect, code-switching in BSCO foregrounds and deploys taboo-switches that adjust the indignant and maddened tone from the beginning until the end as well as the punning irony, which becomes accentuated in the last verse.[169] Sarcastically transcribed in the language of the *alfabetización* process itself.

---

[166] Keller, "The Literary Stratagems Available to the Bilingual Chicano Writer": 309.

[167] Horn, "Ästhetische Funktionen der Sprachmischung": 235.

[168] See McKinney, "Costa Rica's Black Body": 19, n. 11, where the author considers "doctorado" to be self-referential and thus a marker of influence, stating the "intriguing space between the 'campesinos' who refuse the 'damn doctorado'" and the poet "Dr. Eulalia Bernard" (as the compilation is authored), which "makes her voice more likely to be heard".

[169] Scholars have noted the valuable humorous function CS has in written literature. For example, Sturm-Trigonakis names it as "parodistische Züge" (*Global Playing in der Literatur*: 156), which for Bisanti carries out a "funzione comico-umoristica" that deploys a comic, humorous, parodic or ridiculous ("caricaturale") effect in the text ("Retorica e plurilinguismo letterario": 269). And as already discussed *supra*, Horn recognizes that "die Sprachmischung ein mögliches Mittel der Komik sein kann" ("Ästhetische Funktionen der Sprachmischung": 234).

It must now be mentioned here that the switch to "alfabetización" in verse nineteen was recited with anglophone pronunciation in the oral version of "Bilingual Campesinos Speak Out", recorded in the *Negritud* vinyl (1976). Thus, the track plays back "alfabetización" as *alphabetization*.[170] As a result, the original oral version of the printed word refers and construes a distinct historical imagination than the one outlined here with "alfabetización", which nevertheless complements it. While the above discussion focused on the educational reforms which eradicated English schools in Limón – as implied by a *written* code-switch to the official state language –, a complementary approach to the oral version of BCSO throws light upon the failure of the Plan Educativo de Limón (1974), whose purpose was, ironically, to reintegrate English in the province's primary schools afterwards. As stated previously, Bernard directed the teacher training seminars supported by the Ministry of Education, where she used LC as a communication tool for teaching and helping children learn English at school. However, as Herzfeld reported it, the pilot project was terminated because parents and teachers rejected this pedagogic strategy, fearing it would continue to hinder their integration to Costa Rican society and culture.[171] Bernard's switch to *alphabetization* in *Negritud* evokes this *aurally*.

As noted by Winkler, the linguistic continuum of Black Costa Ricans is nowadays heavily influenced by Spa borrowings that are introduced into the English-based matrix, very much like BCSO poetically reenacts it.[172] This, in turn, explains Bernard's choice for the oral pronunciation of verse nineteen. Since "alphabetize" in Standard English means to arrange a number of things in alphabetical order, the original recording of BCSO reflects in this isolated situation a case of linguistic *borrowing*. In other words, *alphabetization* as pronounced in *Negritud* corresponds to a loanword from Spanish that has been adapted phonologically to the English system.[173] The switch is not gratuitous but a conscious performance of social protest, which Bernard purposively emphasizes in the vinyl track orally with resonant stress, sarcasm, and, above all, *anglophone sonority*. In so doing, she enacts on the one hand the inherent dynamics of the linguistic continuum of trilingual Black Costa Ricans. While on the other hand, the aural nature of the recorded version adds a semantic dimension that is *inaudible* in the printed version. Mainly, the negative feelings expressed by Afro-Costa Ricans opposite the Plan Educativo are mimicked *sarcastically* by Bernard through the 'anglophone' switch. By unfolding her claim bilingually through the loanword *alphabetization*, Bernard adds an ironic pun that emphasizes the lack of English skills by the bilingual campesinos themselves who, in Bernard's representation, must borrow from Spanish (i.e. "alfabetización") to condemn the Ministry of Education's English literacy campaign.

An interesting issue remains to be explored in the future. Why would Bernard, having obtained a doctoral degree in Afrolimonese phonology from the University of Wales in

---

[170] Bernard, *Negritud*: Track 17, min. 0:55–0:56.
[171] Herzfeld, "Language and Identity": 129.
[172] Winkler, "Cambio de códigos": 191.
[173] Reinhard Kiesler (1993) defines loanwords as a phonological and/or graphical adaptation of a foreign word by the receiving linguistic system (Kiesler, "La tipología de los préstamos lingüísticos: no sólo un problema de terminología": 505).

1969,[174] choose to transcribe in Spanish the original loanword, i.e. *alphabetization* as "alfabetización", which ultimately makes the unique linguistic play imperceptible? Though an answer to this question is not available, it is however irrefutable that a complementary close reading of "alfabetization" and [*alphabetization*] in "Bilingual Campesinos Speak Out" unearths the complex effects of the internal colonialism that the Caribbean province underwent at the hands of the state – firstly by eradicating English schools, later by a successful acculturation through Spanish that rejected English and Limon Creole. As *freestyled* by Afro-Costa Rican artist Huba, *education was the dilemma.*

> ¿Por qué no enseñan de Marcus Garvey,
> por qué no enseñan de las pirámides de Ihmotep? Eso sí es bueno…
> o inglés.
> Quitaron la escuela de inglés en Limón
> y ahora vean la condición; hay call centers en San José
> y en Limón no hay trabajo,
> fíjese.
> ¿Y cuál es el problema,
> que me hablan?
> Educación es el dilema.
> > Huba, "Cocorí Freestyle"[175]

Political Poetics of Language

Bernard's ironized outrage in becoming a PhD expert in unemployment undertakes another meaning when we take into consideration Romaine's assertion that after finishing school, minority children present a "greater chance of being unemployed" since, paradoxically, education in the official language does not guarantee them employment.[176] When interpreted against the educational reforms that sought to "nationalize" Black Costa Ricans and then re-educate them in English, Bernard's heated sarcasm in BCSO speaks against the blind outcomes of literacy campaigns and delivers the pun of absurdness precisely through the language switch. By sarcastically expressing herself through code-switched "Hombre desocupado", Bernard is protesting the marginalization that anglophone Afro-Costa Ricans suffered because of linguistic struggles. Consequently, I read code-switching at "alfabetización", together with "Bull Shit" (v. 1 and v. 3), "A la mierda with Eso" (v. 5), "Rubbish, shit; pura paja" (v. 8), "aula de mierda" (v. 26), "damn doctorado" (v. 27), and "Hombre desocupado" (v. 28) as a linguistic strategy expressing social protest regarding the educational reforms that were launched at Afro-Costa Ricans in the twentieth century, which in turn granted each of her languages different power and prestige in the province of Limón.

---

[174] I thank Marianela Muñoz-Muñoz for her cooperative dialogue on the subject (Muñoz-Muñoz, *Bilingüismo Político*: 69: "De donde se gradúa en 1969, al defender la tesis *Phonological Study of the Costa Rican Creole English*").

[175] Retrieved from https://www.youtube.com/watch?v=RZyLmd7eV-M.

[176] Romaine, *Language in Society*: 192.

Concerned with how code-switching works in the context of unequal linguistic relations of power, Monica Heller (1992) explains it as a societal language practice which displays an overt form of resistance that either crosses or levels the boundaries between minority languages and state languages that determine their status within the state.[177] Heller understands code-switching as relevant to the nation's politics of language, that is, to "the ways in which language practices are bound up in the creation, exercise, maintenance or change of relations of power".[178] The dominance shift between languages in Limón during the twentieth century makes Heller's affirmation evident, as well as Romaine's claim, who states that in the relationship between mono- and multilingualism in a territory's sociopolitical context, "usually the more powerful groups in any society are able to force their language upon the less powerful".[179]

The linguistic reforms in Limón's educational system are exemplary of this, against which Bernard's taboo switches in "Bilingual Campesinos" protest. Clearly, Bernard's relationship with each one of these linguistic systems is not equal because of their symbolic power and prestige in the province's history. Each refers to a particular and differentiated lived experience (i.e. borderland) in Costa Rica during the twentieth century. Standard English was first a prestige language that defined socio-economic upward mobility, especially for Blacks in Limón. It was later displaced by Spanish, which acquired the status of the official state-language "whose knowledge is necessary for full participation in society".[180] On the other hand, Limon Creole remained the mother tongue of the largest ethnic minority group in Costa Rica, "one with a relatively small number of speakers living within the domain of a more widely spoken language",[181] that is, Spanish. Lastly, fear of hindered integration led to negative charge attitudes opposite Limon Creole and English, becoming Spanish the dominant language. Gal considers spoken code-switching practices to be a symbolic response to relations of dominance in a systemic context of unequal social and linguistic realities,[182] such as attempted domination by state-authorized languages.[183] Following these authors, code-switching in Bernard is understood hence as a symbolic practice repudiating linguistic domination and marginalization as a consequence thereof. Anzaldúa's *mestiza*-consciousness provides the cultural comprehension for this linguistic performance. One that resists cultural assimilation and opts instead for a shifting, pluricentrical, ethnolinguistic identity.

In "Bilingual Campesinos Speak Out" Bernard goes further than in "What fi do?" by formulating social protest as its main theme, relating the content to the symbolic practice of straddling the borderlands linguistically. Code-switching in Bernard performs the *mestiza*-consciousness insofar the *formal* aspect of her bilingual poetry reflects how her ethnolinguistic identity is "sandwiched between two cultures" and therefore "undergoes a struggle of flesh, a struggle of borders, an inner war."[184] Pluricentrical belonging becomes

---

[177] Heller, "The politics of codeswitching and language choice": 133.
[178] Ibid.: 159.
[179] Romaine, *Language in Society*: 34.
[180] Ibid.: 35.
[181] Ibid.
[182] Gal, "The political economy of code choice": 247.
[183] García, *Bilingual Education in the 21ˢᵗ Century*: 250.
[184] Anzaldúa, *Borderlands*: 100.

obvious so much through the linguistic element as through the content matter. If *ethnic identity is twin skin to linguistic identity*, then Bernard's 'struggle of flesh' has to do with the exile of one of her mother tongues into an infranational position, defined as 'non'-Costa Rican. Her 'inner war' is a poetic one whose taboo words declaim unemployment and educational failure. The struggle of borders her pluricentrical belonging represents is fought out bilingually with the purpose of protesting linguistic assimilation. Hence, the performance of multilingualism resists hegemonic monolingualism by crossing over linguistic, cultural, and ethnonational rigid boundaries.

As we shall see next, in "Bilingual Economy" no linguistic hierarchy exists, rather an equilibrium between the languages is installed. Protest, disapproval, and sarcasm are also developed through it so that code-switching foregrounds an oppositional stance regarding Costa Rica's *democratic* imagined community. Once again, Bernard's multilingual poetry straddles the borderlands she inhabits, stor(y)ing the past from an infranational perspective.

The Cacao People

"BILINGUAL ECONOMY"

1   Bono fi café,
2   Bono fi caña;
3   mi no see no where
4   the bono fi cacao.
5   Es que them say,
6   the gente cacao
7   no necesitao for peseta,
8   only the gente from the meseta;
9   so the man in
10   the Banco Central
11   think of we like animal
12   What a democracia "sa"
13   todo para unos
14   nothing for todos;
15   and we tiene no diputao
16   we cacao man…,
17   What a "democratic" land.

Griot (p. 14)
Originally written in 1978

Bernard's multilingualism is (ironically enough) a "Bilingual Economy" (hereafter BE) that allows her to express herself simultaneously by means of various linguistic domains, as the previous poems shows. For Mosby, the language of BE is Limon Creole "with borrowings from the local Spanish".[185] Beyond Mosby's explanation and considering that Limon Creole

---

[185]   Mosby, *Place, Language, and Identity in Afro-Costa Rican Literature*: 109.

is not a hegemonic linguistic entity but instead represents linguistic variables along a continuum, I explore the poem here as being trilingual because of the linguistic *deep structure* of the poem, where a shift from the SE lexifier to Creole is also intercepted by Spanish.

When compared to the two poems previously analyzed, it is noticeable that this poem takes multilingualism to another level. It was argued that Spa switches in "What fi do?" carry out principally the formal elements that foreground the poem, whereas it could be noted in "Bilingual Campesinos Speak Out" that *alfabetización/alphabetization* and taboo word switches function according to stylistic criteria concerning a comic *gradatio* and the installment of a sarcastic ironic tone. A distinction of linguistic spaces is also reproduced in this manner between the anglophone Caribbean and the Spanish-speaking Central Valley. "Bilingual Economy" reproduces cultural and historical alternatives by way of the deep linguistic structure of the text, which brings to the fore diverse cultural worlds dependent on the linguistic domains themselves.[186] Basically, the rhetorical strategy of writing in a language(s) that goes beyond the imagined community's monolingualism marks an emphasis of the linguistic Other. Because of this, Bernard's *mestiza*-consciousness expresses pluricentrical belonging. Hence, with "Bilingual Economy" we are to conclude *Black Costa Rica* by crossing "the border into a wholly new and separate territory."[187] One where Bernard's performance of her *forked tongue* impacts the nation from a borderland perspective born out of diaspora.

As the preceding poem shows, Bernard's poetic vain has the ability to construct powerful multilingual images[188] that, as we shall see next, refer back to an infranational story of the past centered on the economical, specifically regarding the agrarian economy of bilingual campesinos at the Atlantic seaside. Rhetorically speaking, it is key in delivering social information through a tone of ironic protest, determined aesthetically by a stark sarcastic lyrical voice which switches languages in order to convey a particular message. Argumentatively, Bernard's "Bilingual Economy" is largely demystifying of one of Costa Rica's foundational myths: a social democracy, also detailed as a rural democracy.

Following Acuña's study on the invention of the Costa Rican difference at the independence juncture, as well as Jiménez book on Costa Rican twentieth-century *metaphysical ethnonationalism*, together with Ivan Molina's study (2002) of Costa Rican national identity and cultural change in the nineteenth and twentieth centuries and Carlos Cortés's discussion (2003) of Costa Rica's national myths, a rural democracy constitutes one of the key metaphors of the Costa Rican imagined community. An element that, along with peace, austerity, and the characterization of an industrious and laborious white people, was conceptualized as an assumed essential and exclusive characteristic of a 'special' country in the Central American region (see "Imagining Costa Rica", Part I). Bernard speaks against this rural democracy by implementing it in an adversative couple with *cacao*.

---

[186] "When the base language is English, Spanish can be used to emphasize the Chicano roots of specific concepts and areas. A change of language, thus, can signal a change of domain, a change of worlds. English language: Anglo world; Spanish language: Chicano world" (Valdés-Fallis: "The sociolinguistics of Chicano literature": 31f.).

[187] Anzaldúa, *Borderlands*: 101.

[188] Cf. Keller, "The Literary Stratagems Available to the Bilingual Chicano Writer": 268: "powerful bilingual images", referring to Valdés-Fallis "The sociolinguistics of Chicano literature" (1977).

We Cacao Man

The poem is charged with highly symbolic code-switching. The content of the poem is constructed around the words *café*, *caña*, and *cacao*. Beyond reproducing the identical [ka] sound at the end of the verses, these lexemes add a spatial specificity to the text that reflects simultaneously an economical domain. Mainly, *café* and *caña* are particular to the Costa Rican agrarian nineteenth- and twentieth-century economy, whose plantations were specifically located in the Central Valley highlands (the *meseta central*). In fact, Scottish traveler Robert Glasgow Dunlop had noted in 1844 that every family owned a small coffee or sugar cane plantation, to which we will come back in the next pages.[189] Echoing Bernard, "Bilingual Economy" complains about money bonds (*bono*; also referred to through *peseta*, synecdoche for money) being granted for coffee and sugar cane agriculture. These, however, poetizes Bernard, were denied to *cacao* growers, a product particular to the Atlantic seaside since colonial times. Albeit *café* and *caña* are unmistakably Spanish lexemes, *cacao* is contrariwise ambiguous. Either Spanish or English, it holds at its radical essence both possibilities as inclusive of one another, much like Bernard's rhizomatic belonging.

In "Cacao y esclavitud en Matina, Costa Rica, 1650–1750" (2012), Russell Lohse documents that before the conquest of the American continent by Europeans, cacao was already cultivated by the Indigenous autochthonous populations, as signaled by diverse conquistadores such as Juan Vázquez de Coronado (1563) and Fray Agustín de Cevallos (1610). The colonial elite at the colonial capital of Cartago set in motion a cacao-based economy towards the 1650s and by 1676 it had become the province's principal means of income.[190] The Urinama indigenous people were the main labor force of the cacao plantations (though not the only one), who with help of the Franciscan missionaries were colonized for economical purposes.[191] By 1680, as Lohse documents it, they not only took care of the cacao farms, but also took on the building of the necessary infrastructure for expanding the cacao economy. (Much like Africans took care of the sugar islands and built the cities, ports, plazas, churches, etc. of the Plantation machine.) As explained by Lohse, once the coercion of Urinama indigenous people – removed from the Franciscan missions and brought/seduced into the cacao farms by the Governor and his deputies – was prohibited by the high court, cacao farm owners turned to diversifying their labor force, which led to the gradual transition of an Indigenous manpower to African slaves in the following decades.[192]

On the subject, Rina Cáceres's *Negros, mulatos, esclavos y libertos en la Costa Rica del siglo XVII* (2000) reconstructs the history of African presence in the country in the seventeenth century – specifically in Cartago, but in its economic, political and social interrelations with the rest of the Spanish provinces in the region so as to provide a historical and economical background for the settlement of La Puebla de Pardos. This site corresponds to Costa Rica's principal settlement of freed Afro-mestizo people at the

---

[189] Quoted in Fernández Guardia, *Costa Rica en el siglo XIX*: 113.
[190] Lohse, "Cacao y esclavitud en Matina": 77–80.
[191] Ibid.: 87. Lohse speaks of slaves, of free Black people, mestizos, other indigenous populations, and even Spaniards as working at the cacao farms.
[192] Ibid.: 85–87.

outskirts of Cartago. Slavery in Costa Rica was abolished in 1824, when only 89 freed slaves were accounted for.[193] However, as Cáceres documents it, slaves had arrived as early as the sixteenth century with the Spanish conquistadores, as well as during colonial times throughout the subsequent epochs until the country's independence in the nineteenth century. The lowering of the number of slaves to eighty-nine is, according to Tatiana Lobo (1997), a way of consciously undermining the active participation Blacks had in Costa Rica's colonial economy through cacao production, as well as in cattle farming and in urban tasks such as infrastructure construction (e.g. roads, churches, etc.). Lobo furthermore sustains that slaves in Costa Rica represented important trading merchandise in the colonial epoch. She concludes this from the investigations she carried out in the Costa Rican National Archive, whose documents imply that trafficking of Black slaves was intense, since the documents make visible about two thousand legal slave transactions, while the illegal traffic cannot be, for obvious reasons, quantifiable.[194] Lohse's study of cacao production in Matina at the Caribbean seaside complements these affirmations by verifying that between 1670 and 1710 a "mini boom" in the slave trade took place, which led to a re-Africanization of the colonial slave population in the region.[195] Accordingly, Carlos Meléndez (1978) affirms that slave work was encouraged by cacao cultivation at the Atlantic seaside in the eighteenth century.[196] Mauricio Meléndez (1997) also affirms that the illegal contraband of slaves was tolerated and furthermore promoted by the Spanish authorities between the seventeenth and the beginning of the eighteenth centuries.[197] Therefore, the cacao plantations that had been established in the Costa Rican Atlantic territory by the second half of the seventeenth century played a significant part in the circulation of slaves in the province. Because of this, the province represented a very important periphery regarding the Costa Rican economy. Not only did it take part in the colonial economy with its cacao production, but still in the twentieth century the Atlantic province continued to signify important capitalist enterprises for the Costa Rican economy with the banana and cacao enclaves of the United Fruit Company. This historical recurrence reminds us once again of *la isla que se repite*.

In "Bilingual Economy" and as a first-generation Costa Rican-born Caribbean, Bernard speaks of the Black proletariat that settled in Limón and attempted to make a better life for themselves through land tenure and agriculture. The *cacao* switch is central in conjuring up this infranational historical imagination. Harpelle underlines the fact that land tenure at the first half of the twentieth century was "an important step toward higher social status" in Limón.[198] This was actually possible because, as Chomsky mentions it, "Keith himself and the Costa Rican government facilitated the acquisition of land by many West Indian laborers" during the first decades of the United Fruit's flourishing in order to both attract and retain workers,[199] consequently converting Black Caribbeans from proletariats to

---

[193]   Melendez, "El negro en Costa Rica durante la colonia": 48. His sources are to be found at the National Archive, documented under the title "Sección histórica. Provincial Independiente, Nos. 908–918–966–1295."

[194]   Lobo, "La vida cotidiana": 17.

[195]   Lohse, "Cacao y esclavitud en Matina": 92. Lohse charts how by 1680, slave trade had increased by 44% with respect to the decade before; 51% by 1690; and 48% in the first decade of 1700.

[196]   Meléndez, "El negro en Costa Rica durante la colonia": 26.

[197]   Meléndez Obando, "Las familias": 102.

[198]   Harpelle, *The West Indians of Costa Rica*: 19.

[199]   Chomsky, *West Indian Workers*: 28.

landholders, as affirmed by Olien.[200] This allowed Afro-Caribbeans to abandon agricultural labor in the Company and led to upward mobility for migrant workers because, as documented by Bourgois, "their plots often provided them with a cash income superior to what they could earn as wage laborers."[201] Nonetheless, Black landholders later met difficulties on behalf of the state apparatus when the government started interfering in Limón after the United Fruit Company abandoned the region. "Bilingual Economy" poetizes such difficulties with the opening verses "mi no see no where / the bono fi cacao" (vv. 3f.).

Eye dialect, as for example in "*mi* no see", is used by Bernard in order to foreground her multilingual poems and heighten the orality of her poem.[202] She does this as well in "What fi do?" with the word *basilón* instead of "vacilón" (v. 10: 'hell of a good time', as defined in the glossary).[203] In "Bilingual Economy", Bernard eliminates the <d> from the graphical representation of *diputado* (v. 15, 'a representative in assembly'), which rhymes with the ensuing *cacao* word (v. 16). In so doing, the linguistic variety of the region (where the intervocalic [d] sound is not pronounced) is represented *litteraly* accordingly with Callahan's observations. She carries out the same spelling adaptation with *necesitado* in v. 7 ('in need'), so as to allow it to rhyme with the ending word of v. 6, *cacao* again. Through this spelling deviation, rhyme is created around the *cacao* word, which, together with its counterpart *democracy*, represent the thematic center of "Bilingual Economy".

The poet's creative approach to the marginalization of Blacks in Costa Rica by the state (v: 10: "Banco Central") is carried out by installing the *Alteritäts-effekt* by confronting the Central Valley and the ex-centric province of Limón as regions reaping and sowing divergent products. The *Effekt* is signaled with the adversative relationship between cacao and coffee/sugar cane. The former is coupled with *gente cacao* (v. 6) / *we cacao man* (v. 16),

---

[200] Olien, "The Adaptation of West Indian Blacks: 145.

[201] Bourgois, *Ethnicity at Work*: 73f.

[202] Laura Callahan refers to "eye dialect" as spelling innovations employed by fiction writers who code-switch between Spanish/English in Southwestern Spanish, Caribbean Spanish (Puerto Rican, Cuban), and Caló Chicano (Mexican American) in U.S. Latino literature. She explains it functions as "an attempt to close the gap between orthographic and phonetic representation" in words such as *wuz* or *grasias* to differentiate pronunciation depending on the speaker's mother tongue (Callahan, *Spanish/English Codeswitching*: 131). Like Keller – who refers to this formal aspect in Chicano poetry as an aesthetic "spelling innovation" that occurs, among other reasons, either to show accent or to represent a language variety ("The Literary Stratagems Available to the Bilingual Chicano Writer": 309f.) –, Callahan also attributes to eye dialect the function of representing structural features of linguistic varieties, but however goes further by clarifying that the deviation from standard orthography "heightens the orality of the text via the writing down of forms that are not usually seen in print" (*Spanish/English Codeswitching*: 134).

[203] In WFD, the word "basilón" is not orthographically "correct" (*vacilón*) and instead corresponds to a written adaptation of the bilabial pronunciation of <v> as [b] at the beginning of the word by LC speakers (and of most Spanish speakers as well). To write *vacilón* with "b" is an orthographical mistake that could be looked down upon, especially if it represents a single spelling deviation and not a manifestation found regularly throughout the compilation. It could be interpreted as bad orthography on behalf of the writer, supposed ignorant of written norms, or worse, bad editing work. That is why Callahan's "eye dialect" is relevant to Bernard's "basilón" for it elucidates the choice of spelling deviation as having an aesthetic purpose closely related to *orality*. As such, Bernard is playing with written language to reenact a verisimilar speech through phonemic orthography. Winkler furthermore provides a linguistic explanation for *bacilarin* ("fooling around") as an adjusted loanword that has "Spanish root morphemes [with] LC inflectional affixes which show a high degree of morphological and phonological integration" ("Limonese Creole English": 236).

while the latter with *gente from the meseta* (v. 8). Bernard explains this opposition by introducing it with "Es que them say" (v. 5), *es que* defined by Winkler as a frequently borrowed Spanish discourse marker by LC speakers.[204] Furthermore, Bernard re-presents the opposition of un-identical spaces by foregrounding the poem with multilingual poetic formalities. A perfect rhyme between *peseta* and *meseta* is produced, while *gente* (v. 6 and v. 8) couples to the aforementioned rhyme with a dissimilar consonant sound at [n]. The coordination of these three Spa switches (*peseta* – *meseta* – *gente*) leads to an upbeat tempo between tri-/disyllable and monosyllable words in Spa and SE, respectively.

5   Es que them say,
6   the gente cacao
7   no necesitao for peseta,
8   only the gente from the meseta;

Bernard's *forked tongue* portrays pluricentrical belonging by reuniting the linguistic formality with a specific content matter. First and foremost, she has given form to it by code-switching which, recalling Anzaldúa, "makes visible the struggle of borders" in a *litteral* and aesthetic manner. Secondly, the *Alteritäts-Effekt* reproduces mainly "what it is to live under the hammer blow of the dominant [...] culture",[205] which, when it strikes, forces the *cacao man* into an infranational position. That is, into economic marginalization due to the race~nation dialectic, expressed here multilingually. Lastly, as we will see next, Bernard's *forked tongue* expresses an indignant *mestiza*-consciousness because she poetically underscores how "the cultural and spiritual values of one group" – the dominant Spanish-speaking Central Valley Costa Rican identity – *are not truly transferred* from this group to the other.[206] That is, to the Black Bilingual Campesinos of the Limón province.

"Democracy" in a Bilingual Economy

Spa switches in Bernard serve as stylistic embroidery to convey the tone and tempo of the poem's discourse, as well as being used as a rhetorical device that provides alliteration and rhyme as its poetic features. Nonetheless, if the tempo and tone was upbeat and joyous in WFD while in BCSO confrontational and declarative, code-switching in BE provides otherwise a fed-up tone. This attitude becomes more evident and explicit in the final six verses of the poem (vv. 12–17), where the single noun-switch to *democracia* in v. 12 produces a sardonic emphasis on the concept. This is not at all gratuitous and instead underscores and claims a critical perception of it. In fact, the language shift is central in underlining the argument Bernard is deploying in "Bilingual Economy". The quotation marks used at the final verse substitute instead the language switch and summarize Bernard's critique of "democracy" (v. 17). This orthographical element adds an ironic emphasis in order to protest a deceitful concept of the nationally and internationally praised

---

[204]   Winkler, "Limonese Creole English": 235.
[205]   Anzaldúa, *Borderlands*: 85.
[206]   Ibid.: 100: "[...] la *mestiza* is a product of the transfer of the cultural and spiritual values of one group to the other" (emphasis in original).

Costa Rican democracy. Through sarcasm, which functions as a poetic resistance that claims exploitation, "Bilingual Economy" exposes what McKinney has defined as "the limits of racial tolerance in a country that takes pride in its democratic ideals."[207] And most importantly, it performs the *mestiza*-consciousness whose "counterstance refutes the dominant culture's views and beliefs [...] proudly defiant."[208]

In *Costarricense por dicha* (2002), Iván Molina underlines that education was fundamental in deploying a historical imagination regarding racial homogeneity and whose culmination was the affirmation that the Central Valley was in the eighteenth century the epicenter of a rural democracy in an Eden-like time, as expressed by Carlos Monge in *Historia de Costa Rica* (1939).[209] This was the discursive outcome of imagining Costa Rica's isolated-caused poverty as the main cause for a rural, agrarian, and peasant democracy to develop. This was also possible thanks to the presence of small landowners, a crucial aspect in the invention of the 'Costa Rican difference' (see "Imagining Costa Rica", Part I). Professor Carlos Monge (1909–1979) was one of the founders of the University of Costa Rica, also Dean of the Faculty of Humanities (1948–1953) and Rector of the University of Costa Rica from 1961 to 1970. Historian Patricia Alvarenga Venútolo (2011) defines him as one of the most influential intellectuals of the twentieth century regarding the construction of the Costa Rican society.[210] Monge played a fundamental part in historicizing the Golden Age of colonial poverty and rural democracy, which he exposed in his *Historia*. The book became of obligatory reading in the curricula of secondary schools in the country and that, as underlined by Alvarenga, by 1982 had been re-edited and printed seventeen more times.[211] Monge's key contribution was, according to Molina, to have defined the Costa Rican Golden Age through an innovative socioeconomic specificity, that is, through the egalitarian distribution of private property. Monge states small property and a feeling of equality are the fundamental features of Costa Rica's eighteenth-century rural democracy. Which is why Costa Rica was imagined as a country of small peasant farmers (*labradores*) whose social structure was of egalitarian nature:

> Pequeña propiedad y sentimiento de igualdad son los rasgos fundamentales de la democracia rural del siglo XVIII. Por eso Costa Rica fue país de labradores, dueños de pequeñas parcelas...[212]

Alvarenga Venútolo underlines that the figure of the *"labrador colonial"*, later rearticulated as coffee-grower, is central to Monge's *Historia* because it represents the source of Costa Rica's democratic heritage. Coherent with Jiménez observations on the metaphysical language of Costa Rican nationalism, Monge stated that 'in his *soul* a history

---

[207]   McKinney, "Costa Rica's Black Body": 15.
[208]   Anzaldúa, *Borderlands*: 100.
[209]   Molina, *Costarricense por dicha*: 65f.
[210]   Alvarenga Venútolo, "Las diversas entonaciones": 49. The author discusses how Monge's theses vary from one edition to another with the purpose of making visible how Monge was not a monolithic writer (p. 67). Instead, he deploys ambivalent narratives across time regarding his conceptual analysis of history, citizenship, and the construction of the nation as interrelated aspects of the Costa Rica society.
[211]   Ibid.: 60.
[212]   Quoted in Molina, *Costarricense por dicha*: 67.

of democracy was conceived'.[213] Likewise, Acuña refers to the peasant farmer who farmed his own small parcel of land as the expression of an austere and humble, yet laborious nineteenth-century imagined Costa Rican people. Alvarenga traces how the conceptualization of the *labriego sencillo* (as sung in the National Hymn)[214] is transformed along the diverse versions of Monge's *Historia*, firstly represented as the pillar of Costa Rican democracy, later identified with equality, and finally with liberty.[215] Mainly, the *labrador* became the idealized representation of Costa Rica's democracy and in turn, as Molina underlines it, the rural estates of the small coffee-growers of the eighteenth century were imagined as the foundation of Costa Rican social democracy at the beginning of the twentieth century.[216]

Molina underlines the fact that Monge identifies Costa Rica as the region pertaining solely to the meseta central, excluding the people settled at the Pacific seaside, on the one hand, the Indigenous communities located outside the central plateau on the other, as well as the slave-descendant populations based at the Caribbean seaside.[217] Consequently, as Carmen Murillo (1998) explains it, the country was segregated into a center and a periphery under the logic of a 'here' (Central Valley) and a 'there' (the periphery). *Here* are "we" (i.e. the Costa Ricans: the "tico meseteño"), *there*, "the others".[218] Bernard ironically represents this with the *peseta – gente – meseta* triad. In so doing, she makes visible, as Mosby states, how, "[i]n the shining example of Central American democracy and economic stability, there is no representation for [her] marginalized group."[219]

Thus, what Bernard accomplishes aesthetically is only surpassed by the conjunction of it with the content. She has given poetic form to Murillo's geographical us~them reflection through her code-switching, as well as making evident the multiple ideological and economical stories of the past in the opening four verses of "Bilingual Economy", the title itself being decidedly significant and signifying. It is in fact just as efficient as the content matter of "Bilingual Campesinos" in calling attention to the sociolinguistic circumstances of Afrolimonenses as marginalized bilingual Costa Ricans inhabiting a borderland. Moreover, the mirrored noun-switches in the following verses (vv. 5–8) between the *gente from the meseta* and *the gente cacao* become at the light of former suggestions metaphorically historical. They bring together the discourse concerning the social democracy of the Costa Rican imagined community (vv. 12–17) with discrimination and marginalization of the country's *Black Other*. Once again, Bernard's multilingualism performs a *mestiza*-consciousness insofar she and her fellow Afro-Costa Ricans, "[l]ike others having or living in more than one culture, [...] get multiple, often opposing

---

[213] Quoted in Alvarenga Venútolo, "Las diversas entonaciones de una sola voz": 62: "En el alma de ese labrador se gestaba una gran historia de la democracia." (Cf. p. 58.)

[214] The *labriegos sencillos* are defined as the *sons* of the *noble fatherland*: "En la lucha tenaz, de fecunda labor, / que enrojece del hombre la faz; / conquistaron tus hijos – labriegos sencillos – / eterno prestigio, estima y honor [...]" (2° Strophe).

[215] Alvarenga Venútolo, "Las diversas entonaciones de una sola voz": 62.

[216] Molina, *Costarricense por dicha*: 37.

[217] Ibid.: 67 and 68.

[218] Murillo, "La piel de la patria": 50.

[219] Mosby, *Place, Language, and Identity in Afro-Costa Rican Literature*: 110.

messages."[220] Let us not forget that Monge's *Historia* was obligatory school reading when Bernard attended high school. Her protest aimed against this illusory social democracy arises precisely from the imagined community's messages (myths) and the contradictory reality of her sidelined community. Her *forked tongue* reenacts the *mestiza*-consciousness by creating a "cultural collision" underscoring a forced alienation, an imposed double consciousness. Mainly because that which is taught in school does not apply to *all Costa Ricans*. Through code-switching, hence, Bernard protests against the reality of the people belonging to her birthplace Limón, herself daughter of Jamaicans, furthermore connected to the colonial past of Indigenous and slave labor regarding cacao production. As such, the poem makes visible a pluricultural heritage that goes beyond the meseta central's imagined social democracy where, as defined by Carlos Monge, land ownership did not succumb to social nor economic discord, since there was enough land for anyone who had the desire to farm it.[221]

This claim is strongly dismantled in "Bilingual Economy." Not only by poeticizing the denial of economic endorsement to cacao growers to acquire land, farm it, and sustain a lifestyle as any other Costa Rican. But also in the light of the historical considerations I have outlined in the previous pages. Attempting to define the role of the Black, mulatto, and pardo populations in Costa Rica before the cacao-boom of the eighteenth century,[222] Cáceres concludes that the seventeenth century represented an important site of political and economic changes, not only in Costa Rica but in the international scenery as well, when the Atlantic became a place of interchange of people, products, and ideas between Europe, the Americas, and Africa.[223] And it should not be forgotten either that Monge and fellow intellectuals had for decades silenced this reality when imagining the nation as racially homogeneous. "¡Todo con tal de sostener el mito de la democracia rural!"[224]

Opposite Monge's imaginations, Bernard performs intra- and intersential code-switching between verses 13 and 14 that play an important part in delivering the cutting and divergent tone, since the poet goes on to condemn with a multilingual word play an *unequal democracy*: "todo para unos / nothing for todos" (vv. 13f.). Hence, the *formal* feature of multilingualism adds *semantic* strength to the double-edged remark by ironically defining it as the opposite of its inherent meaning bilingually. Also, verse 15: "we tiene no diputao", carries out the same formal/semantic couple in order to declaim a fallacious democracy by protesting lack of representation at the institutional level.[225] Furthermore, the

---

[220] Anzaldúa, *Borderlands*: 100.

[221] Quoted in Molina, *Costarricense por dicha*: 65: "la tierra no dividió a los habitantes en grupos cerrados ni produjo discordias sociales ni económicas. Para todos había tierra; quien lo deseare podía ser propietario".

[222] Cáceres, *Negros, mulatos, libertos y pardos*: 91f. The author argues that towards the middle of the seventeenth century (beginning at 1635–1638) a process of concentration of Blacks, mulattos, and pardos in the country was put into place at the marginalized areas of Cartago, which lastly conformed the formal settlement of La Puebla de Pardos. She goes on to detail their participation in Costa Rica's colonial socioeconomic structure, hence contributing to the reconstruction of the *afromestiza* population in the province's society during this time.

[223] Ibid.: 6.

[224] Lobo, "La vida cotidiana": 17.

[225] Alex Curling Delisser (1908–1987), son of Jamaican immigrants, is the first Afro-Costa Rican to hold office as *diputado* (deputy/substitute) in the country (1953–1958). Regarding Afro-Costa Rican participation in the political scenery, see Unicef, *Afrodescendientes de Valía* (2010).

risky switch at the negative construction between the subject pronoun and its verb in "Bilingual Economy" (v. 15: "we tiene no diputao") engages symbolically 'bizarre pidgin-like utterances'. It may seem slow, dim, and imperfectly developed Spanish, as Segreda characterized the Spanish spoken in Limón, but actually, by switching at this risky position, Bernard is playing ingeniously with ungrammaticality. Like in verse 10 of "Bilingual Campesinos" ("We don't quiere"), she is disrupting grammatical normativity for the sake of style, rhetoric, and tone. Lastly, Bernard resists power relations symbolically and performs against the borderland conflict, appropriating herstory and voicing how "democracy" is but an illusion of equality in this bilingual economy: "todo para unos / nothing for todos".

One last aspect should be included here by way of conclusion. In "Bilingual Campesinos", Bernard code-switches to *Pueblo* constantly in the opening verses. By switching to the state language, she identifies linguistically as part of the Costa Rican people, that is, as a citizen not pertaining to the elite classes in power. The deep structure of this switch reveals its sarcastic essence. Alvarenga Venútolo notices a synecdoche relationship between the humble, austere peasant and the "pueblo" in Monge's *Historia*. As rescued by the author, the pueblo is mainly defined by Monge as an idealized and abstract concept, which represents the Costa Rican community as a homogeneous political subject and whose central actor in the political, cultural, social, and economic history of the country is the *labrador*.[226]

That of *café*.

Recapitulation

As seen across these pages, Bernard adds a problematizing view concerning the idyllic imagination of Costa Rica from the Limonese perspective, both performatively through code-switching as argumentatively through the poetic content. It speaks specifically against assimilation. Schooled and raised as white Costa Ricans through an education system that transmitted a particular national mythology, Afro-Costa Ricans experience double consciousness because their Blackness is termed 'non'-Costa Rican; their Limon Creole constitutes a 'broken English' representing backwardness; while the belief in social equality and equal opportunity thanks to a national social democracy becomes fallacious when their upward mobility is compromised due to ethnonational discrimination. Hence, both "Bilingual Campesinos" and "Bilingual Economy" articulate to a large extent social voices that speak multilingually "the language of and for the working-class, the proletariat, [...] and the marginalized".[227]

---

[226] As Monge writes it, the peasant farmer is the "figura central en la historia política, social, económica y cultural…" (quoted in Alvarenga Venútolo, "Las diversas entonaciones de una sola voz": 61).

[227] Aparicio, "From Ethnicity to Multiculturalism": 27. Aparicio's article focuses on the history of the Puerto Rican literature in the U.S., which she defines as being silenced by literary criticism carried out by the cultural elite, and considers it represents Puerto Ricans as "important cultural agents in the re-making of America" (p. 19). She refers to CS as one of the inherent features taking part in the development of Puerto Rican literature in the context of cultural resistance. Bernard's code-switching can be explained analogously.

Bernard installs a juncture between her lyrical multilingual voice and sociopolitical preoccupations,[228] deploring inequality while playing with language poetically. Therefore, as Mosby has defined it, Bernard's literary combat is "a 'writing back' to the dominant culture and 'writing in' of the black experience in Costa Rica."[229] Multilingualism in Bernard functions as a means for coping with inequality and relations of power within the country regarding what Ian Smart has rescued from her poetry as "the process of adjustment [of the ethnolinguistic minority group] to the host environment."[230] Lastly, her *mestiza-consciousness* in both "Bilingual Economy" as in "Bilingual Campesinos Speak Out" speaks and "communicates that rupture, documents the struggle. She reinterprets history and using new symbols, she shapes new myths."[231] With her *creole talk*, Bernard goes beyond the rupture and the struggle, beyond the history of borderland exclusion and marginalization. With her *forked tongue* she deconstructs and constructs an*other* Costa Rica. In conclusion, Bernard undergoes the path towards recognition through multilingualism.

---

[228]   Aparicio, "From Ethnicity to Multiculturalism": 32.
[229]   Mosby, *Place, Language, and Identity in Afro-Costa Rican Literature*: 78f.
[230]   Smart, "Eulalia Bernard": 80.
[231]   Anzaldúa, *Borderlands*: 104.

EPILOGUE

THE SUM AND THE SUBSTANCE

The Journey's End

I am a turtle, wherever I go I carry "home" on my back.
Gloria Anzaldúa, *Borderlands*

Throughout these pages and by a historically-backwards looking gaze, a dialogue between Costa Rica's imagined community and the ethnonational Caribbean diaspora has been structured upon and across a threefold historical imagination by way of poetic figures mirroring pluricentrical belonging. This study has attempted to demonstrate how pluricentrical belonging represents a borderland criss-crossing-movement across times past, between historical memories, and from within language, which expresses itself through varied lyrical figures of speech. By engaging these pre-texts' poetic aspects and attempting to answer how they express the glocal, pluricentrical belonging has been charted as a continuum that shifts along a multinational story of the past. This hermeneutical approach has as a consequence made evident how these Afra-Costa Rican writers poetize a pluricentrical sense of belonging that flows outward past the limits of a single national imagination, without however compromising the latter.

In order to tell the recent story of *Black Costa Rica*, I have begun by referring to the myth of whiteness central to Costa Rica's imagined community. This was followed by a succinct cultural description of the Caribbean proletarian diaspora in Limón and the way the communities coped with their settlement in another land as a cultural/deterritorialized diaspora. Next, it was necessary to refer to the clash of these two imagined communities during the first decades of the twentieth century, where the dialects of race and nation had a fundamental role in their mutual confrontation. This with the purpose of understanding what Trevor Purcell keenly noted, economics, race and culture are linked structurally in the history of the Costa Rican Black community, which explains in turn why for Ronald Harpelle the agency of Afro-Costa Ricans has remained a forgotten footnote in white-washed Costa Rican cultural heritage. With the purpose of overturning Harpelle's assessment, Afra-Costa Rican poetry was approached accordingly with the details of the sociohistorical process concerning the coming of age of the country's largest ethnic minority. This in turn permitted the national specificity of this Afro-Central American community to be simultaneously comprehended as a localized reproduction of global phenomena regarding diaspora/s (McDonald), exclusion and racism (Campbell), and assimilation and marginalization (Bernard). As a result, Afra-Costa Rican poetry has been used as the medium for making visible how the diasporic cuts across and traverses the imagined community, *revis(it)ing it*. In this critical expedition, it has been demonstrated how poetry by Black Costa Rican women does not inscribe itself within one single space of identification, but rather sets itself out beyond the static signifiers of a nation. It creates thus a diaspora literacy lodged between the local and the global across a fluid historical, linguistic, and cultural continuum. Because of this, Afra-Costa Rican poetry contributes to a Central American diaspora literacy that expresses multiple and plural sites of identification which are determined spatially, meta-historically, and linguistically. An interpretative and critical analysis of the semiotic, argumentative, and linguistic aspects of these women's poetry has furthermore taken into consideration the relationships between the national and the diasporic with a triple-layered historical imagination at its foundation. In so doing, *Black Costa Rica* has thus revealed how pluricentrical belonging mimics a literary identity that is "neither a seamless wholeness nor a debilitating schizophrenia but [rather] something closer to the fruitfully multiple stagings of identity".[1] A literary identity that necessarily shifts continuously between the individual and the collective; across the national and the diasporic; between the local and the global; from the past to the present and towards the future.

As a result, *Black Costa Rica* has extracted certain figures of speech that deploy multifold historical aspects giving form to pluricentrical belonging. Oxymoron, metonymy, and multilingualism are the lyrical figures that have been identified as the deep structure that bring to the surface the specificity of the coming of age of Afro-Costa Ricans as a reproduction of Black circum-Atlantic dynamic/s. McDonald's modernized-nature oxymoron reveals an outernational story of Costa Rica's past whose sites of historical meaning refer to economic histories of capitalism that repeat themselves in the Caribbean region with the train and the Plantation structure at its center. Her poetics of landscape reveals a *repeating island* in Limón as the outcome of diasporic displacement on account of transnational capitalism. The repetitive essence of an open, complex, and unstable meta-archipelago located beyond its own maritime womb has thus been made visible in the Central American isthmus. Campbell's poetry, instead, finds its own *home in diaspora* through the skin-history metonymy, whereby she deploys a meta-historical intertextuality that makes evident how the experience of racism and marginalization, as well as of invisibility and of misrepresentation of Blacks in the master discourses of the West, can be detailed across national specificities. Simultaneously circumscribed to the nation's boundaries and yet pointing to a supranational historical imagination, the *Mothers of the Diaspora* were identified as its spokespeople. Furthermore, the skin-history metonymy gives specific content to Gilroy's claim regarding Blacks as people in but not necessarily belonging to the modern democratic societies they are citizens of. This as a consequence of the outernational position diaspora/s hold opposite the host land's imagined communities and their difficult integration to the new home. Therefore, the journey which began with diaspora and suffered against the dialectics of race and nation was brought to an open end with the representation of the unrealized democracy through Bernard's multilingual political poetics declaiming the second-class citizen position trilingual Black Costa Ricans held. Bernard's multilingualism also makes evident both *rootedness* and *multiplicity* by aligning plural connections with more than one cultural code and history through language. Through it, she exposes furthermore an infranational experience regarding linguistic assimilation and economic marginalization of anglophone Afro-Costa Ricans.

Home is not exclusively a national narrative.[2] It is however one of its constituent parts by necessity, something that these pages have strived to display by extracting the multinational lyrical dimensions that tell the story of Costa Rica's nation~diaspora dynamic/s. Consequently, McDonald, Campbell, and Bernard have been articulated as

---

[1]   Walters, *At Home in Diaspora*: xxii.
[2]   Ibid.: xxv.

glocal poets from whose poetic vein an alternate Costa Rican historical imagination can be unearthed. What are its poetic themes? History, oppression, invisibility; linguistic terrorism and economic marginalization; diaspora and economic histories of transnational capitalism in Costa Rica. What kind of stories of the past do these themes communicate? Diasporic, ethnolinguistic, and those made invisible by cultural insiderism and ethnic absolutism. How do they reveal a glocal historical imagination? Through spatial representations of an ex-centric Costa Rica; with meta-historical poetics; and by border language performance, all of which bring together what was imagined as national and outernational into one single story of the past. McDonald's modernized-nature oxymoron, together with Campbell's skin-history metonymy and Bernard's code-switching deploy a historical imagination that shifts along a continuum where *diaspora* and *home* actualize a play of intrinsic cultural differences across shared historical similarities. The analysis of the glocal has in this manner disclosed a cultural memory pointing to the system of cultural interchanges between the Caribbean, Costa Rica, and Africa in Afra-Costa Rican poetry. A series of relationships between various languages, regions, and repeating economic histories give form to lyrical pluricentrical belonging as a system of multiplicity in the form of a literary rhizomatic palimpsest. This is manifested in a network of connections that bring together lands, cultures, histories, and languages in the coming of age of the Black minority in Costa Rica. Hence, the figures of speech here identified carry out a lyrical stor(y)ing of the na-tion~diaspora/s dynamics in the form of historical imaginations regarding displacement, the confrontations born out of it as contending ethnonational discourses, and the procedures of assimilation and of marginalization of diasporic Black minorities in the host lands. In such a manner, McDonald's modernized-nature oxymoron, Campbell's skin-history metonymy, and Bernard's poetic multilingualism make visible how, paraphrasing Anzaldúa, *Blacks are Costa Rica's double; they exist in the shadow of the country; they are irrevocably tied to her.*[3]

In conclusion, the poems I have chosen to articulate *Black Costa Rica* have been closely read with the aim of reinterpreting these women's poetry from a strictly historical perspective. McDonald's poetics of landscape becomes an interesting asset to Costa Rica's story of the past in so far it re-presents Limón at the center of Costa Rica's irruption into Modernity. Likewise, Campbell's supranational approach to *historia* through *piel* destabi-lizes the Costa Rican metaphysical ethnonationalism concerning the population's exemplary and exceptional white difference in the same manner that Bernard's *creole talk* emphasizes Black routes and roots of the Black circum-Atlantic in Limón, Costa Rica. Together, their lyrical pluricentrical belonging straddles spatio-temporal, racial, and linguistic borderlands and in so doing, their poetry represents in a full-blown manner another Costa Rica, whereby Caribbean descendants are granted a central place in its *revis(it)ed* historical imagination.

---

[3] Anzaldúa, *Borderlands*: 108: "Admit that Mexico is your double, that she exists in the shadow of this country, that we are irrevocably tied to her. Gringo accept the doppelganger in your psyche. By taking back your col-lective shadow the intracultural split will heal. And finally, tell us what you need from us."

I define national literature
as the urge for each group to assert itself:
that is, the need not to disappear from the world scene
and on the contrary to share in its diversification.

Édouard Glissant, *Caribbean Discourse*

Works Cited

Primary Sources

Argüello Mora, Manuel. 1963. "El huerfanillo de Jericó." In *Obras literarias e históricas. Libro II: Novelas y cuentos*, ed. Victoria Azofeifa Camacho, 119–140. San José (CR): Editorial de Costa Rica.

Bernard Little, Eulalia. 1976. *Negritud*. San José?: Indica. [Vinyl]

_____. 1981. *Nuevo ensayo sobre la existencia y la libertad política*. San José (CR): Ministerio de Cultura, Juventud y Deportes.

_____. 1991. *My Black King. A collection of poetry*. Eugene (OR): World Peace University.

_____. 1996. *Ritmohéroe*. San José (CR): Editorial de Costa Rica.

_____. 1997. *Griot*. San José: Seventh Day Adventist Youth Society.

_____. 2001. *Ciénaga/Marsh*. San José (CR): Editorial Guayacán Centroamericana.

_____. 2011. *Tatuaje*. San José (CR): Ediciones Guayacán.

Campbell Barr, Shirley.1988. *Naciendo*. San José (CR): S. Campbell.

_____. 2006. *Rotundamente negra*. San José (CR): Ediciones Perro Azul.

_____. 2013. *Rotundamente Negra y otros poemas*. Madrid: Torremozas.

_____. 2014. "Poemas. Shirley Campbell." *Revista Casa de la Mujer* 20.2: 173–190.

Cicero, Tullius M. 1911. *Rhetorica, Tomus II*. Trans. A. S. Wilkins. Scriptorum Classicorum Bibliotheca Oxoniensis 1911. Retrieved from http://www.perseus.tufts.edu/hopper/text?doc=Cic.%20Orat.%2027.93&lang=original.

Duncan, Quince. 2013. *Dos novelas. Los cuatro espejos. La paz del pueblo*. Bloomington (ID): Edición Palibrio.

Fallas, Carlos Luis. 2010. *Mamita Yunai*. San José (CR): Editorial de Costa Rica.

Gutiérrez, Joaquín. 2011. *Puerto Limón*. San José (CR): Editorial Legado.

_____. 2014. *Cocorí*. San José (CR): Editorial Legado.

Henry, O. 1904. "The Admiral." In *Cabbages and Kings*, 130–143. New York: Doubleday, Page & Company.

Hopkinson, Nalo. 2000. *Midnight Robber*. New York/Boston: Grand Central Publishers.

Lyra, Carmen. 2012. "La negra y la rubia." In *Cuentos de mi tía Panchita*, ed. Juan Manuel Sánchez, 131–141. San José (CR): Editorial de Costa Rica.

_____. 2011. "Bananos y hombres." In *Narrativa de Carmen Lyra. Relatos escogidos*, ed. Marianela Camacho Alfaro, 119–137. San José (CR): Editorial de Costa Rica.

McDonald, Dlia. 1994. *El séptimo círculo del obelisco*. San José (CR): D. McDonald.

_____. 1995. *Sangre de madera*. San José (CR): D. McDonald.

_____, ed. 2006. *Pregoneros de la memoria*. San José (CR): Alianza Francesa/Ediciones Perro Azul.

_____. 2006. *Instinto tribal*. San José (CR): Editorial Odisea.

_____. 2012. *Todas las voces que canta el mar*. La Perla, Nezahualcóyotl: Sediento Ediciones.

_____ and Shirley Campbell Barr. 2011. *Palabras indelebles de poetas negras*. Heredia (CR): Editorial Universidad Nacional.

Montout, Dolores J. 1984. *Tres relatos sobre el Caribe costarricense*. San José (CR): Ministerio de Cultura, Juventud y Deporte.

NourbeSe Philip, Marlene. 2008. *Zong! As told to the author by Setay Adamu Boateng*. Middletown (CT): Wesleyan University Press.

Reid Chambers, Marcia. 2008–2009. "Poetry." *Sargasso. Linguistic Explorations of Gender and Sexuality* 1, Special Issue with Don E. Walicek: 169–170. Retrieved from https://dloc.com/UF00096005/00032/11x.

_____. 2010. "Nátral Fílinz." *Káñina, Revista Artes y Letras (Universidad de Costa Rica)* 34: 207–211.

Roa Bastos, Augusto. 1974. *Yo el Supremo*. Buenos Aires: Siglo Veintiuno Argentina Editores.

Queen Nzinga. 2012. *Afrokon. WombVoliushan Poetry*. San José (CR): Q.N. Maxwell Edwards.

Secondary Sources

Acuña, Víctor Hugo. 2002. "La invención de la diferencia costarricense, 1810–1970." *Revista de Historia* 45: 191–228.

Ainsa, Fernando. 2010. "Los guardianes de la memoria." *Amerika* 3. Retrieved from http://amerika.revues.org/1442.

Allsopp, Richard. 1996. *Dictionary of Caribbean English Usage*. Oxford: Oxford University Press.

Alvarenga Venútolo, Patricia. 2007. "La inmigración extranjera en la historia costarricense." In *El mito roto. Inmigración y Emigración en Costa Rica*, eds. Carlos Sandoval and Patricia Alvarenga Venútolo, 3–23. San José (CR): Editorial Universidad de Costa Rica.

_____. 2011. "Las diversas entonaciones de una sola voz. Historia, ciudadanía y nación en Carlos Monge Alfaro." *Letras* 50: 49–67.

Álvarez Masís, Yanory, ed. 2010. *Cuentos y leyendas. Anécdotas e historias de Costa Rica. Provincia de Limón*. San José (CR): Ministerio de Cultura y Juventud, Centro de investigación y conservación del patrimonio cultural.

"Amer", Leonidas Briceño, Jenaro Cardona, Benjamín Céspedes, Carlos Gagini, Ricardo Fernández Guardia, and Manuel González Zeledón. 1984. "Polémica entre nacionalismo y literatura." *Letras. Revista electrónica de literatura y ciencias del lenguaje* 1.7/8: 289–337. Retrieved from http://www.revistas.una.ac.cr/index.php/letras/article/viewFile/4396/4226.

Anderson, Alan. 1998. "Diaspora and Exile: A Canadian and Comparative Perspective." *International Journal of Canadian Studies* 18: 13–30.

Anderson, Benedict. 1996. *Imagined Communities. Reflections on the Origin and Spread of Nationalism*. London/New York: Verso.

Andrews, Kehinde. 2016. "Black is a Country: Building Solidarity Across Borders." *World Policy Journal* 33.1: 15–19.

Anim-Addo, Joan. 1996. *Framing the Word: Gender and Genre in Caribbean Women's Writing*. London: Whiting and Birch.

Anzaldúa, Gloria. 2007. *Borderlands: The New Mestiza. La frontera*. San Francisco: Aunt Lute Books.

Aparicio, Frances R. 1994. "From Ethnicity to Multiculturalism: An Historical Overview of Puerto Rican Literature in the United States." In *Handbook of Hispanic Cultures in the United States: Literature and Art*, ed. Francisco Lomelí, 19–39. Houston (TX): Arte Publico Press Jan.

Appiah, Kwame Anthony. 1996. "Race, Culture, Identity: Misunderstood Connections." In *Color Conscious. The Political Morality of Race*, eds. Kwame A. Appiah and Amy Gutmann, 30–105. Princeton: Princeton University Press.

Araya Araya, Karla 2015. *Anglophone Afro-Costa Rican Literature: Texts and counter-discourses in the unpublished literary work of Dolores Joseph Montout*. Master thesis. University of Costa Rica.

Aristotle. 1965. *The Poetics*. Trans. W. Hamilton Fyfe. London: Heinemann.

Ashcroft, Bill, Gareth Griffiths, and Helen Tifflin. 1989. *The Empire Strikes Back: Theory and Practice in Post-Colonial Literatures*. London: Routledge.

Assman, Aleida. 2011. *Cultural Memory and Western Civilization. Functions, Media, Archives*. Cambridge: Cambridge University Press [*Erinnerungskulturen* 1999].

Assmann, Jan. 1988. "Kollektives Gedächtnis und kulturelle Identität." In *Kultur und Gedächtnis*, eds. Jan Assmann and Antonio Hölscher, 9–19. Frankfurt a. M.: Suhrkamp.

_____. 1995. "Collective Memory and Cultural Identity." Trans. John Czaplicka. *New German Critique* 65: 125–133.

Astorga, Lucía. 2019. "Con la colocación de la primera piedra, se inicia la historia del nuevo Black Star Line." *La nación* online edition, August 31. Retrieved from: https://www.nacion.com/el-pais/patrimonio/con-la-colocacion-de-la-primera-piedra-se-inicia/6VWIYCON25EKHHJQDMU7N7WZXI/story/.

Augé, Marc. 1992. *Non-lieux: introduction à une anthropologie de la surmodernité*. Paris: Éditions du Seul.

Baker, Colin. 2001. *Foundations of bilingual Education and Bilingualism*. Bristol: Multilingual Matters.

Barbas-Rhoden, Laura. 2003. *Writing Women in Central America: Gender and the Fictionalization of History*. Athens (OH): Ohio University Press.

Barrow, Christine. 1996. *Family in the Caribbean. Themes and Perspectives*. Kingston/Oxford: Randle.

_____. 2001. "Men, Women and the Family in the Caribbean." In *Caribbean Sociology. Introductory Readings*, eds. Christine Barrow and Rhoda Reddock, 419–426. Kingston: Randle.

Bauman, Zygmunt. 1986. "The Left as the Counter-Culture of Modernity." *Telos* 70: 81–93.

_____. 1997. "From Pilgrim to Tourist – Or a Short History of Identity." In *Questions of Cultural Identity*, eds. Stuart Hall and Paul du Gay, 18–36. London: Sage.

Benjamin, Walter. 1989. "Theses on the Philosophy of History." Trans. Harry Zohn. In *Critical Theory and Society. A Reader*, eds. Stephen Eric Bronner and Douglas MacKay Kellner, 255–263. New York: Routledge.

Benítez-Rojo, Antonio. 1996. *The Repeating Island: The Caribbean and the Postmodern Perspective*. Trans. James Maraniss. Durham: Duke University Press [*La isla que se repite* 1989].

Bernabé, Jean, Patrick Chamoiseau, and Raphaël Confiant. 1999. *Éloge de la Créolité / In Praise of Creoleness*. Trans. M.B. Taleb-Khyar. Paris: Gallimard.

Bhabha, Homi K. 1990. "Introduction." In *Nation and Narration*, ed. Homi Bhabha, 1–7. London/New York: Routledge.

Bisanti, Tatiana. 2006. "Retorica e plurilinguismo letterario." In *Retorica: Ordnungen und Brüche*, eds. Rita Franceschini, Rainer Stillers, Maria Moog-Grünewald, Franz Penzenstadler, Norbert Becker, and Martin Hannelore, 265–280. Tübingen: Gunter Narr Verlag Tübingen.

Bitter, Willhelm. 1921. *Die wirtschaftliche Eroberung Mittelamerikas durch den Bananen-Trust Organisation und imperialistische Bedeutung der United Fruit Company*. Darmstadt: Wissenschaftliche Buchgesellschaft.

Blank, Andreas. 1999. "Co-presence and Succession. A Cognitive Typology of Metonymy." In *Metonymy in Language and Thought*, eds. Klaus-Uwe Panther and Günther Radder, 169–191. Amsterdam: Benjamins.

Blom, Jan-Petter and John Gumperz. 2000. "Social meaning in linguistic structure: code-switching in Norway." In *The Bilingualism Reader*, ed. Li Wei, 111–136. New York: Routledge.

Bock–Morss, Susan. 2000. "Hegel and Haiti." *Critical Inquiry* 26.4: 821–865.

Bosch, Velia. 2000. *Clásicos de la literatura infantil-juvenil de América Latina y el Caribe*. Caracas: Biblioteca Ayacucho.

Bourgois, Philippe I. 1989. *Ethnicity at Work: A Divided Labor on a Central American Banana Plantation*. Baltimore: John Hopkins University Press.

Boyarin, Daniel and Jonathan Boyarin. 1993. "Generation and the Ground of Jewish Identity." *Critical Inquiry* 19.4: 693–725.

Boyce Davies, Carole and Elaine Savory Fido. 1990. "Introduction." In *Out of the Kumbla*, eds. Carole Boyce Davies and Elaine Savory Fido, 1–24. Trenton: Africa World Press.

Bragado, Javier. 2017. "No éramos negros hasta que entramos en contacto con los europeos, éramos solo personas." Interview with Shirley Campbell Barr. *El Norte de Castilla* online edition, January 29. Retrieved from http://www.elnortedecastilla.es/internacional/america-latina/201701/29/eramos-negros-hasta-entramos-20170129014913-rc.html.

Brathwaite, Edward Kamau. 2011. *History of the Voice. The Development of Nation Language in Anglophone Caribbean Poetry*. London: New Beacon Books.

Bravo, Víctor. 2001. "La verdad y el juego en la novela histórica." *Estudios. Revista de investigaciones Literarias y Culturales* 9.18: 89–102.

Braziel, Jana and Nicasio Urbina. 2016. "Circum-Caribbean Poetics: Tracing Black Atlantic Routes in the Américas." *Cincinnati Romance Review* 40: 1–22.

Brisson, Luc. 1998. *Plato, The Myth Maker.* Translated, edited and with an introduction from Gerhard Naddaf. Chicago: University of Chicago Press [*Platon, les mots et les mythes: Comment et pourquoi Platon nomma le mythe?* 1994].

Bryce-Laporte, Roy Simon. 1962. *Social Relations and Cultural Persistence (or change) among Jamaicans in a rural area of Costa Rica.* Doctoral dissertation, University of Puerto Rico.

Bryce-Laporte, Roy Simon and Trevor Purcell. 1982. "A Lesser Known Chapter of the Diaspora: West Indians in Costa Rica, Central America." In *Global Dimensions of the African Diaspora*, ed. Joseph E. Harris, 219–240. Washington D.C.: Harvard University Press.

Busia, Abena. 1990. "This Gift of Metaphor. Symbolic Strategies and the Triumph of Survival in Simone Schwartz-Bart's *The Bridge of Beyond.*" In *Out of the Kumbla*, eds. Carole Boyce Davies and Elaine Savory Fido, 289–302. Trenton: Africa World Press.

Butler, Kim D. 2001. "Defining Diaspora, Refining a Discourse." *Diaspora* 10.2: 189–219.

Cáceres, Rita. 2000. *Negros, mulatos, esclavos y libertos en la Costa Rica del siglo XVII.* México D.F.: Instituto Panamericano de Geografía e Historia.

Callahan, Laura. 2004. *Spanish/English Codeswitching in a Written Corpus.* Amsterdam: John Benjamins Publisher.

Cassidy, Frederic and Robert Le Page, eds. 1980. *Dictionary of Jamaican English.* Cambridge: Cambridge University Press.

Castro-Gómez, Santiago and Ramón Grosfoguel, eds. 2007. *El giro decolonial. Reflexiones para una diversidad epistémica más allá del capitalismo global.* Bogotá: Siglo del Hombre Editores.

Castro Madriz, José María. 1999. "Discurso pronunciado por el H. Sr. Secretario de Fomento, Licdo. don Manuel Argüello, y constatación del H. Sr. Dr. José María Castro, a nombre del Excmo., Sr. Presidente de la República, en el acto de la inauguración de la vía mixta al Atlántico, verificada el día 7 de mayo de 1882." In *Crónicas y relatos para la historia de Puerto Limón*, eds. Fernando González and Elías Zeledón, 139–148. San José (CR): Ministerio de Cultura, Juventud y Deportes, Centro de investigación y conservación de patrimonio cultural.

Cavers, David W. 2011. "Nationalism, Ethnicity, and the Cultural Politics of Identity." *Totem: The University of Western Ontario Journal of Anthropology* 1.1: 22–31.

Ch'ien, Evelyn Nien-Ming. 2004. *Weird English.* Cambridge: Harvard University Press.

Chancy, Myriam J.A. 1997. *Framing Silence. Revolutionary Novels by Haitian Women.* New Jersey: Rutgers University Press.

Chaverri, Amelia. "América central debe ser nombrada." In *Literaturas Centroamericanas hoy: desde la dolorosa cintura de América,* eds. Karl Kohut and Werner Mackenbach, 201–218. Frankfurt a.m: Vervuert.

Chomsky, Aviva. 1996. *West Indian Workers and the United Fruit Company in Costa Rica, 1870-1940.* Baton Rouge: Louisiana State University Press.

Clifford, James. 1992. "Travelling Cultures." In *Cultural Studies,* ed. Lawrence Grossberg, 96–116. New York: Routledge.

_____. 1996. *Routes. Travel and Translation in the Late Twentieth Century.* Cambridge: Harvard University Press.

Cohen, Robin. 1992. "The Diaspora of a Diaspora: The Case of the Caribbean." *Social Science Information* 31.1: 159–169.

_____. 2008. *Global Diasporas. An Introduction.* London: Routledge. [1997, London: UCL Press].

Compagnon, Antoine. 2011. "Histoire et littérature, symptôme de la crise des disciplines." *Le Débat* 3.165: 62–70.

Condé, Maryse. 1993. *La parole des femmes. Essai sur des romancières des Antilles de langue française.* Paris: Gallimard.

_____. 1999. "Introduction." In *Caribbean Women Writers: Fiction in English,* eds. Maryse Condé and Thorunn Lonsdale, 1–9. New York: St. Martin's Press.

_____. 2004. "The Stealers of Fire: The French-Speaking Writers of the Caribbean and their Strategies of Liberation." *Journal of Black Studies* 35.2: 154–64.

Contreras, Fernando. 1998. "Territorios y fronteras." In *Costa Rica imaginaria,* eds. Alexánder Jiménez and Jesús Oyamboru, 59–69. San José (CR): Centro Cultural de España.

Corrales Arias, Adriano, ed. 2007. *Sostener la palabra. Antología de poesía costarricense contemporánea.* San José (CR): Arboleda.

Cortés, Carlos. 2003. "La invención de un país imaginario." In *La invención de Costa Rica,* 13–42. San José (CR): Editorial de Costa Rica.

Cortez, Beatriz, Alexandra Ortiz Wallner, and Verónica Ríos Quesada, eds. 2012. *Hacia una historia de las literaturas centroamericanas III. (Per)Versiones de la Modernidad. Literaturas, identidades, desplazamientos.* Guatemala: F & G Editores.

Cudjoe, Selwyn R. 1990. "Introduction." In *Caribbean Women Writers. Essays from the First International Conference*, ed. Selwyn Cudjoe, 5–48. Wellesley (MA): Calaloux Publications.

Decamp, David. 1971. "Introduction: The Study of Pidgin and Creole Languages." In *Pidginization and Creolization of Languages. Proceedings of a Conference Held at the University of the West Indies. Mona, Jamaica, April 1968*, ed. Dell Hymes, 13–39. London: Cambridge University Press.

De Certeau, Michel. 1988. *The Practice of Everyday Life*. Trans. Steven Randall. Berkeley/Los Angeles/London: University of California Press. [*L'invention du quotidien* 1980].

———. 1988. *The Writing of History*. Trans. Tom Conley. New York: Columbia University Press. [*L'écriture de l'histoire* 1975].

De Costa-Willis, Miriam. 1993. "Afra-Hispanic Writers and Feminist Discourse." *NWSA Journal* 5.2: 204–17.

———, ed. 2003. *Daughters of the Diaspora*. Kingston: Ian Randle Publishers.

De Unamuno, Miguel. 1971. "La tradición eterna." In *En torno al casticismo*, ed. Francisco Fernández Turienzo, 89–120. Madrid: Alcalá.

Deleuze, Gilles and Félix Guattari. 1993. "Introduction." In *A Thousand Plateaus. Capitalism and Schizophrenia*. Trans. Brian Massumi. Minneapolis/London: University of Minnesota Press. [*Mille Plateaux* 1980].

Delgado, Richard. 1999. "Citizenship." In *Race, Identity, and Citizenship. A Reader*, eds. Rodolfo D. Torres, Louis F. Mirón, and Jonathan Xavier Inda, 247–252. Massachusetts/Oxford: Blackwell Publishers.

Díaz-Diocaretz, Myriam. 1990. "'I will be a Scandal in Your Boat': Women poets and the tradition." In *Knives and Angels. Women Writers in Latin America*, ed. Susan Bassnett, 86–109. London/New Jersey: Zed Books.

Domenella, Ana Rosa, ed. 2002. *(Re)escribir la historia desde la novela de fin de siglo. Argentina, Caribe, México*. México D.F.: Universidad Autónoma Metropolitana.

Du Bois, William Edward Burghardt. 1995. *The Souls of Black Folks*. New York et al: Pocket Books.

Duncan, Quince. 2015. "Qué aprendí leyendo a Cocorí… En defensa de don Joaquín." *Elpaís.cr* online edition, April 24. Retrieved from http://www.elpais.cr/2015/04/24/que-aprendi-leyendo-a-cocori-en-defensa-de-don-joaquin/.

_____. 2009. "Corrientes literarias afrocentroamericanas." In *Hacia una historia de las literaturas centroamericanas II. Tensiones de la modernidad: del Modernismo al Realismo*, eds. Valeria Grinberg Pla and Ricardo Roque Badovinos, 513–530. Guatemala: F & G Editores.

_____. 2012. "Corrientes literarias afrolimonenses." In *Puerto Limón (Costa Rica). Formas y prácticas de auto/representación. Apuestas imaginarias y políticas. / Puerto Limón (Costa Rica). Formes et practiques d'auto/répresentation. Enjeux imaginaires, culturels et politiques*, eds. Quince Duncan Moodie and Victorien Lavou Zoungbo, 61–82. Perpignan: Presses universitaires de Perpignan.

Duncan, Quince and Carlos Meléndez. 1978. *El negro en Costa Rica*. San José (CR): Editorial de Costa Rica.

_____, Julián González, Guillermo Jiménez, and Mayela Mora, eds. 1995. *Historia crítica de la narrativa costarricense*. San José (CR): Editorial Costa Rica.

_____ and Lorein Powell. 1988. *Teoría y práctica del racismo*. San José (CR): Editorial DEI.

Erll, Astrid. 2002. "Literatur und kulturelles Gedächtnis: Zur Begriffs- und Forschungsgeschichte, zum Leistungsvemögen und zur literaturwissenschaftlichen Relevanz eines neuen Paradigmas der Kulturwissenschaft." *Literaturwissenschaftliches Jahrbuch* 23: 249–276.

_____. 2005. *Kollektives Gedächtnis und Erinnerungskulturen. Eine Einführung*. Stuttgart: Metzler.

Esman, Milton J. 1986. "Diasporas and International Relations." In *Modern Diasporas in International Diasporas*, ed. Gabriel Sheffer, 333–349. London/Sydney: Croom Helm.

Ette, Ottmar, ed. 2008. *Caribbean(s) on the Move – Archipiélagos literarios del Caribe. A TransArea Symposium*. Frankfurt a. M. et al: Peter Lang.

Ette, Ottman. 2003. *Literature on the Move*. Katharina Vester, trans. Amsterdam/New York: Rodopi [*Literatur in Bewegung* 2001].

_____. 2016. *TransArea. A Literary History of Globalization*. Mark W. Person, trans. Berlin/Boston: de Gruyter [*TransArea: Eine literarische Globalisierungsgeschichte* 2012].

_____. 2016. *Writing-Between-Worlds. TransArea Studies and the Literatures-without-a-fixed-Abode*. Vera M. Kutzinski, trans. Berlin/Boston: de Gruyter [*Zwischen Welten Schreiben: Literaturen ohne festen Wohnsitz* 2005].

_____, Werner Mackenbach, Gesine Müller, and Alexandra Ortiz Wallner, eds. 2011. *Trans(it)Areas. Convivencias en Centroamérica y el Caribe. Un simposio transareal*. Berlin: Editorial Tranvía.

_____, Anne Kraume, Werner Mackenbach, and Gesine Müller, eds. 2012. *El Caribe como Paradigma. Convivencias y coincidencias históricas, culturales y estéticas. Un simposio transareal.* Berlin: Editorial Tranvía.

_____ and Gesine Müller, eds. 2012. *Worldwide. Archipels de la mondialisation. Archipiélagos de la globalización. A TransArea Symposium.* Frankfurt a. M./Madrid: Vervuert/Iberoamericana.

Eze, Emmanuel C, ed. 1997. *Race and the Enlightenment: A Reader.* Oxford: Wiley-Blackwell.

Fanon, Frantz. 1952. *Peau noire, masques blancs.* Paris: Les Éditiones du Seuil. Retrieved from http://classiques.uqac.ca/classiques/fanon_franz/peau_noire_masques_blancs/peau_noire_masques_blancs.pdf.

_____. 2008. *Black Skin, White Masks.* Trans. Charles Lam Markmann. London: Pluto Press.

_____. 2002. *Les damnés de la terre.* Paris: Éditions La Découverte. Retrieved from http://classiques.uqac.ca/classiques/fanon_franz/damnes_de_la_terre/damnes_de_la_terre.pdf.

_____. 2004. *The Wretched of the Earth.* Trans. Richard Philcox. New York: Grove Press.

Feldner, Maximilian. 2019. *Narrating the New African Diaspora. 21st Century Nigerian Literature in Context.* Palgrave Macmillan: Cham.

Fernández Guardia, Ricardo. 1985. *Costa Rica en el siglo XIX. Antología de viajeros.* San José (CR): Editorial Universitaria Centroamericana.

_____. 1985. "Robert Glasgow Dunlop, Viajes en Centro América." In *Costa Rica en el siglo XIX. Antología de viajeros*, 103–121. San José (CR): Editorial Universitaria Centroamericana.

_____. 1985. "Thomas Frances Meagher, Vacaciones en Costa Rica." In *Costa Rica en el siglo XIX. Antología de viajeros*, 333–448. San José (CR): Editorial Universitaria Centroamericana.

Finley, Cheryl. 2018. *Committed to Memory. The Art of the Slave Ship Icon.* Princeton/Oxford: Princeton University Press.

Flores, Juan. 2005. "Triple Consciousness? Afro-Latinos on the Color Line." *Wadabagei: A Journal of the Caribbean and its Diaspora* 8.1, 80–85.

_____. 2009. *The Diaspora Strikes Back. Caribeño Tales of Learning and Turning.* New York: Routledge.

Foley, Barbara. 1986. *Telling the Truth: The Theory and Practice of Documentary Fiction.* Ithaca (NY)/London: Cornell University Press.

Foucault, Michel. 1986. "Of Other Spaces." Trans. Jay Miskowiec. *Diacritics* 16.1: 22–27 ["Des espaces autres" 1984].

Fox, Richard G. 1990. "Introduction." In *Nationalist Ideologies and the Production of National Cultures*, ed. Richard G. Fox, 1–14. Washington D.C.: American Anthropological Association.

Gal, Susan. 1988. "The political economy of code choice." In *Codeswitching: Anthropological and Sociolinguistic Perspectives*, ed. Monica Heller, 245–264. Berlin: De Gruyter.

Gallardo, Helio. 1993. *500 años. Fenomenología del mestizo (violencia y resistencia).* San José (CR): Editorial DEI.

Gallego, Mar. 2012. "On Both Sides of the Atlantic: Hybrid Identity and the Spanish-Speaking Diaspora in Agnès Agboton, Mónica Carillo and Eulalia Bernard." In *Migration, Narration, Identity. Cross-Cultural Perspectives*, eds. Peter Leese, Carly McLaughlin, and Wladyslaw Witalisz, 73–89. Frankfurt a.M.: Peter Lang.

García, Ofelia. 2009. *Bilingual Education in the 21ˢᵗ Century. A Global Perspective.* Malden (MA): Wiley-Blackwell.

García Canclini, Néstor. 1995. *Hybrid Cultures. Strategies for Entering and Leaving Modernity.* Trans. Christopher L. Chiappari and Silvia L. López. Minneapolis/London: University of Minnesota Press. [*Culturas híbridas. Estrategias para entrar y salir de la modernidad* 1989].

García Valverde, Orlando. 2010. *Vocabulario básico y cotidiano abreviado del castellano y costarriqueñismos en uso en Costa Rica: inglés-español.* San José (CR): O. García Valverde.

Gellner, Ernst. 1983. *Nations and Nationalisms.* New York: Cornell University Press.

Giglioli, Giovanna. 1996. "¿Mito o idiosincracia? Un análisis crítico de la literatura sobre el carácter nacional." In *Identidades y producciones culturales en América Latina*, ed. María Salvadora Ortiz, 167–206. San José (CR): Editorial de la Universidad de Costa Rica.

———. 1998. "Los colores de la idiosincrasia." In *Costa Rica imaginaria*, eds. Alexánder Jiménez and Jesús Oyamboru, 17–32. San José (CR): Centro Cultural de España.

Gilroy, Paul. 1990. "Nationalism, History and Ethnic Absolutism." *History Workshop* 30: 114–120.

_____. 1992. "Cultural Studies and Ethnic Absolutism." In *Cultural Studies*, ed. Lawrence Grossberg, 187–198. New York: Routledge.

_____. 1994. "Diaspora." *Paragraph* 17.3: 207–212.

_____. 2002. *The Black Atlantic. Modernity and Double Consciousness*. London: Verso.

_____. 2004. "Foreword: Migrancy, Culture, and a New Map of Europe." In *Blackening Europe: The African American Presence*, ed. Heike Raphael-Hernandez, xi-xxii. New York/London: Routledge.

_____. 2007. *There Ain't No Black in the Union Jack. The Cultural Politics of Race and Nation*. London: Routledge.

Glissant, Édouard. 1981. "Histoire, histoires." In *Le discours antillais*, 221–279. Paris: Gallimard.

_____. 1999. *Caribbean Discourse: Selected Essays*. Trans. J. Michael Dash. Charlottesville: University Press of Virginia.

_____. 1999. "History–Histories–Stories." In *Caribbean Discourse*, 61–95. Charlottesville: University Press of Virginia.

_____. 1999. "Cross-Cultural Poetics." In *Caribbean Discourse,* 97–157. Charlottesville: University Press of Virginia.

_____. 2010. *Poetics of Relation*. Trans. Betsy Wing. Ann Arbor: University of Michigan Press [*Poétique de la Relation* 1990].

González, Ann. 2009. *Resistance and Survival. Children's Narrative from Central America and the Caribbean*. Tucson: University of Arizona Press.

González, Melissa. 2019. "Reconstrucción del Black Star Line iniciará este mes." *La República.net* online edition, September 1. Retrieved from https://www.larepublica.net/noticia/reconstruccion-del-black-star-line-iniciara-este-mes.

Gordon, Donald K. 1991. "Expressions of the Costa Rican Black Experience: The Short Stories of Dolores Joseph and the Poetry of Shirley Campbell." *Afro-Hispanic Review* 10.3: 21–26.

_____. 2003. "Shirley Campbell's *Rotundamente negra*: Content and Technique." In *Daughters of the Diaspora*, ed. Miriam De Costa-Willis, 435–440. Kingston: Ian Randle Publishers.

Grewal, Shabnam, Jackie Kay, Liliane Landor, Gail Lewis, and Pratibha Parmar, eds. 1988. *Charting the Journey. Writings by Black and Third World Women*. London: Sheba Feminist Publishers.

Grinberg Pla, Valeria. 2008. "La nueva novela histórica de las últimas décadas y las nuevas corrientes historiográficas." In *Historia y ficción en la novela centroamericana contemporánea*, eds. Werner Mackenbach, Rolando Fonseca, and Magda Zavala, 13–48. Tegucigalpa: Subirana.

_____. 2012. "Una mirada a las letras en los periódicos afroantillanos de Limón." In *Puerto Limón (Costa Rica). Formas y prácticas de auto/representación. Apuestas imaginarias y políticas. / Puerto Limón (Costa Rica). Formes et practiques d'auto/répresentation. Enjeux imaginaires, culturels et politiques*, eds. Quince Duncan Moodie and Victorien Lavou Zoungbo, 83–102. Perpignan: Presses universitaires de Perpignan.

_____, and Werner Mackenbach. 2006. "*Banana novel revis(it)ed*: etnia, género y espacio en la novela bananera centroamericana. El caso de *Mamita Yunai*." *Iberoamericana* 6.23: 161–176.

Gudmunson, Lowell. 1984. "'Black' into 'White' in Nineteenth Century Spanish America: Afro-American Assimilation." *Slavery and Abolition* 5.1: 34–49.

Guardia, Tomás. 1999. "Exposición dirigida por el presidente de la República de Costa Rica general Tomás Guardia en actual desempeño de encargos financieros de aquella República al presidente del Consejo de Tenedores de Bonos Extranjeros. (1882)." In *Crónicas y relatos para la historia de Puerto Limón*, eds. Fernando González and Elías Zeledón, 134–138. San José (CR): Ministerio de Cultura, Juventud y Deportes, Centro de investigación y conservación de patrimonio cultural.

Guerrero, José. 1930. "Cómo se quiere que sea Costa Rica, blanca o negra?" *Repertorio Americano*, September 13, 149–150. Retrieved from http://hdl.handle.net/11056/9330.

Guillaumin, Colette. 1980. "The idea of race and its elevation to autonomous, scientific and legal status." In *Sociological theories: race and colonialism*, Unesco, 37–68. Paris: Unesco.

Gumperz, John. 1982. *Discourse Strategies*. Cambridge: Cambridge University Press.

Habermas, Jürgen. 1997. "Modernity: An Unfinished Project." In *Habermas and the Unfinished Project of Modernity: Critical Essays on the Philosophical Discourse of Modernity*, ed. Maurizio Passerin D'Entrèves, 38–55. Cambridge: MIT Press.

Haigh, Sam. 2000. *Mapping a Tradition. Francophone Women's Writing from Guadeloupe*. London: Maney.

Halbwachs, Maurice. 1967. *La mémoire collective*. Paris: Presses Universitaires de France. Retrieved from http://classiques.uqac.ca/classiques/Halbwachs_maurice/memoire_collective/memoire_collective.pdf.

Hall, Stuart. 1980. "Race, articulation, and societies structured in dominance." In *Sociological Theories: race and colonialism*, Unesco, 305–345. Paris: Unesco.

_____. 1990. "Cultural Identity and Diaspora." In *Identity: Community, Culture, Difference*, ed. Jonathan Rutherford, 222–237. London: Lawrence and Wishart.

_____. 1993. "Culture, Community, Nation." *Cultural Studies* 7.3: 349–363.

_____. 1996. "When was 'the Post-Colonial'? Thinking at the Limit." In *The Post-Colonial Question: Common Skies, Divided Horizons*, eds. Iain Chamber and Lidia Curtis, 242–260. London/New York: Routledge.

Harlan, David. 1989. "Intellectual History and the Return of Literature." *The American Historical Review* 94.3: 581–609.

Harlow, Barbara. 1987. *Resistance Literature*. New York/London: Methuen.

Harpelle, Ronald. 2001. *The West Indians of Costa Rica. Race, Class, and the Integration of an Ethnic Minority*. Quebec: McGill-Queen's University Press.

Harris, Wilson. 2010. *The Palace of the Peacock*. London: Faber and Faber.

Hegel, Georg Wilhelm Friedrich. 2001. *The Philosophy of History*. Trans. J. Sibree, with Prefaces by Charles Hegel. Kitchener (ON): Batoche.

Heller, Monica. 1988. "Introduction." In *Code-switching: Anthropological and Sociolinguistic Perspectives*, ed. Monica Heller, 1–24. Berlin: De Gruyter.

_____. 1992. "The politics of codeswitching and language choice." *Journal of Multilingual and Multicultural Development* 13.1/2: 123–142.

Hellinger, Marlis. 1986. "On writing English-related Creoles in the Caribbean." In *Focus on the Caribbean*, eds. Manfred Görlach and John Holm, 53–70. Amsterdam: Benjamins.

Helmich, Werner. 2016. *Ästhetik der Mehrsprachigkeit. Zum Sprachwechsel in der neueren romanischen und deutschen Literatur*. Heidelber: Winter Verlag.

Henriques, Fernando. 1949. "West Indian Family Organization." *American Journal of Sociology* 55.1: 30–37.

Herzfeld, Anita. 1977a. "Second Language Acrolect Replacement in Limon Creole." *Kansas Working Papers in Linguistics* 2: 193–222.

_____. 1977b. "Towards the Description of a Creole." *Vínculos* 3.1/2: 105–115.

_____. 1978. "Vida o muerte del criollo limonense." *Revista de Filología y Lingüística de la Universidad de Costa Rica* 4.2: 17–24.

_____. 1983. "The Creoles of Costa Rica and Panama." In *Central American English*, ed. John Holm, 131–156. Heidelberg: Groos.

_____. 1994. "Language and Identity: The Black Minority of Costa Rica." *Revista de Filología y Lingüística (Universidad de Costa Rica)* 20.1: 113–142.

_____. 2002. *Mekaytelyuw: la lengua criolla de Limón*. San José: Editorial de Universidad de Costa Rica.

_____. 2011. "Una evaluación de la vitalidad lingüística del inglés criollo de Limón: su vigencia o su desplazamiento." *Filología y Lingüística* 37.2: 107–131.

Hirsch, Marianne. 2008. "The Generation of Postmemory." *Poetics Today* 29.1: 103–128.

Ho, Christine G.T. 1999. "Caribbean Transnationalism as a Gendered Process." *Latin American Perspectives* 26.5: 34–54.

Hobsbawm, Eric. 1994. *Nations and Nationalism since 1780: Programme, Myth, Reality*, Cambridge: Cambridge University Press.

_____. 1996. "Introduction: Inventing Traditions." In *The Invention of Tradition*, eds. Eric Hobsbawm and Terence Ranger, 1-14. Cambridge: Cambridge University Press.

_____. 1996. "Mass-Producing Traditions: Europe, 1870–1914." In *The Invention of Tradition*, Eric Hobsbawm and Terence Ranger, eds., 263–307. Cambridge: Cambridge University Press.

Holm, John, ed. 1983. *Central American English*, Heidelberg: Groos.

Horn, András. 1981. "Ästhetische Funktionen der Sprachmischung in der Literatur." *Arcadia* 16: 225–241.

Hutcheon, Linda. 1996. *A Poetics of Postmodernism: History, Theory, Fiction*. New York/London: Routledge.

Hymes, Dell. 1974. "Preface." In *Pidgins and Creolization of Languages: Proceedings of a Conference Held at the University of the West Indies. Mona, Jamaica, April 1968*, ed. Dell Hymes, 3–11. Cambridge: Cambridge University Press.

Inec (Instituto Nacional de Estadística y Censo). 2014. *Costa Rica a la luz del censo 2011*. San José (CR): INEC. Retrieved from http://www.inec.go.cr/sites/default/files/documentos/inec_institucional/publicaciones/anpoblaccenso2011-01.pdf_2.pdf.

Jackson, Richard L. 1979. *Black Writers in Latin America*. Albuquerque: University of New Mexico Press.

_____. 1997. *Black Writers and the Hispanic Canon*. New York: Twayne.

Jackson, Shirley. 2003. "'Our Weapon is Strong Language.' A Conversation with Eulalia Bernard." In *Daughters of the Diaspora*, ed. Miriam DeCosta-Willis, 122–128. Kingston: Ian Randle Publishers.

Jiménez, Alexánder. 2013. *El imposible país de los filósofos*. San José (CR): Editorial Universidad de Costa Rica.

_____ and Jesús Oyamboru, eds. 1998. *Costa Rica imaginaria*. San José (CR): Centro Cultural de España.

Jones, Janet. 1995. "Portraits of a Diasporan People: The Poetry of Shirley Campbell and Rita Dove." *Afro-Hispanic Review* 14.1: 33–39.

Jordaan, Gert J.C. 2013. *Ancient Greek Inside Out. The Semantics of Grammatical Constructions. Guide for Exegetes and Students in Classical and New Testament Greek*. Vienna: Lit-Verlag.

Keller, Gary. 1979. "The Literary Stratagems Available to the Bilingual Chicano Writer." In *The Identification and Analysis of Chicano Literature*, ed. Franciso Jiménez, 263–316. New York: Bilingual Press.

Kepner, Charles and Jay Soothill. 1967. *The Banana Empire. A Case Study of Economic Imperialism*. New York: Vanguard Press.

Kiesler, Reinhard. 1993. "La tipología de los préstamos lingüísticos: no sólo un problema de terminología." *Zeitschrift für romanische Philologie* 109.5/6: 505–525.

Kim, Sandra So Hee Chi. 2007. "Redefining Diaspora through a Phenomenology of Postmemory." *Diaspora* 16.3: 337–352.

Koch, Charles. 1995. *Ethnicity and Livelihoods, a Social Geography of Costa Rica's Atlantic Zone*. Doctoral dissertation in Philosophy, University of Kansas.

Koch, Peter. 1999. "Frame and Contiguity: On the Cognitive Bases of Metonymy and Certain Types of Word Formation." In *Metonymy in Language and Thought*, eds. Klaus-Uwe Panther and Günther Radder, 139–167. Amsterdam: Benjamins.

Kohut, Karl, ed. 1997. *La invención del pasado. La novela histórica en el marco de la posmodernidad*. Frankfurt a.M.: Vervuert.

_____. 2001. "Mirando al huerto del vecino: los historiadores frente a lo literario." *Estudios. Revista de Investigaciones Literarias y Culturales* 9.18: 57–88.

Kumar, Nita N. 2009. "Form as a Site of Contest: Yoruba Tragedy turns Revolutionary in Amiri Baraka's Slave Ship." *IRWLE* 5.1: 46–52.

Kurtze, Francisco. 1999. "La Ruta Ferroviaria Interoceánica a través de la república de Costa Rica." In *Crónicas y relatos para la historia de Puerto Limón*, eds. Fernando González and Elías Zeledón, 113–121. San José (CR): Ministerio de Cultura, Juventud y Deportes, Centro de investigación y conservación de patrimonio cultural.

Guevara Cárdenas, Juan. 1940. "Las escuelas particulares de la zona Atlántica." *La Voz del Atlántico* online edition, November 16, p. 5. Retrieved from http://www.sinabi.go.cr/ver/biblioteca%20digital/periodicos/la%20voz%20del%20atlantico/la%20voz%20del%20atlantico%201940/kp-16%20de%20noviembre.pdf#.XvLeqS2BrOQ.

Lamarque, Peter and Stein Haugom Olsen. 1996. *Truth, Fiction, and Literature*. Oxford: Clarendon Press.

Láscaris, Constantino. 1975. *El costarricense*. San José (CR): Editorial Educa.

Le Goff, Jacques. 1992. *History and Memory*. Trans. Steven Rendall and Elizabeth Claman. New York: Columbia University Press.

Lewis, Charlton T. and Charles Short. 1879. *A Latin Dictionary*. Oxford: Clarendon Press.

Lipski, John M. 1982. "Spanish-English Language Switching in Speech and Literature: Theories and Models." *Bilingual Review / La Revista Bilingüe* 9.3: 191–212.

Lobo, Tatiana. 1997. "La vida cotidiana." In *Negros y blancos: todo mezclado,* Tatiana Lobo and Mauricio Meléndez Obando, 8–79. San José (CR): Editorial Universidad de Costa Rica.

_____ and Mauricio Meléndez. 1997. *Negros y blancos: todo mezclado*. San José (CR): Editorial Universidad de Costa Rica.

Lohse, Russell. 2012. "Cacao y esclavitud en Matina, Costa Rica 1650-1750." In *La negritud en Centroamérica. Entre raza y raíces*, eds. Lowell Gudmunson and Justin Wolfe, 75–120. San José (CR): EUNED.

Lomnitz, Claudio. 2001. "Nationalism as a Practical System: Benedict Anderson's Theory of Nationalism from the Vantage Point of Spanish America." In *The Other Mirror. Grand Theory Through the Lens of Latin America*, eds. Miguel Ángel Centeno and Fernando López-Álvez, 329–360. Princeton: Princeton University Press.

Madrigal, Lorena. 2006. *Human Biology of Afro-Caribbean Populations*. Cambridge: Cambridge University Press.

Mackenbach, Werner. 2006. "Banana novel revisited: *Mamita Yunai* o los límites de la construcción de la nación desde abajo." *Káñina. Revista de Artes y Letras (Universidad de Costa Rica)* 30.2: 129–138.

_____. 2008a. "El Caribe y la literatura Centroamericana: de la doble exclusión al doble espejo." In *Caribbean(s) on the Move*, ed. Ottmar Ette, 107–119. Frankfurt a.M.: Peter Lang.

_____. 2008b. "Representaciones del Caribe en la narrativa centroamericana contemporánea: Entre una perspectiva exterior y una perspectiva interior." *Revista Mosaico* 1.1: 41–52.

_____. 2012. "Narrativas de la memoria en Centroamérica: Entre política, historia y ficción." In *Hacia una historia de las literaturas centroamericanas III. (Per)versiones de la Modernidad: literatura, identidades y desplazamientos*, eds. Beatriz Cortez, Alexandra Ortiz, and Verónica Ríos, 231–257. Guatemala: F & G Editores.

Maldonado-Torres, Nelson. 2007. "On the Coloniality of Being. Contributions to the Development of a Concept." *Cultural Studies* 21.2/3: 240–270.

_____. 2011. "Thinking through the Decolonial Turn: Post-Continental Interventions in Theory, Philosophy, and Critique – An Introduction." *Transmodernity: Journal of Peripheral Cultural Prouction of the Luso-Hispanic World* 1.2. Retrieved from http://escholarship.org/uc/item/59w8j02x.

Mance, Ajuan Maria. 2007. *Inventing Black Women. African American Women Poets and Self-Representation, 1877-2000*. Knoxville: University of Tennessee Press.

Marcelo, Cristián. 1994. "Prólogo." In *El séptimo círculo del obelisco*, Dlia McDonald, 3–4. San José (CR): D. McDonald.

Marley, Bob and The Wailers. 1980. *Uprising*. Kingston: Tuff Gong/Island Records.

Martin-Ogunsola, Dellita L. 1987. "Invisibility, Double Consciousness, and the Crisis of Identity in *Los cuatro espejos*." *Afro-Hispanic Review* 6.2: 9–15.

Martinez-San Miguel, Yolanda. 2014. *Coloniality of Diasporas. Rethinking Intra-Colonial Migrations in a Pan-Caribbean Context*. New York: Palgrave Macmillan.

Massiah, Joycelin. 1983. *Women as Heads of Household in the Caribbean: Family Structure and Feminine Status*. Paris: Unesco.

McKinney, Kitzie. 1996. "Costa Rica's Black Body: The Politics and Poetics of Difference in Eulalia Bernard." *Afro-Hispanic Review* 15.2: 11–20.

McWhorter, John. 1995. "The Scarcity of Spanish-based Creoles Explained." *Language in Society* 24: 213–244.

Mechán, Juan. 1999. "Informe del Ingeniero Juan Mechán sobre el Limón y el camino a construir." In *Crónicas y relatos para la historia de Puerto Limón*, eds. Fernando González and Elías Zeledón, 91–100. San José (CR): Ministerio de Cultura, Juventud y Deportes, Centro de investigación y conservación de patrimonio cultural.

Meléndez, Carlos. 1978. "El negro en Costa Rica durante la colonia." In *El negro en Costa Rica*, eds. Quince Duncan and Carlos Meléndez, 11–58. San José (CR): Editorial de Costa Rica.

_____. 1978. "Aspectos sobre la inmigración jamaicana." In *El negro en Costa Rica*, eds. Quince Duncan and Carlos Meléndez, 59–95. San José (CR): Editorial de Costa Rica.

Meléndez Obando, Mauricio. 1997. "Segunda Parte. Las familias." In *Negros y blancos: todo mezclado*, Tatiana Lobo and Mauricio Meléndez, eds., 81–171. San José (CR): Editorial Universidad de Costa Rica.

Méndez, Alejandro and Raúl Cascante. 2016. "Incendio consume edificio Black Star Line en Limón." *La Nación*, April 29. Retrieved from https://www.nacion.com/sucesos/incendio-consume-edificio-black-star-line-en-limon/G2AJY7JMPZCWPE5LESWIOUZOJM/story/.

Meza Márquez, Consuelo. 2015. "Memoria, identidad y utopía en la poesía de las escritoras afrocentroamericanas: relatos de vida." In *Mujeres en las literaturas indígenas y afrodescendientes en América Central*, eds. Consuelo Meza Márquez and Magda Zavala González, 119–185. Aguascalientes: Universidad Autónoma de Aguascalientes.

_____ and Magda Zavala González, eds. 2015. *Mujeres en las literaturas indígenas y afrodescendientes en América Central*. Aguascalientes: Universidad Autónoma de Aguascalientes.

Menton, Seymour. 1993. *Latin America's New Historical Novel*. Austin: University of Texas Press.

Mignolo, Walter. 2000. "La colonialidad a lo largo y ancho: el hemisferio occidental en el horizonte colonial de la modernidad." In *Colonialidad del saber: eurocentrismo y ciencias sociales. Perspectivas latinoamericanas*, ed. Edgardo Lander, 55–85. Buenos Aires: CLACSO.

_____. 2003. *The Darker Side of the Renaissance: Literacy, Territoriality, and Colonization*. Ann Arbor: University of Michigan Press.

Miles, Robert. 1982. *Racism and Migrant Labour*. London: Routledge and Kegan Paul.

_____. 1987. "Recent Marxist Theories of Nationalism and the Issue of Racism." *The British Journal of Sociology* 38.1: 24–43.

_____. 1995. *Racism*. London/New York: Routledge.

Miller, Paul B. 2010. *Elusive Origins. The Enlightenment in the Modern Caribbean Historical Imagination*. Charlottesville: University of Virginia Press.

Ministerio de Cultura, Juventud y Deportes. Dirección General de Cultura, Costa Rica. 2000. "Poemas del Taller Francisco Zúñiga Díaz." *Imago. La revista cultural de biblioteca y colección* 7 (October): 43–45. San José (CR): Ministerio de Cultural, Juventud y Deportes, Dirección General de Cultural.

Mintz, Sydney W. 1966. "The Caribbean as a Socio-Cultural Area." *Cahiers d'Histoire Mondiale* 9.4: 912–938.

Molina Jiménez, Iván. 2002. *Costarricense por dicha: identidad nacional y cambio cultural en Costa Rica durante los siglos XIX y XX*. San José (CR): Editorial Universidad de Costa Rica.

Montes-Alcalá, Cecilia. 2015. "Code-switching in US Latino literature: The role of biculturalism." *Language and Literature* 24.3: 264–281.

Mora, Sonia Marta and Flora Ovares, eds. 1994. *Indómitas voces: las poetas de Costa Rica. Antología/Selección*. San José (CR): Editorial Mujeres.

Mosby, Dorothy. 2003. *Place, Language, and Identity in Afro-Costa Rican Literature*. Columbia: University of Missouri Press.

_____. 2012. "Roots and Routes: Transnational Blackness in Afro-Costa Rican Literature." In *Critical Perspectives on Afro-Latin American Literature*, ed. Antonio D. Tillis, 5–29. New York/London: Routledge.

_____. 2012. "Raíces y rutas: Identidad, ciudadanía y negritud transnacional en la literatura de afrodescendientes centroamericanos." In *Hacia una historia de las literaturas centroamericanas III. (Per)versiones de la Modernidad: literatura, identidades y desplazamientos*, eds. Beatriz Cortez, Alexandra Ortiz, and Verónica Ríos, 317–344. Guatemala: F & G Editores.

_____. 2014. *Quince Duncan. Writing Afro-Costa Rican and Caribbean Identity*. Alabama: University of Alabama Press.

Mukařovský, Jan. 2014. "Standard Language and Poetic Language." In *Chapters from the history of Czech functional linguistics*, ed. Jan Chovanec, 41–53. Brno: Masarykova Univerzita.

Muñoz-Muñoz, Marianela. 2018. *Bilingüismo político: Afrocaribeñas en el estado blanco y multicultural costarricense (1978-2017)*. Doctoral dissertation, presented to the Faculty of the Graduate School of the University of Texas at Austin in Partial Fulfillment of the Requirements for the Degree of Doctor in Philosophy, May 2018.

_____. 2019a. "Nacionalismo blanco, prensa e inversión de las víctimas durante la 'polémica Cocorí'." *Revista de Filología y Lingüística de la Universidad de Costa Rica* 45.2: 73–98.

_____. 2019b. "Una poética-política de la negritud en Costa Rica: El caso de Eulalia Bernard." In *Congreso sobre creación artística en la década de 1970 (2019 octubre 16-17, San José, C.R.). Memoria, recurso electrónico*, ed. María José Monge Picado, 153-158. San José: Fundación Museos Banco Central de Costa Rica.

Murillo, Álvaro. 2015. "Un libro infantil agita el racismo en Costa Rica." *El País. El periódico global*, online edition, May 18. Retrieved from https://internacional.elpais.com/internacional/2015/05/18/actualidad/1431980282_802085.html.

Murillo, Carmen. 1998. "La piel de la patria: sobre las representaciones de la diversidad cultural en Costa Rica." In *Costa Rica imaginaria*, eds. Alexánder Jiménez and Jesús Oyamboru, 45–58. San José (CR): Centro Cultural de España.

_____. 1999. "Vaivén de arraigos y desarraigos: identidad afrocaribeña en Costa Rica, 1870-1940." *Revista de Historia (Universidad Nacional de Costa Rica)* 39: 187–206.

Myers-Scotton, Carol. 1993. *Duelling Languages. Grammatical Structure in Codeswitching*. Oxford: Clarendon Press.

N.A. 1999. "Inauguración oficial de los trabajos del ferrocarril al Reventazón." In *Crónicas y relatos para la historia de Puerto Limón*, eds. Fernando González and Elías Zeledón, 149–158. San José (CR): Ministerio de Cultura, Juventud y Deportes, Centro de investigación y conservación de patrimonio cultural.

Nesbitt, Nick. 2008. *Universal Emancipation: The Haitian Revolution and Radical Enlightenment. (New World Studies)*. Charlottesville: University of Virginia Press.

Neumann, Birgit and Ansgar Nünning. 2012. "Travelling Concepts as a Model for the Study of Culture." In *Travelling Concepts for the Study of Culture*, eds. Birgit Neumann and Ansgar Nünning, 1–22. Berlin/Boston: De Gruyter.

Nora, Pierre. 1989. "Between Memory and History: Les Lieux de Mémoire." Trans. Marc Roudebush. *Representations* 26 (Special Issue Memory and Counter-Memory): 7–24.

O'Callaghan, Evelyn. 1993. *Woman Version: Theoretical Approaches to West Indian Fiction by Women*. London/Basingstoke: Macmillan Press.

Olien, Michael D. 1977. "The Adaptation of West Indian Blacks to North American and Hispanic Culture in Costa Rica." In *Old Roots New Lands. Historical and Anthropological Perspectives on Black Experiences in the Americas*, ed. Ann M. Pescatello, 132–156. Westport: Greenwood Press.

Oreamuno, Yolanda. 2011. "El negro, sentido de la alegría." In *A lo largo del corto camino*, 110–111. San José (CR): Editorial Costa Rica.

Orr, Linda. 1986/87. "The Revenge of Literature: A History of History." *NLH. A Journal of Theory and Interpretation* 18: 1–22.

Ortiz Wallner, Alexandra. 2012. *El arte de ficcionar: la novela contemporánea en Centroamérica*. Madrid: Iberoamericana.

Ovares, Flora, Margarita Rojas, Carlos Santander, and María Elena Carballo. 1993. *La casa paterna. Escritura y nación en Costa Rica*. San José (CR): Editorial Universidad de Costa Rica.

Pakkasvirta, Jussi. 1997. *¿Un continente, una nación? Intelectuales latinoamericanos, comunidad política y las revistas culturales en Costa Rica y Perú (1919–1930)*. Helsinki: Suomalainen tiedeakatemia.

_____. 1993. "Particularidad nacional en una revista continental. Costa Rica y Repertorio Americano, 1919–1930." *Revista de Historia* 28: 89–115.

Palmer, Paula. 2005. *"What Happen." A Folk-History of Costa Rica's Talamanca Coast*. Miami: Zona Tropical.

Palmer, Steven. 1995. "Hacia la 'auto-inmigración': El nacionalismo oficial en Costa Rica, 1870–1930." In *Identidades nacionales y Estado moderno en Centroamérica*, eds. Arturo Taracena and Jean Piel, 75–85. México: Centro de estudios mexicanos y centroamericanos, Flacso San Salvador, Editorial de la Universidad de Costa Rica.

_____. 1996. "Racismo intelectual en Costa Rica y Guatemala, 1870–1920." *Mesoamérica* 31: 99–121.

_____. 2004. "Sociedad anónima, cultural oficial: inventando la nación en Costa Rica 1848–1900." In *Héroes al gusto y libros de moda: sociedad y cambio cultural en Costa Rica (1750–1900)*, eds. Iván Molina Jiménez and Steven Palmer, 257–323. San José (CR): EUNED.

Palmer, Steven and Iván Molina, eds. *The Costa Rica Reader. History, Culture, Politics*, Durham: Duke University Press.

Paz, Octavio. 2006. "Paisaje y novela en México." In *Corriente alterna*, 16–18. México et al: Siglo XXI Editores.

Pérez-Brignoli, Héctor. 2018. *Historia global de América Latina del siglo XXI a la independencia*. Madrid: Alianza Editorial.

Perkowska, Magdalena. 2008. *Historias híbridas. La nueva novela histórica latinoamericana (1985–2000) ante las teorías posmodernas de la historia*. Madrid: Iberoamericana.

Persico, Alan. 1991. "Quince Duncan's *Los cuatro espejos*: Time, History, and a New Novel." *Afro-Hispanic Review* 10.1: 15–20.

Pfaff, Carol. 1979. "Constraints on Language Mixing: Intrasentential Code-Switching and Borrowing in Spanish / English." *Language* 55.2: 291–318.

Picado, Clodomiro. 2004. "Our Blood Is Blackening." In *The Costa Rica Reader. History, Culture, Politics*, eds. Steven Palmer and Iván Molina, 243–244. Durham: Duke University Press.

Piedra, Paula, ed. 2007. *Noches de poesía en el farolito: una mirada a la poesía costarricense en el 2007*. San José (CR): Editorial Perro Azul.

Pittman, Elizabeth. 2014. *"Force. Spirit. Feeling:" Rewriting the Slave Ship in Contemporary African American Literature*. Doctoral dissertation, The Columbian College of Arts and Sciences. Retrieved from https://pqdtopen.proquest.com/pubnum/3609013.html.

Pons, Maria Cristina. 1996. *Memorias del olvido. Del Paso, García Márquez, Saer y la novela histórica de fines del siglo XX*. México D.F.: Siglo XXI Editores.

Poplack, Shana. 1980. "Sometimes I'll start a sentence in Spanish Y TERMINO EN ESPAÑOL: toward a typology of code-switching." *Linguistics* 18: 581–618.

Portilla, Mario. 2000. "Hispanismos en el diccionario de ingles criollo de Costa Rica." *Revista de Filología y Lingüística* 26.1: 71–79.

Pratt, Mary Louise. 1997. *Imperial Eyes: travel writing and transculturation*. London: Routledge.

Pulgarin, Amalia. 1995. *Metaficción historiográfica: La novela histórica en la narrativa hispánica posmodernista*. Madrid: Editorial Fundamentos.

Purcell, Trevor. 1982. *Conformity and Dissension: Social Inequality, Values, and Mobility among West Indian Migrants in Limón, Costa Rica*. Doctoral dissertation, Department of Anthropology, John Hopkins University.

_____. 1993. *Banana Fallout: Class, Color, and Culture among West Indians in Costa Rica*. Los Angeles: Center for Afro-American Studies, University of California.

Putnam, Lara Elizabeth. 1999. "Ideología racial, práctica social y Estado Liberal en Costa Rica." *Revista de Historia (Universidad Nacional de Costa Rica)* 39: 139–186.

_____. 2002. *The Company They Kept. Migrants and the Politics of Gender in Caribbean Costa Rica, 1870–1960*. Chapel Hill: University of North Carolina Press.

_____. 2004. "La población afrocostarricense según los datos del censo de 2000." In *Costa Rica a la luz del censo del 2000*, ed. Rosero Bixby, 375–398. San José: Centro Centroamericano de Población de la Universidad de Costa Rica.

Quesada, Álvaro. 1994. "Nación y enajenación: génesis de la literatura nacional costarricense." *La palabra y el hombre (Revista de la Universidad Veracruzana)* 89: 115–127.

_____. 1995. *La formación de la narrativa nacional costarricense*. San José (CR): Editorial Universidad de Costa Rica.

_____. 2002. *Unos y los otros: identidad y literatura en Costa Rica, 1890-1940*. San José (CR): Editorial Universidad de Costa Rica.

Quijano, Aníbal. 1992. "Colonialidad y modernidad/racionalidad." *Perú indígena* 13.29: 11–20.

_____. 2000. "Colonialidad del poder, eurocentrismo y América Latina." In *Colonialidad del saber: eurocentrismo y ciencias sociales. Perspectivas latinoamericanas*, ed. Edgardo Lander, 201–246. Buenos Aires: CLACSO.

_____. 2007. "Colonialidad del poder y clasificación social." In *El giro decolonial*, eds. Santiago Castro-Gómez and Ramón Grosfoguel, 93–126. Bogotá: Siglo del Hombre Editores.

Ramírez, Sergio. 1983. "Balcanes y volcanes." In *Balcanes y volcanes, y otros ensayos y trabajos*, 11–114. Managua: Editorial Nueva Nicaragua.

Ravasio, Paola. 2014. "El caso de *Mamita Yunai*: La construcción de un testimonio sobre el Caribe." In *Nueva literatura para un siglo nuevo. El Popol Wuuj, el libro del amanecer. Actas del VIII Encuentro Mesoamericano "Escritura-Cultura", VI Coloquio "Escritoras y escritores latinoamericanos"*, eds. Helena Ospina, Erika Chinchilla Ramírez, and Gabriel Quesada Mora, 529–544. San José (CR): Promesa.

_____. 2020. "*Negritud* de Eulalia Bernard." In *Caribbean Worlds – Mundos Caribeños – Mondes Caribéens*, eds. Gabriele Knauer and Ineke Phaf-Rheinberger, 345–369. Madrid/Frankfurt a.M.: Iberoamericana/Vervuert.

Renan, Ernest. 1993. "What is a nation?" In *Nation and Narration*, ed. Homi K. Bhabha, 8–22. London/New York: Routledge.

Restrepo, Eduardo. 2012. *Intervenciones en teoría cultural*. Popayán (CO): Editorial Universidad del Cauca.

Ricœur, Paul. 2000. "L'écriture de l'histoire et la réprésentation du passé." *Annales. Histoire, Sciences Sociales* 55.4: 731–747.

Roach, Joseph. 1996. *Cities of the Dead. Circum-Atlantic Performance*. New York: Columbia University Press.

Roberts, Nicole. 2008. *Main Themes in Twentieth Century Afro-Hispanic Caribbean Poetry*. Lewiston/Queenston/Lampeter: Edwin Mellen Press.

Rodríguez Jiménez, Olga Marta. 2004. "¿Hay elementos racistas en Cocorí?" *Káñina. Revista Artes y Letras (Universidad de Costa Rica)* 28: 55–59.

Rosaldo, Renato. 1995. "Foreword." In *Hybrid Cultures. Strategies for Entering and Leaving Modernity*, Néstor García Canclini, trans. Christopher L. Chiappari and Silvia L. López, xi-xvii. Minneapolis/London: University of Minnesota Press.

Rosario, Reina. 2015. *Identidades de la población de origen jamaiquino en el Caribe costarricense (segunda mitad del siglo XX)*. República Dominicana: Cocolo Editorial.

Rojas, Margarita and Flora Ovares. 1995. *Cien años de literatura costarricense*. San José (CR): Editorial Costa Rica.

Romaine, Suzanne. 1994. *Language in Society*. Oxford: Oxford University Press.

Rossi, Anacristina. 2005. "El Caribe perdido: literatura y exclusión en Costa Rica." In *Literaturas Centroamericanas hoy: desde la dolorosa cintura de América,* eds. Karl Kohut and Werner Mackenbach, 155–167. Frankfurt a.M.: Vervuert.

Safran, William. 1991. "Diasporas in Modern Societies: Myths of Homeland and Return." *Diaspora* 1.1: 83–99.

Sandoval, Carlos and Patricia Alvarenga Venútolo, eds. 2007. *El mito roto. Inmigración y Emigración en Costa Rica*. San José (CR): Editorial Universidad de Costa Rica.

Sarlo, Beatriz. 2006. *Tiempo pasado: cultura de la memoria y giro subjetivo. Una discusión*. Mexico: Siglo XXI Editores.

Sartre, Jean-Paul. 2004. "Preface." In *The Wretched of the Earth*, Frantz Fanon, Trans. Richard Philcox, xliiii–lxii. New York: Grove Press.

Sauma, Osvaldo, ed. 1998. *Martes de poesía en el Cuartel de la Boca del Monte. Tomo I*. San José (CR): Lunes.

Schmeling, Manfred and Monika Schmitz-Emans, eds. 2002. *Multilinguale Literatur im 20. Jahrhundert*. Würzburg: Könnigshausen & Neumann.

Sebba, Mark. 2012. "Writing Switching in British Creole." In *Language Mixing and Code-Switching in Writing: Approaches to Mixed-Language Written Discourse*, eds. Mark Sebba, Shahrzad Mahootian and Carol Jonsson, 89–105. New York/London: Routledge.

Segreda, Luis Dobles. 1996. "El estado y la cultura de los hombres de color." In *Temas educacionales, semblanzas políticas. Tomo II*, Luis Dobles Segreda, ed. Carlos Meléndez, 401–403. San José (CR): EUNED.

Senior, Diana. 2011. *Ciudadanía afrocostarricense. El gran escenario comprendido entre 1927 y 1963*. San José (CR): EUNED.

Seton-Watson, Hugh. 1977. *Nations and States. An Enquiry into the Origins of Nations and the Politics of Nationalism*. Boulder: Westview Press.

Sharpley-Whiting, T. Denean. 2002. *Negritude Women*. Minneapolis: University of Minnesota Press.

Sheffer, Gabriel. 2006. "Transnationalism and Ethnonational Diasporism." *Diaspora* 15.1: 121–145.

Silk, Michael. 2003. "Metaphor and Metonymy: Aristotle, Jakobson, Ricoeur, and Others." In *Metaphor, Allegory, and the Classical Tradition. Ancient Thought and Modern Revisions*, ed. George R. Boys-Stones, 115–150. Oxford: Oxford University Press.

Singh, Nikhil Pal. 2004. *Black is a Country. Race and the Unfinished Struggle for Democracy*. Cambridge: Harvard University Press.

Smart, Ian. 1984. *Central American Writers of West Indian Origin. A New Hispanic Literature*. Washington D.C.: Three Continents Press.

_____. 1987. "Eulalia Bernard: A Caribbean Woman Writer and the Dynamics of Liberation." *Letras Femeninas* 13.1/2: 79–85.

Smith, Michael G. 1962. *West Indian Family Structure*. Seattle: University of Washington Press.

Smith, Valerie. 1994. "Reading the Intersection of Race and Gender in Narratives of Passing." *Diacritics* 24.2/3: 43–57.

Solano Rivera, Silvia. 2014. "El giro identitario en la poesía de Shirley Campbell Barr." *Repertorio Americano* 24: 371–393.

Solano Rivera, Silvia and Jorge Ramírez Caro. 2016. "Poética de la liberación en Shirley Campbell Barr." *Cincinnati Romance Review* 40: 155–200.

_____. 2017. *Racismo y antirracismo en literatura. Lectura etnocrítica*. San José (CR): Editorial Arlekín.

Sommer, Doris. 1993. *Foundational Fictions: The National Romances of Latin America*. Berkeley: University of California Press.

_____. 1999. *Proceed with Caution, When Engaged by Minority Writing in the Americas*. Cambridge: Harvard University Press.

Soto-Quiros, Ronald. 1998. "Desaparecidos de la Nación. Los indígenas en la construcción de la identidad nacional costarricense, 1851-1942." *Revista de Ciencias Sociales (Universidad de Costa Rica)* 82: 31–53.

_____. 2012. "Desarrollo, etnia y marginalización: imágenes del puerto caribeño de Limón Costa Rica (1838-1967)." *Études caribéennes,* online journal, April 21. Retrieved from https://doi.org/10.4000/etudescaribeennes.5715.

_____. 2012. "La difusión del etnotipo costarricense: los Apuntamientos de J. B. Calvo, del texto educativo a la propaganda internacional." Boletín AFEHC [Asociación para el Fomento de los Estudios Históricos en Centroamérica], 54. Retrieved from http://www.afehc-historia-centroamericana.org/index_action_bul_aff.html.

Spivak, Gayatri C. 1988. "Can the Subaltern Speak?" In *Marxism and the Interpretation of Culture*, eds. Cary Nelson and Lawrence Grossberg, 271–311. Chicago: University of Illinois Press.

Squier, Ephraim George. 1858. *The States of Central America*. New York: Harper & Brothers Publishers.

Sablo Sutton, Soraya. 2008. "Spoken Word: Performance Poetry in the Black Community." In *What they don't learn in School. Literacy in the Lives of Urban Youth*, ed. Jabari Mahiri, 213–242. New York: Lang.

Sturm-Trigonakis, Elke. 2007. *Global Playing in der Literatur. Ein Versuch über die Neue Weltliteratur*. Würzburg: Könnigshausen & Neumann.

Taketani, Etsuko. 2014. *The Black Pacific Narrative. Geographic Imaginings of Race and Empire between the World Wars*. Hanover (NH): Dartmouth College Press.

Thomason, Sarah G. 2001. *Language Contact: An Introduction*. Washington D.C.: Georgetown University Press.

Timm, Leonora. 1975. "Spanish-English code-switching: El porqué y How-Not-To." *Romance Philology* 28.4: 473–482.

Todd, Loretto. 1974. *Pidgins and Creoles*. London/Boston: Routledge & Kegan Paul.

Tölölyan, Khachig. 1991. "The Nation-State and its Others: In Lieu of a Preface." *Diaspora: A Journal of Transnational Studies* 1.1: 3–7.

_____. 1996. "Rethinking Diaspora(s): Stateless Power in the Transnational Moment." *Diaspora: A Journal of Transnational Studies* 5.1: 3–36.

Torres, Lourdes. 2007. "In the Contact-Zone: Code-Switching Strategies by Latino/a Writers." *MELUS* 32.1: 75–96.

Trouillot, Michel-Rolph. 1995. *Silencing the Past. Power and the Production of History*. Boston: Beacon Press.

Tsagarousianou, Roza. 2004. "Rethinking the concept of diaspora: mobility, connectivity and communication in a globalised world." *Westminster Papers in Communication and Culture*, 1.1: 52–65.

Unicef and Unia (Universal Negro Improvement Association). 2010. *Afrodescendientes de valía*. Limón (CR): UNIA. Retrieved from https://www.unicef.org/costarica/docs/cr_pub_Afrodescendientes_de_valia.pdf.

Valdés-Fallis, Guadalupe. 1976. "Code-Switching in Bilingual Chicano Poetry." *Hispania* 59.4: 877–886.

_____. 1977. "The sociolinguistics of Chicano literature: Towards an analysis of the role and function of language alternation in contemporary bilingual poetry." *Point of Contact / Punto de Contacto* 1.14: 30–39.

Van Hear, Nicholas. 1998. *New Diasporas. The Mass Exodus, Dispersal and Regrouping of Migrant Communities*. London: UCL Press.

_____. 2014. "Refugees, Diasporas, and Transnationalism." In *The Oxford Handbook of Refugee and Forced Migration Studies*, eds. Elena Fiddian-Qasmiyeh, Gil Loescher, Katy Long, and Nando Sigona, 176–187. Oxford: Oxford University Press.

Varadarajan, Latha. 2010. *The Domestic Abroad. Diasporas in International Relations*. Oxford: Oxford University Press.

Vega Carballo, Jose Luis. 1981. *Orden y progreso: la formación del estado nacional en Costa Rica*. San José (CR): Instituto Centroamericano de Administración Pública.

Verg, Erik. 1962. *Mañana ist es zu spät. Zwölf neue Welten um das Karibische Meer*. Berlin: Ullstein.

Viales, Ronny J. 1998. *Después del enclave. Un estudio de la Región Atlántica Costarricense*. San José (CR): Editorial Universidad de Costa Rica.

_____. 2000. *Los Liberales y la Colonización de las Áreas de Frontera no Cafetaleras: El caso de la Región Atlántica (Caribe) costarricense entre 1870 y 1930*. Doctoral dissertation, Universitat Autònoma de Barcelona.

_____ 2013. "La segunda colonización de la región Atlántico/Caribe Costarricense. Del siglo XVI hasta la construcción de la red ferroviaria." In *La conformación histórica de la región Atlántico/Caribe costarricense: (Re)interpretaciones sobre su trayectoria entre el siglo XVI y XXI* (2013), ed. Ronny Viales, 89–126. San José (CR): Editorial Nuevas Perspectivas.

Villalobos Saborío, Paulo. 2019. "Reconstrucción del Black Star Line de Limón iniciará en abril." *Ameliarueda.com*, March 4. Retrieved from https://www.ameliarueda.com/nota/reconstruccion-black-star-line-limon-iniciara-abril.

Villanueva, Djenane. 2015. "El libro infantil Cocorí, ¿una obra racista?" *CNNespañol*, online edition, May 25. Retrieved from http://cnnespanol.cnn.com/2015/05/25/el-libro-infantil-cocori-una-obra-racista/.

Wade, Peter. 2006. "Afro-Latin Studies: Reflections on the Field." *Latin American and Caribbean Ethnic Studies* 1.1: 105–124.

Walfran, Mr. L. 1999. "Informe de Mr. L. Walfran, ingeniero encargado de la expedición de los puertos y del camino al Atlántico." In *Crónicas y relatos para la historia de Puerto Limón*, eds. Fernando González and Elías Zeledón, 87–90. San José (CR): Ministerio de Cultura, Juventud y Deportes, Centro de investigación y conservación de patrimonio cultural.

Walters, Wendy. 2005. *At Home in Diaspora. Black International Writing*. Minneapolis: University of Minnesota Press.

Watson, Ingrid. 1991. *Afro-Hispanic Literature. An Anthology of Hispanic Writers of African Ancestry*. Miami: Ediciones Universal.

Weinreich, Uriel. 1953. *Languages in Contact*. The Hague et al: Mouton Publishers.

Whimster, Sam. 1998. "The Nation-State, the Protestant Ethic and Modernization." In *Max Weber, Democracy and Modernization*, ed. Ralph Schroeder, 61–78. New York: St. Martin's Press.

White, Hayden. 2000. *Figural Realism. Studies in the Mimesis Effect*. Baltimore: John Hopkins University Press.

_____. 2010. "Romanticism, Historicism, and Realism: *Toward a Period Concept for Early Nineteenth-Century Intellectual History*." In *The Fiction of Narrative: Essays on History, Literature, an Theory, 1957-2007*, Hayden White, ed. Robert Doran, 68–79. Baltimore: John Hopkins University Press.

_____. 2010. "The Tasks of Intellectual History." In *The Fiction of Narrative: Essays on History, Literature, and Theory, 1957-2007*, Hayden White, ed. Robert Doran, 80–97. Baltimore: John Hopkins University Press.

Williams, Raymond. 1977. *Marxism and Literature*. London: Oxford University Press.

_____. 1980. "Ideas of Nature." In *Problems in Materialism and Culture. Selected Essays*, 67–85. London: NLB.

Winkler, Elizabeth. 1998. *Limonese Creole: A Case of Contact-Induced Language Change*. Doctoral dissertation, Indiana University Bloomington.

_____. 2000. "Cambio de códigos en el criollo limonense." *Filología y Lingüística* 26.1: 189–196.

_____. 2013. "Limonese Creole English." In *World Englishes. Volume III: Central America*, eds. Tometro Hopkins and Ken Decker, 205–250. London: Bloomsbury.

Winkler, Elizabeth and Samuel Gyasi Obeng. 2000. "West Africanisms in Limonese Creole English." In *World Englishes* 19.2: 155–171.

Young, James. 1997. "Toward a Received History of the Holocaust." *History and Theory* 36.4: 21–43.

Zapata Duarte, Enrique and Edgar E. Blanco Obando. 2013. "La región Atlántico/Caribe de Costa Rica. Las políticas de desarrollo desde el gobierno central y desde la región: su planteamiento inicial y los resultados finales. 1950-2009." In *La conformación histórica de la región Atlántico/Caribe costarricense: (Re)interpretaciones sobre su trayectoria entre el siglo XVI y XXI* (2013), ed. Ronny Viales, 439–476. San José (CR): Editorial Nuevas Perspectivas.

Zavala González, Magda. 2008. "Novela de la nación en crisis." In *Historia y ficción en la novela centroamericana contemporánea*, eds. Werner Mackenbach, Rolando Fonseca, and Magda Zavala, 49–58. Tegucigalpa: Subirana.

_____. 2015. "Para conocer a las poetas afrodescendientes centroamericanas." In *Mujeres en las literaturas indígenas y afrodescendientes en América Central*, eds. Consuelo Meza Márquez and Magda Zavala González, 97–113. Aguascalientes: Universidad Autónoma de Aguascalientes.

Zimmer, Tanja. 2011. *El español hablado por los afrocostarricenses. Estudio lingüístico y sociológico*. Kassel: Kassel University Press.